SON OF HAVANA

A BASEBALL JOURNEY FROM CUBA TO THE BIG LEAGUES AND BACK

09.23.19

To Joel —
Best wishes,
LOOO-EEE

LUIS TIANT WITH SAUL WISNIA

FOREWORD BY CARL YASTRZEMSKI

DIVERSION

To Maria, my best friend and partner on this long journey of nearly 60 years.

—Luis Tiant

To Michelle, with love and a promise: it really is done.

—Saul Wisnia

For more information, email info@diversionbooks.com

Diversion Books
A division of Diversion Publishing Corp.
443 Park Avenue South, suite 1004
New York, NY 10016
www.diversionbooks.com

First Diversion Books edition May 2019
Hardcover ISBN: 978-1-63576-543-4
eBook ISBN: 978-1-63576-542-7

Printed in The United States of America

1 3 5 7 9 10 8 6 4 2

Library of Congress cataloging-in-publication data is available on file.

Contents

FOREWORD

I HAVE SAID IT before and I'll always say it: If you wanted one pitcher to start a big game, it would be Luis Tiant. Nobody was a tougher competitor—or a better teammate. He meant so much to us, and to the fans. We all loved him.

Luis played for the Indians when I first met him. He threw real hard, in the mid-nineties. The mound was higher then, and he pitched up; he had a good breaking ball and a rising fastball.

He threw that rising fastball a lot, and one Saturday afternoon at Fenway Park in May 1967 he struck me out three times. After the game I was taking [extra] batting practice, so of course he had to walk out on the field and get my attention. I looked over at him, and he just said one thing:

"You need it."

That was Luis. Even when you weren't his teammate, you knew he was a funny guy. He seemed to have nicknames for everyone. He'd call me "Polack" with his crazy Cuban accent and I'd just laugh. You couldn't get mad at him.

About a month later at Fenway, I faced him again and hit a home run. As I was rounding the bases, he turned to me yelling, "You dumb Polack!" I was laughing, and yelled back, "You big Black Cuban!" Then he came up to me the next day and said, "I guess the batting practice paid off."

When the Red Sox picked Luis up in 1971 he was coming off a bad shoulder, but I thought if his arm came around he could help us. He was smart, had great control, and knew how to pitch. Even if he had lost a little something on his fastball, I felt he could rely on his pitching knowledge to get guys out.

That first year, he was still hurting, but in '72 his arm was sound. He was just outstanding that summer, nearly pitching us to a pennant, and the fans at Fenway Park started in with all the "LOO-EEE! LOO-EEE! LOO-EEE!" chants. I never heard anything like it, or saw fans react to a ballplayer in that way. It sent chills down my spine. Fans recognize effort, and they knew how hard he had worked to come back. They understood him, and they loved him. It was beautiful.

I think that unique windup he had helped him because it was so herky-jerky. He'd turn his back to the plate, which hid the ball well from batters. With a right-handed hitter, his back would be turned toward them, so they couldn't see the ball at all. Lefties like me could pick the ball up a little quicker, but it was still tough. That was a big part of his success.

Luis was great under pressure, especially in the '75 postseason. When he pitched the way he did in the first game of the American League Championship Series, beating Oakland, it gave us all a big lift. We had just lost Jim Rice to a broken hand, and I know the team was down by not having Jimmy in the lineup. By beating the three-time defending champs, Luis picked us all up.

Then in the World Series, he shut out the Reds in the opener at Fenway and got the big hit to start our winning rally. Game Four at Cincinnati was tougher, because Luis didn't have his best stuff. I can remember Darrell Johnson coming out to the mound in the ninth inning and asking him how he felt, because he had thrown so many pitches. Luis told him he started the game and he was going to finish it.

That's the way he was; he wasn't looking for any help from the bullpen. And he *did* finish it, getting us another big win.

When Luis's mom and dad came to Boston from Cuba that summer of '75, after all those years apart from him, it was heartwarming. It not only made the Tiants happy, it made the whole team happy. Especially in that atmosphere in Boston, and the way the fans loved Luis, I'm sure it was a huge thrill for his parents. And, of course, they got to see him win those big games.

We loved Luis so much in the clubhouse. He was absolutely hysterical, and always had something to say that was funny. Luis kept the team relaxed with his big Cuban cigars and practical jokes. He was just a very funny, positive person, win or lose.

That's another thing I always liked about Luis. If he had a bad game, he'd say, "Yaz, I'll get 'em next time." That was his attitude. He never got upset. Just "I'll get 'em next time." Maybe deep down, it hurt him—I'm sure it did—when he had a bad outing. But he didn't show it. He kept his cool.

I was very surprised about Luis signing with the Yankees as a free agent after 1978, because of the fan loyalty he had in Boston and how much they loved him. He loved Boston too, so it came as a big, big surprise when he went to New York. It was strange to everyone, I think, seeing him in pinstripes, but I understood *why* he went.

That move had a big impact on our team, beyond wins and losses. I was quoted as saying that "When they let Tiant go, they took out our heart and soul." Things were never quite the same, and it hurt us as a unit. Nobody could fill his shoes when it came to keeping guys loose.

I've always thought that Luis should be in the Hall of Fame. No doubt about it. He has the statistics, and then you include the tremendous games he pitched in tight situations for us. Certainly nobody loved being out there with everything on the line more than Luis did.

To this day, he still calls me "Polack." I'll see him at spring training, down in Fort Myers, and he'll go, "Hiya, Polack, how ya doin'?"

All you can do is laugh.

CARL YASTRZEMSKI
Boston Red Sox, 1961–83
National Baseball Hall of Fame

1

SHUTTING UP PETE ROSE

ON A RAINY OCTOBER AFTERNOON in 1975, the right-field bullpen door at Fenway Park swung open and the cheering began. Like a wave of sound, years before anyone had heard of the wave, the capacity crowd stood and screamed for the bow-legged man walking in toward the diamond: LOO-EEE! LOO-EEE! LOO-EEE!

In his bright white polyester uniform, with his thick belly and Fu Manchu mustache, Luis Tiant looked more like a guy rolling out of bed for a Sunday-morning beer league than a professional baseball player. The Cincinnati Reds, the "Big Red Machine" that had torn through the National League and were prohibitive favorites in this '75 World Series, had not shown Boston's Game One starting pitcher much respect. Pete Rose, the Reds' talented leadoff man and spark plug, told reporters he couldn't wait to face Boston's ace right-hander.

Other than a few isolated moments in All-Star games years before, however, Rose and his overconfident teammates had only seen Tiant perform on TV or tape. They underestimated the warrior who had won the hearts of New Englanders with his matador-like demeanor and ability to baffle hitters with an assortment of curves, blooper pitches, and a sneaky-quick fastball. All were delivered from an exaggerated, seemingly impossible high-kicking, spinning windup that further complicated matters for batters.

The fans affectionately called him "El Tiante." He may not have looked like a baseball player, or pitched like anybody they had seen. Still, there was nobody they depended on more in a big game—or that his teammates loved more, on the field or in the clubhouse.

Part of what made Tiant so special, and led to his broad appeal, was his fascinating back story. He was an only child, the son and namesake of a legendary, dark-skinned Cuban pitcher denied the chance to play in the white major leagues a generation before. Tiant had achieved his father's broken dreams and the fame that came with them, but at a heavy cost; with Fidel Castro restricting all travel in and out of Cuba, he had gone 14 years without seeing his family of origin in their beloved island home.

Now, as he scanned the stands behind the Red Sox dugout, Tiant spotted his own private cheering section—his beautiful wife, his children, and his aging parents, whose first-ever visit to Boston that summer had required diplomatic intervention that resulted in an emotional airport reunion played out on the front pages. He looked to the plate, where Rose was adjusting his tight red batting helmet and digging in, cocky as ever. And then a last time to the stands, at fans whose opposing views on the merits of busing Black students to white neighborhoods each school day had sparked a year of mounting racial tension and violent protests that would eventually reach City Hall Plaza. His own son was starting to hear a lot of bad stuff from other kids.

Yet here at Fenway, Tiant noticed, the fans always looked too happy to fight when he was pitching. They were united in their universal affection for both the team and for him—the darkest man on the field. Even the rain and cold didn't seem to bother them; tucking their umbrellas under their seats, they began yelling his name over and over into empty, red-white-and-blue popcorn holders that doubled as megaphones.

Tiant felt his entire life had been building to this point. The heartbreak of separation from his home and family. The isolation, fueled by racism and language barriers, that he encountered in the minor leagues of the Deep South. The crippling injuries that tore away his shoulder ligaments and nearly his livelihood. All of it had led to this place and this time.

He looked in at catcher Carlton Fisk for a signal, and took a deep breath. Then Luis Clemente Tiant started his windup.

SOMETIMES I'D STAND THERE on the mound, and think to myself: these people were just outside killing each other, and now they're all here yelling for me. This is *CRAZY!*

But that's Boston. Fans here love baseball, and they love effort. It doesn't matter who you are if you show them you'll do whatever it takes to win. And if you *deliver*, then you've got them behind you forever.

We used to have a saying where I grew up in Cuba: The good rooster fights anywhere. If you had a cock fighter, you could put him into any ring against any opponent and he would give it his all. It was the same way with me and baseball. If you're good, you'll fight anywhere and against anybody. I believed in myself, so that's what I did. You might feel the same way, and that's fine. Let's get in that ring and see who wins the cockfight.

In the World Series, Cincinnati was definitely the favorite. But I told my teammates, "Don't believe that. We've got a good team, and we can beat *anybody*. We showed that against Oakland, and we can do it again." The Oakland A's were the three-time defending World Series champs, and also heavily favored against us in the American League Championship Series. But we swept them three straight, so here we were.

Coming out strong in that first game against the Reds was very important for us. We were at home, and wanted to set the tone for the series. All the papers were saying how Cincinnati's right-handed power hitters like Johnny Bench and George Foster were going to smash the ball to left, and that Joe Morgan and Dave Concepción were going to run wild on the bases. But I knew if I pitched low and outside to the righties that it would be tough for them to bring their swing all the way around and get lift on the ball toward the Green Monster. If guys tried to steal, I had a lot of faith in Carlton Fisk's arm behind the plate—and my pickoff move to first wasn't too bad either.

My back had been bothering me earlier in the summer, but once we got some breathing room in the division I was able to skip a few starts in early September. I never liked too much rest but I'm glad Darrell Johnson, our manager, insisted on it. I'd come back feeling stronger than ever.

I always felt great pitching at Fenway. The fans were so close you could really hear them, and they were very supportive. All the LOO-EEE, LOO-EEE stuff was good for me; I fed off it. Boston fans are like the fans in Cuba and Mexico: very loud, very passionate, and very knowledgeable. That's a nice combination, especially if you produce—and always give your best. They can tell if you don't.

We didn't have all the big names the Reds did, but our guys knew how to play too. So when Pete Rose started talking shit, it was alright with me. That's why they play the games. He got up that first time and didn't know what was coming at him—which is just the way I wanted it. If you've got a hitter guessing, it doesn't matter whether you have your best stuff or not. You can find a way to get him out.

My first pitch to Rose was high and a touch outside, and he didn't bite. He fouled off a couple fastballs, took another high and away, and then I froze him in his spikes with my hesitation pitch—a dipping, slow-moving pitch that when thrown well would seem almost to pause mid-flight before breaking sharply down into the catcher's mitt. Fisk caught it and then immediately gunned it back to me, faster than it had come in. I could tell he was excited.

The crowd loved it, but not Rose. He stomped away from the plate like it was on fire, and his tough-guy look was gone. He tried to fake a laugh as he turned to umpire Art Frantz, like he couldn't believe what he had just seen. Frantz said the pitch was perfectly legal, and lucky for Rose it was ball three.

He stepped back into the box and glared at me again.

The count was now full. I threw a couple more fastballs, trying to catch Rose guessing wrong, but he managed to foul them into the left-side seats. He looked at his bat, but it wasn't going to give him any answers. This was just between me and him, and when I gave him a breaking ball with my next pitch it jammed him. Swinging defensively, he tapped a weak grounder to second baseman Denny Doyle, who threw it to Cecil Cooper at first. Easy out.

As Morgan, Cincinnati's number-two hitter, walked to the plate, I could see Rose already yapping at his teammates in the dugout. He was telling them I had nothing, I found out later, and they could beat me if they waited out my breaking stuff. Get me to throw more fastballs, and then knock them all over Fenway.

He should have saved his breath. I wasn't stupid, and I wasn't going to let them dictate the action. I had waited too long to get here—to get my *whole family* here. Nobody was taking the food off my table so easily.

Rose was still jawing after the game. "In the National League," he sneered at reporters, "we don't face anyone who throws a spinning curve that takes two minutes to come down." Maybe so, but that was his problem. So was his big "0-for-4" at the top of the Reds box score.

Pete was a great hitter, but not that day. None of the Reds were, as the scoreboard showed:

INNING	123	456	789	R	H	E
CINCINNATI	000	000	000	0	5	0
BOSTON	000	000	600	6	12	0

This old rooster still had a little fight in him.

2

SEÑOR SKINNY

IN A SMALL TOWN OUTSIDE Havana, young Luis Clemente Tiant was the best athlete among his friends. He excelled at a variety of sports, especially baseball, but there was a shadow looming over him: his father, Luis Eleuterio Tiant, a pitching legend on the island.

Playing year round—in Cuba, Mexico, and other tropical climes during the fall and winter, and in the Negro National League of the United States in the spring and summer—the elder Luis was a wiry left-hander and fan favorite known for his colorful pitching persona. He spent the 1930s and '40s delighting crowds and frustrating batsmen with a vast repertoire of pitches delivered from different wind-ups and angles. And when given the opportunity in exhibition games, he held his own against top hitters of the era—including Babe Ruth.

The problem for Luis E. and other dark-skinned players of his generation was finding such opportunities. The highest and by far most lucrative level of organized baseball was closed off to them, as an unwritten but vigorously defended color line barred non-whites from playing in the U.S. major leagues. Some Latino and Black stars with strong skills and lighter hues "passed" as white and made it onto major league rosters for brief or long stints; Luis E., whose physique earned him the nickname Señor Skinny, did not have this option.

So on he played, waiting and praying for change while enduring the long bus rides, low pay, and biting racism in the Deep South. He felt his time would someday come, but when the color line was finally broken in the late 1940s, Señor Skinny was already past 40 years old—and his chances for a major league contract barely matched his build.

Luis C. Tiant was a young boy when his father threw his last pitch as a professional, but he inherited from his namesake a love for family, friends, and hard work that would serve as the foundation on which he would build his own diamond dreams.

THERE WAS A TIME when if you asked someone in Cuba if they had ever heard of Luis Tiant the baseball player, they might have said, "Which one?" Or, if they were a *real* old-timer, they may have asked, "the lefty or the righty?"

The first, born in Havana on August 27, 1906, was the left-hander. My father.

Luis Eleuterio Tiant was one of the best pitchers on the island—and one of the smartest. I only saw him play at the very end of his career, but I grew up hearing how great he had been. Baseball has always been *the* sport of Cuba, and Dad was a national hero.

He wasn't a big man. Maybe 5-foot-10 and 150 pounds, he was nicknamed "Señor Skinny." I know what you're thinking: I filled out a uniform pretty good, so how can I be the son of Señor Skinny? I don't know, but I've got the photos to prove it. My mother, Isabel, was a terrific cook, but even she couldn't fatten him up.

His size kept him from having an overpowering fastball, but Dad made up for it by pitching with his head and his heart. Sportswriters and guys who played against him said his herky-jerky motion kept hitters off-balance, and he had more ways of gripping the ball and more different deliveries than they could ever figure out. It's the same way the writers would later describe me as a pitcher. I didn't learn it from him, but I guess some things just get passed on.

Another thing Dad had was a great pick-off move. Runners on first had a tough time taking leads, never knowing when he might throw over there. He was said to be so confident in his move that he would intentionally walk batters just so he could try to pick them off. They say he even did this to Cool Papa Bell, a Hall of Famer who one teammate said was so fast he could "flip the light switch and be in bed before the room got dark."

Fans loved the Señor Skinny show—but not hitters. One time, the legend goes, Dad started his regular windup from the stretch and then threw to first so suddenly that the batter was completely fooled and took a full swing at a ball that wasn't there. While the hitter wondered how the pitch got by him, the umpire told him he was lucky he didn't call him out for stupidity.

Dad always kept them guessing.

"You had to watch him," remembered Armando Vazquez, a teammate of my father. "When you expected him to throw a curveball, he threw you a fastball; when you expected him to throw you a fastball, he threw you a screwball. Smart guy."

That screwball—also known as a fadeaway—was Dad's best pitch. It would break away from the hitter, the opposite of a curveball, and then dip down at the last instant. The top major league screwball pitcher in the 1930s was Carl Hubbell, the great left-hander for the New York Giants. So, they also called Dad the Cuban Carl Hubbell.

He would have loved to have faced Hubbell in a big-league game, but he never got the chance. This was before Jackie Robinson broke the color line, and my father was too dark-skinned to "pass" like some Cubans and play in the white major leagues during those days. No matter how good a pitcher he was, it just wasn't going to happen.

Dad couldn't sit around feeling sorry for himself; he had to put food on the table. So he went where he *could* play. For many years he pitched year-round: winters at home against the top ballplayers in the Cuban League, and summers in the United States against Bell, Josh Gibson, Satchel Paige, and the other great Black players in the Negro Leagues. He also pitched at different times in Mexico, the Dominican Republic, and on barnstorming clubs in the U.S.—including the famous House of David team that all wore long beards, and another one called the Havana Red Sox. Altogether he put in more than 20 years as a professional ballplayer from 1926 to 1948.

Early in his pro career, Dad was on a team called the Cuban Stars. All the players on the Stars were from the island, and they toured the U.S. playing white semipro teams and top Black clubs from the Negro Leagues. Even if they truly loved the game, like my father, they had two strikes against them from the start.

"Unlike the U.S. Negro League teams, the Cubans had no home city; they were on the road constantly," John Holway, a Black baseball historian and author, explained. "Discrimination in hotels and restaurants—which American Blacks could avoid at least while they were playing at home—was a constant fact of life for Cubans."

Eventually Dad and other players from the island hooked on with the Negro League's New York Cubans. The Cubans had a place to call home; starting in 1940, they played at the Polo Grounds when the Giants were on the road. But while the two clubs shared a ballpark, that was it. The white major leaguers made good money and traveled first class by trains with dining cars and sleeping compartments; the Negro Leaguers rode buses and had trouble finding greasy spoons and fleabag hotels that would serve Blacks. Sometimes they just ate sandwiches and slept on the bus.

My dad told me that at one point in his career he made 50 cents a game, and sometimes played three games in a day. They would have one game in the morning, ride by bus to another ballpark, play *that* game, and then get back on the bus and head to a third ballpark to play that night.

"We didn't have much money," said Armando Vazquez, "but we had a little freedom."

The Cubans were managed by one of the island's most legendary athletes, my father's hero Martín Dihigo. He could do it all; pitch, play the infield and outfield, and hit for power and average. At home they called Dihigo *El Inmortal*—The Immortal—and he was Cuba's Babe Ruth. In the Negro League's 1935 East-West All-Star game, Dad pitched the first 9 innings, and then was relieved by Dihigo in the 10th. El Inmortal gave up the game-winning home run, but it was still a big thrill for Dad. Dihigo later became the first player enshrined in baseball Halls of Fame in Cuba, Mexico, and the United States.

Most people agree that Satchel Paige was the best of all Negro League pitchers, but at his peak my father might have been just as good. Five times, Dad led the Cuban League in shutouts, including a record 12 in the winter of 1936-37. One summer, 1935, he got the most votes of any Negro League pitcher—including Paige—for the East-West All-Star Game. A sportswriter for the *Chicago Defender*, a top Black newspaper, wrote that "Lefty Tiant is a pitcher without weakness."

Frank Forbes, the general manager for the Cubans, said my father was so skinny he "looked like he suffered from consumption." But that didn't stop him from making some of the best players in the world look silly.

Buck Leonard, one of the greatest hitters of all time, was a Negro League legend who would eventually make the Hall of Fame. They called him "the Black Lou Gehrig" but he sure didn't hit like Gehrig against Dad.

"He'd give Buck a fit," Wilmer Fields, Leonard's teammate from the Homestead Grays, later remembered. "Buck was a fastball hitter, and Tiant would throw that junk up there—screwball, slider, curveball—very seldom you saw that fastball. And you know, it's hard to hit that junk, especially in a park like Griffith Stadium [home of the Washington Senators, which the Grays also called home]; that was a big place."

Only when my father had completely frustrated Leonard, Fields said, would he suddenly sneak in the heat. "He'd really hum that ball—every now and then he'd burn it in."

The Negro Leaguers felt they were just as good as the white players, and they loved to prove it. John Holway was one of the first to research games between the two groups, and of the first 444 box scores he could find from what he called baseball's "apartheid era," the Blacks won 268 and the whites 168. There were eight ties.

These weren't just any white players, either; entire major league teams would come to Cuba on offseason barnstorming trips to play against all-star teams from the island. In April 1935 my father beat the St. Louis Cardinals, 2-1, in an 11-inning game at Havana. These were the defending World Series champions, with Hall of Famers Dizzy Dean, Pepper Martin, and Joe Medwick—the famous "Gas House Gang." He stopped them cold.

Later that same year my father pitched against the real Babe Ruth in an exhibition game held in the States. Ruth was at the end of his career, and the promoter for the event told Dad to lay the ball in nice and easy so the Babe could hit it over the fence and give the crowd a show.

"OK," my father said. "Don't worry about it."

Then the game started. Depending on who was telling the story, Ruth either got one ground-rule double and three flyball outs, or Dad blew it right by him—striking the Babe out three or four times. The details don't matter; what does is that the Babe *didn't* homer. The promoter was mad, but my father made his point.

"I wasn't going to let nobody hit a home run off me like that," he told me.

You see, my dad didn't care *who* was at the plate—or whether the game counted. They *all* counted to him. The batter was the enemy and had to earn his way on base. Dad threw inside when he wanted, always keeping you off the plate, and beaned more than his share of guys.

Ted Page of the Philadelphia Stars, a pretty tough guy known as "Terrible Ted," said that my father "gave no mercy to any batter." Page would know; he used to tell about the time he got a hit off one of Dad's curves, and then the next time he came to the plate got knocked out cold with a pitch to the head.

"He laid me out. They poured water on me, they poured ice on me, everything," Page said later. "Tiant couldn't speak much English. But the guy playing third base, Arango, in his very poor English said, 'You no hit *dat* one!' I'm lying on the ground: 'You no hit *dat* one!' I could just hear him. My head was getting bigger and bigger. I didn't know how big it was going to get."

If anybody doubted the story, Ted would show them the proof.

"See that spot on my temple? No hair. The guy that hit me there was Luis Tiant."

Newspaper stories about my father's games played up his smarts and quirky delivery, calling him a "clever southpaw" with "weird slants." He didn't have an engine that conked out after nine innings either. On December 2, 1943, Cuban Winter League rivals Marianao and Cienfuegos played a 20-inning game—the longest in the history of Cuban professional baseball—and Dad threw 14 scoreless innings before allowing a single unearned run and exiting after 15.

After all those years of work, he seemed to get better with age. In 1947, when he was 41, Dad had a perfect 10-0 record, pitched in front of 38,402 fans at the Polo Grounds in the East-West All-Star Game, and led the Cubans to the Negro National League pennant. Their opponents in the Negro World Series were the Cleveland Buckeyes, who had future major leaguers Sam Jethroe and Al Smith in the outfield and future Dodgers pitcher Chet Brewer on the mound. A real strong club.

The best-of-seven series was played in different cities and ballparks to draw bigger crowds, and my father started Game Two at Yankee Stadium. He didn't pitch great, and left trailing, but the Cubans came back and won, 10-7. It was the same thing during his next start at Cleveland's League Park, in Game Six: The Buckeyes got out to a 5-0 lead, but the Cubans bailed him out and won, 6-5, to clinch the series. Dad had gone through the entire regular season and playoffs without losing a game for a championship team.

It was a good time to have a career year. That same season, Jackie Robinson had broken the color line and made the Brooklyn Dodgers as the first acknowledged Black major leaguer since Morris Fleetwood Walker nearly sixty years before. Robinson led the Dodgers to the 1947 National League pennant, was named Rookie of the Year, and paved the way for other big-league teams to start signing Black ballplayers. Many of the best were in the Negro Leagues, including dark-skinned Cubans like my father.

Dad probably figured his chance had finally come, but things don't always work out the way you want—or the way they *should*. First, the Cubans released him in the winter of 1947-48. All he ever told me later was that the manager didn't like him—but how can you not like a guy who never loses? The whole thing seemed crazy, but he just said that's the way it was. I never pushed him to tell me more.

He spent that winter playing in a second-level Cuban league, and then with a few Mexican teams the next summer. The Negro National League folded, partly because of Jackie, so Dad couldn't go back there. And unless your name was Satchel Paige, who the Cleveland Indians signed in 1948 as a 42-year-old "rookie," nobody wanted a spot on their roster taken up by someone anywhere near that age—whether he was Black, white, or purple.

Young teammates of my father from the '47 Cubans, including Minnie Miñoso, catcher Ray Noble, and pitcher Lino Donoso, would later make the majors. But not Dad. Señor Skinny's baseball career was over.

"Tiant would have pitched in the major leagues easy, easy," Armando Vazquez said of his teammate and friend. "Everybody talked about Tiant; he was a hell of a pitcher. Magnificent." Monte Irvin, a Hall of Fame outfielder who starred in the Negro Leagues and later with Willie Mays on the New York Giants, agreed, saying Dad would have been a "great, great star" in the majors.

Peter J. Bjarkman, the author of several books on Cuban baseball history, summed up my father's fate.

"Tiant's only flaw as a topflight moundsman," wrote Bjarkman, "seemed to be that he was black-skinned."

By this time, there was another mouth to feed in the Tiant house. I was born in Havana on November 23, 1940, and grew up with my parents just outside the capital in the borough of Marianao. I was the third "Luis" in the family, after my grandfather and father. My oldest son and my grandson both carry the name now too. (To make things easiest for readers, we'll refer to my father as Luis Sr., me as Luis, and my son as Luis Jr.—or Little Luis—from this point on.)

There has been a lot of kidding around about my age, going back to my playing days. Red Smith, the great New York sportswriter, once wrote that I was "34 going on 44," and every time I joined a new team during my career the papers would mention my "reported" age like it couldn't be true. Hall of Famer Tony Perez, a great friend, used to joke that he grew up in Cuba hearing about the "legendary Luis Tiant"—even though Tony is almost the same age as me. Nobody asked if he was talking about my father.

I can take a joke, but I don't care what anybody says. A lot of players *did* take years off their age back then when they were trying to break in, especially guys from poorer countries like Cuba where they didn't keep good birth records. A scout was much more likely to sign an 18-year-old prospect than a 22-year-old. But if my mother said I was born in 1940, then that's good enough for me.

Besides, I was still a little kid when my father stopped pitching. The only times I remember seeing him play were in a few Cuban Winter League games right near the end of his career. One of my uncles used to take me. We'd sit down behind the dugout, and my father would peek out and tell my uncle, "C'mon, bring him down." Then my uncle would bring me down and seat me right in the dugout. I was about seven years old, and this was around 1948, so the years match up.

Still don't believe me? Look at the back of my baseball card.

Marianao was a small town. There were people living around us—lawyers, businessmen, a president of a soda company—who were rich, and some of my best friends growing up came from families with a lot of money. But most of us were poor. We had clothes, and nobody went hungry, but things were tight. So, everybody helped each other. If you didn't have something to eat, or you needed anything, you could come and knock on our door and say, "Do you have this?" and we'd give it to you. Then, a little later on, we might need to do the same thing at your door.

Dad played ball for almost 20 years straight, winter and summer, and had barely saved any money. Even though he was loved and well-known in Cuba, there were no high-paying coaching jobs or a big pension to fall back on when he was through. When his career was over, Dad had to hang up his glove and go right to work like everybody else.

He managed to scrape together enough to buy a truck with two of my uncles. One of the uncles worked for a moving company, so after they bought the truck, the three of them worked there. It was tough. Sometimes they had to work all day moving furniture in the heat, going on maybe three or four trips for one job. Later, when he got a little older and couldn't lift as much, Dad pumped gas at a station right on the main road. Everyone driving by could see him in his bright white uniform.

I've got nothing against pumping gas, but I'm sure it was tough to go from pitching in Yankee Stadium to filling up cars.

When I was growing up, Sundays were about getting together with the neighbors. Everybody would throw in some money, and we would cook—each week at a different house. My mother's specialty was croquettes, and there was always family around to enjoy them with us. I had two twin aunts down the block, married to the uncles who got the truck with my father, and my grandmother and grandfather—my father's parents—lived a half-block past them.

After these grandparents moved to another town about five miles away, I would often take the bus over and stay with them for two or three days. My grandfather, the first Luis, used to be a policeman; now he was working for a rich family taking care of a big place that they had. It seemed to take up almost a whole block, and we would ride a horse all around the grounds. Granddad was small, but my grandmother was a tall woman—maybe 5-9 or 5-10. She was beautiful, with green eyes.

Family was everything. My mother was tough, but she could be funny too. If she liked you, she'd joke with you. I probably got my funny side from her.

My father was a proud man. He loved putting on a suit and hat and walking down the avenue where we lived shaking hands with everyone. If it was a hot day, he might change his suit three times and walk all over town in the morning, noon, and late afternoon. I was proud of him, too, and loved hearing people talk about how great a pitcher he had been.

What he *didn't* talk about much was what a hard life it was—what he went through on the road, and how his career ended.

As I'd learn later, dark-skinned Cuban players, just like Black players in the United States, dealt with a lot of racism trying to make it in white baseball. A few light-skinned Cubans like pitcher Adolfo "Dolf" Luque, a 20-game winner for the Cincinnati Reds in 1939, were able to "pass" and reach the major leagues. Dad was happy for them, but it was very, very tough to not get his own chance.

Sometimes he got together with his old teammates, including Minnie Miñoso—a great Cuban outfielder who, because he was younger, would get a chance to star in the majors after the color line was broken. My father was Minnie's first roommate, and they became good friends. Minnie used to come around to see him, and they would just start talking and talking. But I never saw any trophies or anything else in our house related to Dad's baseball career.

Really, I don't think he ever got over being released by the Cubans. He had not been a drinker when he played; when he and his teammates went out after games, they told me, he always got milk. But now he would drink with my uncles, maybe to help forget.

A lot of the time, when he wasn't at work, my father took care of me while my mother worked. She cooked for a rich family in a big, beautiful house near where we lived. It wasn't a long walk for her to get there, maybe five blocks, but it was like being in another world. She'd clean for them every once in a while, too, and one day I was coming home from school and saw her cleaning the front steps of the other family's house. I must have been 12 or 13.

"No more!" I yelled at her. "I don't want to see you over here doing that, or I'm going to get mad!"

It's funny. This family was great to my mother; it was like the kids cared more about her than *their* mother because she was always over there. She cooked for them for a long, long time, and that was OK. I just didn't want to see her cleaning their stairs, and I said so.

You know what I did after that? Every day, when I got out of school, I would go and clean those stairs myself.

I wanted something better for her, and for my father, and they wanted the same for me. Take school. Many of my friends went to private schools, but we didn't have the money. My father believed knowing English would lead me to success, so somehow, he got me into a private school that taught English. The problem was that I didn't learn much—just a few words like "table," "seat," and "window." It wasn't that I was dumb; my heart just wasn't in it.

Here's why: at the age of 13 or 14, I was the same size I am now. When we went into a classroom, I was by far the biggest kid there. And every time I said something wrong in English, everybody laughed. It got me really mad.

One day I told the teacher, "You know, you better tell these kids to stop laughing at me when I say something wrong. I don't know English like *they* don't know English, so I don't know what they are laughing at. But if they keep messing around with me, I'm going to beat them up. That's what I'm going to do."

The teacher did nothing, and I kept getting more frustrated. Then one day I went to my dad.

"You know what?" I told him. "I don't want to go to school anymore. I hate English class."

Dad made me stay in school and graduate, but he did let me stop going to English. Then look at what happened. I came to the United States, and I needed to know English after all. He was right; I wish I had listened to him then.

3

CUBA DREAMS

UNDETERRED BY THE INEVITABLE COMPARISONS to his father, Luis Tiant gravitated to the pitcher's mound. There he met with success—and scrutiny.

He threw the ball so hard—and with so much movement—that in his early teens he was temporarily restricted from pitching in dimly lit night games to protect hitters and catchers from injury. After excelling in Cuba's Little League and Juvenile League programs, he was selected at age 16 to travel to Mexico City for an international tournament. It was 1957. Fans who saw him there noted that he had inherited his father's talent, and he felt pride rather than pressure.

The next natural step for a bright, rising ballplayer on the island was ascension to one of four professional teams comprising the Cuban Winter League—a circuit so strong that pro ballplayers from the United States, even major league stars like Willie Mays and Jim Bunning, crossed the Gulf of Mexico and joined the league during their off-seasons. And since one of its four teams—the Havana Sugar Kings—also played a full summer schedule as a top minor-league affiliate for a major league club, a dream formed in Luis's mind: If he could get the Sugar Kings interested in him, it could lead to a professional contract and the chance, someday, to pitch in the majors.

After turning 18, he told his parents of his desire to try out for the Sugar Kings. Luis Sr. was wary of the plan. Still haunted by memories of the racism and rough living conditions he encountered during the 1930s and '40s as a Cuban professional ballplayer in the U.S., he feared his only child would receive similar frustration and disappointment were he to travel there.

WHEN I CAME TO understand the harsh treatment my father endured in baseball, I felt bad about it. But it never changed my mind about people. I didn't worry about race—liking this guy or not liking that guy. Everybody was equal in my eyes; it's what they *did* that mattered. I never liked abuse, but I didn't take crap from anyone either.

If you were bad to some of my friends, you and I had a problem. I was a big kid, and I never liked it when another big kid hit a little kid. If I saw it, I'd fight him. I fought for my friends all the time. I was good to them and they were good to me. We would fight for each other.

One day I fought with a kid who had just moved in. He was trying to be smart, to establish himself as a tough guy by taking on a bigger kid—me. I was in the park, and he hit me with a rock. It broke against my skull, and there was blood everywhere. So, I got a rock and went after him; I wanted to kill him.

There was a woman who used to take care of the kid, like a maid, and she saw me chasing him.

"No, no! Don't do it!" she yelled. "You're going to kill him!"

"Look what he did to me!" I yelled back. "If I get him, I'll beat the shit out of him!"

I *didn't* catch him, and on the way home I had to go past where my grandmother lived. I was bleeding all over my shirt and everything, and she came out and cleaned me up. What did my friends do? They all got together and went to the kid's house. They started throwing rocks at it, and I had to go over there and tell them to stop.

Then, about three days later, I came up to the kid on the sidewalk. This time, I beat the shit out of him.

Because I was an only child, my friends were like brothers to me. No matter what we did, good or bad, we were always together. We didn't have a lot, and some of us much less than others, but we didn't care. Friends and family was enough.

Mostly, we played sports. At first, I did a little soccer, a little boxing, and a little running. Then, over time, things started happening.

Somebody punched me in one of my eyes, and that was it for boxing.

I was a 400-meter runner in track, and one day the guy who ran the 800 meters was sick. The coach came up to me.

"Do you think you can run the 800, too?"

"I don't know, but I'll try."

Well, I started that thing, and oh boy. It was a real hot day, and by the end of the race I couldn't even walk. They had to throw water on my face to get me moving. That was it for track.

Soccer also meant a whole lot of running, but there was one game where a big kid like me could really do all right: *el remachado.* This was a different thing all the way, more of a punishment than a game. You wanted to punish the other guy.

Everybody started in the middle, and then one guy threw a ball up in the air. You tried to get it, and if you did then you threw it at someone close to you. I mean, you *gunned* it.

The ball we made ourselves; we took a cigarette box, and then we put a rock inside some paper and wrapped the cigarette box around it. If that thing hit you, it *hurt.* The good thing was that we had a rule: you had to hit the guy from the waist down. Still, you could always miss and hit the guy in the back—or even on his head.

Remaches means "rivets" in English; when you played el remachado, and got hit, it felt like somebody was drilling a screw into *you.*

One day I went to a friend's house. He had a banana tree, and we ate some bananas. Then we went and played el remachado. During the game, I picked up the ball, gunned it at him, and hit him in the back (my aim was off that day). He started throwing up and turned blue.

"Oh my God," I thought. "I killed him."

Luckily, he wasn't hurt too bad. We stopped the game after that, and we stayed good friends. Most of the kids, we took care of each other. We grew up in the same area and we played all the time.

After a while I started focusing on baseball, which was my favorite sport anyway. This was the way it was with most of my friends, and most kids in Cuba. Baseball was like a religion in our country, and still is today. The first official game between two all-Cuban teams was played there in 1874, about ten years after students who learned it while attending college in the United States, as well as U.S. military men, started bringing baseball to the island. By the time I was coming up in the 1940s and '50s there were pro teams that played in integrated leagues all through the winter and summer. Young kids started in the Juvenile League, which is like the Little League in the U.S., and progressed up from there onto amateur clubs with hopes of going pro.

When fans weren't going to the ballpark, they listened to big-league games on the radio. Most of the broadcasts were Yankees games, so most Cubans became Yankees fans. I was too—sorry, Boston—and Mickey Mantle was my favorite player. Since there were a bunch of daily newspapers on the Island that carried box scores from the U.S., I could see how Mickey and dad's old teammate Minnie Miñoso—who mostly played for the White Sox—were doing.

As kids we didn't have fancy gloves, shoes, or equipment. A lot of times we didn't even have a decent place to get a game going. At the good parks, people often wouldn't let you play because they were afraid you would hit one of the little kids with a ball by mistake. We'd just find someplace else. There might be rocks in the field, or a hole in it, but we didn't care. We would even play in the street.

Whatever it took, we were going to *play*. If we didn't have a bat and ball, we'd get a cork, put some little nails into it, and then tape it up. Then we'd use a broomstick to hit it with. And if we could only get four or five guys to a side, we'd play a game called four corners. A guy would pitch the ball to you, you'd hit it with your hand, and then you'd run to a base. If the guy hit you in the leg with the ball before you reached base, you were out.

Because I was big, I started as a catcher. I didn't have a chest protector or cup, just a mask and glove. One time when I was behind the plate, a guy hit a foul tip and it got me right in the privates. I hurt for a LONGGGG time. That was it for catching.

Next, I played some infield: third base and some first base, and even second and short. I liked every position they put me at, and I was a good hitter. But if your father was Luis Tiant, everyone expected you to become a pitcher. So eventually I tried it, and I was hooked. It was not long before I was on the mound most of the time.

I felt good on the mound because I was in control. I wanted to be there. I wanted to be *the guy*. Not just out there, but playing an important part in the game. When I went out and won, I knew I put part of my life out there. We didn't just win because of this or that guy. I was *part of that win*.

My dad didn't give me too many pitching lessons, but I must have picked up something from watching him because from the start people said my motion was similar to his with all the different movements and the shaking. They say he kicked his leg up a little bit like Juan Marichal would later on, but I don't remember that from when I saw Dad play as a little kid—and he never taught it to me later.

What he did teach me was this: *Don't go starting anything you don't think you can finish.* I've carried that through all my life, on and off the field, up until now.

Once I got going in baseball, some of the guys who had played with my father started coming up to me.

"You're pretty good," they would say, "but your father was better."

His friends said it too, but it didn't bother me. I would just smile and say, "OK." Honestly, I was proud to be mentioned alongside him. It meant I was doing all right.

My father never used to watch me pitch when I started out. Maybe it was because of how he felt about his own career. But his friends saw me, and they told him, "You better go see your boy. He's getting good."

I was fourteen or fifteen years old by then, playing on a team called the Buena Vista Social Club. We played in a ballpark in Buena Vista with a bus stop behind it—they called it the Route Twenty-Eight Stadium. The buses would stop across the street, and the pitcher's mound looked straight through to the bus stop. I looked over one time from the back of the mound and saw my father getting off a bus. He hid behind one of the big columns at the bus stop and started watching me pitch.

He didn't think I saw him, and I didn't let on that I did.

After the game—which I won with a shutout—I looked over again and saw him coming across the avenue. He came up to me and shook my hand. Then he hugged me.

"You were good," he said.

That meant the world to me, knowing that he liked what he saw. He had pitched as a pro for 20 years, so he knew a good pitcher when he saw one. It didn't matter if I was his son, either; he was not the type to say nice things just to make me smile. He was tough, but also honest.

After that, he came to a lot of my games. I'd look over from the mound to the bus stop and he'd be standing there. He never actually went into the ballpark, even though it was wide open with free admission. Was he nervous? Superstitious? I never found out why.

When I got a little older, our team used to play under the lights a lot. The lights didn't work that great, which caused problems. One time I was pitching at night and the catcher couldn't handle me in the bad light. Every time I'd strike a guy out he'd make it to first base when the ball got by the catcher. So, he didn't count as an out, and I'd have to face an extra guy. I wound up striking out six guys in one inning!

Finally, the boss of the league told me I couldn't pitch anymore at night because I was going to hurt somebody. My coach put me back at third and first base for night games, until we changed to another park with better lights.

Once I was back to pitching days *and* nights, I started winning a lot. That was it; I never played another position again.

Word spread, and in 1957, when I was 16, I was selected to go to the World Series of Mexico. Cuba's top amateur team played against the Dominican Republic, Puerto Rico, the United States, Mexico, Panama, and Venezuela. I needed my parents' permission to make the trip, and I figured they would be excited about the opportunity.

I was half-right.

My mother, who always supported me, was OK with it. But not my father.

"You're not going," he said.

My mother jumped all over him.

"Why not?" she yelled. "This doesn't happen all the time! It's what he wants to do—let him play!"

Dad didn't budge.

"Nah, nah, nah," he said. "He's not going anywhere."

"But maybe it's the last time he gets a chance to go somewhere like this," Mom yelled back. "Let him go and compete and have a good time."

He kept saying, "No, no, no," but my mother fought hard.

Finally, Dad gave in and agreed to let me go. This was my first time out of the country, and my first time on a plane. It was a DC-7, a little Army transport plane with propellers. Because it was a cargo plane, there were no seats; the whole team just sat on the floor with our backs to the walls. All we needed were parachutes and we could have made a World War II movie.

Once we got out of that flying coffin, the trip was great. I pitched in some games, did well, and we almost won the whole tournament. But when I got back home I hurt my elbow. I went to the doctor, a Mexican guy living in Cuba. Somebody had told me he was good with sports injuries.

You know the ultrasound machines they have today? There was nothing like that back then. Every machine he had in his office looked like he had made it himself—like he was a mad scientist or something. He would rub this cream on my elbow, put it in a hot bowl, and then zap me with electricity. MANNNNN, it hurt. But it also seemed to *work*, at least at first. I went to him for two months, and felt better, but when I tried to pitch my elbow still bothered me.

Around this time, I met another doctor who wanted me to pitch for his team. I was very discouraged, and told him I couldn't do it. I couldn't throw without pain.

"No, you'll be fine," he said. "Come see me."

So, I went to see him in the hospital. He told me, "Sit down, I'll be right back." When he came back he brought a tray with a huge needle on it. It was so big it was hanging off the tray, and it was real thick all the way around.

"OK," he said, "Now I'm going to give you a cortisone shot."

I knew nothing about cortisone shots, but I knew I didn't want any part of that needle. He put some cream on my elbow, and then he left the room for a while to give it time to take before the shot.

This was my chance.

BOOM! I jumped up, ran out the door, and took off down the hall. He came running after me, but he didn't catch me because I was thinking about that needle.

My arm was still numb, and I knew I was going to have to go back there eventually. So, I called him up.

"What are you, chicken?" he said.

"Yeah, I'm chicken!"

He said I could go back the next day, and I did—and *then* he got me with that needle. Oh man... that hurt. The thing is, he kept moving the needle around, and that hurt *more*. And after he finished, he told me I had to keep throwing.

"Doctor," I said, "how do you expect me to throw when I can't even bend my arm?"

I couldn't even stretch it out; my arm felt like it had a piece of wood in it.

"You've just got to stretch out and throw," he said.

"Doctor, I'm not doing anything."

I had to go to him another time, and he put in another needle. After *that* shot, he told me to take it easy for a few weeks and then throw. I kept working it out and working it out, stretching my arm, and over time the pain in my elbow went away.

It never bothered me again, either, but I didn't pitch for the doctor's team. I didn't think he had been fair to me, pushing me to throw when I was still in pain. He was thinking more about his team than my health.

That's what happened in 1959. After coming back from my elbow injury, I had another good year in the Juvenile League in '58. Now I wanted to try out for the most respected of all Cuban teams: the Havana Sugar Kings.

Owned by a huge sugar plantation owner, the Sugar Kings were part of the Cuban Winter League. The league had four teams—Almendares, Cienfuegos, Havana, and Marianao—that played as many as five games a week. Most games were in the Gran Estadio de La Habana, a wonderful ballpark in Havana. The talent in the league was terrific; all the best native players, plus major league stars like Willie Mays and Jim Bunning who were looking to stay sharp and in shape during their off-season. Many great Negro League players like Josh Gibson, Ray Dandridge, and my dad had also played there through the years.

This was Cuban baseball at its best—and most colorful. Steve Fainaru and Ray Sanchez describe the era perfectly in their book, *The Duke of Havana*:

> "Before the revolution, baseball in Cuba, particularly in Havana, was played with an intensity found only in New York before the Dodgers and Giants moved west. The range of the sport may have been unrivaled. The sport was as colorful as the culture in which it thrived. This was back when the mob ran Havana and there were numbers runners on every street corner. Gambling was encouraged at the ballpark. The bookies were like hot-dog vendors. As [Almendares pitcher Max] Lanier ran off the field about beating the Havana Reds in the famous 1947 Cuban League finals, the bettors mobbed him, stuffing dollars into his uniform as if he were a stripper exiting the runway. By the time he reached the clubhouse he was $1,500 richer."

Great baseball, great fans, and great money? I wanted a part of that.

By the time I was coming up, the Sugar Kings also played during the summer in the International League, competing with pro teams from the U.S., Canada, and Mexico. The Sugar Kings had become a Triple-A affiliate of the Washington Senators, a major-league club. So, if I signed with Havana, I would be just one step away from the majors—with a chance to either make it to Washington or get seen by a scout from another big-league team and hope for a trade. Cuban pitchers Camilo Pascual and Pedro Ramos had been signed by the Senators a few years before, and were now in the big leagues facing Mantle and Miñoso.

My father came with me to the Havana tryouts in the spring of 1959, but I didn't make the Sugar Kings. Later, an official from the Senators told my father what he thought of my talent:

"Señor Tiant, your boy will never make it. He should accept that now, and maybe get a job in the fruit market as a salesman."

Before this, I didn't understand why my father was so against my playing in that Mexico tournament back in '57. *He* played, I'd think to myself, so how come he doesn't want *me* to play?

Now I was starting to get it.

Despite being a great pitcher, he never got a chance to play in the major leagues. He had to deal with racism for all those years in the U.S., and he didn't want me to go through what he went through. Even if times were changing, and there were Black players in the majors, there was still plenty of racism there too. Plus, the big-league owners controlled everything in baseball; no-trade clauses, multiyear contracts, and free agency were way, way in the future. You could get cut or traded at any time. Just like what happened to him.

That's why he didn't want me to play. He wanted me to go to school and get an education so *I* could be the one in control. Maybe become a doctor, a lawyer, or an engineer. Not follow the same path as him, which led to pain and disappointment.

Only it wasn't that easy. Like him, I loved the game. I loved the feeling of being out on that mound. To me, *that* was control. And when another chance came, if it did, I was going to take it.

4

YOU CAN'T GO HOME AGAIN

ONCE LUIS TIANT'S FATHER BEGRUDGINGLY accepted his son's choice of vocation, a career opportunity developed almost immediately.

It was, in fact, the elder Tiant whose connections helped pave the way. Back in the 1940s, a young Mexican named Bobby Avila had been a batboy and bull-pen pitcher for teams on which Luis Tiant Sr. had played. Eventually Avila made his own way in the game, reaching the major leagues with the Cleveland Indians—part of the first wave of talented young Black ballplayers to emerge in the years just after Jackie Robinson's 1947 debut. He stayed in touch with the Tiants and watched with delight as Señor Skinny's son grew into a promising pitcher.

Avila was back home during the winter of 1959, playing in the Mexican League and scouting for the Indians. He recommended young Luis to the Mexico City Tigers, who signed him to a contract. The Tigers enjoyed a working relationship with the Cleveland organization, much like the Havana Sugar Kings of the Cuban League had with the Washington Senators. It was just the break Tiant was seeking to keep his big-league dreams alive.

Moving to a new country, with little money but high expectations, Tiant struggled in his initial season as a pro. Then he exploded, becoming the Mexican League's top winner in 1960. He won the heart of a young lady named Maria del Refugio Navarro, whom he met in a most appropriate locale. He even earned a coveted spot with a Cuban League team for the coming winter. Tiant's career and love life were looking up, but beyond that things were far less certain.

Cuban revolutionaries led by Fidel Castro had stormed Havana and overthrown dictator Fulgencio Batista on New Year's Day, 1959, a move which brought the populace initial joy quickly followed by concern and fear. Castro promised Democracy and prosperity, but by aligning himself with Russia he seemed more intent on Communism. The U.S. government, once a partner with Cuba in diplomacy and on the baseball diamond, quickly became a Cold War-fueled enemy.

It was with mixed feelings that Tiant—on his way to his third season in the Mexican League—flew out of Havana in May 1961. Not knowing what the future held for Cuba, he had plans of his own that included making a life with Maria. He hoped to ask for her hand, get married, and that fall bring his new bride home to meet his family and enjoy an island honeymoon. His parents, he was sure, would love her, and when his big-league dreams came true Tiant could provide them all with a safer, more comfortable life.

Then came a letter from his father that changed everything—breaking the young pitcher's heart but deepening his resolve.

IT'S FUNNY HOW THINGS happen. My father originally didn't want me to play professional baseball, and it winds up being his old friend who helps get me my first big break. Bobby Avila used to catch my dad in the bullpen, and then went on to become a batting champion for the Indians. Avila remained close with our family, and when he told general manager Carlos Gonzalez of the Mexico City Tigers about me, Gonzalez signed me to my first contract—for $150 a month. I was on my way.

The Tigers were part of the Mexican League, which went back to the 1920s and was stacked with great Black ballplayers from the Negro Leagues, Cuba, and everywhere else. Mexico was so mad for baseball that in the 1940s a nutty rich guy named Jorge Pasquel offered top white players like Joe DiMaggio and Ted Williams huge contracts to jump their MLB teams and play in Mexico. The plan didn't work out, but in the mid-fifties the Mexican League became part of organized professional baseball's farm system as a Double-A league—two notches below the majors.

When I got to Mexico City in the spring of 1959 to play for the Tigers, I maybe had $20 in my pocket. That was it. It's crazy when you think about going through something like that. You don't know anybody, and you don't know the country. The people are speaking Spanish, but they are using different words than we use back home. You go to talk to people, and they don't know what you are saying. It's you against everybody.

You don't know if you're going to succeed. What if you get hurt or don't make the team—then what will you do? You don't have the money to fly home. You're 19 years old, and you don't know shit. You just want to play. I thank God He gave me the kind of mentality and heart to make me unafraid of anything. I pushed myself to the limit—and just kept telling myself that I could *do* this.

My first manager in Mexico City was Santos Amaro—a Cuban native who had played on my father's teams, primarily in right field, and was a legendary line-drive hitter with a fantastic arm. Baseball was his life, and both his son Rubén Sr. and grandson Rubén Jr. would go on to play in the majors. Santos was a terrific gentleman, a great dresser, and a fine manager, but even he could not do much with the 1959 Tigers. We were awful. Our record was 39-104, and by the end of the season we had gone through *three* managers.

My father never saw me pitch for Mexico City. The problem? He would get nervous, and the doctor told him not to come to my games. So he stayed back in Cuba. He used to play dominoes in the park around the corner from our house, and when I was pitching he would run home where my mother had the radio on with the game.

"Vieja?"—that means "Old Lady"—"Vieja? How's the kid doing?"

"He's doing good, he's winning now," she would answer.

Then he would leave and go back to his dominoes. He would play a game, check on *my* game, and then go back to play another. That's how he followed me.

That first year with Mexico City, my parents didn't hear me win too often. I went 5-19 with a 5.92 ERA and walked 107 batters while only striking out 98. Control and durability, two things that would become important parts of my game, were talents I hadn't yet developed. In 27 starts, I only completed 11—although three were shutouts. It was my first time facing professional competition, and I had to adjust and up my game. I definitely couldn't get away with mistakes. We had the worst team batting average and fewest home runs in the league, and gave up nearly two more runs a game than any other team. There was little room for error.

It was tough, but I never lost confidence in my ability. That winter I went home and tried again to join the Cuban League. I knew the owner of one team from when I'd played in the Juvenile League, but he just strung me along for a month and then said they didn't have any room on their roster for another pitcher.

So, I went back for another shot with Havana and managed to last a week with them at the end of training camp. Then they started the season losing a bunch of games in a row, and cut me without ever letting me pitch. The coach who was working with me just told me not to come back the next day; maybe they thought I was bad luck. Fermin Guerra, Havana's manager, said he would call me when they needed some more pitching. But I never heard from him, and wound up playing in the Venezuela League that winter before returning to Mexico City for my second year with the Tigers.

Everything came together for me in 1960. I won my first three games, and by the beginning of June already had as many victories (at 5-1) as I did the entire previous year. "If there is such a thing as a sophomore jinx," wrote Mexico City sportswriter Roberto Hernandez, "it has not affected Luis Tiant." I made the Pan-American All-Star team, and wound up tied for the league lead in wins and winning percentage with a 17-7 record (.708)—although my control was still an issue and I also led the way with 124 walks.

This is when I really started developing a reputation for having a rubber arm. In addition to my regular turn in the rotation, I also came on several times in relief—sometimes on the same day. In one doubleheader with Veracruz, I started the first game, got knocked out in the third inning, but then came back in the second game with five shutout innings out of the bullpen. Some guys hated the extra work, but I felt I did better the more I threw.

The Mexican League was a hitter's league then, and on the Tigers we had some of the best. Old family friend Bobby Avila, the same guy whose good word helped get me signed by the Tigers the year before, joined me on the All-Star team with a .333 average and a league-record 125 runs scored in his last year as a pro. Jose Echeverria, who somehow never got past Double-A, batted .369 with 131 RBI in 129 games. Two other guys drove in around 100 runs, and as a team we scored more than six a game—which will make most pitchers look good.

I was getting lots of attention now, appearing in weekly sports magazines and really bonding with the people of Mexico City. There were requests to give baseball clinics to kids throughout the area, and I was happy to do it. No matter what level you are at, the fans are the reason you are there. Without them, you're nothing, so I always felt it was important to give back. Besides, I liked making other people smile. Maybe it went back to watching my father, walking around shaking everyone's hand. It just felt right.

Everyone said "The Cuban Kid" was going places, and so were the Tigers. After finishing in last place the year before, we won the Mexican League championship. They called it "a Cinderella transformation" for both me and the team, and the fans loved it. Our attendance was up 175 percent from the previous year, the biggest increase in all of minor league baseball. The Tulsa Oilers of the Texas League beat us in the Pan-American playoffs, but our fans screamed so loudly that the Texans said it reminded them of a college football game. We even had cheerleaders who came out in the cold and rain to lead the shouting at our home games at Social Security Stadium. Four games in the series were decided by one run, including the finale, which I lost, 3-2, to Dick Hughes. Both of us would go on to start World Series games in the majors later on, me for the Red Sox (in 1975) and Hughes for the Cardinals *against* the Red Sox (in '67).

That 1960 season was big for me in another way. On July 28, I was at a women's softball game with some of my teammates, and saw a pretty girl playing left field. Her name, I found out, was Maria del Refugio Navarro. I started blowing her kisses from the stands.

"I was coming in from the field with a friend, and he was outside the fence," recalls Maria. "Our eyes met, and when he did that with the kisses I said to my friend, 'What's the matter with this guy? Is he crazy or what?'"

I don't think she liked me at first.

"Nah, not really," says Maria with a laugh. "But then a few days later, some girls on the team who he knew had a birthday party, and invited the whole team. I went with a friend, and he was there. He was dressed nice and had beautiful eyes. We started dancing, and that was it. That was the connection right there."

We started dating. She was Mexican, from Mexico City, and her family was into soccer and other sports. One of her brothers used to go to our games, and he liked me. *All* her brothers liked me, and her mother too. She was a widow and used to tell Maria, "You take care of Luisito (we had gotten close, so she called me that)—take care of him!" Maria would get mad and say, "My mother loves you more than she loves me!"

I'm not sure if Maria's mother knew about the reputation ballplayers had with the ladies, but I guess she realized I only had eyes for Maria. We dated the rest of that season, and then, on October first, I had to leave her behind in Mexico City and go home to play winter ball.

It was a scary time in Cuba. Growing up, I had never paid much attention to politics. The country was ruled by Fulgencio Batista then; he pretended to run a Democratic government, and was backed by the U.S., but everybody knew he was corrupt and fixed the elections. Those who said otherwise paid for it, so there was not much anybody could do. You just worked as best you could for yourself and your family.

The first I heard of Fidel Castro was when I was a teenager; he and a group called "The Bearded Revolutionaries" had tried to overthrow Batista in 1953 and were sent to jail. Because Castro was a powerful speaker who told people what they wanted to hear, he became a national hero to many Cubans. His band of guerilla soldiers spent years in the mountains planning and carrying out attacks on Batista, and when they finally drove him out of Havana and took control on New Year's Day, 1959, people were hopeful.

Castro said the country would soon become a true Democracy, but it was a lie. He and his men had former Batista supporters and officials put in jail, tortured, or executed. They shut down newspapers and radio stations that spoke out against them. All this started happening when I was playing in Mexico City, and I was worried about my parents, my uncles and aunts, and all my other relatives and friends back home.

When Castro took over, he was always talking about how much he loved baseball. He would go to games and wave at the crowds, or throw out the first pitch, and stories started to spread inside and outside Cuba that he had been a star pitcher in college who had big-league scouts trying to sign him. The rumors weren't true, but they were repeated so much that over time many people started to believe they *were* true. After Castro pitched for a pickup team he called Los Barbudos—The Bearded Rebels—and shutout a team of military police for a couple innings in a meaningless exhibition game, the stories increased.

That's just what Castro wanted. Baseball was a great source of pride for our country, and he saw it as a way to connect with the people. We grew up with the game from a very young age, playing in organized leagues. We had other sports like American football and soccer, but they were just for fun. If you were a good athlete, and you lived in Cuba, you wanted—and were encouraged—to be a baseball player. Castro understood this.

So did big-league teams. They knew they could take advantage of our desire to use baseball as a way out of poverty. So they signed up the best players on the island when they were still young, at way below their value. Even if you knew what was happening, there wasn't much you could do about it. If you complained about a contract, or not getting a big bonus, it was "see you later." There was always another player waiting his turn.

"It used to be that I had that territory all to myself but I stumble all over scouts in Cuba now," Joe Cambria, a top scout for the Washington Senators, told sportswriters in 1960. "Why do so many big league teams want Cubans? It's easy. You can get them cheaper than the American kids and they try harder. A Cuban kid at 15 or 16 already is a polished fielder. He works at the game all the time. He's still 'hungry.' The American kid is lazy and has so many distractions."

Cambria and other scouts found plenty of talent on the island when I was growing up. From the time Minnie Miñoso joined the White Sox in 1949, through 1959, nearly 40 Cubans made their big-league debuts. Some just had a cup of coffee, but others like Miñoso, Tony Taylor, and Zoilo Versalles had long, successful careers. As a pitcher, I had Camilo Pascual and Pedro Ramos to inspire me. Starting in the mid-fifties, both were members of Washington's starting rotation. And in '59, both were on the American League All-Star team along with Miñoso.

Guys weren't just leaving Cuba to play organized baseball in the summer now—they were *coming in*, too. In 1954 the Havana Sugar Kings joined the International League (IL) as an affiliate of the Cincinnati Reds. The IL had teams in U.S. cities like Rochester and Syracuse, New York and up into Canada with Montreal and Toronto. This was Triple-A, just one level below the majors, and there were lots of former major leaguers playing in the IL. Others, like Cubans Cookie Rojas and Mike Cuellar, would soon go the other way—from the Sugar Kings up to the majors.

After the big leagues expanded into Los Angeles and San Francisco in the late '50s, there was even some talk that Havana could soon get an MLB team. Why not? Cuba was a popular tourist destination with beautiful weather, delicious food, and plenty of entertainment including great music and gambling. Plus there was the passion people had for baseball on the is-land; that meant huge crowds.

Castro's revolution ended those big-league dreams. Government curfews, violent protests, and bombings cut into attendance at Gran Stadium, the Sugar Kings' home ballpark in Havana. This was just a warm-up to what happened during the 1959 season, six months after Castro took power. A doubleheader between the Sugar Kings and Rochester Red Wings started late on the night of July 25, part of a celebration marking the sixth anniver-sary of one of Castro's first rebel attacks. But when the early game went into extra innings, things got out of hand.

"Promptly at midnight, rockets in the background behind the stadium signaled the start of Cuba's first July 26 celebration," the *Rochester Democrat and Chronicle* reported. "The Cuban anthem played and everyone rose to sing. At the same time, weapons inside and outside the ballpark began firing."

Frank Verdi, a coach for Rochester, recalled that "bullets were flying out of the sky everywhere, thousands of 'em. We didn't know what the hell was happening. Players were diving for cover everywhere. There was a Jeep that was used for driving the pitchers in from the bullpen and that's where I took cover with a bunch of other guys. After about five minutes, it all subsided and the game resumed."

That was a mistake. Verdi was coaching third base in the top of the 12th inning for Rochester when more stray shots were fired. One .45 shell hit Verdi in the head, injuring his neck and ear; another got Sugar Kings short-stop Leo Cardenas—a future big-leaguer—in the shoulder blade. Before things could get even worse, the game was stopped and declared a 4-4 tie.

"If that bullet had been two inches to the left, the boys on the ball club would have had to chip in $5 apiece for flowers," Verdi said. "I was wearing a rubber and plastic lining in my cap [due to a prior beaning]. It saved my life. I have a wife and four kids at home. So far as I'm concerned, I've had it in Havana. We went there to play ball, not to be shot at."

The headline in the Rochester newspaper the next day was NIGHTMARE IN HAVANA—WINGS IN REAL DANGER. The incident was front-page news across the U.S.

You can't blame Verdi for being so upset. I don't think the soldiers were *trying* to shoot any ballplayers, and other people there that night said it wasn't as bad as he described. Nobody got badly hurt, Cuba apologized to the Red Wings organization, and the season continued. Havana even went on to win the 1959 International League championship, and then upset the Minneapolis Millers of the American Association—a Red Sox affiliate led by my future teammate Carl Yastrzemski—in the Little World Series.

But a lot of fans and officials in organized baseball were scared by what happened. IL officials were discussing dropping Havana from the league, pointing to the violence and declining attendance. Castro talked big, prom-ising that he and his government would do whatever it took to help. "The Sugar Kings are a part of the Cuban people," he said. "It is important for us to have a connection with Triple-A ball."

It didn't matter. By 1960 U.S.-Cuban relations were getting worse by the month, and in July the International League moved its Havana franchise to New Jersey—right in the middle of the season. The Sugar Kings would still have a team in the Cuban Winter League, but the country's professional ties with American organized baseball were over.

I felt bad about what happened, but there were other things on my mind as I flew home from Mexico City that fall. First there was Maria, who I had to leave behind with her family. I knew I was going to miss her very much. Then there was my career. After my big year for Mexico City, I felt I needed to take it to the next level in winter ball.

Then my plane landed in Havana, and I got the surprise of my life.

Waiting for me at the airport, along with my mother and father, was Sugar Kings manager Fermin Guerra. This was the same guy who, just the year before, had left me waiting for his phone call that never came. Now that I was a star in the Mexican League, I guess he figured I was good enough for his team.

My father looked on with a big smile as Guerra went into all the reasons why he wanted me to play for him in the Winter League. It was what I had always wanted to hear, but I was still angry at how Guerra had treated me before. He didn't have the respect to even call me last year, so why should I play for him now?

The reason was simple: this was my dream. Pride is a wonderful thing, but I had to follow my heart too. Playing for Guerra, and *winning* for him, would be good for my career and would make my father proud. Both those things were very important, so I shook Guerra's hand and joined the Sugar Kings.

It was a good move for both of us. Although Havana finished under .500 for the winter season, I went 10-8 with a 2.50 ERA and showed the people of my country how far I had progressed. Seeing my name on the list of the league's top pitchers along with veteran big-leaguers like Pedro Ramos and Mike Fornieles made me very proud.

My father's old teammates still told me "you're good, but he was better," and it still didn't bother me at all. What *did* bother me was that suddenly some people who didn't have the time of day for me before were acting different.

Like I said, I never cared what color anybody was, but there were some people in Cuba who cared a lot. There was this one private club in my hometown of Mariano that wouldn't let Blacks in. The guys who ran the club knew my family; they had grown up with my parents and my uncles. But they were white, and my parents were Black. When I went there with a group of my friends, we had to wait around outside. If we went in and tried to play ping-pong, we got kicked out on our asses. The guy at the door had been a friend of my family, but it didn't matter.

Then one day, after I signed with Havana, my friends and I went by the club. There were about five of us, and the same guy was outside.

"How are you doing, boys?" he says. "You want to come in?"

"Forget it," I said.

"C'mon, Luisito—come in."

He called me Luisito, like all my friends did when we were young. But he wasn't my friend, no way.

I lit into him.

"You remember when we used to come here *every frigging Saturday*, or if you had a party on Friday, and you never let us in? Wouldn't even let us play ping-pong? Now I'm playing pro ball, and you want to let me in?"

He just stood there, not knowing what to say.

"Well forget it," I said. "I don't want nothing to do with you guys. You can take your club and *shove it*."

It was crazy. Growing up, most of my friends where I lived were white. Their fathers had good jobs—doctors, lawyers, businessmen—and my friends went to good colleges. My parents couldn't afford that, and neither could most Blacks. I only knew two Blacks who went to college. We couldn't get in *that* club, and we couldn't get in *this* club—a block and a half from my parents' house!

It was crazy how we had to live, and that's one of the reasons I think it's important to tell my story. I'm sick and tired of people telling me, "You were lucky to play baseball." Lucky my foot! They don't know what I had to go through. I'm thankful to God for what He gave me, and the opportunities I had to provide for my family, but it wasn't luck.

When things like this happened, they made me stronger. I loved my home, but I couldn't wait to get back to Mexico City for another season with the Tigers. Not just to keep pitching, but also because it meant I could see Maria again. We wrote each other all winter and called when we could. The problem was you never knew if Castro had people listening in or reading the mail you sent. If they didn't like what you wrote, they threw the letter out before the person ever saw it. If your letters *did* get through, the person you sent them to could usually tell they had been opened and resealed. I guess they didn't mind what Maria wrote, because I think I got all her letters.

Even though I tried to stay out of politics, you couldn't ignore what was happening. Castro had started making trade deals with Russia, and Cuba was getting shipments of goods and arms from the USSR. This was during the Cold War, when anybody who was for Russia was automatically the United States' enemy. Soon there were rumors that the U.S. Army was going to invade Havana. Castro's government was also seizing land from citizens, and more people than ever were out of work. Hundreds of thousands of Cubans were leaving the island, not knowing when they would return.

I was due back in Mexico in the spring of 1961. But tension was rising between the U.S. and Cuba. Then there was the failed invasion in April by U.S.-backed Cuban rebels hoping to overthrow Castro at the Bay of Pigs. It all made getting off the island nearly impossible. For a month and a half, there were no flights going in or out.

Then, on May 25, after the minor league season had already started, Castro opened things up for a bit. I had gotten my visa and everything together, and as soon as it was possible—BANG!—I went on the first plane I could. Then the next day, right after I got out, they canceled the flights again. I think only a few planes got out—mine was one of them. Then nobody could get out anymore.

After missing the early part of the season, I jumped right into action with the Tigers. Coming out of the bullpen or starting, it really made no difference to me. I *preferred* to start, but whatever the team wanted me to do, I would do. So like the year before, Mexico City took advantage of my live arm and used me as a swingman.

In one doubleheader against our intercity rivals, the Mexico City Reds, I pitched five-and-two-thirds scoreless innings of relief in the first game to get the victory, and then came back and pitched five more out of the bullpen to win the nightcap. When the second game went to extra innings, I started the winning rally in the 11th with a single. Even then, I could help myself with the bat.

In July I was named to the Mexican League All-Star team for the second year in a row. This meant playing in the Pan-American Association All-Star Game, a matchup of the best talent from the Mexican League with the best from the Texas League. There were actually two games—the first in Mexico City, the second in San Antonio, Texas—and I got into the second one. The Texas lineup was stacked with future major leaguers, but I did all right; pitching in relief, I struck out six in three innings and let up only two singles to get the win.

Besides helping my team and feeling good about my performance—I figured there were big-league scouts in the stands—there was something else special about that game. The starting pitcher for the Mexican League, who I relieved in the fourth, was a little right-hander named Julio Moreno. He was a real old-timer from the Havana area, and was known as "the Cuban Bob Feller" for his overpowering fastball. But that was back in the 1930s;

Moreno had pitched year-round in various leagues for close to 20 years, like my father, and at one time they were teammates. Unlike Dad, who was a little older, Moreno made it to the majors and had played three seasons with the Washington Senators in the early 1950s.

By the time we shared the mound in San Antonio, Moreno was 40; his fastball was mostly gone, but he was still capable of getting guys out. Now they called him *Jiquí*, after the strongest and sturdiest of Cuban trees. He was a battler, just like my father had been, and one of the many reminders I got during my early career that I was following proudly in Dad's footsteps.

Some things had not changed much since my father's days in the Negro Leagues. While we were in Texas, we saw signs saying "NO MEXICANS" in the windows of the downtown shops. San Antonio was a couple hundred miles from the Mexico border, and I guess they wanted people coming over the line to know where they stood. It was like the "COLORED ONLY" and "WHITE ONLY" signs Dad had told me about seeing when he was playing in the Deep South. I'd see plenty of those soon enough.

After the All-Star game, rumors started to spread about the chances of my getting signed by a major league team. *The Sporting News*, which came out every week, was known as "The Baseball Bible" because it covered every team at every level of the game. In August, this note appeared on the Mexican League page:

> Two peso circuit pitchers have caught the eyes of major league scouts this season, one of them being Luis Tiant of the Mexico City Tigers…Manager Memo Garibay of the Tigers reported that the Los Angeles Dodgers had made "a good offer" for both pitchers. The Chicago Cubs are also interested in Tiant.

My English was not so good yet, so I didn't read this myself, but I definitely heard about it. It was all exciting, but the best part of my summer came off the field. I knew more than ever that Maria was the one I wanted to share my life with, but when it came to asking her mother and brothers for her hand in marriage, I was nervous. This is what teammates are for, right? So I called Luis Zayas, who had played with me on the Tigers the year before. He was with me the night I met Maria at the softball field, and now I needed him again.

One night that June, Maria opened the door and saw two guys staring back at her: me and Zayas. He helped give me the confidence I needed to propose that night. Lucky for me, she said yes.

Exactly two months later, on August 12, 1961, Maria and I were married in Mexico City. It was just me and her and her family, since my parents and the rest of my relatives were back in Cuba. We planned to go there in September so she could meet them. We'd celebrate with my family, and then honeymoon off the southern coast on Island de Pinos. Another winter season pitching for the Sugar Kings was also in my plans.

Then my father sent me a letter.

"Don't come home," he wrote. "Castro is not going to allow any more professional sports here—no baseball or boxing. If you do come home, I don't think you'll be able to get out again. They are not letting many people leave the island, especially young men of military age. Just make a life in Mexico for you and your family. I'll let you know when you can come home."

I showed the letter to Maria, and she didn't know what to say. I *wanted* to go home, but what could we do? Like my dad said, there was no guarantee we'd ever be able to get back out; it had been hard enough for me to get out that spring. Baseball was what I loved, and at home there was no longer the opportunity to make a living at it. Castro had shut the Cuban Winter League down, and starting in 1962 all teams on the island would be amateur clubs funded and overseen by the government year-round.

Thinking back now, as a father and grandfather, I realize how hard it must have been for my dad to write that letter. I was his only son, his only child, and by telling me these things he was taking the chance that he might never see me again. You have to love that about parents. All they want is what's best for you, no matter how much it hurts them. Your happiness is their happiness; your dreams are their dreams. He knew how much baseball meant to me, as it had to him, and he wanted me to reach the top—no matter what.

In the end, I respected my father's wishes. That winter, instead of having our honeymoon in Cuba, Maria and I went to Puerto Rico and I pitched there. It broke my heart just to think about home, but I believed then, as I have always believed, that God was looking out for me. He had a plan.

I never found out whether the Dodgers or Cubs tried to sign me, but it turns out that a Cuban League executive who also scouted for the Cleveland Indians, Julio "Monchy" de Arcos, had been at the Pan-American All-Star game in San Antonio when I struck all those guys out in relief. He told his bosses about me, and Cleveland purchased my contract from Mexico City for $35,000. That was a lot of money then, but I didn't get one Mexican penny—not one cent!

It was another slight, but I really didn't care. This was the chance I had been waiting for, and I was determined to get to the big leagues and make some *real* money. Then I would find a way to bring my whole family together.

5

FROM THE BUSHES TO THE BRONX

GETTING OPPOSING BATTERS OUT WAS in many ways the easiest part of life in the minor leagues for Luis Tiant. On the field he could battle on equal terms with the man at the plate, and by working harder and longer could gain an edge. Outside the white lines, however, the road to success was not so easily paved.

Being young and Black, and in the earliest stages of learning English, he was an outcast in the small, dusty towns of the Deep South where the Cleveland Indians sent him to hone his craft. There were dirty stares on the street, ugly slurs from the stands, and lonely nights in his room missing his family—some trapped in Castro's Cuba and some growing in Mexico City. He could not combat racism on his terms, with his fists and his wits, for the mores of Jim Crow did not allow it. Jail or worse awaited those who challenged the status quo. Fellow players, whites as well as African-Americans, didn't know what to make of him.

So Tiant fought back with the weapons at his disposal. He used his ability to throw a baseball fast and strong to win over fans, and his talent for friendship and fun to gain the respect—and love—of his teammates. Off-seasons spent with his beloved Maria and baby boy Luis Jr. sustained him, as did the more welcoming conditions for athletes of all colors in the winter leagues of Puerto Rico, Mexico, and Nicaragua.

By the time he rose to the highest level of the Cleveland farm system, Tiant's skills were bursting at the seams of his woolen uniform. Strikeouts and victories piled up to the point where the goal he had been working toward as long as he could remember—the same goal his father had been unfairly denied before him—was finally close enough to almost touch.

And when he *did* touch it, the result would shock everyone—except himself.

ONE MINUTE I WAS counting the weeks until my mother and father could meet my beautiful new bride. Now—in the summer of 1961—I was wondering if they would *ever* meet her, and if I'd ever see them or anyone else in my family again.

Cuba is only 90 miles from the United States, but it might as well have been on another planet as far as I was concerned. With Castro in control, I couldn't go back to the island unless I wanted to give up being a pro ballplayer. Going back also meant risking that I couldn't get back out. My parents, cousins, uncles, and aunts were all trapped too. If you wanted to leave Cuba on a plane, you needed money and connections. Our family had neither. For poor folks like us, the only way out was on one of those crowded, rickety old boats that were sneaking off the shores into the Atlantic, headed for Miami. My parents weren't young or strong enough for that trip, and even if they were, many of the boats never made it.

People don't understand how really bad something like that is unless you are faced with it. You take the good and the bad. When you go through it, it's then that you think—*damn*, that's tough. You just hope you're going to see your family someday. My friend's father passed away in Cuba, and he couldn't go there for his funeral. In later years, I would see a lot of my friends die in the United States, and their families couldn't even send their bodies back to be *buried* in Cuba.

That's not right. That's not the way to treat a human being. Every few weeks, you'd hear that so-and-so had died, someone you knew because you'd grown up with them. But you couldn't do anything about it. That's why I asked God every day to just let me see my mom and dad again.

With so much on my mind, I had to find a way to put it all aside and channel everything into my pitching. The Indians were giving me a chance and I did not want to blow it. If I had to wait all the way from October until spring training I might have gone crazy worrying about my career and my family, but there was winter ball to help me keep focused.

I spent the 1961-62 winter season with Caguas of the Puerto Rican League. It was almost like pitching in the majors. Orlando Cepeda of the

Giants, Roberto Clemente of the Pirates, and Bob Gibson of the Cardinals, all established stars and future Hall of Famers, came to play in Puerto Rico because they knew the importance of staying in shape and staying sharp year-round. That's how they remained on top, and I intended to do the same thing.

Facing the best brought out the best in me, and in one game I set a league record with 20 strikeouts. For the playoffs, at the end of January, 10,000 fans came out to see me battle the Mayaguez team and ace Juan Pizarro, a 14-game winner in the majors the year before. They saw a good show; it was scoreless until the sixth, when a guy named Martin Beltran got to me for a homer and gave Pizarro the 1-0 win. The fans were happy; both Pizarro and Beltran were native Puerto Ricans.

I hated to lose, but knew I had pitched well. So did Mayaguez. They signed me up for the Inter-American Series, where we faced top teams from the leagues in Panama, Nicaragua, and Venezuela. This was pretty common; because the seasons were shorter, lots of times you could play with two or even three clubs in one winter. You made some more money and got to show more people what you could do.

In this case I showed them plenty. I won two games in the Inter-American Series, hit a three-run homer in one of them—I told you I could hit!—and pitched in the championship final against Bob Gibson. He was just starting to show his stuff in the big leagues with the Cardinals, and I could tell he was the real deal. Yankees relief ace Luis Arroyo, who had saved the clinching game of the World Series just a few months before, saved one of my victories. Besides all the major leaguers in the series, there were also 13 Cubans—most of them guys like me looking for a new start. I wished my father could have seen it.

In February 1962, after Maria and I flew back from Puerto Rico to Miami, she went on to Mexico City to be with her family and I flew to Tucson where the Indians trained. It was exciting to be joining a big-league organization, but it was a tough time for me. I thought about Maria, of course, and I thought about my parents. They sounded safe in their letters and phone calls, but remember, those were all being read or listened to by Castro's people—just like my letters to them.

When I was a kid, my father didn't want me coming to America because of what he'd gone through. After I *did* come, I knew why.

My first minor league stop was in Charleston, South Carolina, the Indians' Class A club in the Eastern League. This was my introduction to the

American South. The Black players, including Cubans, faced terrible racism. When we were on the road and stopped to get something to eat, the white ballplayers would have to bring the food to us on the bus because we couldn't go in. We couldn't eat in the same restaurant or stay in the same hotel as them.

They rented a house for us in the Black section of the city, which was far away from where the white players stayed. And when you got to the ballpark, forget it. They called us niggers, saying they were going to send us back to Africa or hang us. How we looked like monkeys. All kinds of barbarian things; it's amazing what you'd hear, even at home games!

People don't realize what we had to go through. They make you feel like an animal—*worse* than an animal. I think in those days, in the South, they treated animals *better* than they treated Blacks. I tell you, it was sad. I would sit down and just shake my head. I couldn't believe what they would say and do to you. "You can't go here. You can't eat there. You can't stay here." *Damn.*

In my country, if somebody called you a nigger, you punched him in the face. You couldn't do that in the South in 1962. Whatever happened between you and a white person, if the police came along they'd beat the shit out of you. Then they'd put you in jail. You lose, and then you lose again. So you just tried to keep your cool and look the other way.

It was tough for all the Black players, but at least the American Blacks spoke English. Now I knew why my father had pushed me to stay in English school; I should have listened to him. I couldn't understand anything, and couldn't even ask for food. "Lettuce and tomato and scrambled eggs." That's all I knew, and so that's all I ate for about a month. None of the coaches spoke Spanish, and there were no interpreters or anything like they have today. Besides, I couldn't eat too much anyway with only about $1.50 per day in meal money.

How did I start to learn more English? From TV. You would watch a show and get some idea of what they were trying to say, and then you would listen for the same words when people were talking around you. What I used to do was try to learn one word at a time, and what it meant. Then I could try and put it together with other words. You could also learn from the other players, but the problem there was it was "Baseball English"—and it had a lot of bad words. You couldn't start many sentences off with those words, especially if you were being interviewed on the radio. I'd get in a little trouble for that later on.

Through everything, I kept writing my parents, and calling them once a month. I would send what little extra money and other things home that I could, but later I learned they didn't get a lot of what I sent. Once my father sent me a letter, saying I had forgotten about them and didn't care about them anymore, because he didn't get one of my packages. That made me terribly sad.

Maria was back in our Mexico City apartment with her family, so she didn't know what was happening. All I told her was that things were not so good between Blacks and whites, and it was tough finding a place to live. I left out the details because I didn't want her to worry, especially with her expecting our first baby in September. We talked a lot on the phone, and she sent me pictures of herself with her big belly, but it was hard for both of us to be separated during such a special time.

It was all so much to handle. I used to go to my room every day and cry, because I felt I couldn't do or say anything about what was happening to me and my family. But in my mind and my heart, I was also using these experiences to drive me. I knew I had to make it someday if I wanted things to change.

That first year I didn't blow anybody away, but I didn't embarrass myself either. After facing guys like Cepeda and Clemente over the winter I was real fired up to start the season and won my first five decisions. Then I had some trouble with a stiff elbow that I tried to pitch through, and the strong young hitters in the league like Dick Allen, Ken "Hawk" Harrelson, and Jim Ray Hart brought me back down to earth quick. Overall I held my own, going 7-8 with a 3.63 ERA on a team that finished under .500. We had some solid pitching. Besides me, our rotation had future big-league stars Tommy John and Sonny Siebert, but we finished last in the league in home runs. It turned out to be good practice for the way things would be in Cleveland a few years later.

My teammates were mostly okay; some made fun of my thick Cuban accent and how I struggled with my English, but riding guys is part of being on a team so I didn't let it bother me. I learned to give as good as I got, with Blacks *and* whites, and found I could make people laugh without doing much of anything. A guy who clowns around all the time, on and off the field, will never get respect. But when my teammates saw how hard I worked on the mound, and how serious I was about winning, they understood I was no clown.

Even at that point the Indians seemed to think I had a pretty good future.

In the middle of the season, when I was dealing with my stiff elbow, they called me up to their Triple-A team in Jacksonville of the International League. Because I was injured I didn't even want to go, but Charleston manager Johnny Lipon convinced me that you just didn't say no to a promotion. So I went up, got into one game, and then spent a month riding the bench and staying in shape by running. It felt like being on a track team, but I had learned in Cuba that running was great for a pitcher's legs and stamina.

When I was back in Charleston and the season was winding down I got a telegram with big news from Mexico City: Maria had given birth on September 2 to our first son, Luis Jr. Even though I would have to wait 48 long days to meet him, just hearing about him meant so much. If I had felt I was really *alone*, and on my own, during that first year playing in the South, I might have gone into a hole. But I knew I had responsibilities: a wife, a baby, a house. I had to take care of them. And that made me feel happy.

That fall, and all the way through Christmas, we were together in Mexico City—me, Maria, Little Luis, and Maria's mother, brothers, and their kids. It was wonderful, but it also made me think of my parents and family back in Cuba, who were celebrating their first Christmas without me. When we called my mom and dad during the holidays, we told them about how beautiful Luis was, and how fast he was growing. There was no need to talk about the sad things; we all knew what they were, and we couldn't do anything to change them.

The months went by very fast, and then it was off to another season of winter ball in Puerto Rico. I had an eight-game winning streak there, which helped get me invited to the Indians' major league camp for the first time during spring training. Even though I didn't stay on the big-league roster, it was another sign that they saw me as a real prospect. When the regular season began I was sent to Burlington, North Carolina, in the Carolina League; this was another Class A team, like Charleston, but a step up the minor-league ladder. I was ready.

Right from the start, I was one of the top pitchers in the league, leading in strikeouts and ERA. Burlington in 1963 wasn't any better than Charleston in '62 when it came to how people treated Black ballplayers. But now, maybe because I had that year with the organization under my belt, and was doing real good, I felt like I could fight back more.

Once in Burlington I went into a store to buy a little toy for my boy—a car that ran on batteries. A white customer was in there too, and when he saw me paying he left all his stuff on the counter and walked right out of the store. He wouldn't buy from any place that sold to me. After I paid I went outside and saw him talking to another white person, and I cussed him out with every English word I knew.

Another time, in a fancier department store, I was looking at some of the watches and jewelry they had under locked glass. I pointed to something, asked the woman behind the counter, "Can I please see that?" and she said, "Well, you know that costs a lot, right?" Just because of my color, she assumed I couldn't afford it. So I walked out.

The fans around the Carolina League weren't much better to me or any of the Black players. My English still wasn't too good, but I found a way of getting my point across. And just like I stuck up for my friends back home when it came to bullies and prejudice, I felt a responsibility to my teammates.

Our second baseman at Burlington, Barry Levinson, is still a close friend. He remembered one incident in Raleigh, North Carolina, that summer that shows what I'm talking about.

"Luis wasn't starting that day, so he was coaching first base," Barry recalled. "One fan called one of our Black players a nigger, and Luis went right over and vented as best he could to the guy. Our manager [Pat Colgran] came over when the incident was somewhat calmed down, and he said to Luis, 'Stop! They'll kill you!'"

They didn't go that far, but fans were still calling us every name in the book. It was hard to keep my anger in, but like the year before, I tried to channel it into my pitching. I wanted to show them that color had nothing to do with *what* you could do. No matter what our color, or which language we spoke, we could do the same things as everybody else.

Those fans gave me more power to fight back, and *show them*, and so that's what I did. I came there to play baseball, not fight, and if I was good enough I felt I could turn them around.

On May 2, I pitched a four-hit shutout and helped myself with two RBI singles. Five days later, in front of the home fans in Burlington, I threw a no-hitter against Winston Salem. Then, in my next start, I almost threw *another* no-hitter. After that, the fans filled the park every time I pitched, and they didn't call me anything you wouldn't want a little kid to hear.

Looking back, I thank God I never gave up. He gave me the strength to get through the hatred I experienced, and He provided me the confidence to do what I did to turn that hatred into respect. That was a big turning point for me. From that point on, because I knew what I could do, I was never going to let anybody step on me or do things to make me less than anybody else.

"Luis Tiant could be a name worth remembering," sports columnist Gordon Cobbledick wrote in the Cleveland *Plain Dealer* after my no-hitter. I was determined to prove him right.

By this point I had been pitching professionally year-round for five years, and at a top amateur level for several years before that. I wasn't just chasing my own dreams, but my father's too. So even though I was just 22 years old, I was much more experienced than the majority of guys in the minor leagues. My teammates could sense it.

"Luis was a real student of the game for a young man," Barry Levinson remembered. "When I played with him, he already knew how to pitch—how to change speeds, and all about location. Most kids his age didn't get that yet. That's why they were there, to get it drilled into them, but he had it already.

"I never played with anyone who competed as hard as Luis. When he almost pitched the two straight no-hitters, the one hit against him in the second game was a Texas Leaguer. I just missed the damn thing [behind second base]. It was in the bottom of the last inning; I don't remember if there were one or two outs, but Luis didn't even blink. He just got the last outs he needed.

"The next time we played that team, Rocky Mount, the kid who got the hit was batting third. It was the first inning, the kid comes up, and BOOM! He goes right on his ass.

"I walk in to the mound from second to talk to Luis.

"'What are you doing hitting that guy? It's only the first inning!'

"Luis says, 'SOB got the hit.'"

"Luis was talking about the blooper that killed his no-hitter. He had not forgotten.

"For however old we were in '63, to have that competitive spirit…that really showed me: 'Boy, this kid has really *got it.*'"

That kind of intensity and determination was the way to win over fans and teammates, and it was the only way I knew how to play. But you can't be intense *all* the time. I knew the importance of keeping things loose, and the guys on the team appreciated that too.

One time we were driving back on the bus from a road trip late at night. It was pitch black, and we came to a railroad crossing. You could see the light from the train coming in the distance. We had this old bus driver, Sam, and he was pushing the pedal to the metal to get us across the tracks in time. That light is coming closer and closer, and then all of a sudden I jumped up and yelled, "LOOK OUT SAM, YOU SON OF A BITCH!"

The whole bus broke up laughing. Up until then, I don't think a lot of guys on the team thought I knew that much English!

Most people think of me, and they think about my cigars. I do love them, and that goes back to my days in the minors. One time it helped Barry get me good on a prank.

"My dad used to send me cigars, and we had these open lockers where you could see everything," Barry remembered. "Luis would always steal my cigars, but I could never catch him in the act. So one day I decided to cure him of the habit.

"I went to the hobby shop and got one of those things you put in cigars to make them explode. I pushed it into one of mine with a toothpick, put the cellophane back on, and put it on top of my locker.

"Luis was pitching that night, and when he pitched there was no way I was going to get my cigar. So I took my time getting into the locker room, and sure enough I walk in just when he's coming out of the shower with a towel draped around him. He goes over to my cigars, grabs one, and lights it.

"'MMMMMM,' he says as he drags on it. 'That's GOOOOOOOOD.'

"I pretend I'm mad as hell, and then all of a sudden the thing explodes. It was perfect.

"He wouldn't take a cigar from me for weeks after that. 'C'mon, Luis,' I'd say. 'Have one.'

"'No! No! NO!'"

Barry got me that time, but I enjoyed plenty of victory cigars in 1963. By the end of the season I was 14-9 with a 2.56 ERA and led the league with 207 strikeouts in 204 innings. I was also gaining a reputation for finishing what I started, with 17 complete games in 24 starts, and including the no-hitter I had six shutouts. That was tops in the league too. It was my best year in pro ball so far.

By now the sportswriters in Cleveland were calling me one of the organization's top prospects, and this gave me confidence that I carried over into the 1963-64 winter season. Pitching for the Lara Cardinals of the Occidental League in Venezuela, I threw a one-hitter in my first start, had 16 strikeouts in another game, and overall went 7-0 with five shutouts to help Lara to a championship. In 63 innings I struck out 89 batters, nearly 13 a game. Just like the previous year, it was not hard finding a second club to hook on with once the Occidental season ended. I joined Valencia of the Venezuelan League and stretched my winter winning string to nine straight—all complete games.

Tiant Toys With Batters—Five Runs in 79 Frames read a headline in *The Sporting News* after my ninth victory. This time Cobbledick of the *Plain Dealer* called me the "hottest item among the Indians and Indians-to-be in Latin America." It took Gaylord Perry, a future Hall of Famer I'd face many times later on in the big leagues, to stop the streak.

Any streak like that—and I had them at several different stages of my career—depends on much more than the pitcher. You need a team of guys all doing their jobs, and that starts behind the plate. Having a catcher you can depend on is so important, and Elrod Hendricks—who later caught for several pennant-winning teams in Baltimore—was behind the plate for most of my starts for Valencia. He called a great game and was a strong hitter, too, coming through for me when it counted. Another teammate who would win a title with the Orioles later on was Luis Aparicio, a future Hall of Famer and as good a defensive shortstop as there was in baseball. Guys like that made it a lot easier to win, and playing with them did a lot for my confidence.

Around this same time, news got out that showed not just how far I had come, but how little faith Indians general manager Gabe Paul had in me just a year before. It turns out that after I struggled with injuries my first few months with the organization, he thought I was damaged goods.

"Luis Tiant keeps pitching shutouts in Venezuela. Gabe can now breathe a sigh of relief about Tiant's success," *The Sporting News* reported during my winter hot streak. "The pitcher had been unprotected in the draft and luckily he wasn't claimed. The Tribe purchased him from the Mexican League a few years ago for a good price, but when he arrived in Tucson [for spring training in 1962] he wasn't throwing as hard as the reports indicated. It developed he had arm trouble. Apparently his fast ball has come back."

Imagine that—any team could have had me for next to nothing, and nobody picked me up. Now, like the paper said, my fastball *was* back, and one thing was for sure: if I kept this up, there was no way Cleveland or anybody else was going to make a mistake like that about me again.

After going 10-4 for the winter, with an ERA under 3.00, I went to spring training with the Indians in Arizona determined to make the big-league club out of camp. But Gabe Paul and management frustrated me again by sending me down to the Portland Beavers, Cleveland's top minor league team. Portland played in the Pacific Coast League, a Triple-A circuit many believed was very close to the majors in terms of skill level. Winning there, I figured, would be my ticket to the big time.

It was, but it took a lot more winning than it should have.

Even back then, a lot of ballplayers got huge signing bonuses before ever playing a game professionally. These were the guys that big-league clubs were grooming for stardom, the sure things, and for the Indians in the early 1960s Sam McDowell was one of those guys. He was a big left-handed pitcher from Pittsburgh, and the Indians reportedly signed him for a bonus of $75,000 right out of high school, outbidding 14 other teams in the process.

McDowell was up and down between Cleveland and the minor leagues a bunch of times early in his career, mostly because of trouble with his control. They called him "Sudden Sam" because of how fast his pitches snuck up on batters, but getting the ball over the plate consistently was tough for McDowell. Just like when Nolan Ryan came up with the Mets, Sam was often wild and always nasty. Most guys couldn't hit either one of them. If you look at the records today, you'll see McDowell is still in the top ten for all pitchers lifetime in fewest hits allowed per nine innings—just over seven (7.0344). Ryan is first (6.5553).

I never knew about how much money Sudden supposedly got, and I didn't care. If I could pitch as well as him, I figured, Gabe Paul would notice. The first game I played for Portland, our season opener at Arkansas, McDowell was the starter. He got into trouble in the sixth, so manager Johnny Lipon—who had also moved up from Charleston—brought me into a 4-4 game. For the next five-and-two-thirds innings I pitched one-hit ball, and we won 6-4 in 11 innings.

That was the closest either of us would come to losing for a long, long time.

By late May, McDowell and I were each 7-0 and tearing up the league. Sudden was pitching with better control than ever before, and was called up to Cleveland after getting his eighth win. I matched him a few days later with *my* eighth win, but even with an ERA of 1.94, I stayed put in Portland. It's not like the Indians couldn't have used me. Gabe Paul predicted before the season that Cleveland would battle the Yankees for the American League pennant, and the Indians were just four games out at 21-16 after sweeping a doubleheader at Washington on May 31. I'm sure I could have helped close the gap even more, but Paul kept me in the minors.

McDowell beat Washington in relief on the 31st, then moved into the rotation and had 14 strikeouts and just three walks in his first start. I was happy for Sudden, but also felt cheated. I was so mad that when I got to 8-0, I told Lipon to call Gabe Paul in Cleveland.

"You get me more money," I said, "or I'm going home."

I was making $400 a month, but I knew I was pitching better than all these guys making more than me. That wasn't right.

"I'll go home and wait until you reach him."

I lived behind the ballpark, so I started to walk home.

"No, no, you stay here," Lipon yelled. He kept calling Gabe Paul, and when he got through he got me more money—a raise to $800 per month.

Right after that I lost my first game of the season on a double by the other team's pitcher, but then I won seven more in a row. This was one of the best leagues in the minors—if not *the best*—with guys like Tommie Agee, Rico Petrocelli, and Tony Perez who would be starring in the majors a few years later. I felt like nobody could beat me.

Plenty of teams were beating the Indians. They had strong young pitchers like McDowell, Sonny Siebert, and Gary Bell, but had trouble scoring runs. They dropped 11 of 12 games in one stretch and by the middle of July had fallen into eighth place, 15 games behind the Yankees.

At least one guy knew I could be of some help.

"Sam McDowell pulls out all the stops in appraising Luis Tiant, a pitching staff mate at Portland the property of the Indians," the Cleveland *Plain Dealer* reported on June 20. "It's Sudden Sam's opinion that the Cuban right-hander, a speedballer, can't miss in the big time."

A few weeks later, my record with Portland was up to 15-1 when we flew into San Diego for a series against the Padres. (This was five years before the city got a major league team of the same name; these Padres were Triple-A.) We get there around seven o'clock in the morning, and I was supposed to pitch that night. The Padres had Tony Perez, who was leading the PCL in home runs, and I was excited to battle my fellow Cuban countryman.

I picked up a newspaper at the airport, and it was filled with talk about me facing Perez—the league's best pitcher against its best power hitter. I went back to the hotel, hoping to get a nap, and as soon as I walked in my room the phone rang. It was the trainer, saying Lipon wanted to see me right away.

"Goddamn, it's early!" I yelled into the phone. "I've got to pitch tonight! I need some rest!"

"No," the trainer says. "He *really* wants to see you."

Lipon, the manager, was like a father to me. He had pitched in Cuba, too, and in the big leagues. He was good to me and my family. But why did Johnny want to see me? I wasn't sure; I thought maybe they were going to release me. Yeah, I was 15-1, but I had pulled that stunt when I was 8-0 and demanded more money. Maybe they thought I was a troublemaker.

When I got to Lipon's room, he told me the news:

"The Cleveland Indians want you in the big leagues."

I'm sure what I said next surprised him.

"They want me in the big leagues, huh? You tell that son of a bitch Gabe Paul I want to finish what I started here."

"No, no, you *have* to go!" Lipon says. "This might be your last chance—the only chance you're going to get!"

"I don't give a shit. I'm not going anywhere! I wasn't good enough when I was 8-0, and they brought up McDowell with the same record. Now I'm 15-1 and suddenly I'm good enough? No—let me finish what I started here."

"No, no, no," said Lipon. "You better go."

Lipon was fighting with me like he was my dad, and that's why I loved him. I still laugh thinking about it. When Maria and I used to go to Mexico, years later, we would make a stop at Johnny's house in San Antonio and stay there for a few days. He was a good man to me and my family.

I might have been the first guy to say no to a big-league promotion. Looking back, it was a matter of pride, and maybe a little anger. The Indians *should* have brought me up earlier, but I wasn't a big bonus boy like McDowell. Now I had a chance to win 20 games for Portland and lead the team to a PCL pennant. If I did that, the Indians would *have* to take me to the big leagues.

Eventually, Lipon talked me into moving up. Thank goodness he did. I'm not sure what Gabe Paul would have done if he heard I didn't want to report. That might have been it for me.

I went from the hotel over to the San Diego ballpark, and said goodbye to my teammates in the visitor's clubhouse. Then I caught a plane to meet up with the Indians on the road in New York. My first time wearing a big-league uniform, I'd be in Yankee Stadium, home of the greatest team in baseball history. The team I read about and heard on the radio growing up, revered in Cuba and the rest of the world. The team of Ruth and Gehrig, DiMaggio and Mantle. The four-time defending American League champions.

Did I feel any pressure? Not really. I had proven myself against the best before, in winter ball, and I had nothing left to show them in the minor leagues. Besides, I figured Cleveland would work me in slowly, against a less challenging opponent.

It was Friday, July 17. I flew on the red eye all night to New York, and got in at 7:00 in the morning. I headed over to the Biltmore Hotel, and as soon as I was in my room, the goddamned phone rang. I swear those things know just when you're coming.

The trainer was on the line.

"Gabe Paul wants to see you."

"Goddamn it! I just flew all night from San Diego. Why does he want to see me now? It can wait till later."

"No it can't. He wants to see you in his room. You have to sign your contract."

"Oh shit, OK. I'll be right over."

The major-league minimum salary at the time was $6,000, and they gave me $5,000. Even though I came up mid-way through the season, that was $1,000 less than I was supposed to get. But what was I going to do about it right there, on the spot? I was worried if I said something they'd threaten to send me back to Cuba. That's what they did back then; they scared you into doing whatever they wanted. Nobody had agents, so they knew they could take advantage of you—especially the Latino players who had trouble with English.

So I kept my mouth shut, signed the contract, and went back to my room to try to get a little rest.

That afternoon I took the team bus to Yankee Stadium. When I got there, the first thing I did was go in to meet the Indians manager, George "Birdie" Tebbetts. Birdie was a baseball lifer, a tough former catcher back in uniform a few months after having a heart attack and bypass surgery in April. He was a big bear of a man with a high-pitched voice like a bird that led to his nickname.

Birdie didn't mess around with small talk.

"You ready to pitch?"

"Damn right I'm ready to pitch. I was supposed to pitch last night for San Diego."

"OK, you're going to pitch tomorrow, in the second game."

"Fine, no problem."

It happened so fast I didn't have time to be nervous. The Indians were playing a Sunday doubleheader against the Yankees the next day at the Stadium; McDowell would start the first game for us against Rollie Sheldon, and I'd start the second game . . . against Whitey Ford!

So much for easing me in slowly.

Ford was the ace of the Yankees, a left-hander who had gone 24-7 and started Game One of the World Series the year before. He had won his 200th career game earlier in the 1964 season, and even in his mid-30s had a great curve he threw more than half of the time. Whitey also liked to scuff up the ball now and then, and as a native New Yorker was probably the most popular guy on the team next to Mickey Mantle.

After talking to Birdie I went to the clubhouse to say hello to my new teammates. I knew most of the guys from spring training, and had played with a lot of them in the minors. Cleveland had a real young team without any big stars. The oldest position player, and the one I was the closest to, was outfielder Al Smith. It was great to see him. Al had played with my father in the Negro Leagues and was an old family friend. In the '50s he had been an All-Star on strong Indians teams, but now he was more like a coach, playing once or twice a week and passing on his wisdom. In my case, he was really looking out for me.

When Al found out Tebbetts was going to pitch me against Whitey Ford right out of the gate, he was mad.

"Goddamn it! They are throwing you to the dogs with your hands tied!"

"I don't care. I'll just do what I gotta do."

"But why didn't they put you in against Kansas City or another bad team?"

"You know what? The way I've been throwing the ball in Portland, I don't care *who* I'm pitching against. It makes no difference to me."

"But why do they put you against the *best* team, and the best pitcher?"

"It doesn't matter. If I lose, I lose against the best. If I win, I *beat the best*. I have to go out there, do my thing, and show them what I can do. I really have nothing to lose."

Al still didn't like it, but that's really how I felt. I mean, there was nothing I *could* do about it, right? I wanted my chance, and here it was. I just had to make the most of it.

I slept well that night, and got to the ballpark early. When you were the starting pitcher, back in those days, you always found a brand new ball in your locker. That was a sign from the manager—the game was yours. When I picked up that ball, and moved it around in my hands, I started to feel a little nervous tension. I'm not afraid of anything, except maybe really big needles, and I never lost my head. I knew what I wanted to do, I just didn't know if it was going to work. That's the problem; to believe is one thing, but to *play* is another.

Yogi Berra, the great Yankees catcher, was now the team's player-manager. Everybody knows what a funny guy Yogi was, but he was also smart. When the New York sportswriters asked him if he knew anything about me, he said "Yeah, he must be real old, because I remember playing against him a long time ago." When I saw him I said, "You played against *my father*, not me."

He just smiled. I'm sure he knew, but it was still funny.

That was one of the ways I felt like my father was with me in this game. Another was that we were playing just across the Harlem River from the Polo Grounds, where my dad had pitched so many years for the New York Cubans of the Negro Leagues without getting the chance to play in the white man's league. Later I learned that he actually pitched one of his last games right there, at Yankee Stadium, during the 1947 Negro World Series. Al Smith was in that game, too, playing against my father for the Cleveland Buckeyes. If he remembered, he didn't say anything to me. Maybe he thought I had enough on my mind already.

There was a big Sunday crowd at the Stadium, more than 30,000. The Yankees lineup was packed with All-Stars—Mantle, Elston Howard, Bobby Richardson, Tom Tresh—and they knocked Sudden Sam around in the opening game of the doubleheader. They got 10 hits off him in less than six innings, and won, 6-2. Beating up on the Indians was nothing new to these guys; in 10 games against New York so far in the '64 season, Cleveland had only won once.

But the Yankees had never faced *me*.

I had one thing going for me before I even took the mound in the second game: a 1-0 lead. Ford was wild in the top of the first inning and walked three guys. One of them came around to score, and guess who it was? Al Smith! I guess he felt like he had to take things into his own hands to help me out. Pitching with a lead always made me bear down harder, so I appreciated it.

The first guy up for New York was Tony Kubek, their great shortstop. I had heard of him, but I really didn't know most of the Yankees or how to pitch to them. There had been no time to prepare, and my English still wasn't too good. But my catcher that day was Joe Azcue, a Cuban, so I could communicate with him easily. He was young but had played a bunch of games against the Yankees and knew their lineup. He helped me out a lot.

Kubek had sat out the first game of the doubleheader, so he was fresh. I struck him out anyway. Next was Phi Linz, and he grounded out. "Shit, this ain't so tough," I said to myself. "The guys don't matter. It's the same here as it is down in Portland. Just keep going."

Hector Lopez walked, bringing up the cleanup hitter: Roger Maris. I sure knew who *he* was, the 61-homer man, but *he* didn't know *me*. I struck him out too. Later on, you start thinking about it, and that's when you realize how crazy it is. But when you're doing it, the scared part goes away. All you want to do is play.

And so that's what I did; I just kept going—boom, boom, boom. I felt so good; it was unreal. I remember thinking, this is so easy, I could have been here before. That's really what I was thinking: *I could have been here before.*

We grew up in Cuba listening to baseball on the radio, and since it was usually Yankees games, most Cuban fans rooted for New York. Now here I was at Yankee Stadium striking out Roger Maris, the home run king, in front of a big crowd. Maybe *this* game was on back home, and men like my father were listening while playing dominoes. Everybody wants their family to see their major league debut; I didn't have that option, but I wanted to believe that *somehow* they were listening.

Through five innings the Yankees only had one hit off of me, a single by Tresh. We scored another two runs on a groundout and a Leon Wagner home run, so we were up 3-0 when they pinch-hit for Ford in the fifth. It didn't matter who they put in there, this was *my* day. The score was still 3-0 when I struck out Maris again to end the eighth, and I got them one-two-three in the ninth. I finished with a four-hit shutout and 11 strikeouts.

It turns out there were some Cuban guys in the stands right next to the visitor's dugout who knew me from when I was a kid. When the game was over, and I was coming in, somebody called out "Hey Lusito!" I heard that and knew it had to be somebody from home. So I looked over, and Goddamn it, it was a guy named Manuela Cabrera who was friendly with my father when I was growing up. That felt good.

In his story the next day, Leonard Koppett of *the New York Times* wrote that "Luis Tiant, a 23-year-old Cuban refugee...yesterday made the sort of major league debut that little boys dream about, even in Havana."

He was right. They let me do what my father never could do. It started right there, in that moment and that time. All the things they did against my father in the Negro Leagues, saying he couldn't play in the big leagues…. This put Señor Skinny back on top. We had finally made it.

The day before, Yogi Berra had called Birdie Tebbetts and asked who the Indians were starting in Sunday's doubleheader. Yogi probably figured since the Indians were in eighth place, 16 games out, Birdie wouldn't care about keeping it a secret. It was already mid-July, and we weren't going to catch the Yankees or the Orioles in the American League pennant race without a rocket.

"McDowell and Luis Tiant," Birdie told Yogi.

"Who's Tiant?"

"We just smuggled him in from Cuba," Birdie said seriously. "He's so good, Castro wouldn't let him out. You guys better stay loose."

I'm sure Yogi knew Birdie was joking, like when Yogi told reporters he played against me and not my father twenty years before. He was having some fun riding the rookie before the Yanks would try to knock me back to Havana the next day. Maybe trying to rattle me.

It didn't bother me a bit; I had confidence in myself. And now I had gotten the last laugh, too, by beating his team.

"I was good enough to win, but not against this kid today," Whitey Ford told reporters after the game. That was classy of him to say, and it made me proud to hear it coming from the best pitcher in the league.

Besides being a great catcher, and translating to Spanish when the manager and other guys visited me on the mound during games, Joe Azcue helped me out with sportswriters in those days.

After that first game, they asked if facing the Yankees scared me.

"I was nervous at the beginning," I said through Joe, "but as soon as I struck out Kubek, I felt better."

Was this my first time in Yankee Stadium? I said it was.

"It certainly is impressive," I added. "But I wasn't scared out there. I have confidence in myself."

In all the excitement of the moment, I tried to be careful how I talked. I wanted to be respectful, but also let them know that no matter how many championships the Yankees had won, they didn't intimidate me. Ballplayers said they didn't read the papers, but they heard what other players said about them.

"This was the moment I've been dreaming of, and I wanted to make the most of it," I added. "Now that I'm here, I plan to stay here—because they didn't let my father play in this league." Maybe all of that didn't make it on the air, or into the papers, but I said it and meant it.

Did I think my father had heard about the game on the radio back in Cuba?

"Maybe," I said. "Sometimes there is some wire service report on the Cuban boys here," I said through Joe, "and sometimes they may hear the Voice of America."

Later, when things calmed down, I thought about it some more. I sure hoped Dad *did* hear it—and Mom, too.

I was there because of them.

6

COMING OF AGE IN CLEVELAND

AFTER CONQUERING THE MIGHTY YANKEES, Tiant spent the last two months of the 1964 season showing the Indians organization the folly of keeping him stashed away in Portland so long. "Cleveland's Cuban Cutie" dominated big-league lineups with the cool, cunning savvy of a veteran, and the refrain "He can't be just 23" was repeated in dugouts and press boxes from Boston to Anaheim. A consensus decision was made regarding the balding, mature-looking hurler, one which despite his firm and proud denials reverberated for decades:

Tiant must be lying about his age.

For the next three seasons, performing admirably and at times brilliantly for an offensively-challenged Indians lineup, he strived to make the leap from rookie star to consistent contributor. It was not easy on a team with a revolving door of managers, each with his own views about how to best use the hard-throwing righty. One month he was a starter, the next a mid-game innings-eater, and the next a closer. Tiant wanted desperately to stay in the rotation permanently, and shined when given this opportunity. His strong performances, however, often came on the short end of 2-1 and 3-2 scores; this being a pre-sabermetrics era when gaudy win-loss records were the primary measure of a pitcher's worth, Luis remained a second-tier star.

Frustrated, he kept it all in context. The cutting racism of his minor league days was mostly behind him, his salary was good, and he was living his dream. And even as his English was slow to improve, Tiant became an indispensable source of love and laughter for his teammates. They respected his skills, honored his friendship, and delighted in his festive approach to the game and life. Even opponents whom he mowed down and mocked in the heat of a pennant race find it hard to get angry; he was too damn funny.

Through it all, Tiant continued to endure a long exile from his homeland and parents. He and his wife Maria now had a son and daughter, giving Luis three precious gems his mother and father had never met. The new clan provided him with strength and a sense of duty, and he took almost no time off—pitching all spring and summer in Cleveland and all fall and winter in the warmer climes of Venezuela and Puerto Rico. The grind was tiring, and worried his big-league employers, but he believed it was the best way to hone his craft. Someday, he dreamed, he would shine so bright that nobody could deny him the riches and power needed to reunite his loved ones.

BACK WHEN MY FATHER was still playing, Cleveland was a baseball city. But by the time I came up in '64, with the NFL growing in popularity, football was king. The Cleveland Browns had a future Hall of Fame running back in Jim Brown, and they were always competing for championships and drawing crowds of 50,000 or more to home games. The Browns and Indians shared Cleveland Municipal Stadium, and when the Indians won a couple pennants and a World Series in the 1940s and '50s, they drew big crowds there too. Fans loved watching pitchers Bob Feller, Bob Lemon, and Early Wynn, and great hitters like Larry Doby, Al Rosen, and my buddies Bobby Avila and Al Smith. After all those guys retired or were past their prime, though, things changed.

The Indians of 1964 were a middle-of-the-pack team. They didn't have too many big names anymore, and usually drew real small crowds. Sometimes there were only a couple thousand fans in the huge stadium. Sportswriters said interest in the team actually was *up*, and that a lot of fans were listening to the games on radios, in their cars, or watching them on TV when they were on. But it's still sad as a ballplayer to see all those empty seats. You feel like your home fans are not supporting you.

Things were so bad that the group of businessmen who owned the Indians were talking about moving the team. As many as a dozen cities were supposedly interested. "Our problem is a simple one. We need more dollars," general manager Gabe Paul told Cleveland Mayor Ralph Lacher in the summer of '64. "Our loss last year, which was checked by Ernst and Ernst auditors, was $1,200,000. Our loss this year, up to August 31, was in excess of $800,000. We just can't go on year after year like this."

My win against the Yankees got a lot of press, especially back in Cleveland. One sportswriter called me "Lightening Luis Tiant, the Indians' pitching papoose" and when I told reporters I thought I could pitch faster than I did in New York, I guess fans wanted to see for themselves. Four days after the Yankees game, one of the best home crowds of the season came out for my first start at Cleveland Stadium. They saw a good one.

It's funny that the team I would be most associated with later on—the Boston Red Sox—was the second I ever faced in the big leagues. The Red Sox had two guys in uniform who would become two of my favorite people in baseball: Johnny Pesky and Carl Yastrzemski. Back then I knew them only by what they had done. Pesky, the Boston manager, had been an All-Star shortstop for the Red Sox before and after World War II, batting in front of Hall of Famers Ted Williams and Bobby Doerr; I remembered him from listening to Yankees-Red Sox games on the radio as a kid. Yastrzemski, who everyone called "Yaz," was a young guy just a year older than me. He didn't quite have the power he'd develop later on, but he was a great left fielder and doubles hitter who had led the American League in batting the year before.

Another funny thing about that game was that it was only the second time I had ever set foot in the ballpark I would call my home field for the next six seasons. Two years before, as a minor leaguer, I came to watch a game at Cleveland Municipal Stadium while in town to have a shoulder injury checked out by the Indians medical team. Back then, Gabe Paul was worried I was damaged goods. He wasn't worrying anymore.

Boston was in seventh place, just ahead of the Indians in the AL standings, but was one of the league's top hitting clubs. Led by Yaz, Dick Stuart, Felix Mantilla, and rookie star Tony Conigliaro, they lead all AL teams in batting in 1964 and were second in home runs. None of it mattered to me. Still feeding off the confidence from my first time out, I pretty much stopped them cold with a six-hit, 6-1 win. I also got *my* first big-league hit—a single off of Bob Heffner.

"Luis Clemente Tiant is for real," the Cleveland *Plain Dealer* announced the next morning. That wasn't bad praise for a guy with only 18 innings in the big leagues, and showed how hungry the city was for baseball players worth playing up.

The sportswriters weren't the only ones impressed.

"Man is he strong. You got to like him," said Red Sox manager Pesky. "He threw just as hard in the ninth as in the first, if not harder, and he got the ball over."

Pesky's players called me "Little Bull" as a way of saying I was strong, and

Red Sox pitching coach Bob Turley agreed. Turley also said I "got away with" some bad curve balls, so I tried to remember that for the future.

What was most important to me those first couple games, besides winning, was how well I got along with my new teammates on and off the field. It happened real fast.

"How come you couldn't pitch a shutout this time the way you did against the Yankees?" one guy joked in the clubhouse after the Boston game, loud enough for reporters to hear.

"Yeah, I told you to pitch a shutout," kidded another.

"You can't throw shutouts all the time," I shot back.

"How come you let Mantilla hit that home run?"

"This is no game for little boys," I said. "Sometimes they hit homers."

Joking around has always been a sign of belonging in sports, of becoming one of the guys. It's also an important way to build up a team. I knew I wasn't going to win every time out, but if you play hard and do your best, and know how to leave the game on the field, your teammates will respect you. That's especially true for pitchers; guys who respect you will play harder behind you.

On the Indians, we needed all the hard workers we could get to come up with runs. We didn't have a lot of heavy hitters like the Red Sox. Outfielder Leon Wagner, a friendly, outgoing player who everyone called "Daddy Wags", hit 31 homers for us that year, but nobody else even had 20. We only batted .247 as a team, so our pitchers really had to bear down to keep us in games. Three guys in the starting rotation the second half of the year—me, Sam McDowell, and Sonny Siebert—were all rookies. And since I did well as soon as I came up, Birdie Tebbetts didn't think twice about using me whenever necessary.

I had to leave my third start, a 4-3 loss to the Los Angeles Angels, with a stiff shoulder, so Birdie skipped my next scheduled spot in the rotation four days later and instead pitched me in relief two days in a row—the last two innings of a 2-1, 11-inning victory over Detroit and the last two batters of a 4-2 win against Washington. I picked up a win and a save, but I was glad he put me back in the rotation after that.

"I don't know how good a pitcher we have, but we've got a good thrower," Tebbetts said during my first month with the club. "It helps when a boy comes from a baseball family. I think this kid should do very well."

As a former catcher who had played back in the 1940s, Tebbetts probably also appreciated my ability to finish or go very deep into ballgames. In the '60s, there was still a lot of satisfaction and pride in finishing a game that you started. It was a badge of honor. Today the managers all want to pull a pitcher after six or even five innings no matter how well he's doing, because the stats show the value in saving your best arms for what has become a much longer postseason with three playoff rounds plus the wild card play-in game. In the '60s, before the leagues split up into East and West divisions, the AL and NL champions went straight to the World Series—and you had your best guys out there on the mound as long as they could go.

Everybody knew the Indians were not going to the World Series in 1964, but I still tried to look at every game like it was important. If you gave me that ball in the first inning, I wanted to be out there at the end. Usually I was; seven of my first eight wins in the big leagues were complete games. I conditioned myself all year long, doing lots and lots of running, playing catch with a heavy ball, and some exercises with barbells, so that I would have the energy to get through a long season. I may not have looked like it, but I was always in great shape.

When I won my fifth game with the Indians in mid-August, a complete-game shutout against the Angels, someone pointed out that I was the first pitcher in organized professional baseball to reach 20 victories in '64— combined with my 15-1 half-season in Portland, my record so far in '64 was 20-2. Each week the Sports pages ran the statistics of every pitcher in both leagues, from the best earned-run-average down to the worst, in one long column. Names like "Ford, New York," "Koufax, Los Angeles," and "Marichal, San Francisco" were always bunched around the top, but by September "Tiant, Cleveland" was up there as well. I sent some of the clippings home to Cuba so my parents could see them.

My $5,000 salary may have been under the big-league minimum, but it was more money than I had ever had in my life by a long shot. I sent most of it home to Maria and Little Luis, and some to my parents—in hopes they would get it and not Castro's soldiers. With a little of what was left I bought my first car. It was four years old, but I was still so excited I drove it straight from the dealer over to the ballpark.

It started making funny noises the closer I got to Cleveland Stadium. And as soon as I reached the parking lot and turned off the engine, the radiator blew up! Welcome to the big leagues!

Near the end of the year, with a chance for the Indians to finish over .500 and as high as fourth place in the ten-team league, Birdie put me back in the bullpen and told me be ready to pitch anytime during the upcoming four-game series at home against the league-leading Yankees. Players whose teams finished first through fourth in both leagues all got a share of World Series bonus money then, so there was added incentive for us to win besides pride.

I did get into one of the games late, and took the loss when Elston Howard got to me for a home run in extra innings. That one hurt, but I did get to live out another one of my dreams. As a kid I fantasized about pitching against Minnie Miñoso—the greatest of all Cuban players then in the big leagues—and Mickey Mantle. Now I had done both. First I faced Miñoso in winter ball, and in this game I went up against Mantle for the first time. He flew out to right.

The Yankees swept the series, and we lost seven straight overall to ruin our chances at .500, but I finished the season strong. My first time pitching at what would become my favorite place to play, I threw a shutout against the Red Sox in Fenway Park on September 30. Dick Stuart was gunning for the home run and RBI titles for Boston, but he was 0-for-4 with three strikeouts. Yaz and Tony C were both 0-for-4 too, and overall I let up only four hits while striking out 11. Maybe the most incredible number about the game was the attendance at Fenway: 934 in a 35,000-seat ballpark. They had some big hitters, but thanks to bad pitching and bad management, the ninth-place Red Sox were in even worse shape than the Indians.

The crowd was a lot bigger four days later when we played at Yankee Stadium in our last game of the year. I got the start on three days' rest, and Tebbetts pulled me after six innings with the score 1-1 thanks to my first big-league homer: a shot into the right-field seats off future *Ball Four* author Jim Bouton. McDowell pitched the rest of the way, and we wound up winning, 2-1, in 13 innings. Maybe Tebbetts should have left me in; a year later I hit my second career homer, and it was off Bouton, too!

Our victory kept the Yankees from winning 100 games, but they still went to the World Series while we finished sixth at 79-83. They really had our number; if you throw out our 3-15 record against New York, the Indians would have been well above .500 and considered a very competitive club. This frustrated me like all my teammates, but as my big-league career got going I began to notice something: I pitched some of my top games against the top teams.

In my three games against the Yankees that year, I had a 1.06 ERA, my lowest against any opponent. Facing the best brought out the best in *me*, and so did tight situations. In one game that September, I had a 5-4 lead on the White Sox when they loaded the bases against me with one out in the eighth inning. All they needed was a flyball or a grounder to the right side to tie the game, but I got a foul popup to the catcher and a grounder to short to get out of the jam.

All of this told me one thing: when the time came, whether in Cleveland or somewhere else, I believed I would rise to the occasion and win big games in a pennant race.

My final record with the Indians as a rookie was 10-4, with a 2.83 ERA, nine complete games, and three shutouts in 19 games (16 of them starts). When you add that to my numbers in Portland (15-1) and in the 1963-64 winter league season in Venezuela (11-3), I was 36-8 overall in less than 12 months. I pitched more than 350 innings for four teams, and I felt great.

So did Gabe Paul, who had almost let me go the year before. The press wouldn't let him forget it.

"The most exciting pitcher in the American League today is a Cuban boy named Luis Tiant," wrote Cleveland sportswriter Regis McAuley. "And those tears you hear splashing around the major leagues are being shed by the general managers of 19 clubs who could have grabbed this sensational righthander for the waiver price [of $8,000] at last winter's minor league meetings in San Diego. They all missed the boat. ... The main reason Tiant is pitching for the Indians today is because Gabe Paul made a great big boo-boo and got away with it."

Now he had learned his lesson. Two days after the '64 season ended I signed an $11,000 Cleveland contract for 1965, more than double the $5,000 I had made the year before. I was very happy with the raise, and knew it would help me and Maria as we thought about giving Little Luis a sister or brother. At the same time, I was sad that I couldn't easily share my good fortune with my parents and other family back in Cuba. Even if I mailed them cash, it was unlikely to make it into their hands.

I wasn't the only one in this situation; a lot of young Cuban ballplayers who managed to get out after Castro came in were now making the majors, including three who would go on to long careers and meet up in the playoffs and All-Star games.

Tony Perez, the slugger I was getting ready to face in San Diego the day I got called up, joined the Cincinnati Reds seven days after my debut and soon became one of the National League's top RBI men. Bert Campaneris, a shortstop in the Kansas City Athletics system, debuted the same week as Perez did and hit two home runs in his very first game with KC. He'd be a great fielder, base stealer, and leadoff hitter for close to 20 seasons, many of them with World Series-winning teams after the A's moved to Oakland. Perez is in the Hall of Fame, and I think Campy should be, too.

But of all the Cubans to come up in 1964, the best pure hitter was my future teammate Tony Oliva. Joining me and Campy on the Topps All-Rookie team that year, he hit .323 for the Minnesota Twins to become the first rookie batting champion in big-league history, and also led the league with 209 hits, 43 doubles, and 109 runs scored. Oliva was one of many play-ers from Cuba signed by scout Joe Cambria for the old Washington Sena-tors—who in 1961 moved to Minnesota and became the Twins. What most people don't know is that Olivia's real first name is Pedro; Tony is his brother.

Here's the story. Pedro was a great young ballplayer who Cambria wanted to sign to a Twins contract just a few weeks before spring training in 1961. This is when worsening relations between Castro and the United States were making it tougher than ever to fly out of Cuba, something I had to deal with myself after getting signed by Cleveland. Pedro didn't have a birth certificate, which was needed for a passport, but Tony did. So Pedro bor-rowed it, got a passport, and flew to the U.S. with a new name.

We were the lucky ones. The *real* Tony, also a top player, never got out of Cuba.

One thing many Latino players had to deal with during our careers was talk about our ages. In my case it started right when I first came up. Because I was doing so good, people figured I couldn't be just 23.

"He was so far ahead of everybody else who came along at that stage," Cleveland sportswriter Russ Schneider, an old-timer who went back to the days of Babe Ruth, said later, "I was convinced he had knocked about five years off. It just seemed obvious. This was no naïve kid. Luis knew his way around. Plus he looked even older because he was already starting to lose his hair."

First off, I knew my way around because I had been pitching all spring, summer, and winter, including to big-league ballplayers, for five years! Sec-ond, he may have thought it was a compliment saying I pitched like I was older and wiser, but I didn't like being called a liar.

Think about it this way: Did they ever question whether Ted Williams was really 21 when he drove in 145 runs as a rookie, or if Mickey Mantle was 20 when he hit .311 and led the Yankees to a World Series title? Frank Rob-inson was as Black as me, but born in Texas. He had 38 homers his first year, and nobody asked to see *his* birth certificate. Frank said he was 21, so they believed him. But with the Latino players, especially the Cubans, if you didn't look like a young kid, they figured you were lying.

It never was the Latinos' fault. The American scouts would go down to our country, see a guy play, and think, "Hey, he's got it going—maybe he can make it." If they couldn't verify how old the guy was, they'd figure they could take four or five years off his age. "He says he's 24? OK, let's make him 20 or maybe 19." The scouts would even change the birth certificates, or make fake ones.

The players didn't know anything about the rules and passports; we'd never had one before, so we didn't know the difference. I'm sure with computerized records in lots of countries that this is harder to do now, but I wouldn't be surprised if scouts still try to do it.

However old they thought I was, Indians fans were excited about my future—and the team—going into 1965.

Mostly, people were excited about our pitching. Our four top returning starters—McDowell, Siebert, me, and Jack Kralick—all had ERAs under 3.25 in '64, when the Indians set a major league record with 1,129 strikeouts as a staff (I got the record-breaker in my Fenway start). We were young too; McDowell was still only 22 years old, I was 24, Siebert was 28, and Kralick was the old man of the staff at 29. With us as the "Big Four" for a full season, many baseball people including our manager Birdie Tebbetts predicted we would have one of the strongest rotations in the American League.

"When we started to pitch them in regular rotation [after the 1964 All-Star Game] and before the final two weeks of the season, we were the best team in the league," said Tebbetts. "Give these kids a chance to mature and they're going to win a lot of games for a long time."

To keep us sharp during the long off-season, the Indians arranged for Siebert, me, and another young pitcher they were high on—Steve Hargan—to play on the same winter league team: the Ponce Lions of the Puerto Rican League. Ponce had a working agreement with the Indians; Johnny Lipon, who had managed many of us in the minors at Charleston and Portland, was the Lions' manager in 1964-65, and young Cleveland position players like Tommie Agee and Duke Sims were also on the roster. Although Lipon was born and raised in the Midwest, he spoke pretty good Spanish before most U.S.-born managers did, and that made a big difference to those of us who were still struggling to learn English. Lipon did a lot for us.

The league was very competitive and filled with current and future stars. We were picked as the team to beat, but that winter's champions were the Santurce Crabbers, whose lineup included Orlando Cepeda, a native Puerto Rican who was already one of the top home run hitters in the National

League playing alongside Willie Mays on the San Francisco Giants. Leading pitchers for the Crabbers were Cuban Juan Pizarro, a 19-game winner that year for the White Sox, and Rubén Gómez, another local hero who had helped the Giants to the 1954 World Series title. He only played in the majors for 10 years, but he spent 29 *years* in the Puerto Rican Winter League.

Some of the young guys on rosters that winter who would soon be big-league stars included Joe Morgan of Santurce, Willie Horton of the Mayaguez Indians, and Bert Campaneris—who I loved having behind me as shortstop on the Lions. Tony Perez, who played 10 winters for the Crabbers, has said that Puerto Rican baseball was "almost major league caliber" in the '60s. I agree. That's one reason I never liked taking winters off when I was young, no matter how many innings I pitched during the summer. There was no better way to stay in shape and stay sharp.

I didn't have a very good winter for Ponce, going 5-6, and Siebert was only 5-4. But Cleveland management was still confident enough in our pitching staff, and worried enough about our offense, to pull off a huge trade just before spring training. Gabe Paul sent promising left-hander Tommy John, who had failed to stick in the big leagues the previous two seasons, to the White Sox in a three-team swap with Kansas City that brought outfielder Rocky Colavito back to Cleveland. Rocky was a great home run man with a rifle arm, and had been one of the most popular players in Indians history before being traded away back in 1960. He could still hit the long ball at age 31, and I'm guessing Paul hoped he would both help us win and help our attendance.

The deal not only cost us John, who would go on to win 288 games in the big leagues, but also starting catcher Johnny Romano and outfielder Agee, a speedster with a great glove and bat who would later be Rookie of the Year for Chicago. But at the time everybody in Cleveland was really excited about the move. The switchboard operators at Indians team offices said they were getting hundreds of phone calls in support of the trade, the most since all the angry calls they got the day Rocky was dealt five years before. Some experts predicted the move might even win us the pennant.

It didn't, but we did improve a lot in 1965—finishing with an 87-75 record that was the best for a Cleveland team in six years. Rocky did his part, leading the AL with 108 RBI and hitting 26 homers. As a club we finished third in the ten-team league in homers and batting average, and our attendance went up nearly 35 percent, which stopped the talk of moving the team. In June we won 10 straight and 16 of 18, making believers out of a lot of fans, but in the second half of the season we lost a lot of close ballgames when we couldn't get the key hit, double play, or big catch when it mattered.

The guy affected the most was Sudden Sam McDowell. He topped the AL with a 2.18 ERA and 325 strikeouts, and he made both the All-Star team and the cover of *Sports Illustrated*. But his record was only a so-so 17-11, and although the magazine compared him to Sandy Koufax, to me Sudden was a lot more like Nolan Ryan would be a few years later when he first went to the Angels. Both were faster than anybody else in the American League, and nearly unhittable, but had trouble with their control. McDowell topped all AL pitchers with 132 walks and 17 wild pitches, and that was a lot of free bases to give away when you were suffering from a severe lack of run support. In seven of his 11 losses, the Indians were either shut out or limited to just one run.

I knew how he felt. My record was 11-11, and eight of my losses were by one or two runs. But I'm not going to blame anybody else for that season; my job was to keep the other team off the scoreboard, and I didn't do it good enough in 1965. My ERA was 3.53, a big jump from my rookie year, and I only had 10 complete games in 30 starts.

Part of my problem was getting hurt early on. In spring training I strained a muscle in my pitching arm, throwing a curveball in the first intrasquad game, and I tried to come back from it too soon. For a month all I could do was run and lob a baseball, and for the rest of the year the arm never really stopped hurting.

Tebbetts put me in the bullpen at the beginning of the regular season to work me back slowly, and I didn't make my first start until May 1. Then, after getting my record up to 9-3 by late July, including a one-hitter and a two-hitter, I lost eight of my last 10 decisions with a 4.05 ERA over the final two months. My slump was a big reason the Indians, who were just half a game out of second place starting August, finished in fifth, 15 games behind the pennant-winning Minnesota Twins. If it wasn't for Siebert (16-8 with a 2.43 ERA) and terrific relief work from Gary Bell, Don McMahon, and Lee Stange, things might have been much worse.

In a real up-and-down season, the one place I pitched consistently well was Boston. I had a 1.63 ERA in three starts at Fenway Park, and my win there on June 28 moved us into a first-place tie with Chicago. In my next Fenway appearance, on September 16, I walked none and struck out 11—including Yastrzemski three times—and in one stretch put down 17 straight batters. But I got out-pitched by another young fireballer: Dave Morehead.

While I was holding Yaz and Co. to six hits and two runs, Morehead was pitching a no-hitter to beat me 2-0.

Just that kind of season.

It turned out to be a big day in Red Sox history, and not just because of the no-hitter. While Morehead and his teammates were celebrating after the game, Boston owner Tom Yawkey fired general manager Mike "Pinky" Higgins. It was a move long overdue. Higgins had been either GM or manager of the Red Sox for most of the past decade, never coming close to winning a pennant. He was also known by Black players throughout baseball as a terrible racist. Higgins supposedly said, "they'll be no niggers on this team as long as I have anything to say about it."

Sure enough, Boston was the last big-league team to integrate, in 1959, and they had only had a handful of African-American or Latino players through '65. Their first Black pitcher, right-hander Earl Wilson, was just emerging as a star when he was traded to Detroit for telling a reporter off the record that he had been denied service at a bar during spring training in Florida. That reporter told another writer, who wrote a story, and Wilson was deemed a troublemaker. After the trade, he became a 20-game winner and helped the Tigers to a World Series title.

In his autobiography, *I Never Had it Made*, Jackie Robinson described his own phony tryout with the Red Sox in 1945—two years *before* he broke the color line with Brooklyn. Jackie said he and two other Negro League guys did great in their tryout, but none even heard back from Boston. "Tom Yawkey," Robinson wrote, "was one of the most bigoted guys in baseball."

I'm not saying I agree with Jackie; I have no proof Mr. Yawkey was a racist, and he was always good to me when I joined the Red Sox. But even though I never met Pinky Higgins, I heard enough bad things about him to believe he was probably the guy at the center of the problem. Mr. Yawkey's biggest mistake was probably that he didn't fire Higgins sooner; by the time he gave him the boot, Boston was finishing up a 62-100 season, its worst in more than 30 years.

The guy who took Higgins's place as Red Sox GM was Dick O'Connell—and he was the right guy for the job. In his first two years he completely turned the team around, rebuilding the farm system and making a bunch of smart trades. He didn't care if a guy was white, Black, or blue, as long as he could help the club. And because Mr. Yawkey had plenty of money he was willing to spend, O'Connell could take risks on guys he had a good feeling about.

I didn't know it at the time, but that GM move in Boston would have a big impact on my own career and my life a few years down the road.

Meanwhile, as the '65 season was winding down, I began to think about taking the winter off. I had been pitching year-round for six years, and while I enjoyed doing it, and always felt strong as the summer wore on, I also had my share of injuries. The extra money definitely came in handy, but by taking a vacation from playing I could spend more time with Maria and Little Luis back in Mexico City. Gabe Paul and the front office were also in favor of my skipping winter ball, so I did. I worked out off a mound two or three times a week, and I ran a lot, but didn't pitch any games from October through January.

The other big thing I did that winter was change my eating habits. I was never a *fat* guy, but because of my stocky physique people always joked about my size. When I struggled during 1965, even my dad wrote me from Cuba saying I had to lose weight. That was easy for Señor Skinny to say, but not so easy for me to do. One sportswriter wrote that I had "a tendency to gain weight by merely looking at a big dinner."

I figured if I wasn't playing a lot, I had to be careful. Maria is a great cook, but I really watched myself. No greasy foods, chocolate, potatoes, or bread. Beans and rice was my favorite meal, but Maria only let me have it once a week. Team management was worried that I was gaining weight in Mexico City, but I was actually *losing* 20 pounds. And when I showed up in Tucson for spring training, this was the headline: "TIANT TANTALIZES TRIBE BY CUTTING DOWN ON WEIGHT."

Nobody was more shocked than Birdie Tebbetts.

"Holy smokes ... how about that?" the manager told reporters after first seeing me. "I was almost afraid to look at him. I'd heard he got so fat."

I loved it.

"I feel goooooood," I told the shocked writers. "How do I look?"

Then I went into the clubhouse and picked up a pair of size 32 pants, down from 36 the year before.

The writers all started calling me the "new" Luis Tiant, and there was a great feeling about the team in general heading into the season. After the jump to 87 wins the year before, the expectations were for even bigger things. "This could be the team to watch in 1966," the New York Times predicted in its baseball preview issue. "The Indians have the basic ingredients of success—pitching and power."

Both were clicking when the season started. We tied what was then a major-league record by opening the year with 10 straight wins, and after sweeping New York three in a row at Yankee Stadium were 14-1 on May 5. I had three wins already—all of them complete-game shutouts. Our pitching coach Early Wynn was a 300-game winner, but I was also getting tips by mail from another good source: my dad. He stressed the importance of getting the first batter out each inning, and never, ever pitching the ball high to anyone.

I tried to follow his advice, and the "new" Luis Tiant was the talk of baseball. When one sportswriter asked me how I was doing it, I smiled and replied simply: "I am skinny and I am lucky."

Of course it wasn't all luck. It seemed like the time off over the winter had been a good idea. My arm was completely pain-free for the first time that I could remember, and my ERA was 1.71 at the end of May. I was pitching so well that Tebbetts again used me in relief a few times between starts, and it didn't bother me at all. He even thought about making me a full-time reliever, because he knew I didn't mind throwing every day. But this was before guys like Goose Gossage and Bruce Sutter got real big contacts as relievers, so I hoped to stay a starter where I could make more money for my family.

Besides, why mess with something that isn't broken? McDowell, Siebert, Bell, and our other pitchers were all doing great, and guys like first baseman Fred Whitfield, shortstop Chico Salmon, and my Cuban catching buddy Joe Azcue were coming through big at the plate. It looked like nobody could stop us. When Bell four-hit the Twins on May 28, we had a 27-10 record and were in first place by four-and-a-half half games.

But what's funny about baseball is that you never know when things are going to shift. It's a long season, and injuries can pile up. Maybe a bunch of guys get cold at once, or you can just run into plain bad luck. Whatever the reason, after being the hottest team in the league for the first two months, we went belly-up in June and July. During one stretch we lost 20 of 29 games, and we quickly fell from first place to nearly 15 games behind the Baltimore Orioles.

That was big trouble. The Orioles had been developing into a contender with guys like third baseman Brooks Robinson, first baseman Boog Powell, and a great young pitching staff. Trading for Frank Robinson before that year put them over the top.

After a decade as one of the best hitters in the National League, Frank immediately became the best in the AL. Off the field he was the type of leader who could control a clubhouse, and his teammates called him "Da

Judge" because he ran a "Kangaroo Court" where fines were given out for things like missing the cutoff man or not moving a runner along. Frank made everyone around him better, and in '66 he won the Triple Crown by leading the AL in batting (.316), home runs (49), and RBI (116).

I did my small part to help him get there. We were playing the Orioles at Baltimore's Memorial Stadium on May 8, and had just lost the first game of a Sunday doubleheader. I was trying to keep us in first place by a game over the Birds, and pitch my fourth straight shutout to begin the season. Robby came up in the first inning with Luis Aparicio on base, and I started him off with a fastball that broke low and inside. Real tough to hit—just like Dad preached.

It didn't fool him.

"The ball jumped off his bat, rocketing toward left field in a towering arc," Baltimore sportswriter Doug Brown wrote. "The only question was whether it would stay fair and third base umpire Cal Drummond signaled that it had. The ball landed in the parking lot behind the left field bleachers and was retrieved by two teenagers, Bill Wheatley and Mike Sparaco, from under the wheel of a car, 540 feet from home plate. It traveled a measured 451 feet on the fly."

The Orioles had been playing at Memorial Stadium for 12 years, and when the public address man announced to the crowd of nearly 50,000 fans that it was first time a ball had ever been hit completely out of the ballpark, they gave Frank a standing ovation.

"I'd never heard anything like it before," Robinson said later. "The ovation started and it mounted and it was a little touching. I was a little embarrassed, though tremendously pleased. It was one of the greatest things that ever happened to me. It was so unexpected."

Happy I could help!

After the game, the two kids who found the ball after it had rolled 100 feet to a stop under a white Cadillac brought it back to Frank; each got a season's pass and an autographed ball in trade.

That's not even the whole story. A week later the Orioles had a pregame ceremony where they put an orange and black flag at the spot where the ball left the park on the fly. The flag read "HERE," and they left it there until Memorial Stadium closed in 1991. Frank gave the ball a place of honor in his trophy case.

Me? All I got for making it possible was a loss—and ribbing from teammate Gary Bell and Mike Cuellar of the Orioles every time we came to

Baltimore. "Luis, what's that up there?" they'd say, pointing at the flag. "Do you know?"

I do know *this*: Frank Robinson hit about .150 off me the rest of his career.

Later in the season, after reliever Dick Radatz got hurt, Tebbetts put me in the bullpen again, this time for six weeks. While I didn't complain, I really didn't like it too much. I wanted to be out there to *start* the game, not just to finish it. But the manager is No. 1, and what he says goes. Especially if you're a young player trying to stick in the league.

Birdie was a good man, and a good manager, but he couldn't turn things around when they went south. On August 19, with the team in third place, 14 games out, he resigned for, as he put it, "the good of baseball in Cleveland." Coach George Strickland, who had filled in as manager in '64 when Birdie had a heart attack, took over again on an interim basis. The change didn't help; after going 65-57 under Tebbetts, we were well under .500 the rest of the way and finished in fifth place at 81-81. The only good thing to come out of the switch for me was that Strickland let me start a couple times down the stretch, and I threw two solid complete games.

In the end, the year was a mixed bag. I finished just 12-11 after my hot start, but my 2.79 ERA was still a big improvement over '65. Even though I started only 16 games, I tied for the league lead with five shutouts. And when Birdie put me in the bullpen, I finished 22 games and picked up eight saves. We all underachieved as a team, but I felt I had done OK with all the shuffling between roles. My biggest problem, honestly, may have been all the weight I had lost before the season. As the summer wore on, I got more and more tired.

I didn't know who would be the Indians' new manager in 1967—most thought it *wouldn't* be Strickland—but if I wanted to prove that the best place for me was in the starting rotation, I figured the time to start doing that was now. No more long vacations. When the American League season ended, I signed on for the winter with the Caracas Lions of the Venezuela League. That was the same league where my success playing with Valencia three years before had proved the launching pad for my journey to the majors.

There was plenty of strong competition to measure yourself against in Venezuela, and I responded to the challenge. I got off to a great start and helped the Lions make a push for the playoffs. My partner in crime was outfielder Jose Tartabull, a Cuban who played with the Kansas City A's during the summer. In one two-week stretch Jose hit .457, and he was gunning for the batting title as we battled Valencia for first place.

The Latin fans were always passionate, but sometimes things could get out of hand. In one game I pitched against the Aragua Tigers, their left fielder Dick Dietz—who normally caught—made two errors that led to four runs. The crowd really let Dietz have it, throwing bottles, oranges, and whatever else they could find at him. Even after he singled in the ninth inning, they kept at it. When a cup of ice hit Dietz as he stood on first base, he called time, left the field, and quit the team.

That was one of seven straight wins I picked up for Caracas en route to a 12-6 record and 1.84 ERA during the regular winter season. I also had some fun at the plate, helping win several games with my bat and knocking in five runs on three hits (including a homer) in one game. We wound up tying Valencia for the pennant, and in the playoffs I had three complete-game wins as we won the Venezuela championship over the LaGuaira Sharks. There were 35,000 fans at our title-winning game in Caracas's University Stadium, as big as any crowd we drew in Cleveland.

I was ready for a fresh start with the Indians in 1967, especially when I heard the team's new manager was from outside the organization. Joe Adcock was real young for a skipper, only 39, and had been an outfielder with the California Angels the year before. As a player he was known as a nice guy, but he ran us hard in spring training.

"The boys can expect me to be strict and I'll stress fundamentals," he said after getting the job. "I think there are a lot of mental errors made that shouldn't be." Perhaps to show he meant business, he fined McDowell $500 for missing curfew during spring training.

Adcock planned to use a five-man rotation, and I wanted to be in it along with McDowell, Siebert, Bell, and Steve Hargan, a terrific rookie for us in '66 with a 2.48 ERA (third best in the league). I told the manager how I felt, and he told me "he'd see"—which I took to mean he wanted me to prove to him I deserved it.

When we opened the exhibition season, Adcock gave me the start in our first game. This meant a lot. Not only did it show he was giving me a fair shot at being a starter, but the game was in Mexico City. This was the birthplace of my wife, and it was my adopted home. We were also playing the team I'd started my career with: The Mexico City Tigers. Sure, it was spring training, and the Tigers were not a big-league club. But it still felt special to me, and when I threw five shutout innings with just one walk, Adcock told reporters he was impressed with my control. "Looie looked like he was in mid-season form," he said.

After pitching 195 innings in three months of winter ball, I hoped to pace myself in Tucson and not throw hard *all* the time. I had worked on a knuckleball in Venezuela, and wanted to try it out, along with some other breaking stuff, when the games didn't count. This didn't go over too well with Adcock and the new Cleveland pitching coach, Clay Bryant.

In one game against the hard-hitting Giants, I relieved Siebert to start the fifth and let up two hits and a walk that inning. Even though nobody scored, I got an earful from Bryant.

"Looie was throwing blankety-blank lollipops up there and I had to straighten him out quick," the coach told reporters after the game. "He acted like he didn't want to throw the blankety-blank ball, and I told him to either do it or get out.

"If he's going to be that way, he'll not pitch for me."

This went on for a while. When I let up five hits including a homer to Ron Santo against the Cubs, blowing a 4-1 lead, I got more abuse from Bryant.

"You don't get in shape by throwing lollipops," he said after this game, which we came back to win. "It's all right if you're trying something, but the only thing Tiant should be doing now is getting himself ready."

This thinking made no sense to me. I was already in shape from playing three months of winter ball. Trying things *was* how I got myself ready for the season ahead. I had been working on some new stuff in Venezuela, and now I wanted to try it against whole lineups of big-leaguers. I realize, looking back, that he and Adcock were trying to toughen me up and help me get back to the level of success I'd had as a rookie. They were trying to piss me off, and it worked.

During my last starts of the spring I threw more fastballs and less "lollipops"—which pleased the coaching staff enough to secure my spot in the starting rotation. The decision on an Opening Day pitcher was initially kept a secret, and some people thought I might even get it over McDowell. But Sudden Sam was still the golden boy, even after a 14-15 season, and he got the nod. After two postponements—one a rainout and one from a power outage—I started the second game and got whipped 10-1 by the Angels. Then I got knocked around in my next start.

Things got better after that, at least for me. I went on a six-game winning streak that included back-to-back 12- and 13-strikeout efforts against the

Senators and Tigers, but the team was playing barely .500 baseball. Gabe Paul decided something had to be done. Pitching continued to be the club's greatest strength, but our hitting and defense needed work.

The previous November, during the winter baseball meetings, Paul had said he was willing to listen to trade proposals for pitchers—with me and 10-year-veteran Gary Bell rumored as the candidates most likely leaving. We both survived the winter, but with the team limping along in mid-1967, Paul finally pulled the trigger. On June 4, with the Indians in fifth place, he sent Bell to the Red Sox in exchange for young, hard-hitting first baseman Tony Horton and longtime outfielder Don Demeter.

It was tough to lose a great guy like Bell, who was dependable whether starting or relieving and was hilarious in the clubhouse. Everybody called him "Ding Dong," and we had a lot of fun together. But good pitching only worked if you could score some runs, too, and we hoped Horton and Demeter would provide us some much-needed power.

"I just hope the Indians continue to hit against me the way they hit for me," Bell joked on the way out.

Ding Dong got his wish. He immediately moved into Boston's starting rotation and won 12 games in just over half a season for the Red Sox, including three wins against Cleveland. Horton hit OK for us, but Demeter was barely above .200; overall, we played much worse after the trade than before it. Just as fast as I won six games in a row, I *lost six* straight in July and August, earning me another short stay in the bullpen. My ERA was still right near the top 10 in the league, but my record was 8-9. Offensive production was dropping throughout the majors, so there was less room for error.

The American League pennant race that summer was crazy. Five teams—Chicago, California, Minnesota, Detroit, and Boston—were all bunched at the top of the standings. The Red Sox were the biggest surprise; they had finished ninth the year before, but had a tough young club led by two superstars: pitcher Jim Lonborg and leftfielder Carl Yastrzemski. Lonborg, a tall, thin right-hander with a great fastball and the courage to pitch inside, was leading the AL in strikeouts and wins; Yaz, already an excellent player, was taking his game to the next level and chasing a Triple Crown just like Frank Robby the year before. Plus, Yaz played Gold Glove defense.

It's a long season, full of stress, and you need ways to keep yourself from going crazy when you're going bad. On every team I played on, I tried to be a guy who not only played hard, but also knew how to have fun. Taking my cigar in the shower always made guys laugh, I'm not sure why. My imitations had 'em chuckling, too. Even when my English wasn't too good, I could do a pretty good version of Sam McDowell arguing with Joe Adcock about coming out of a game. Poking fun of guys, giving them the needle, it was all fair game. Even guys on other teams—hey, they were stressed out too, right?

In May we had come to Boston before the fans there really caught on that the 1967 Red Sox might be something special. I struggled with my control, walking eight, but also struck out nine—including Yastrzemski three straight times on fastballs. We won in 10 innings, 5-3, and Yaz was so angry he had them wheel out the cage after the game so he could take extra batting practice. It was impressive dedication, it really was, but I couldn't help getting a little jab at him for it.

I walked by while he was in the cage, looked him in the eye, and said simply, "You need it." (If you've already read the foreword to this book, you know how that story ends.)

Unlike the year before, we pretty much knew by August that we had no chance to make the World Series. Still, even if we couldn't win, I wanted to prove my value by pitching well against the teams that *could*. Sometimes our bats didn't make it easy. On August 22, I struck out 16 Angels, but it took a homer in the bottom of the ninth by pal Joe Azcue to get me the 3-2 win. Ten days later I pitched nine shutout innings against the Angels, this time on the road, but we lost 1-0 in the 12th. That was a tough one to get over.

Overall I made six starts in September, and that game in Anaheim was the only one I didn't finish. I was 4-0 with a 1.55 ERA for the month, and beat the Twins, White Sox, and Red Sox—all of whom were going for the pennant. I tried to think of it like *we* were going for the pennant; if we couldn't win, at least we could have a say. The newspapers got into the act, too; after we beat Chicago in 13 innings, the big headline in the *Plain Dealer* was "Tribe Drops Chisox Two Behind."

The final week of September we went to Boston. Fenway Park felt much different than when we'd ended the season there two years before. Only about 1,200 people saw Dave Morehead's no-hitter against me in '65; now the Red Sox were in first place, with a chance to go to their first World Series in 21 years, and were leading the league in attendance. Fenway had no second deck, and very little foul territory, so you felt like the crowd was right on top of you. You could tell by how they cheered that they really *knew* the game. It reminded me of the atmosphere at games back in Cuba, and I loved it whether I was pitching for the home team or the visitors.

It's important to try to let yourself go a little in a tense pennant race, but it's much easier to keep loose when you're *not* in one. I was real loose on this day, and I was bringing it. I struck out three guys in the first inning, seven through the first five, and we knocked out our old pal Gary Bell, Boston's starter, with two homers in the fourth.

As we built a 6-0 lead, I couldn't help having some fun.

"We couldn't hit him, and each time he struck somebody out, he'd look over at our dugout and say, 'You guys are tight, huh? You're looking like re-alllll tight assholes!'" remembers Rico Petrocelli, shortstop for the Red Sox that day. "He was a character, you know? You couldn't help but like him, even when he was beating you."

Yaz got to me late in the game for a three-run homer, his 43rd of the year, but we still won, 6-3. That knocked Boston one game behind league-leading Minnesota and a percentage-point behind Chicago with three games to play.

"Tiant was good; I have to tip my cap to him," Yastrzemski said after the game.

What did *I* think?

"I have to make money, too," I told the big group of reporters around my locker. "I eat like these guys eat."

We beat Boston again the next day, but they still won the pennant by sweeping the Twins over the weekend while the White Sox and Tigers were losing. Yaz, Rico, and Gary Bell each earned more than $5,000 in World Series bonus money, which could buy plenty to eat. I was left watching the Series on TV, *again*.

Still, it wasn't a bad year for me personally. My 12-9 record wasn't anything great, but I finished in the AL's top 10 in strikeouts (219) and ERA (2.74). Nobody in the majors struck out more batters per nine innings than my 9.225, and I even *hit* .254—sixth-best on the team. But when your club finishes eighth at 75-87, no one really cares about your stats.

The best news for me that fall came off the field: Maria gave birth to our daughter in October. We named her Isabel, after my mother, and I couldn't help wondering if she and her big brother Luis Jr. would ever meet the grandparents whose names they carried. As another Christmas approached, with another mouth to feed, I also wondered what the future had in store for me.

Would I ever break through with the kind of season that would get me the big money—and get *me* on TV for the big games?

7

POOR MAN'S MCLAIN

AFTER A STEADY CLIMB UPWARD during the first decade of his professional baseball career, Luis Tiant was about to see his fortunes rise as dramatically as one of his most electrifying pitches.

The 1968 MLB season is remembered as "The Year of the Pitcher," and one can make a strong argument that Tiant outperformed even 31-game winner Denny McLain of the Detroit Tigers that summer in the American League. Fans who regularly combed the agate-type lists of league leaders in their daily newspapers grew accustomed to seeing Tiant's earned-run-average appear above those of McLain and all other AL hurlers, while Tiant's shutout and strikeout feats earned him both frequent appearances in bold-faced headlines and a spot on baseball's grandest mid-summer stage.

Many attributed his new level of success to changes he had made to his already unique pitching motion. Always looking for an edge, Tiant added more head bobs and upper-body twists during his delivery, moves made to keep hitters off-balance. Fans loved the show, but for Tiant it was always about strategy rather than showmanship. He was pitching for his team, and for his family, not the cameras.

McLain got the glory, in the form of postseason awards and a World Series title. But with a far less-potent lineup supporting him, and with thoughts never far from his aging parents trapped in Castro's Cuba, El Tiante was peerless as a competitor. It seemed at times like he had the weight of the world atop his strong, overworked shoulders, but he still managed to be a revered and hilarious teammate as well as a dedicated father, son, and husband.

Those were the things, he knew, that have the greatest value—even if measured by heart instead of hardware.

IT DIDN'T TAKE GABE PAUL long to make his move when the 1967 season ended. Right after we lost our last game to Baltimore, 4-0, finishing the year eighth with a 75-87 record, the Indians GM fired manager Joe Adcock and replaced him with Alvin Dark. The news ran in the paper the next day along with a story about the Red Sox beating the Twins to win the AL pennant. It turns out my win the week before had not buried the Sox, as Carl Yastrzemski feared; he and his teammates were going to their first World Series since 1946, and Boston fans had stormed the field at Fenway Park to celebrate after the last game.

The headline about our new manager, above Yaz's smiling mug, was big and bold:

CAN DARK MAKE TRIBE SEE LIGHT?

I already knew a little about my new boss. An All-Star shortstop for the New York Giants in the '50s, Dark managed that team after it moved to San Francisco. He won a National League pennant in 1962 when his club featured Willie Mays, Juan Marichal, Orlando Cepeda, and Willie McCovey, and for the past three years he had managed in the AL with the rebuilding Kansas City A's. He had a reputation as a strong strategist and a great handler of pitchers, but was fired by A's owner Charlie Finley in August of '67 after KC fell into last place.

There were rumors that Dark didn't get along with the Black and Latino players on the Giants, but Marichal told Indians second baseman Pedro Gonzalez, a fellow Dominican, that they weren't true.

"Juan Marichal is my best friend," Gonzalez said to a reporter. "He is my countryman. He is dark-skinned like me. He pitched for Al in San Francisco. He tells me Dark is a great manager. He tells me this many, many times."

That sounded good to me, but I still wondered how I'd get along with Dark—or if I figured into his plans.

During the winter, Dark told reporters that it was "unlikely" the Indians would trade any of their starting pitchers, but "we would if the right kind of deal presented itself." With a wife and now *two* kids to support, I couldn't afford to start over with a new organization. There was only one thing to do: devote myself to being *so* good that Dark and Paul would never think of trading me.

After a month in Mexico City with Maria, Luis, and baby Isabel, I went to Venezuela to pitch a second winter with the Caracas Lions. I was determined to prove myself, and I did—leading the league with a 1.34 ERA and helping Caracas to the championship. Two of my major-league teammates also played for the Lions that year: Indians outfielder Vic Davalillo, a native Venezuelan, hit .395 to win the league batting title, and Diego Segui, a Cuban who pitched for Dark in Kansas City and later with me on the Red Sox, went 12-1 with a 1.56 ERA. Today Diego and Vic, both great ballplayers and gentlemen, are in the Venezuelan Baseball Hall of Fame.

Dark made a trip down to Caracas to see me and Vic play, and told reporters he was worried about my weight. There was nothing to worry about. I reported to Tucson in great shape and pitched well in the exhibition games. And even though Dark ran a more relaxed camp than Adcock, with less drills, I knew how important strong legs would be for me late in the season. So, I ran as much as I could.

One day a reporter overheard Dark and new pitching coach Jack Sanford talking as they saw me running around the field.

"Look at the way that guy is working," said Dark.

"I'll bet you a case of golf balls right now that Looie is at least 18-6 this season," Sanford replied.

"I won't bet against him," said Dark, "but that's one I'd sure like to lose."

There was a lot of energy around the team, and a lot of new faces besides the coaching staff. The Indians had picked up speedy young outfielders Tommy Harper and Jose Cardenal, who would make our lineup one of the fastest in baseball. The big addition to the pitching staff was Eddie Fisher, a veteran knuckleballer Dark figured would be real tough for batters to face after getting fastballs in the upper 90s from me, Sudden Sam McDowell, and Sonny Siebert.

"Man, we're all just floating into this season," outfielder Leon Wagner said with a huge smile on the first day of training camp. "I tell you baby, it's just awful beautiful."

Daddy Wags was right. First it was awful, and *then* it was beautiful—for a while.

On April 4, just before the season started, Martin Luther King was shot and killed. There were riots in lots of the big cities, including Cleveland, and many teams postponed their openers. I could understand why Black people were angry; I remembered how it felt being yelled at and treated like shit because of the color of my skin. In Cuba, a friend of mine was one of the thousands executed by Castro's firing squads for standing up for what was right. But it was supposed to be different in the United States, and this made me wonder. It was sad to see so much hate.

The start of our season didn't cheer anybody up. I pitched lousy in the home opener when Dark brought me in to relieve Sudden Sam, letting up a home run to former teammate Chuck Hinton and taking the loss. The team went 6-11 in April overall, and I hoped that Dark would move me into the rotation and leave me there.

He did, and I got hot—along with the club. We won 11 of our first 12 in May to move into second place. What we couldn't do is overtake the Detroit Tigers at the top. We had good speed, and great pitching, but just didn't have any power. Paul had traded our top home run hitter, Colavito, over the winter, feeling he was starting to decline. Wagner, our other big slugger, "promised" a 40-homer year during spring training and then came out flat. He was also showing his age, and nobody stepped up to take his or Rocky's place.

On defense our guys tried their best, but sometimes it seemed we couldn't hit *or* catch the ball. This put a lot of pressure on the pitchers. You knew every time out that one mistake could cost you the game.

A start I made at Boston early in the year is a good example. I let up a three-run homer to Reggie Smith in the fourth inning, we shut them out the rest of the way, and we lost, 3-2. Of course, you can't lose if the other team doesn't score, and that's how I won my next four games—by scores of 2-0, 4-0, 8-0, and 2-0. The four consecutive complete-game shutouts got me within one of the major league record for one pitcher, which had held since 1904.

I wasn't just pitching good, I was *dealing*—allowing just 14 hits and seven walks while striking out 35 over the 36 innings of the streak. Batters hit a combined .118 off me during those games, but I wasn't paying attention. I never looked at numbers when I pitched, and didn't care what I did the last time out. The only thing I wanted to do was get ready for the next start.

The press made that tough. After the fourth straight shutout at Baltimore a photographer got cute and took a shot of me holding up four metal bat weights, or donuts, that looked like zeros. The picture ran all across the country.

We always had a hard time turning double plays on the Indians, and that's what happened in my next start—we failed to get one when we needed it. This was also against Baltimore; I was up 1-0 with one out in the sixth when Frank Robinson hit a grounder to second base, a sure double-play ball to get me out of the inning. Larry Brown picked it up and threw to second, but shortstop Chico Salmon dropped the ball as the runner slid in.

Everybody was safe, and big Boog Powell was coming up next. That was trouble. Boog hit a three-run homer, and we wound up losing, 6-2. My scoreless innings streak was over at 41 1/3; there would be no fifth donut.

Here's where being a good teammate comes into play. Sure, I was mad we lost, but I knew that Chico—who was my roommate on the road—felt even worse. He didn't drop the ball on purpose, so what good would it do to chew him out? It was like being back home as a kid. I took care of my friends, because they were the closest thing I had to brothers. Now I felt the same way about my teammates.

When the writers asked me my thoughts about what happened, I reminded them that Chico had made a great play at Yankee Stadium earlier in my shutout streak to help keep it alive.

"Errors are part of the game," I said, looking over to where Chico had his head hung in his locker. "I like to have a shutout, but I'm pitching to win. You have to be lucky to get shutouts. You have to be lucky to win, too."

I shouldn't have been surprised the Orioles found a way to break the streak, just like they broke my chance at a fourth straight shutout back in '66 on Frank's moon-shot homer. They were just an incredible team. Their lineup was dangerous nearly all the way through, from Don Buford and Davey Johnson up top through Boog and the Robinson boys—Frank and Brooks. In the field they had Gold Glovers at second base (Johnson), third (Brooks Robinson), shortstop (Mark Belanger), and center field (Paul Blair). They called Brooks "Hoover", like the vacuum cleaner, because he picked everything up. When the ball hit the bat, I swear to God, he knew by the sound it made where that ball was going. He was BADDDD.

For years the Orioles had Jim Palmer, Dave McNally, and Mike Cuellar atop their rotation, all of them 20-game winners, but that team could make *any* pitcher look good. In Baltimore the saying was that manager Earl Weaver's strategy consisted of three things: pitching, defense, and three-run homers. That's all he needed.

On the Indians all we really had was the pitching, but it was so good it was keeping us near the top the first half of the season. McDowell, who had the best fastball in the majors and was always considered our ace, was leading the league in strikeouts and had an ERA below 2.00. He and our other starters Siebert, Stan Williams, and Steve Hargan were all doing great, but for the first time since we both joined the Indians in 1964, it wasn't Sudden Sam getting most of the attention.

There were stretches before where I pitched great for a month or even six weeks straight, but never for this long. After the loss to Baltimore I won seven of my next nine starts, all complete games, never allowing more than two runs. Boston manager Dick Williams, after winning the 1967 pennant, would be managing the American League in the All-Star Game the next month. Players voted for the All-Star starting lineup then, not the fans, but managers got to select the pitching staff. I gave Williams something think about when I struck out 13 of his Red Sox in an 8-1 victory at Fenway Park. That gave me a 12-5 record, tying my previous high in wins for a full season—and it was still only June. The win also dropped my ERA to 1.19.

I felt I deserved to be an All-Star, and I hoped Williams wasn't still mad at me for beating Boston during the final week of '67. If he was, he didn't show it. He named me to the team, my first time as an All-Star.

They called 1968 "The Year of the Pitcher" and it really was; besides my long shutout streak, Bob Gibson of the Cardinals had one of 47 innings and Don Drysdale of the Dodgers set a new record of 58 2/3 straight just before the break. The Tigers' Denny McLain, whose team we were chasing for first place, was on pace to be the first 30-game winner since Dizzy Dean in 1934. Among hitters, two Red Sox—Carl Yastrzemski (.307) and Ken Harrelson (.302)—were the only American Leaguers batting .300 at the halfway mark.

There were different ideas for what was causing the offensive dip. Some thought that the bigger fielding gloves now being used were cutting down on hits, or that the new, bigger ballparks were too hard to homer in. Even Hank Aaron, closing in on his 500th homer that summer, was seeing a dip in his offense. He suggested giving batters four strikes to improve their chances. "What worries me," Aaron said, "is that lack of hitting is cutting deeply into our attendance."

Harry Walker, a former batting champion and big-league manager, blamed organized youth baseball programs like Little League. He said that instead of hitting all day by themselves or with a couple friends, like he and others from the previous generation did, Little Leaguers were taking only a very limited number of swings each practice and game. Their coaches, he believed, cared more about winning than teaching them how to hit.

"They tell the boys the pitcher is wild, and he'll walk 'em, so DON'T SWING," said Walker. "I've seen kids stand at the plate all day without swinging a bat. The pitchers get to throw, but the hitters don't get to hit."

I didn't buy that. We weren't facing little kids; these were big-league ballplayers who got plenty of swings every day for years in the majors and the minors. Great athletes who were the best in the world at what they did.

These things went in cycles; hitters mashed the ball in the early '60s, and now pitchers had the edge.

For me, that edge was never bigger than on the night of July 3, 1968. We were facing the Minnesota Twins, runner-ups to Boston for the pennant the previous year. A good home crowd of 21,135 turned out to see if we could stay in second place, and I got off strong with seven strikeouts over the first four shutout innings.

I was just warming up.

In the fifth, I struck out the side. Cesar Tovar led off the sixth for Minnesota with a hard hit into center field, but we got him trying to stretch out a triple. I had one more strikeout that inning, and then another in the seventh. Stan Williams was on our bench charting every pitch, but I had no idea how many strikeouts I had. All I cared about was keeping us in the game, because Minnesota starter Jim Merritt was doing great, too. It was still 0-0 in the eighth when I struck out the side again.

Then, with one out in the ninth inning, the Twins sent up Harmon Killebrew to pinch-hit. Everyone called him Killer; he was strong as a bull and the best power hitter in baseball. He hit 40 homers practically every season, and wound up with 574 lifetime including five off me. But this time he went down swinging, and I eventually got out of the inning when Tony Oliva—another great hitter, and a fellow Cuban who should be in the Hall of Fame with Killebrew—flew out to right.

Nine innings, it turns out, wasn't enough. Merritt was still shutting us down, and so we kept going.

The fans were on their feet when I came out to start the top of the tenth, maybe the loudest I had ever heard them at Cleveland Stadium. We never made the World Series, but I was thinking this must be what it sounded and felt like. My heart was really pumping, and I let up a double on my first pitch to Rich Reese. He was the go-ahead run, and Frank Quillici got him to third with a bunt single, but I kept him there by striking out the side for a third time.

Only after my Cuban buddy Joe Azcue won the game for us with a single in the bottom of the tenth did I find out how many strikeouts I actually had: *nineteen!*

When they told me I was one of only a few pitchers to ever get that many since 1900, it felt great. Bob Feller, an Indians legend who had a 348-strikeout season right after World War II, never did it. Neither did all-time career strikeout champ Walter Johnson, or Bob Gibson, or even Sandy Koufax! A guy named Tom Chesbro had 21 in a 1961 game, but he pitched 16 innings to get them. Other than him, the only ones to reach 20 all came later on: Roger Clemens (twice), Kerry Wood, Randy Johnson, and Max Scherzer. A few other guys have gotten 19 since '68, including Nolan Ryan four times, but it's still a short list. The most I had other than that night was 16.

Combined with my 13 strikeouts against Boston in my previous start, I now had 32 in my last two games—which broke Koufax's two-game record of 31 set in 1959. Sandy had also struck out 41 batters in a *three*-game stretch, and I tied him on that one. John Roseboro, Minnesota's catcher, said he had "never seen a fastball thrown so hard, for so many innings," as he did facing me that game. He would be a good judge, because before joining the Twins, he had caught Koufax on the Dodgers.

What's funny is that I didn't even feel like I had my best stuff that night. In the clubhouse afterwards, I was having my regular victory cigar and getting my pitching arm iced down by trainer Wally Bock when Stan Williams heard me saying I wasn't happy with my control. So he came over and told me that out of 135 pitches I threw during the game, 101 of them were strikes—and I didn't walk a single batter. So whatever I thought, the results were OK.

If you weren't in Cleveland, or maybe Baltimore, you didn't see that game. This was way before MLB.com, ESPN, or cable superstations, so the Game of the Week on national TV was the only chance fans had to watch games their teams weren't playing in. If your city didn't have a big-league club, the Game of the Week was *it* for baseball, and only teams having a good season usually made it onto the national telecasts.

After we started winning in '68, we showed up a few times on the Game of the Week—which some people managed to pick up down in Cuba from a Florida station. There was a friend of mine I grew up with whose father was a butcher. His family knew my father and mother, and they had a big TV. If the authorities caught you with one, you'd get put in jail, so they kept it out of sight. But every time I pitched on TV, on the Game of the Week, the butcher would send somebody to my parents' house to tell them. Then they would go to the butcher's and watch.

My father told me later that every time they put me on the screen during those games, my mother would go up and touch it—to try and touch *me*. Then she would cry. That's why I tell people you have to go through it to really know the feeling of what it is like to be separated from your family like that. It makes you sad, but it also makes you appreciate what you have.

Every season during those years, once the school year ended, Maria always came up from Mexico City with the kids to live in whatever city I was playing in. I had very few chances to see my father pitch, or to even be around him when he played, and I wanted things to be different for my children. So in '68, Maria, five-year-old Luis, and baby Isabel spent the summer in Cleveland.

Little Luis loved it.

"We would run around the whole stadium, which was usually pretty empty," Luis Jr. remembers about those days. "I spent a lot of time down in the clubhouse, playing with the other players' sons. We would hang out and play baseball or whatever games we could come up with, and Cy Bynick, the clubhouse man, used to take care of us. He'd buy us hot dogs and ice cream, and let us break the old lights hanging down from the ceiling with our balls. Tony Horton, the Indians first baseman, was one guy I could remember vividly; I used to call him my big brother."

Maria tried to bring the kids to every game I started at home that summer. Given our crowds, they were easy to spot.

One time, after a tough win against Detroit, I was telling reporters about how some of the Tigers players had talked trash to me during the game. I was getting real heated up, like I had been on the field, until Little Luis walked over and gave me a big kiss. Then I just smiled. That picture made the papers, too.

"It was one of the funnest times of my life," says Luis Jr. "I was at the ballpark all the time, and even got to fly on the plane with the team on a short road trip. When my father went head-to-head with Denny McLain in Detroit, I sat in the first row of a packed Tiger Stadium, right by the Indians dugout. Dad shut McLain out, 2-0."

Little Luis, his baby sister, and their mother came to the All-Star Game, too, which that year was in the Houston Astrodome. Most of us American League players had never seen the first domed stadium in the majors, and I was excited to represent the Indians along with Sudden Sam and Azcue. Joe and I had come a long way together since he caught my first start in Yankee Stadium and translated interviews for me back in '64. My dream then was to face Mickey Mantle just once; now I was going to be his teammate for a night. Making it even more special was that Dick Williams had named me his starting pitcher for the American League.

There were 48,321 fans in the stands, plus 160 million more watching on TV—60 million across the United States, and the rest on the Spanish-language broadcast shown in South and Central America and the Caribbean. I think I was a little hyped up, trying too hard to be perfect. Maybe it was also something about playing indoors for the first time. I just wasn't myself, and that cost me.

Willie Mays led off for the NL with a single. He loved to run, so I figured he might take a big lead and try to steal. After going to my set, I spun around and looked to first. He *did* have a big lead, and I had him picked off easily, but I rushed my throw to Killebrew and it went off his glove as Mays raced to second. Then I got my signals crossed up with Tigers catcher Bill Freehan, and threw a wild pitch on ball four to Curt Flood. Freehan was expecting a curve, I threw a high fastball, and Mays went to third and Flood to first as Freehan chased it down. The next batter, Willie McCovey, hit a double-play grounder, scoring Mays from third.

That was the only run I let up in my two innings, and it was all the NL needed; they won, 1-0. I took the loss due to my own errors, but had held my own against a lineup with five future Hall of Famers: Mays, McCovey, Henry Aaron, Ron Santo, and baseball's best hitting pitcher, Don Drysdale. When I talked to my parents on the phone after the game, which they were able to watch, my mother was very happy.

My father wanted to know why I threw a wild pitch!

After the All-Star break, it seemed like there were more reporters wanting to interview me than ever before. And they were all asking the same thing: What was I doing different this season?

Part of it, I told them, was why I didn't win more in the past: luck. For years mine was not so hot, but now it was OK. Plus I had added more movement to my delivery—and that seemed to be bothering hitters.

My delivery. More than 35 years after I stopped pitching, it's the thing people remember most about me. That's OK. Everybody has something that makes them different, that makes them *unique*, and for me it was how I went about my business on the mound.

Most guys keep their body sideways to the batter throughout their windup, and then swing around to face the plate as they release the ball. I usually turned my body completely backward during my windup, so that it almost looked like I was facing center field. Then I'd spin completely back around again for my release. I felt it gave me more power, and more deception, and gave the hitter less time to react to the ball.

Some think my motion was patterned after my father, who also had some funny things he did with his windup. He did give me a few tips, but mostly I developed my own style over time—adding in new things as I went along. It was always about gaining whatever edge I could against the hitters. The big thing I added in '68 was more head motion, bobbing it up and down during each stage of my windup. Some guys said it looked like I was gazing up at the moon. I didn't do it for show, although I'm glad people enjoyed it.

My hesitation pitch really bothered batters. I would go into my regular windup, and then stop for a moment in mid-motion right before I threw the ball. It was totally legal, but I only did it with the bases empty. If there was someone on, I figured, an ump might call it a balk. So I was careful, and for my first 11 years in the majors I was never called for a balk once. Some managers and players on opposing teams said that I *should be*, including Orioles manager Earl Weaver, but they never won that argument.

Rico Petrocelli, later my teammate with the Red Sox, is one guy who remembers my hesitation pitch well.

"It was almost comical," Petrocelli says. "What he would do is wind up and take his stride—the left foot going on the ground—and then he would drag his right foot off the mound and throw a slow pitch. He threw it once to George Scott and we were all laughing. It was a riot, unless you were the one trying to hit it."

One pitch I started in Cleveland I called "The Jaw Breaker." I'd shake and stop my head *seven* times, look up, look down, and then point my jaw toward second base, third, the centerfield corner, and behind my back. A lot of times, I didn't even know what I was going to do until just before I did it. It depended on the situation, or how I felt, or what I thought the batter was thinking.

One big difference in my early years was my velocity. Back then, before my shoulder injuries, I could throw real fast—close to 100 miles per hour. Maybe 75 percent of my pitches were fastballs, but they weren't all the same. The fastball is the best pitch in baseball because it's really like *five* pitches, if you move it around. There was nobody who threw quite like I did, although Al Dark said I reminded him of my dad's old Negro League rival, Satchel Paige. Tommy Harper thought I was more like Giants ace Juan Marichal, who had a real high leg kick and also did a great job concealing the ball. Not bad company.

Everybody seemed to have a different ways of describing my windup. Here are a few from the summer of '68:

"He's the toughest pitcher in the league to follow. You think he's throwing from one direction and all of a sudden he's throwing from another."

—Mickey Mantle

"I still have nightmares about that pitch of his. To me, standing there in the batter's box, it seemed like he threw everything at me but the ball."

—Frank Howard of the Senators, after I struck him out with my hesitation pitch ("I gave him the shoulder, back, foot, and the ball last," I told reporters afterward.)

"Tiant uses the pitcher's rubber like a swivel. He plants his right foot on top of it and moves his body in all sorts of directions. His arms go toward third base, his head goes toward centerfield and his left leg goes up and down. Somewhere, from the midst of all this motion, out comes a baseball."

—sportswriter Leigh Montville of the *Boston Globe*, who would later cover me on the Red Sox

"When Tiant can throw that fastball from his spinning motion, he is unbelievable."

—Yankees manager Ralph Houk, whose team I shut out three times that year

Pitching is important, but it can only take you so far. I kept doing well in the second half of the season, and so did the rest of our staff. But our hitting never came around, and eventually that caught up with us—especially me.

McLain got his 20th win on July 27, and I got my 17th the next day. Then, in August, the team scored 10 runs for me in seven starts—and I only won once. By mid-August we were nearly 15 games behind the Tigers, and knew we couldn't catch them. It became a matter of pride for guys in the rotation to keep pushing each other to win.

"There was so much competition between the pitchers," McDowell said later. "One guy would throw a shutout, and then you'd want to do it. If Tiant threw a four-hitter, then I wanted to throw a *three*-hitter. If Siebert struck out fourteen, I was going for *sixteen*. All of our pitchers threw hard. We could knock the bat right out of people's hands."

Gabe Paul helped, too, when he started giving $100 clothing bonuses to every Indians pitcher who threw a complete-game shutout. "I hope we have the best-dressed pitching staff in the major league," he joked early in the season, and we did. By the end of the year we had twenty shutouts—tied with the Dodgers for the most in the majors. I led the AL with nine, Sonny Siebert had four, and McDowell had three. That's a lot of suits.

Because I knew that every shutout was a team effort, I shared my clothing bonuses with the guys who made key hits or fielding plays in my games. And while Paul didn't pay us extra for strikeouts, we had plenty of those too. McDowell topped the majors with 283, and I was third in the AL with 264—behind him and McLain (280).

Sudden Sam was really something. I've never seen anybody, including Nolan Ryan, throw harder than him. His pitches looked like they were going 105 miles an hour, and he'd throw one over or behind your head to keep you guessing. He also had a great curveball, and hitters used to come up with phantom injuries so they wouldn't have to face him.

McDowell had two problems, though: he didn't take care of himself, and he was always trying crazy stuff on the mound. Like he would throw two fastballs to a hitter so he couldn't even get the bat off his shoulder, and then he'd come back with a change-up and the guy would hit a home run. He loved to challenge guys in different ways, rather than just blow them away.

That was the one season that people looked to me as Cleveland's ace, not McDowell. And in mid-August, after I lost 3-0 to the Tigers in Cleveland, McLain and Freehan both said some real nice things about me.

"Luis and I would each be fighting for thirty wins if he had our kind of hitting to go with his kind of pitching," said Denny, who had picked up his 24th victory the day before.

Then Freehan, McLain's regular catcher, corrected him.

"If Tiant had our lineup on his side," Freehan said, "he'd be shooting for *forty* wins."

They weren't just throwing bull. Denny was great that year, no doubt about it. But as he said himself, he had a great hitting team supporting him. The '68 Tigers had 185 home runs—led by Willie Horton's 36—and scored the most runs in the league. The Indians only hit 75 homers, and our top guy had just 14. My record was 21-9, pretty good, but in my nine losses we scored *a total* of 12 runs. That's barely one run a game, and you're not going to win 30 games with support like that unless you're a magician.

Sometimes I felt like every pitch I threw had to be my best, and I'm sure that put undue strain on my pitching arm. In September I developed a sore elbow and missed three starts. I still managed to get my 20th win at Minnesota, and treated all my teammates to a champagne celebration in the clubhouse. Then, after being out most of two weeks, I shut out the Yankees, 3-0, in my final game. Mickey Mantle's line single in the first inning was New York's only hit, and also the last of his career. Mickey retired during spring training of 1969, after deciding that playing with bad knees and so many other physical problems had become too hard. He didn't like being a .237 hitter (which he was in '68), or being in constant pain. Mickey will always be one of my favorite players, and I was honored to give up his final hit.

With that last win, I signed my name into the Cleveland record books. My ERA of 1.60 was the lowest in franchise history, topping Stanley Coveleski's 1.82 from way back in 1917. It was also the best in the American League since Walter Johnson of the old Washington Senators had a 1.49 mark two years after Coveleski. From what I've heard, Johnson and I had something in common: he also pitched for a team that struggled to score runs, and all his losses that year (he was 20-14) shows it.

McLain didn't have to worry about runs, and he went 31-6 for a Tigers team that won the World Series. He took home the Cy Young Award as the AL's best pitcher in a unanimous vote, while also being named the league MVP. Bob Gibson, who went 22-9 with an incredible 1.12 ERA and 13 shutouts for the National League champion Cardinals, won the same two awards in the NL.

I came in fifth in the AL MVP voting, but I'd rather have gotten to the World Series. Gibson struck out 17 Tigers in the series opener, and Mickey Stanley of Detroit said he didn't think Gibbie was any faster than me. It would have been nice to take him on that October and see for myself.

Even with our drop-off in the second half, it had been a good year for the Indians. We wound up 86-75 and in third place, our highest finish since 1959. That got each player $900 in World Series bonus money, and gave us confidence about the future. We had tied the Orioles for the best ERA in the American League at 2.66, and all our starting pitchers were still in their prime. The White Sox were the only AL club that hit fewer home runs that we did, but Gabe Paul said he was committed to picking up a big power hitter over the winter. That would be a huge help.

Maybe I'd get my chance at Gibson in October of '69.

8

DOWN AND (ALMOST) OUT

HOW DOES ONE IMPROVE UPON a spectacular season, a year when you owned two of the most impressive statistical categories in your league? For Luis Tiant the answer was simple.

Leading the American League in ERA and shutouts was very satisfying, as was a fat new contract he'd soon get. Reuniting with his mother and father, however, would bring far greater happiness than any boldface stats or the riches that accompanied them. After seven long years, Tiant had a taste of this dream in the fall of 1968. It was as wonderful as he imagined, but, like his newfound status as a pitching ace, it ended far too quickly.

His employers had by then already touched the first needle to his brilliant balloon, recommending that their now-hot commodity rest his arm by foregoing his usual off-season routine of pitching in the winter leagues. Tiant pleaded his case, insisting that he performed best when accorded year-round work. For Cleveland management, however, the choice was non-negotiable. "Not really a choice at all," he thought.

As Tiant feared, the consequences were immediate—and nearly disastrous.

Starting in spring training of 1969, he endured a rapid succession of setbacks that hit hard at his won-loss record and his heart. There were injuries and indignities, promises made and not kept, that challenged his resolve. A change of uniforms initially resulted in a change in fortunes, but in the end this too proved a brief respite. One pitch, and one "pop," and his security was again ripped away.

By the summer of 1970, just two years removed from being on top of the baseball world, Luis Tiant would find himself struggling to keep a toehold in the game he loved.

ALVIN DARK AND I had gotten along okay most of the 1968 season. Then in September I scratched myself from a start right before a game against Baltimore, when I felt a stiffness in my elbow during my bullpen warm-ups. He didn't like me making a decision like that for myself and told reporters he was "surprised" by what I did. When I read that in the next morning's paper, I went straight to the manager's office.

I slammed the paper down on his desk and told Dark that I didn't appreciate his suggesting I was not trying my hardest to play. If the game was of any real importance, of course, I *would* have played. But with us out of the pennant race so late in the season, I didn't think it was worth risking a serious injury for me to go out there.

He said he understood, and that he didn't mean anything by what he said. But I still felt like he had disrespected me.

What happened next was even worse. After I came back later in September to win my last two starts, including a one-hitter against the Yankees, Dark and Gabe Paul told me they didn't want me playing winter ball. They felt that after pitching close to 260 innings that season, I needed to rest my arm. As a twenty-game winner, I was more valuable than ever to the team. They couldn't risk my getting hurt.

"Get hurt? You can get hurt anywhere!" I insisted. "A car could hit me. I could slip and fall in my house. I *know* winter ball is the best thing for me—I've done it for ten years!"

The whole discussion was crazy. Yes, I had some pain, and my elbow stiffened up a bit against the Yankees, but it was nothing too serious. And if they were so worried now, why did Dark question my taking myself out against Baltimore? Weren't they worried about me then?

I tried to reason with them. Winter ball was something I looked forward to every year, I told them, and more importantly it made me a better ballplayer. A pitcher's strength comes from his legs, and by playing through the winter I came to spring training with strong legs and a fluid, loose arm. My arm was already feeling stiff. Without that constant work, it might get worse and be that much harder to loosen up in the spring.

It still upsets me to think about it fifty years later. This was my body, and who knew it better than me? After the season I had just given them, I felt I had earned the right to make my own decisions about my off-season. Why not do the same thing that had worked so well already?

Then there was the extra money you could make playing year-round. Maria wanted to build a new house back in Mexico City, so I could really use it. I had pitched well in the Venezuelan League the previous two winters and planned to go back there.

After we talked it out, Paul came up with what he said was the perfect solution. The Indians would pay me the same money I'd make playing in Venezuela, on top of my regular contract, and I could stay home the whole winter with my wife and kids. I didn't like him dictating my life, but there was nothing I could do. He and Dark were in charge.

I decided to try to make the most of it. They told me to spend my time relaxing and watching TV. Forget *that*; if I couldn't play, I'd find other ways to stay in shape.

So that's what I did. I ran up and down the stairs of our house, over and over. I threw a heavy ball back and forth across a field in the park down the street. And to simulate my pitching motion, and try to keep the muscles in my arm loose, I did all kinds of stretching exercises out on our porch. Little Luis and Isabel watched me, and I made sure to find time to play with them every day. Maria made me lots of healthy foods to try to keep me from gaining weight.

"It was nice to have him home the whole winter, especially with the two kids," Maria remembers, then offers a sly smile. "Besides, we had a wonderful surprise for him."

The surprise came on Isabel's first birthday in October. Maria set everything up for a party, with family and friends coming over to watch the Olympics—which were in Mexico City that year. Everybody was laughing and having a good time, and then all of a sudden, the door opened.

I couldn't believe my eyes. It was my MOTHER!

In that moment, I forgot all about working out and making sure my arm stayed sound. I had not seen my mother in more than seven years, and here she was standing right in front of me. She had never even met Maria, or our two children, so it was a very emotional moment for all of us. We started to hug each other and cry.

It turns out Maria had planned the whole thing. She had arranged with the Cuban embassy for my mother to come for a visit during the Olympics in October and then to stay through Christmas and New Year's. I always knew Mom and Maria would get along great, and they did. It would have been even better if my father came, too, but that wasn't to be. Castro would not let both of them visit out of fear that they would not return. Dad staying behind in Havana was Castro's insurance that Mom would come back to him.

We didn't want her to leave, of course. We begged her to stay. Even Dad told her, when we spoke to him on the phone, that she should remain with us. But she was worried about what would happen to him if she did; maybe they would put him in jail, or worse. Besides, she told us, she and Dad had been married for more than forty years. They belonged together and *needed* to be together.

Dad had already lost me, and she didn't think he could handle losing her too.

She was right, and we knew it. So shortly after New Year's Day, 1969, she flew home to Havana. I didn't know when, or if, I'd ever see her again.

My heart was broken, just as it had been when I got my father's letter in '61, but I had to put that aside and focus on the season coming up. The Indians had spent the winter trying to trade for a big bat and almost made a deal for Dick Allen of the Phillies. He was a terrific hitter, but Gabe Paul wouldn't agree to the asking price: me or Sam McDowell. We were, he said, the only "untouchables" on the club.

So I was still an Indian when spring training rolled around—and a richer one, too.

I felt I deserved more money after my breakthrough season, and I got it: a $52,000 contract, up from $32,000 in '68. Nobody got multiyear deals then, but Paul did throw in a new fur-lined overcoat when I came up to Cleveland in January to sign. That was a good thing, because it was only the second time in my life I had ever seen snow, and it was *freezing!*

The pay raise warmed Maria and me up, and so did the award I picked up at dinner that night as "Man of the Year" from the Cleveland baseball writers—beating out Alvin Dark. But with that kind of attention came pressure. I wanted to prove myself worthy of all that money. It didn't help when at the dinner, in front of nearly 1,000 fans, Dark predicted a pennant for the team and said "Luis Tiant could be better" than in '68.

It wouldn't be easy. From the start, spring training was a nightmare for me on and off the field. The problems started before I even got to camp. Marvin Miller, head of the MLB Player's Association, had been working all winter to get owners to pay more into a pension plan that players could start collecting on when they were forty-five. There was a vote by the player reps to have everyone strike and not show up for camp unless a new labor agreement was signed, but after not playing all winter, I wanted to get on the field as soon as possible.

When I showed up for camp in Tucson on February 23, with a new labor agreement still not signed, I made sure a bunch of rookies and minor leaguers were there before going in. Then a reporter asked me what I thought about going against the union and being the first regular to report.

"If I don't play, will Miller pay my bills?" I said. "Will he feed my family? Will he take care of my children?"

Look, I had nothing against the union, or Marvin Miller. He had the best interests of all players in mind. But at that point in my life, with so much on the line, I felt I had to look out for my own.

Once camp *did* start, I got real bad news. Indians traveling secretary Charley Morris, who took care of everything for players when we were on the road, died. He was both a great friend and a second father to me when I first came to the United States, helping me get used to the new culture and new language. I took his death hard.

Then, once the exhibition games started, I had a lot of trouble getting my arm to loosen up. It felt like I was pushing the ball, and I couldn't aim it where I wanted. I allowed seven walks in my first four innings of pitching, and when I *did* get the ball over the plate, it got hit hard somewhere fast. Plus, I felt tightness in my hand and the back of my shoulder. The trainer said it was just sore muscles, but I worried that it was something much worse.

Giants ace Juan Marichal, 26-9 the year before, gave me a gift he said would help: a vial of snake oil. I rubbed the slimy, awful-smelling stuff on my arm, and it did feel better. Marichal said it worked for him, so I joked with reporters that maybe *I'd* be good for twenty-six wins now. Why not?

Opening Day was in Detroit, me against MVP Denny McLain and the World Series champs in front of 53,500 loud fans. I felt relaxed going into the game and even got an early lead when our shortstop Larry Brown hit McLain's third pitch into the upper deck at Tiger Stadium. Maybe things were going to be OK after all.

But then Denny clamped down, retiring twenty-three of the last twenty-four batters he faced from the second through the ninth inning. If this was 1968, I probably would have matched him batter for batter. But it wasn't; I had nothing, and the Tigers hit me hard in a 6–2 loss. I walked four, gave up a big homer to Al Kaline, and allowed five runs before Dark pulled me in the sixth.

I also got a warning from home plate umpire Larry Napp for arguing balls and strikes. I only talked back a little, really, but Napp said he didn't like the way I was "strutting around" on the mound.

"I was just walking around out there," I told him. "I got nothing against *you*, but I want *you* to have nothing against *me*."

A lot of pitchers had something against the strike zone that spring. After all the low-scoring games in '68, the league had made rule changes they hoped would generate more offense and make games more exciting for fans. They lowered the pitching mound from fifteen inches to ten inches and shrunk the strike zone so that it was defined as "between the batter's armpits and the top of his knees when he assumes a natural stance." For the first five years of my career, it had been "from between *the top of the batter's shoulders and his knees*." So this was a big difference.

I guess Napp wanted to make sure I knew exactly what the new rules were, because the next day he came around our dugout before the game to show Dark and me a diagram of the revised strike zone. I didn't say anything, but the look on my face told Napp what he could do with his diagram.

Like me, many of the same pitchers who were blowing hitters away the year before struggled to adjust to the new zone. Then, eventually, guys got used to the change. It did what the league hoped it would; nobody threw four or five shutouts in a row like Drysdale and I had in '68, and batting averages started going back up. But the cream still rose to the top. The best pitchers found a way to dominate.

Not me.

It wasn't the rule changes that killed me in 1969. I could get used to anything. No, what killed me, I'm convinced, was listening to the GM and not pitching winter ball before that season. My arm never felt right, from the first day of spring training until the end of the year, and I also developed a bad back that kept me from throwing as hard as in the past. These things had never happened to me before, and even if I didn't complain, there was no hiding them once the games started.

Beginning with the opener at Detroit, I was winless in my first eight starts of the season—and lost seven of them. During that stretch, my ERA was 7.51, I walked four or more batters five times, and I only had one complete game. The previous year, I had finished five of my first seven starts, never walking more than three.

Alvin Dark was sure that the reason I was struggling, and the reason I got hurt in the first place, was because of my delivery.

"He hasn't lost his control to the point where he can't throw strikes, but he's lost it enough so that he can't pinpoint the ball the way he wants to," he told one writer. "You've got to keep your eye on the target. You can't throw your head up into the air, then look over at the scoreboard and then pitch a baseball."

It's funny; he never said anything the previous year when I was shutting everybody out with the same windup. Now he was sure it was the problem.

Besides, it wasn't just me; the *whole team* was playing lousy. We lost our first five games, scratched out a ten-inning win, and then lost ten more straight. By winning on the last day of April, we finished the month 2–15. This was the first season that the American League and National League were each split into two divisions, and we were in last place in the six-team AL East from Opening Day on.

"We really don't know what is the matter," Dark said when asked for the millionth time about my rough start. "We know he isn't throwing as hard as he was last year, but we don't know why. He has had a little arm trouble, but it hasn't been that serious."

Not serious? That was news to me. The pain was bad, but I felt like if I kept going out there, put the motion back into my delivery, and got used to the smaller strike zone and the lower mound, things might turn around.

They did, at least for a while.

Starting with my first victory, on May 30, I won seven of nine starts with five complete games. My ERA dropped all the way down to 3.89, and I was getting a few more runs to work with, too. Thanks to a big trade with the Red Sox, we finally had a legitimate power hitter on our side in Ken Harrelson. I was glad I didn't have to pitch *against* him anymore, but even the Hawk's thirty homers couldn't save the team, or me, this year.

As suddenly as I got hot, I went cold again. After I won on July 13, I went *sixty days* before my next victory. Things were so bad that even on the day I officially became an American Citizen, August 29, I couldn't get one in the win column. The White Sox beat me, 4–2. As Casey Stengel used to say, you can look it up.

When my next win finally came, on September 11, it was against the Tigers and Denny McLain—the same ace that clobbered me Opening Day. He was on his way to a 24-9 season and another Cy Young Award, which made the victory extra satisfying.

"It felt like waking up from a bad dream that lasted two-and-a-half months," I told reporters afterward. They asked if I planned to celebrate with champagne, like I did after winning my 20th the year before, and I smiled before answering:

"No champagne. I can't afford it."

A big part of the problem was my velocity; Dark was right about that, it was down. Catcher Joe Azcue later said I "lost two feet off my fastball" between 1968 and '69, and hitters who could get around quicker on my pitches started knocking them out of the park. After letting up sixteen home runs the previous year, I gave up thirty-seven in '69—the most in the major leagues. I also let up the most walks, 129, and my strikeouts fell by more than 100 in roughly the same number of innings (249.2). That's a bad combination.

To keep my mind off all the losing, I tried to have fun. Chico Salmon was my roommate, and he would always come in late at night after I was asleep. He'd turn on the light, wake me up, and start talking to me.

"C'mon, I'm pitching tomorrow! Go to sleep!"

"OK, OK."

He'd turn out the light, and about a minute later, he'd be asleep—and *snoring*. Loud enough to keep me up for the next hour.

That pattern went on for a while. Then one night in Detroit, I decided I'd had enough. This time, when he fell asleep, I filled up a bucket of cold water and threw it on him.

He got the point, and I got more rest. Unfortunately, that didn't help my record either. My ERA was never *too* bad after mid-season, and it ended up being 3.71 for the year. But when your team is scoring one or two runs every game that you pitch, letting up 3.71 of them is not going to work.

Heading into the last day of the season, I was 9–19. No pitcher ever wants to lose twenty games, especially a year after *winning* twenty. But I wasn't going to duck a start, so I took the ball at Yankee Stadium.

Instead of a one-hitter like I had there to close out 1968, I lost 4–3. I became the first Indians pitcher since 1902 to lose twenty, and our 62–99 record was the worst by a Cleveland club since 1914. A year after being in second or third almost the entire season, we spent all but one day of '69 in last place.

Usually that kind of year gets a manager fired. But after getting close with the team's owner, Alvin Dark was now pretty much serving as both manager and general manager (although Gabe Paul still had the GM title for a while). Dark wasn't about to fire himself, and being safe made it easy for him to stay upbeat. He told everybody he was building for the future, and that only five players on the club were part of his long-term plans.

I was one of them—or so he said.

"I think Luis will come back and I guess some other people do too, as we've had folks on other clubs asking about him," Dark said right after the season. "This wouldn't be a good time to deal him."

Whether or not he was telling the truth, and whether he liked it or not, one thing was sure: I wasn't going to spend another winter resting my arm. Sure, I enjoyed all that extra time with Maria and the kids the year before, but skipping winter ball was not good for me. So I found a way to do both; I signed up to play with a team in the Mexico Pacific Winter League based in Hermosillo, a little town near the Mexican-U.S. border. This way I could go home to Mexico City and my family more often.

I had already joined the Hermosillo club when I stopped in at a grocery store by the border to pick up some things. The owner was a guy I knew from back in the Mexican League, and he asked me what I thought about the news.

"What news?"

"You've been traded."

There it was, in his newspaper. The Indians had sent two pitchers—me and swingman Stan Williams—to the Twins for four players: pitchers Dean Chance and Bob Miller, outfielder Ted Uhlaender, and third baseman Graig Nettles. Chance, like me, was a former twenty-game winner who had fallen off badly in '69 due to a shoulder injury. Miller was an OK reliever, and Uhlaender was a solid-hitting center fielder, one thing the Indians definitely needed. Nettles, the youngest player in the deal, had hit just .222 as a rookie but was expected to be a star. He was the key to the trade.

Sportswriters covering the Indians, who had always been very good to me, seemed to be in agreement with management that the move favored Cleveland.

"Don't be surprised if Alvin Dark is indicted for theft," Chuck Heaton wrote in the Cleveland *Plain Dealer*. "The trade he consummated with the Minnesota Twins yesterday looks like a steal at this point."

Heaton went on to say that while he expected Chance to return to his winning ways, and Nettles and Uhlaender to fill two important spots for the Indians at center and third, the team was better off without me.

"There were indications that the friendly Cuban couldn't stand the prosperity of that 21–9 campaign of 1968. He didn't appear in top physical shape at the start of last season and seemed to lose some of his determination.

"Luis also irritated Dark by continuing all those pitching gyrations after a firm suggestion that his control might be better if he just unloaded the baseball."

More of that bullshit about my motion, the same one I used when I'd had a 1.60 ERA. I didn't hear anybody complaining about it then. And this "friendly Cuban" never came to camp out of shape or not determined to win; after working so hard to become a starting pitcher, and make good money, why would I want to blow it?

Still, no matter what they said in the paper, which also reported that nearly two hundred fans calling in to the *Plain Dealer* sports desk favored the trade, 4-to-1—I had mixed feelings.

The Indians were the only organization I had ever played for in the U.S. They had given me a chance to live out my dream of making the major leagues. The fans in Cleveland, even when there were not many of them at the ballpark, were great to me. I made a lot of friends on the team, some of whom I'm still in touch with fifty years later.

But things between me and Dark had been getting worse all year. It was hard to play for somebody who didn't respect you, and once Dark took over the GM duties, he had authority to make trades. My fate was sealed.

Luis Jr. might have been more upset about the news than me; after running around there for years, he knew all the best places to sneak into at Cleveland Stadium. Now he'd have to learn all new ones at Metropolitan Stadium, home of the Twins. It was probably going to be tougher for me to spot him and his sister and mother in the stands, though; the Twins drew a lot more fans than the Indians.

How come? Winning is always good for attendance.

That was the best thing about the move: the chance to be with a true contender. I was going from a team that lost ninety-nine games and finished last in the American League East in 1969 to one that won ninety-seven and finished first in the AL West. The only real stars on the Indians had been pitchers; Minnesota had standout performers up and down the roster.

Their lineup was one of the best in baseball, led by a trio of Hall of Fame-caliber players: Harmon Killebrew, Rod Carew, and Tony Oliva. Killebrew was the reigning AL MVP, having topped the majors with 49 home runs and 140 RBI in '69. I was glad I wouldn't have to worry about him smashing bombs off me anymore or getting line-drived to death by the other two. Carew was the returning AL batting champ (.332), while Oliva had won *two* batting crowns with a third to come. Tony also had twenty-homer power, and both he and Rod were Spanish-speakers—Carew from Panama, and Oliva a fellow Cuban. They would become my fast and lifelong friends.

Minnesota's deep pitching staff was led by returning twenty-game winners Jim Perry and Dave Boswell. They had a former twenty-five-game winner in Jim Kaat and All-Star reliever Ron Perranoski backing them all up in the bullpen. The only thing that stopped the Twins from going to the 1969 World Series was running into an even deeper Baltimore team in the playoffs, but I hoped to help them change that.

One thing was sure: the Twins definitely knew what *I* could do. They were the team I had nineteen strikeouts against in '68, and Minnesota manager Bill Rigney said he expected I would go right into his starting rotation. Of course, that didn't stop Minnesota fans from being worried about the trade, too; they remembered how great Chance was for them when he won twenty, and they didn't like seeing a great young prospect like Nettles swapped for a pitcher with a suspect arm.

One guy who came to my defense then, and always, was Stan Williams. I was really happy he was involved in the trade, too, because it meant we would remain teammates. Just like he had bailed me out of a bunch of jams as a relief pitcher, he stuck up for me after the trade, even though he was also under pressure to produce with a new team.

"Tiant is one of the greatest pitchers in baseball," Stan told Minnesota sportswriters. "His arm is sound, and Luis is a great competitor. I think the change of scenery will help him plus the fact he is pitching winter ball this year, something he didn't do a year ago."

Part of the reason I think Stan felt so strongly about my situation, besides our friendship, was because he had gone through similar problems himself. He had originally come up with the Dodgers in the early '60s as a great fastball pitcher who racked up strikeouts like Sandy Koufax and Don Drysdale. Then Stan had a real bad arm injury that forced him to change his style, and he went from being an All-Star starter to a reliever and spot starter. Things got so bad, he said, that many times he pitched with tears running down his cheeks due to the pain.

Eventually Stan's arm got better, he caught on with the Indians, and he worked his way back to the point where he was again considered very valuable. He thought I could do the same thing.

Dean Chance called the trade "too good to be true" because his hometown of Wooster was only fifty miles from Cleveland, but he was classy enough to say nice things about Stan and me.

"Tiant is one of the best in the league and he has to help them," Chance said. "Outside of [Ron] Perranoski, the Twins had no bullpen. That's where Williams is going to be a big plus."

These were great endorsements, but I still had plenty of people thinking I was damaged goods. That winter, I took to the press to defend myself.

"My arm feels fine this winter pitching in Mexico, and I'm not fat," I told the *Minneapolis Star-Tribune,* in December.

My 9–20 record in 1969? I blamed that on both a lack of run support in Cleveland and a lack of winter ball before that season—which caused my back muscles to tighten. My arm itself, I insisted, was now fine.

"I think the Twins will score some runs for me, and we can win the pennant," I said confidently. This wouldn't be anything too new for them, but it sure would make a difference for me after all those losing years with the Indians. So would a $50,000 yearly salary, roughly the same I made with Cleveland. It was another one-year deal, but I wasn't complaining.

In late January, just before the Twins reported for spring training in Orlando—no more long trips to Arizona where the Indians had their camp—another reporter asked whether I thought I had lost my fastball. I really put it on the line with my answer:

"We'll see what they say after this year. I have no arm problem."

Hey, it's always good to be confident, right? Besides, I believed it; I had won a combined nine games in Mexico and the Dominican Republic over the winter and really did feel good heading into the exhibition season. I was confident enough to give more details about what had happened to me the year before, when a bad back really hampered my control.

"I was wild and behind the hitter most of the season due to the injury," I told writers later when '70 spring training opened. "This winter in Mexico and the Dominican Republic, my back didn't trouble me at all."

I met Mr. Griffith that first week of camp. After he introduced himself, the Twins owner said he was excited to see that it looked like I lost about fifteen pounds over the winter. I told him he was right, and that I was going to help pitch the Twins to the pennant. He liked that too.

It didn't seem like much of a stretch, given the club we had, that we could go to the World Series. When I got to know my new teammates, I felt even better about our chances. We all got along great, and I could tell everybody there wanted to win. Soon they were joking with me about my being closer to thirty-five or forty years old than thirty, but that stuff is OK when it comes from your teammates. I just made a note of which guys to get back with pranks later on.

Like me, our manager, Bill Rigney, was new to the club. The Twins hired him after firing Billy Martin, who had already developed several ways of finding trouble early in his managerial career. Martin won wherever he went and was a fantastic strategist, as I learned when I played for him later in my career. But he couldn't keep his opinions to himself, and had a short fuse, and that resulted in fights. In Minnesota during the 1969 season, he had beat up one of his own players—pitcher Dave Boswell—outside a Detroit bar. Boswell wound up with a reported twenty stitches in his face, and Martin was on borrowed time with Mr. Griffith.

At the end of the '69 season, after leading the Twins to a 97–65 record and an AL West title, Martin was fired. This left the new manager, Rigney, with a very strong and deep team. Other than the trade that brought Williams and me to Minnesota, there were no major changes made to the roster for 1970.

So when we started the exhibition season 1–14, Rigney told reporters he wasn't worried—we would win when the *real* games started. You could tell he really meant it, and we loved to hear his confidence. That positive attitude rubbed off on all of us.

I felt strong coming in, thanks to winter ball, but still struggled along with the rest of the team to get on track. In my first fifteen exhibition innings, I gave up eighteen walks, and I'm sure Minnesota fans who were already worried about the Chance-for-Tiant trade were thinking the worst. It didn't help that Chance was looking really good for Cleveland in *their* camp, where he was reportedly throwing much harder than the previous season.

"He [Chance] sure didn't look to me like a guy who has arm trouble," one longtime Cleveland sportswriter noted late in spring training. "I saw Tiant throw twice in Florida before I came here, and he didn't throw nearly as well either time as did Chance."

Rigney and pitching coach Marv Grissom treated my situation well. Rather than just *tell me* to change my delivery like Alvin Dark used to do in Cleveland when I was struggling, or complain to the press about it, they worked closely with me to make subtle adjustments they felt could help. One reason I had a bad back in '69, they showed me, was because I was pushing off the rubber with my heel instead of my toes. They helped me to make that change and then kept watching to make sure I didn't slip into any bad habits again.

Grissom also showed me video of my pitching that was taken that spring and broke down all the components of my delivery for me. This is done all the time now, and hitters like J.D. Martinez are famous for watching hundreds and hundreds of their at-bats to look for sloppy mechanics. But video sessions were new then, and they really helped me. Pretty soon I was back to getting ahead of hitters and walking far fewer guys.

By the start of the regular season, my back felt better, but my right shoulder was still hurting. The Twins trainer, George Lentz, thought it might be a pulled muscle that would eventually pop into place. I hoped he was right and kept my aches and pains to myself.

Rigney announced I had made the starting rotation and would be pitching in the second game of the season right behind staff ace Jim Perry. I was determined to make the most of the opportunity he and the team were giving me. And although I struggled in that first start, walking four and lasting less than five innings, Rigney said he was confident I was on the right track. More importantly, we won the game 6–4.

Six runs? That was more than I sometimes got in a month of starts with the Indians, but it was nothing special here. In fact, nearly the exact same thing happened in my second appearance; I let up five runs in five innings, but my teammates blasted out eighteen hits, and I got my first win with the Twins, 11–5 at Oakland.

This kind of offensive support was great for my nerves. In Cleveland, I felt like I had to pitch a shutout or maybe give up one run to have a chance to win. Here, if I was competitive, and kept us in the ballgame, I had faith that our lineup would take care of the rest.

And that Twins offense certainly helped my record. Starting with that game, I won five straight starts from late April to mid-May. Included were two games against the Indians, one at home and one at Cleveland Stadium where a "crowd" of under 5,500 were on hand for my return. Seeing all those empty seats on a beautiful Saturday afternoon reminded me that even though I felt bad at first about being traded, it had been for the best.

The writers wanted me to say I felt great revenge coming back to beat my old manager and teammates, but I wouldn't bite. I didn't like wins over the Indians any more than wins against other teams. I was happy to be winning, period, although I admit now I didn't mind having Alvin Dark see me doing well.

My ERA was a solid 2.86 after I beat Detroit to reach 5–0, but there were signs something wasn't right. I had a complete-game shutout in an earlier appearance against the Tigers, but the longest I pitched in any other game during this stretch was seven innings. My strikeouts were way down, partly because I couldn't throw my fastball as much as before. I had to depend more on my breaking stuff, which I couldn't always throw as consistently for strikes. In my second start versus Detroit, I walked nine batters in less than six innings, and while I still got the "W," (we scored eight runs that day) it was ugly.

The Twins team doctor, Harvey O'Phelan, thought my problem was muscle adhesions. Adhesions are knots that build up in the ball-and-socket joint of your shoulder, he told me, causing it to swell and stiffen. A cortisone shot lessened the pain enough so I could keep pitching, but it didn't get rid of the knots.

Grissom, the pitching coach, told anybody concerned that I was "sound physically," and if you looked at your Sports section this seemed true. When I took the mound on May 28 against the Milwaukee Brewers, the Twins were first in the American League West at 28–12 . I was leading all AL pitchers with my perfect record, the Twins were undefeated in my nine appearances, and at the plate I was helping myself with a .368 batting average. I always loved to swing the bat, and my hard-hitting teammates seemed to be rubbing off on me.

I was rubbing off on them, too, making sure nobody got too big a head from all of our winning—or got too down after a loss.

Like with the Indians, I kept things loose in the dugout and clubhouse. Nobody asked me to do it; it just came naturally. If a guy was sitting by his locker reading the paper, I might crawl up behind him and light it on fire; if the team was glum after a bad game, I'd start dancing the Funky Chicken in my long underwear while puffing a cigar.

Then there were my nicknames. Everyone called Killebrew "Killer" for the way he smashed baseballs to death. Not me. If he was pressing at the plate, I'd let out a high-pitched yell from the bench in hopes of drawing a laugh and easing his mood.

"C'MON BABY KILLY!"

Winning isn't everything, but it does make things more fun, and playing with the Twins was by far the most fun I'd ever had in the majors to that point. Early on against Milwaukee May 28 was more of the same. I had missed my previous start with a sore shoulder but didn't think it was anything to worry about. We were playing at home and by the fourth inning built up a lead of 11–0, with me contributing to the cause with three singles and three RBI. "Luis Tiant is terrorizing the American League with his bat as well as his pitching arm," one newspaper story would start the next day.

But then it happened. In the seventh inning, as I was delivering a pitch to Brewers first baseman Mike Hegan, I heard a pop.

At first it didn't really hurt; all I felt was a slight twinge in my shoulder. I started looking around, wondering if maybe somebody had taken a shot at me. Then I realized the sound had come from my own arm. I was hoping it was the "good" kind of pop that trainer George Lentz had told me might happen if my stretched-out shoulder muscle popped back into place. I wound up walking Hegan but came back to strikeout Danny Walton. Everything seemed okay.

It wasn't. When I came out for the eighth and started taking my warmup pitches, the shoulder began hurting pretty bad. I motioned for the pitching coach and told him I was taking myself out; Stan Williams replaced me on the mound, and I went to the clubhouse to have the trainer look me over. The initial diagnosis was that it was just a muscle strain, which didn't sound too bad at all.

After the game, I joked with writers that if I had to miss a start or two, I could always play outfield to keep my bat in the lineup. Besides pitching long enough to get the win, making my record 6–0, my three hits raised my batting average to .434. That gave me quite a lead over Carew, who was only at .398 and "officially" leading the American League. So what if he had ninety-five more at-bats? I was one mean dude with that lumber.

"The arm and shoulder feel OK now," I told reporters, flashing my undefeated smile. Deep down, I wasn't so sure, but I'd have my answer soon enough.

A few days later, on Sunday, I went out to the bullpen to test the arm.

I couldn't throw the ball more than a few feet.

Monday was a day off, and the team flew on to New York for a series with the Yankees. I stayed behind with Tony Oliva, who was also having some shoulder trouble, and the two of us went to see Dr. O'Phelan.

The doctor told me to lie on the table and took X-rays of my shoulder. After he was done, Tony was sitting next to me while Dr. O'Phelan and some other doctors looked at my X-rays in the next room. I could see them in there, one looking at the other one, shaking his head, and then pointing at me.

"Tony, Tony, I think there is something wrong," I said.

"Nah, there's nothing wrong!"

I didn't believe him.

They called us in, and Dr. O'Phelan pointed at the X-ray.

"You see this, Luis? You have a crack from here to here—from your shoulder to your armpit. A fractured scapula of your right shoulder blade, also known as a hairline fracture."

As Dr. O'Phelan explained it, my muscle had ripped straight out of the bone; the muscle had stayed back, and the bone had kept going forward. An orthopedic surgeon who later worked with the 1972 U.S. Olympic team, he said he had only seen that type of injury once before—to a guy who threw the javelin—because of the extraordinary strain he put on his arm.

Over time, I realized that this fracture had probably been the cause of my problems in Cleveland. Nobody there was able to diagnose it or wanted to believe me when I said I was in pain. Rather than getting it properly examined and treated, they just kept sending me out to pitch. Of course, I *wanted* to keep pitching, too, but I would have rested if I knew there was a good medical reason for it. Looking back, I think I was probably cracking the bone over and over again during the '69 season.

Through all the repeated strain I put on my shoulder as a pitcher, Dr. O'Phelan said, I was lucky that I didn't *fully* break the shoulder. If I had, my baseball career would have been through. But with a hairline fracture, when the bone healed, it would be stronger than ever. He believed I'd have no problem returning to pitching.

I hoped he was right; he had never seen a baseball player with this injury before, and I was no javelin thrower. There were no past cases to draw on.

And even if the doctor *was* right, it might take a long time to prove it. He said I needed rest, but how much? What if I did all the rehab and worked my way back, and it happened again?

Time is very precious, and I didn't know how long the Twins—or any other team—would be willing to wait.

9

TWIN KILLINGS AND RED SOX

THROUGH ALL THE CHALLENGES HE faced starting in 1969, Luis Tiant never lost his self-confidence. He was a tireless worker who still displayed flashes of his old pitching brilliance on occasion, and those who really knew him—and who recognized his resolve to turn things around—were ready to go to bat for their friend when he needed them.

That opportunity presented itself in the spring of 1971. When his damaged shoulder failed to come around as fast as Minnesota Twins management desired, Tiant suddenly found himself a man without a team. Despite his prior track record of excellence, there were two hurdles to his finding new employment in the major leagues. In addition to having a suspect arm, Tiant was now on the wrong side of age thirty—and rumors continued to persist that he was in fact much older than his baseball card claimed.

Two now-former teammates worked the phones on his behalf and found one team willing to give the rehabbing right-hander a month in the minors to regain his form. Mother Nature helped wash out that trial, but through his resiliency and his many strong relationships within the game, Tiant was able to secure himself one more shot.

The club willing to provide it was the Boston Red Sox, who he had dominated back when they were American League laughingstocks and his fastballs routinely reached the high nineties. Boston was now a team on the rise, and Tiant a pitcher down on his luck—but not, he insisted, as broken-down as many thought. The Red Sox organization had enough true believers in the former ERA champ to provide him with a uniform and a spot on their Triple-A roster. What Tiant did with it would be up to him, but he was pretty sure that there would be no more chances coming.

Three strikes and you're out.

WHEN I WENT ON the twenty-one-day disabled list on June 1, 1970, the Twins brought up a nineteen-year-old rookie right-hander who was blowing them away at Double-A. Bert Blyleven took my spot in the Minnesota rotation, and twenty years later he was still pitching at a high level in the big leagues. He finished with 287 wins and is now in the Hall of Fame.

It's funny how these things go around. When I first joined the Indians in '64, the pitcher whose spot *I* took on the roster went on to win 288 games: Tommy John. The big difference was that it wasn't an injury to Tommy that opened things up for me; he just needed more innings to gain confidence and experience at the big-league level. A trade to the White Sox gave him that chance, and he wound up topping Blyleven and everybody else but Nolan Ryan by pitching for *twenty-six* seasons. Ryan got him by one, with twenty-seven.

John did miss part of 1974 and all of '75 when he was with the Los Angeles Dodgers and tore up his elbow. Pitchers everywhere can thank him for what he did next.

In an attempt to save his career, Tommy asked orthopedic surgeon and Dodgers team physician Frank Jobe to operate on his elbow. What Jobe wound up doing was a new procedure: taking a healthy tendon from Tommy's right forearm and using it to replace the ruptured ulnar collateral ligament (UCL) in his left pitching elbow. After a year of rehab, Tommy came back in 1976 and turned in twenty-win seasons for both the Dodgers and Yankees—eventually pitching fourteen more years.

The surgery became so popular that it was named after him, and today hundreds of pro and amateur ballplayers return to the field after Tommy John surgery. More than 25% of all pitchers who appeared in MLB games during the 2018 season have had the surgery, some more than once. Unfortunately, my shoulder injury was about ten years before arthroscopic procedures like Tommy Johns became commonplace. If you were a pitcher and hurt your arm in 1970, like me, your options were much more limited. Surgery of any kind usually meant the end of your career. Most guys tried to get by as best they could without going under the knife.

In my case, Twins doctor Harvey O'Phelan prescribed complete rest for ten days, followed by muscle-building physical therapy. If I got through all of that okay, *then* I could resume throwing. I followed his plan and added in plenty of running—always a big part of my conditioning regimen. Day after day, as I went through my exercises, all I could think about was getting back out there on the mound.

The timing could not have been worse. I had never been in a big-league pennant race where my team had a legitimate shot to win down the stretch. Now I finally had that chance, and it was being taken away from me. I knew it was best to be patient and work as hard as possible to rehab my shoulder, but it was still very tough to be on the sidelines. And because everything took longer than expected, it wasn't until two months later that I finally got the go-ahead to pitch again.

"The fracture is entirely healed, and Luis can throw in a game any time now," Dr. O'Phelan said in late July. "His biggest obstacle will be to rebuild the muscles in that shoulder. There is a chance he could reinjure the shoulder if he tries to overexert it, but the probability is small."

My first game back was an August 3 start against the Brewers, the same club I was facing when I heard the bone pop back in May. When I got out to the mound, I remember thinking home plate looked very far away. I was on a five-inning limit and under strict doctor's orders: *do not throw the ball too hard, too often*. These two constraints put me at a big disadvantage, and I lost the game. It was my first loss of the year, dropping my record to 6–1, but I still felt good afterwards. Like I was back on track.

I was even more optimistic after my next start, when I pitched into the seventh inning and only allowed one run against the A's to pick up a win—helping my own cause with a double and a run scored. Then another problem developed; even though I kept taking my regular turn in the rotation, I stopped making any real progress. I'd pitch pretty good for four or five innings and then get tired. I just didn't feel *strong*, no matter how much extra conditioning I did. My stamina was shot, and my pitches didn't have the same life they did before the injury.

Big Frank Howard of Washington could tell the difference. After he hit a 440-foot homer and a double to help the Senators beat me at RFK Stadium later in August, he recalled the time two years before when "Tiant...had me swinging at one of his pitches while I was falling down."

Howard put his finger right on it. I didn't have the stuff to make guys fall down and look bad anymore, and it was costing me and my team.

The Twins had a decent lead over second-place Oakland in the AL West most of the season, but we lost nine straight right around the time I came back. As the race got tighter, manager Bill Rigney got more impatient. So after I was hit hard by the Red Sox in an August 16 game at Fenway Park—a place where I usually pitched great—Rigney took me out of the rotation.

More work probably would have helped me eventually, but in the last forty-five games of the season, I only made four relief appearances. My final record of 7–3 with a 3.40 ERA didn't look too bad since I missed half the year, but after coming back I was only 1–3 with more walks than strikeouts. I believed with all my heart that I needed to keep pitching to get sharper, and the manager didn't give me that chance.

It was really a no-win situation. Dr. O'Phelan said I shouldn't pitch too all-out, but that's the only way I knew *how* to pitch. That's how I established my consistency and my confidence. If I wasn't putting everything I had into every pitch, it just didn't feel right.

Through it all, I tried to enjoy the good times with my teammates. Eventually we pulled away in the AL West, and when we clinched on September 22, I celebrated as hard as anyone and was seen by reporters pouring champagne on Rigney's head. It was my first title of any kind in the big leagues, and I wanted to share my joy. Rigney was in his fifteenth year as an MLB manager, and it was *his* first time in the postseason too. Even though he had been tough on me, I knew he wanted to reach the next level—the World Series—as much as I did.

In the end, I guess Rigney didn't feel I was healthy or strong enough to help the Twins get there. During the American League playoffs against Baltimore, I only got into one game—throwing two-thirds of an inning late in an 11–3 loss. The Orioles swept us three straight to win the pennant, and none of our starting pitchers got past the fourth inning. Almost nobody Rigney put out there did the job, including me, and we were outscored 27–10 overall. But that still didn't take away from my frustration. After the hard work we *all* put in to reach the postseason, it really hurt to not get a real chance to help the team more on the big stage.

Looking back, I probably should have kept my mouth shut when Cleveland *Plain Dealer* sports columnist Russell Schneider tried to interview me during the playoffs. But I was angry, and so I spouted off to Schneider—who I had known since my rookie year with the Indians.

"There is nothing wrong with me, but there is something wrong with *him*," I told Schneider, pointing over at Rigney. "I know I won't be here next season. He will trade me because he doesn't like me, and I don't like him. My arm is OK, but the man won't let me pitch. He says I don't throw hard enough, but I say it does not matter how hard you throw if you win. That is all that is important."

I didn't know at the time what my future was with the Twins, and I didn't help myself any with those comments. All I could do now was show every-body that I could still pitch—and win—at a high level. So right after the season, I went home to Mexico City and started working out: running, lift-ing weights, doing push-ups, and swimming for thirty minutes a day. Then, after a month of that, I went back to Venezuela for winter ball.

All that winter, while Rigney and Twins president Calvin Griffith tried to figure out ways they could trade me, I just kept telling myself that I could and *would* make it all the way back and become a regular starting pitcher in the majors again.

The way Griffith talked to the media about my situation made me even more determined—and more angry. As spring training of 1971 neared, he told an Associated Press reporter that after he saw me pitch seven one-hit innings in Venezuela, "we decided to send Tiant a contract." They had ac-tually waited until the last possible day, January 15, to mail it to me, and it was for a salary of $48,000. This was a 20% cut from my 1970 pay, and the maximum cut allowable by the league.

Griffith acted like he was doing me a favor by not releasing me!

At least Rigney told writers he planned to give me a lot of work during the exhibition season, so I felt I would have a fair shake to show him my arm troubles were behind me. When I arrived in Orlando in terrific shape, at a trim 193 pounds, he was full of praise from the very first time he saw me in camp.

"You can't believe Luis Tiant," he told reporters. "It's the Tiant of four or five years ago. Remember that little belly he had—no more."

That was no joke. My clothes were falling off of me.

Once we started working out, Rigney heaped it on even more.

"He [Tiant] has thrown better in spring training than at any time during last year. Last year in camp he used to sweat like crazy. But this year that isn't happening. I think he was throwing in pain then. He wouldn't say anything, though, because he was making good money and didn't want to blow it. Would you?"

The guy who wrote the checks, Griffith, also said he was very encouraged by my progress, but I didn't know what to think about their compliments. Were they trying to make me feel good so I'd pitch better or trying to get other teams excited about me to (hopefully) work a trade?

Making the whole thing even tougher was that another pitcher on the Twins was in the same boat as me: Dave Boswell. He had gone from 20–12 in 1969 to 3–7 in '70 while dealing with back injuries, and like me was hoping to make a comeback. Rigney and Griffith were full of praise for Boswell too but probably wouldn't want to keep us both.

Not all my challenges in Florida were on the field. Spring training down there could sometimes remind you of the Deep South in the early '60s, even without the "COLORED ONLY" signs.

One time me, Stan Williams, and a few other guys went to the dog track on an off-day. There was a place that had day and night racing; after spending the afternoon there, we left to have dinner nearby before heading back for the evening races.

Some folks thought we chose the wrong restaurant.

"The people in there were all pointing and mumbling and cussing because a Black man was having dinner," Williams remembers. "So I got up and said, 'You people really know how to treat a guy, don't ya? If you've got anything more to say, say it to me outside. Come out in twos…no, better make it threes. I want to make sure there is somebody to catch the other two.'"

Stan was six-foot-five, 230 pounds, and went by the nickname "Big Hurt" long before Frank Thomas picked it up. Nobody in the restaurant took Stan up on his offer, but I certainly appreciated it.

We ran into similar shit when Jim Kaat and some other guys on the team invited me to play golf. Twice in 1971, at two different private Orlando clubs, I was denied entry because of my color. The course manager at one club told Kaat that I could only play if I was with a club member, even though he knew that none of the Twins belonged there. I'm guessing the club had no problem letting *them* golf without members because they were white.

"I thought they were kidding when they said Luis couldn't play," Kaat said after the incidents went public. "On days when Luis wants to play, we will go where we are all welcome."

I appreciated Kaat for understanding what was going on, but to me these were more examples of what I learned a long time before. No matter how famous you got, or how much money you made, to some people you were always going to be just another nigger.

My golf game didn't get much action that winter anyway. Right when we were starting to play exhibition contests, I pulled a muscle in my ribcage. It wasn't related to my bigger shoulder issues, but I couldn't pitch for several weeks. It was late March before I got into a game, and when I did, I was crushed for ten hits and six runs in just four innings against Bob Gibson and the Cardinals. Not the results I needed to impress my bosses.

The *good* news was that it was the first time in I don't remember how long that I felt relatively pain-free in both my back and shoulder while pitching. This was very important to me, and I tried to tell Rigney and anybody who would listen that I thought I was finally turning the corner. I felt better physically than I had in three years, and just *knew* that if I had more time to throw and work on my control, I could get back to being the pitcher I'd been.

If they heard me, they didn't believe me.

On March 30, just one day before the Twins broke camp and headed to Houston for three last exhibition games before the regular season, the word came down: both me and Boswell were being released.

"I tried to make a deal for both men," Griffith told the papers. "I believe others were reluctant to give anything because they guessed we would be releasing them and they could pick up their contracts for a dollar."

I didn't believe that for a second, but I'll tell you what Griffith *did* do. By cutting me when he did, he took money right out of the mouths of my family. He only had to pay me one month's salary, rather than the two months he'd have owed me if I stayed on the roster through Opening Day a week later. It was like when the Indians paid me $5,000 on my first contract, rather than the correct league minimum of $6,000. They probably figured I was too afraid to say anything, and they were right. I didn't complain then because I was worried about getting sent back to Cuba.

Now I was a different man. I wasn't afraid of anything, and I told Rigney I thought the cuts were unfair. He said a big reason the Twins made them was that the team was "in the midst of a youth movement," and he even threw some last bullshit praise at reporters as he was showing me the door.

"I've never seen the real Tiant," Rigney told reporters. "He was hurt when we got him from Cleveland last year, and he's been injured all spring. I can't give you an honest opinion of Tiant, but if he can stay healthy, he'll make somebody a good pitcher."

This time they had shut the box and really buried me. How many feet do they bury people in—six? They buried me about fifteen feet! Who would want to sign me with that kind of no-good endorsement?

Word spread quickly about what had happened. Nobody could believe it. I'd pitched so little the whole spring, and guys were all saying the same thing: How could the organization give up on me without more of a chance?

The next day, the rest of the team was leaving Orlando to head to Houston. I was in the lobby of our hotel when all the players came through to get on buses for the airport. They saw me, and everybody got really emotional. Some even started to cry, me included, and a bunch of guys tried to cheer me up.

"Don't worry, you'll get a job somewhere."

"You'll be signed with someone real soon."

I wanted to believe them, but it was only a few days before the start of the regular season. How was I going to find a job with every other team's roster already pretty much set?

"They shit on Luis," remembers Stan Williams, my longtime teammate in both Cleveland and Minnesota. "Calvin Griffith kept looking for ways to save money. He would get a good player and get a good year out of him, for as little as possible, and then trade off his value for kids."

I'll never forget one more thing Griffith said about me and Boswell, which made all the papers:

"With the money we're saving from paying these two, we can get five or six guys."

I had an answer for him, which I kept to myself:

"I'll be back."

Before I could make good on that promise, I had to find another big-league team to sign me. But the first thing I had to do was call Maria in Mexico City. She was expecting to come up to meet me in Houston for the series there. Now I had to explain to her what had happened before she heard about it on the radio or from the papers.

She cried, just like me. I said everything was going to be OK; if I couldn't find a job in the majors, my plan was to go down to Mexico City, live at home with her and the kids, and try to hook on with either my old team—the Tigers—or another Mexican League club. In the meantime, I was going to stay in Orlando and keep working out with a Cuban guy I had met that winter. I'd go over to his house, eat with his family, and then he'd catch for me. A good deal all around.

"I was upset, but I knew Luis was a fighter," Maria says of that time. "I was sure he would find more work one way or the other. He always did."

Some possibilities were more real than others. Rigney told me he'd talk to his friend Charlie Fox, who was manager of the San Francisco Giants, and tell him I was throwing the ball really good. I felt like asking why he would be willing to recommend me to other teams if he didn't think I was throwing good enough for *his* team. But what would be the point?

In the end, I never did hear from Charlie Fox. That was no surprise. But I did have two angels on my shoulder that spring: my friends, fellow pitchers, and now-former Twins teammates Stan Williams and Ron Perranoski. They worked the phones, trying to get me a free-agent shot with another team trying to fill out its roster. Manager Billy Martin from the Tigers didn't call back because it turns out he was already looking into signing Boswell. The Red Sox never answered, either, but Stan and Ron kept right on trying.

"I knew Luis wasn't done, and I knew what a great pitcher he was," Williams remembers. "My friend Ed Roebuck, an old teammate from the Dodgers, was scouting for Atlanta out in Los Angeles. I called him up and I said 'Hey, Eddie, you want to put a feather in your hat? Recommend the Braves pick up Tiant. He's going to be fine; this man can really pitch.'"

Stan told Roebuck that the Twins had made a big mistake releasing me, and he was really pissed at them for it. His passion must have come through because that call got me a shot with Atlanta's Triple-A team, the Richmond Braves of the International League.

Clyde King was the manager in Richmond, and he and I agreed to a thirty-day contract on April 15. It was really more like a month-long tryout. King would put in reports to Eddie Robinson, the Braves farm director, after each of my starts. If, after thirty days, the Braves were committed to keeping me and bringing me up to the big leagues, I'd sign with them for a full year. If not, they would release me, so I could look for another job.

It only took three innings for King to make a decision about whether he thought I could help his club.

"There is nothing wrong with his arm," he said after my Richmond Braves debut, pitching part of an exhibition game against the Charleston Charlies in Florida. "No sir. Nothing. He'll be a starter, and I told him he'll be in there every four days."

King delayed my first regular season start in Richmond a day so Eddie Robinson and Braves general manager Paul Richards could both be there. This time I went seven innings and allowed one run on four hits against the Toledo Mud Hens. Darrell Evans, who would later hit more than 450 homers in the big leagues, got one for me, and Hank Aaron's little brother, Tommie—a really good Triple-A player who never quite put it together in the majors—had two hits including a triple.

"Very impressive," Richards said when a reporter asked him about me. "He threw hard, but the real test will be his next few times out."

That was all I needed to hear. I felt one hundred percent better, and my fastball was popping like it was in 1968. I figured I was on my way back to the majors, and King was right—there was nothing wrong with my arm.

The problem was the rain.

We had terrible April weather with a bunch of rainstorms and even some snow. Instead of pitching every four days, like King planned, it was more like every seven or eight days because of all the postponed games. It wasn't the manager's fault; nobody can control the weather. I just couldn't get into a regular rhythm.

After that game in Richmond, I only made two more starts over the next three weeks. I lost both, including one played on a rain-soaked field with temperatures under forty degrees. I could have definitely pitched better, but as I've said before—I thrive on work. That spring, there wasn't enough work to be had.

As May 15 and the end of my thirty-day trial got close, I started feeling the pressure. If this was a normal season, I wouldn't be worried; once the weather got better, and I got into a groove, I'd be fine. But I had to show the Braves what I could do *right now*. On May 10, at Norfolk, Virginia, I started against a team packed with future big leaguers—the Tidewater Tides. I figured this might be my last chance.

Through four innings, the only hit they got off me was a bunt single that hugged the chalk all the way down the line. Tommie Aaron homered to help us build a 5–0 lead, and when the leadoff man for Tidewater doubled in the bottom of the fifth, I wasn't too worried. But then the next guy hit the ball off someone's glove, the guy after *that* beat out an infield single, and all of a sudden, it was 5-1 and the bases were loaded. I tried to blow a fastball by future Met John Milner, but he already had a major-league swing and smashed it for a game-tying grand slam.

That was it; the manager had seen enough and took me out.

We wound up coming back to win the game, but it looked like I may have lost my shot at the big leagues. My ERA was now 6.26 through five games (four starts), and I had allowed twenty-two hits and sixteen earned runs in 22 2/3 innings. Sure, I had struck out a decent number of guys, but I had also walked nearly as many. It didn't matter that I felt great physically, either; those kinds of numbers were not going to get me my shot.

Then something happened that confirmed what I truly believe: God has a plan for all of us.

From Trenton we headed to Georgia to play the Columbus Colonels, the

Triple-A affiliate of the Red Sox. The manager of the Colonels was Darrell Johnson, who it turns out had heard some good things about me through the baseball pipeline.

Here's how it went down:

First Pedro Ramos, a fellow Cuban-born pitcher and ex-big leaguer who was playing with me in Richmond, told his friend Jose Santiago that he thought my stuff was coming along great—even though my record didn't show it.

Then Santiago, a pitching hero from Boston's '67 "Impossible Dream" team who was in the minors trying to recover from his own sore arm, told *his* friend Lee Stange.

Stange was the key. He was Boston's minor league pitching coordinator and a former teammate of both Santiago's (with the Sox) and mine (with the Indians). He told Johnson, who as Red Sox pitching coach in 1968 and '69 had gone up against me plenty of times when I was with Cleveland. Darrell knew what I was capable of doing when healthy.

Professional baseball rules prevented me from meeting with representatives from one team while still under contract with another, so Johnson used Stange to quietly pass the word along: if the Braves released me when my thirty days were up, I should come see him.

I was supposed to pitch for Richmond on Friday, May 14, the night we got into Columbus. But then Clyde King told me Thursday, "We're not going to pitch you Friday. We want to wait until we can get Braves general manager Paul Richards down here from Atlanta to talk to him more about you."

This worried me for a couple reasons. I didn't know what was up—except my contract the next day—so I figured they were getting ready to release me. Plus, without pitching I would have no chance to show Johnson up close that I was getting better. I'm not sure if King knew yet that Johnson and the Red Sox were interested in me, but I had to confirm whether Atlanta was still serious about offering me a contract; if they *weren't*, I didn't want to ruin my chances with Boston by waiting too long to find out.

So I made a deal with King.

"I'm going to give you until nine o'clock tomorrow morning to make a decision about signing me," I said. "I'll meet you and Paul Richards at the hotel restaurant for breakfast. If you don't show up, I'll know you're not interested."

"OK," King said.

The next morning, May 15, I got down to the restaurant early. King and Richards never showed. I stayed about a half hour, alone at my table, and then looked in the lobby. They weren't there either, and that made it clear in my book: My contract with the Braves was up, and I was now a free agent able to negotiate with other clubs.

I didn't even wait for the Twins to issue my official release, which they would do later that day. I left the hotel, went right to the ballpark, and by ten o'clock was meeting with Darrell Johnson and Lee Stange. They called Boston GM Dick O'Connell, who gave them the go-ahead to sign me on the spot. It was a standard one-year contract, too; no more of this thirty-day stuff with all the extra pressure. Johnson said he'd pitch me every fourth day, and if my arm kept improving, O'Connell would bring me up to the big leagues.

Looking back, that signing was one of the best things I ever did. The Red Sox believed in me enough to take a chance, and I will always be grateful to them for that. Johnson was true to his word, moving me right into Louisville's regular rotation in place of another twenty-game winner who was also on the way back: Jim Lonborg. Lonnie was a Cy Young Award winner for the Sox in 1967, with a one-hitter and three-hitter in the World Series that year, but had been dealing with injuries ever since. Now he was healthy enough to get another chance in Boston, and if I did my job with Columbus, I'd be joining him there soon.

My first start was on May 18 against the Tidewater Tides and John Milner, who had chased me with the grand slam in my last game with Richmond. This time I kept him in the ballpark and pitched the first eight innings of a 7–4 win. Jose Santiago, whose good word had helped get me this chance in the first place, bailed me out with a perfect ninth. The big hits for us included a two-run double by Ben Oglivie—one of four future Boston teammates of mine in the lineup that night along with Rick Miller, Juan Beniquez, and a catcher you may have heard of named Carlton Fisk.

The next time out I had thirteen strikeouts and just one walk in seven innings against the Richmond Braves. This felt extra good since they had given up on me just a few days before, and even though I lost the game, I knew I had pitched well. Johnson told O'Connell I was looking better every day; more importantly, I *felt* better every day.

It was at Rochester, on June 1, that I sealed the deal. I struck out nine in a five-hit shutout and cruised to a 10–0 win with help from homers by Oglivie, Miller, and Fisk. My control was really coming back, and including that game, I now had twenty-nine strikeouts and eleven walks in thirty-one innings with Louisville. I had allowed only twenty-two hits, and my ERA was 2.61.

Haywood Sullivan, director of player personnel and development for the Red Sox, was in the stands that night in Rochester. After the game, he asked me to meet him for breakfast the next morning. I said yes.

This time everyone invited showed up, and Sullivan got down to business right away. Looking across the table, he asked if I was ready to join the Red Sox.

In my mind I flashed back to 1964 when Birdie Tebbetts wondered if I was okay facing the mighty Yankees in my big-league debut—one day after flying in from Triple-A San Diego. I didn't have to think much about it; my answer now was pretty much the same as it had been to Birdie seven years before:

"You're damned right I'm ready."

The difference was that this time I wasn't coming out of nowhere; most American League players, coaches, and fans had either seen or played against me. They knew *what* I could do; they just didn't know if I could still do it. Now they were going to find out.

Would the Red Sox be getting the overpowering Tiant, the broken-down Tiant, or something in between?

Nobody was sure—including me.

10

REBIRTH IN BOSTON

IN THE AFTERMATH OF THEIR 1967 "Impossible Dream" pennant, the Red Sox had given Boston fans three entertaining—but largely unsatisfying—seasons.

Miserable teams playing in a near-empty Fenway Park were a thing of the past, but the level of success predicted for the ballclub anchored by Triple Crown winner Carl Yastrzemski and pitching ace Jim Lonborg had not transpired. Long-suffering New Englanders inspired by the one-year leap from ninth place to the World Series in '67 still packed Fenway, but by 1971 many were growing impatient with the club's inability to return to the postseason.

One could cite a variety of reasons. First baseman George Scott's hitting dropped off dramatically post-1967 as he battled weight and strike zone issues. Lonborg went from twenty-two wins to six after an off-season ski accident. Pitcher Jose Santiago, terrific during the '67 stretch drive, was all but finished by the next summer due to elbow problems. And hometown hero Tony Conigliaro, after missing one and a half seasons with eye and other injuries suffered in a near-fatal beaning, was rumored to again have vision problems—likely hastening the club's 1970 decision to trade the popular outfielder after he just hit thirty-six homers.

The Red Sox remained a strong ballclub despite these challenges, but they lacked the roster depth and cool confidence of the Baltimore Orioles—their American League East rivals currently seeking a third straight pennant. When Luis Tiant first put on a Boston uniform in June of 1971, there were no boldface headlines trumpeting his arrival, just queries as to why the team would acquire an aging, sore-armed pitcher. How could that help them beat Jim Palmer's Orioles?

Tiant's shaky early outings justified the concerns. Then came 1972 when the long years of patience and perspiration dedicated to bringing his pitching arm back to life were rewarded. He led a Red Sox rush for the AL East title with a string of brilliant performances, aided by the heroics of rookie catcher Carlton Fisk and rejuvenated elder statesman Yastrzemski. The feeling around the club went from one of brooding fatalism to a determined self-assurance; Tiant was always confident, win or lose.

Mostly, he won. And at Fenway, where boos once cascaded down on him and his teammates, chants of LOO-EEE! LOO-EEE! now shook the ballpark.

BEFORE I STARTED my first game for the Red Sox, against the Kansas City Royals, a reporter asked me how I felt to be in this position after dealing with injuries for several seasons.

"My arm is fine. Perfect. Everything's OK," I told him. "No reason I can't win again. I should win lots of games for this team."

Damn, I sounded confident. I turned out to be right, too—but it didn't look that way for a while.

Major leaguers will tell you they never read what's written about them in the newspapers, but don't believe them. I guess guys today will say they never pay attention to anything on ESPN or the MLB Channel or on sports talk radio either. No way. It's impossible not to hear at least *some* of what's being written or said, even if English is not your first language. You can say you don't care, but you wouldn't be human if you didn't.

There is only one good thing about what Cliff Keane wrote in the *Boston Globe* after my Red Sox debut on June 11, 1971. Because we were playing on the road, I didn't have to see the paper lying around the visitor's clubhouse in Kansas City. Keane had been speaking his mind about ballplayers since he broke in with the paper during Ted Williams's 1939 rookie season, and he made it clear right away how he felt about the club signing me.

"The latest investment by the Red Sox in Luis Tiant looks about as sound as taking a bagful of money and throwing it off Pier 4 into the Atlantic," Keane wrote. "Luis couldn't wait to get to the mound against the Royals. He raced out onto the field.... But when he left with nobody out in the second inning, he was much more deliberate in his pace."

I look at these words now and I have to laugh; I mean, it was my *first game*, and Keane was acting like he'd just seen me stink up the joint for the tenth straight time. But that's how things were with the Red Sox when I joined the team—players, fans, and even the sportswriters were all frustrated.

After coming out of nowhere to win the '67 pennant with a young club, they figured they would be on top for years. It didn't work out that way.

Boston had not come close to another championship, and a has-been hurler with a bad arm was definitely not what they needed.

"I was ambivalent when Tiant first came here; I thought he could be on the tailside," says Kevin Vahey, a cab driver and part-time student at Graham Junior College across the street from Fenway in the summer of 1971. "As fans we were more excited by a pitcher like Sonny Siebert, who started the year 9–0. There was mass indifference to Luis; he was just there. It was like, 'Great, we're going nowhere.'"

After all those years in Cleveland, I understood why fans felt that way. The Red Sox were not the Indians, but with no wild-cards and play-in games back then, it was much tougher to make the postseason. Boston had to win the American League East just to get to the AL playoffs, and that meant beating out five teams including the best club in baseball: The Baltimore Orioles. Baltimore had won the 1970 World Series and was favored to win its third straight pennant in '71 with All-Stars like Frank and Brooks Robinson, Boog Powell, and Davey Johnson in the lineup and a starting pitching staff stacked with four twenty-game winners that year: Jim Palmer, Dave McNally, Pat Dobson, and Cuban junkballer Mike Cuellar.

The Red Sox had very good pitchers like Ray Culp, Gary Peters, and Siebert, my teammate from the Indians picked up in the trade that sent Hawk Harrelson to Cleveland. But the last twenty-win season by a Boston pitcher was Jim Lonborg's 22–9 in '67, and after he tore up his knee skiing that off-season he fell to 6–10. The Sox had not found a true ace to replace him, and Lonnie was just now showing glimpses of his old form.

Boston always had guys who could crush the ball out of Fenway Park, but their hitting was down a bit too. Yaz had a bad wrist that cut his power in half, and Tony Conigliaro had been traded to the California Angels in a very unpopular move. Tony C's 116 RBIs and swagger were missed, but his eyes were going again, and he quit the Angels that summer. His departure from the Red Sox left Rico Petrocelli, Reggie Smith, and George Scott as the only real power threats in Boston's everyday lineup.

Still, my new team was making a fight of it. I took the mound for that first start in Kansas City with the Red Sox in second place, three games behind the Orioles. It was a risk to put a guy still getting his pitching legs back right into the rotation, but that's what Boston manager Eddie Kasko did. Then even after I gave up three hits, three walks, and five runs—all in a little more than one inning of work, Kasko stuck with me. My next appearance was in relief, but then I made nine straight starts from late June to early August.

I didn't win any of them.

It was tough, real tough, to keep losing like that, especially when you're trying to do your best to help your new teammates. But I knew the guys could tell I was trying. They saw me running all those laps around the ballpark, every day, and dropping nearly twenty pounds to get down near my rookie playing weight. They saw me going back out there, game after game, never complaining about an error or bad play made behind me. And they especially saw it in my best-pitched game of the season, one which most of them knew had extra-special meaning to me.

It was on July 15 at Fenway, against the Twins. I was still angry at Minnesota for releasing me, and I wanted to show them the mistake they had made. So I left it all out there, throwing 154 pitches, striking out nine, and matching zeros with Cy Young winner Jim Perry through ten innings before telling Kasko I had better come out before I hurt my arm. When we picked up the 3–0 win on a walk-off blast by Rico over the Green Monster in the thirteenth, two thoughts crossed my mind: I was sorry my old buddy Stan Williams had to give up Rico's homer for Minnesota, and I hoped Twins president Calvin Griffith was cursing at his TV or radio when he did.

There was just one problem: the Orioles kept winning. That night they won their eleventh straight game, leaving us five and a half back in the East. I could tell my arm was coming around, and so could Kasko, but it wasn't showing on the field. After I lost to the Tigers and Mickey Lolich, 8–2, on August 8, giving up seven hits and five runs in three innings, it dropped me to 0–6 with a 6.64 ERA.

It's funny to think about, with all the LOO-EEE! LOO-EEE! chants that came later on, but the first yelling I heard from fans in Boston as a Red Sox was booing. I never remember dealing with any of the racial stuff that guys like Reggie Smith and Jim Rice heard in the outfield, but it could get pretty nasty. Of course I wasn't the only one; plenty of guys heard booing that year, even Yaz—who had been the most popular player on the team for years. So I figured I was in good company and tried to not let it bother me.

Worse than the booing was what came next. Even though we were still in second place, and still within six games of Baltimore, Kasko pulled me from the rotation after the Detroit loss. There came a point when I guess he felt he had to make a change, given my 0–6 record. Rookie Rogelio Moret was brought up from Louisville to take my spot, and from that point in mid-August until the end of the season, all my appearances came in relief.

Now fans could boo me up close in the bullpen. Plenty did, including these two young girls who would stand behind the bullpen wall screaming for me to "go home to Cuba." Finally I had enough and went looking for their father. It turned out they were the daughters of a cop that worked at Fenway, and when I confronted him, he was embarrassed. I'm not sure what he said to them, but I never saw those girls again.

I was doing what I could to stop the booing myself. My bullpen stats were pretty good: twenty strikeouts in twenty-two innings, over ten games, with only twelve hits and seven walks allowed. My ERA was 1.23 during that span, and I even picked up my first victory in more than a year when I entered a tie game against the Orioles at Fenway and shut them down from the seventh through the ninth—when Yaz won the game with a single off Palmer. It was a great victory, especially for Carl. He had been going through a real bad slump as he dealt with his own injuries, and everybody ran out to meet him at first base like we had just won the pennant. I was happy for him and relieved to get my first "W" in a long, long time.

But don't let this fool you. Even when I did good in relief, I hated it. I just felt there was something special about being out there at the start of a game. You controlled the pace and could set guys up in their early at-bats for how you might pitch them later on. It was like a chess match, and I missed finding the rhythm of each contest and then pushing myself to finish what I started—like my dad had taught me.

In the end, my move to the pen didn't help the club anyway. Right after I left the rotation, we had a terrible August homestand, losing seven straight and eleven of twelve to ruin any chance we had of catching Baltimore. By the end of the season we were in third place, eighteen games back, but I didn't complain to Kasko. I knew Eddie had gone as far as he could with me, and later on he said he appreciated that I never "bitched and moaned" about getting pulled from the rotation. "The man was a professional in every sense of the word," he said.

I'm glad he felt that way, but that didn't mean I wanted to *stay* in the bullpen. I was out to prove I could still be a starter, and that meant I needed more time on the mound—any mound—to get my legs in nine-inning shape.

So after the 1971 season, I went back to Venezuela and another season of winter ball. I had played there with the Caracas Lions each winter for a bunch of years, but now they wouldn't take me back because they knew I had been hurt. So I went with their rivals, the La Guaira Sharks, and in my first three starts I got my butt kicked all over the place. The papers were killing me, saying I was no good and had a broken arm and should go back to Cuba.

Then one Sunday, November 14, we played in Caracas at eleven in the morning against the Lions—the same team that had not taken me back. As I came out to the mound to start the game, I said to myself, "Today, my arm is not really hurt. I am going to be fine. Just let it go."

First inning, they got no hits. Second inning, third inning, fourth inning, fifth inning, sixth inning, seventh inning, still nothing. I was throwing a no-hitter through seven innings, and the Lions fans, who had cheered me for years when I was on *their* team, were yelling shit at me with each pitch.

"You damn Cuban! You're a traitor!"

"What did I do?" I wanted to yell back. "*They* didn't want *me*, not the other way around!"

I didn't say anything, but I did give the fans my middle finger—leading some of them to want to come on the field and kill me. They were screaming all the way around the stands, but I got through the eighth and ninth innings and got my no-hitter. Up until that point, it was the most feel-good game of my life. I wish my parents could have seen it, and Maria. I wish *everybody* could have been there.

You know, people don't realize how hard it is coming back from being defeated, or hurt, or whatever. You're trying to prove, "Hey, I'm not finished. I'm still here." People don't believe it. Then you get beat in a big game and forget it. It drowns you.

Some guys can work their way out of a slump, and some guys can't. See? Some hitters go 0-for-4, and they just say, "I'm going to do well tomorrow." Even if they don't, eventually they know they will. Other guys go 0-for-4, get worried, and then get deeper and deeper into it. The uncertainty gets in their heads, it grabs them, and then they implode. That's what happens to a lot of young players, and I tell them: it's all about confidence. You have to get your confidence back.

I never totally lost my confidence, no matter how low things got, but I did start to have my doubts after going 1–7 for Boston and ending the year in the bullpen. That day in Caracas, when I pitched a no-hitter with all those fans screaming at me, was when the rest of my confidence came rushing back.

Now, more than ever, I felt I was going to make it back *all the way*.

* * *

My no-hitter got a brief mention in the Boston papers, but it didn't really change anybody's feelings heading into 1972. Even with my strong performance in the bullpen the previous August and September, many experts figured I had a fifty-fifty shot to make the team when spring training started at Chain O' Lakes Park in Winter Haven, Florida.

Nobody used the word "closer" then, but the Red Sox had one of the better pitchers serving in that role in lefthander Albert "Sparky" Lyle. Sparky had led the team three straight years in saves, including sixteen in '71 to go along with a fine 2.75 ERA. He also appeared in fifty or more games every year, so I wouldn't be the team's go-to relief pitcher as long as Lyle was around. That was OK by me; I didn't like the job anyway.

But what if I couldn't crack the starting rotation? Since I still made a pretty good salary, that probably increased the chances the Red Sox would try to release me early rather than have to pay me for the whole year just to sit in the bullpen and get in a few games. No relievers, Lyle included, made big money then.

It was a time of uncertainty for me, but one thing that helped make that first spring training with the Red Sox more fun was being reunited with one of my closest friends from our Cleveland days: speedy outfielder Tommy Harper. Tommy came to Boston as part of a big off-season trade between the Red Sox and Milwaukee Brewers in which the Sox sent George Scott, Jim Lonborg, Billy Conigliaro, Joe Lahoud, Ken Brett, and Don Pavletich to Milwaukee in exchange for Tommy, Lew Krausse, Marty Pattin, and minor leaguer Patrick Skrable. We lost one starting pitcher in Lonborg and gained one in Pattin, so the first three spots in the rotation were set heading into the season—Sonny Siebert, Pattin, and Ray Culp. The fourth and fifth spots were still up for grabs.

I did my best to prove myself worthy of a shot at one of them. Over my first several spring training appearances, I let up a total of one earned run. Then, in late March, just a few days before camp broke, I made a big mistake—trying to blow a one-and-two pitch past Mike Jorgensen of the Mets with the bases loaded in a scoreless game. He slammed it 410 feet over the wall in right-center field for a grand slam, and just like that I was a 4–0 loser.

Eddie Kasko was still supportive. "Tiant gave up the home run, but I thought he pitched well," he said after the game. It felt great having the manager in my corner.

Besides that, the Red Sox made another move that I felt improved my chances of sticking with the club. Looking for a veteran first baseman to replace George Scott after the Milwaukee trade, Boston GM Dick O'Connell sent Lyle to the Yankees for Danny Cater on March 22. It wasn't a popular move with the players, who all loved what Sparky gave us, but it filled a big hole.

Cater was a right-handed, line-drive hitter who had always done well at Fenway Park, and O'Connell's hope was that he'd keep that up. He didn't. A .279 lifetime batter with some pop over eight full seasons before coming to Boston, he hit .237 with zero power his first year with us. His Fenway swing disappeared, and before the summer was over, he was on the bench, and Yaz had moved in from left field to play first. Lyle, meanwhile, was going 9–5 with 35 saves and a 1.92 ERA in New York, keeping the Yankees in the pennant race until the final weeks.

Today many consider that deal to be one of the worst in Red Sox history, but it was also an opening for me. O'Connell said at the time that he felt comfortable giving Lyle up because of our pitching depth, and that he saw Bill Lee as the team's primary left-handed reliever going forward. This left room for a veteran *right*-handed arm in the pen, and while I wanted to be starting, I had proven myself capable of filling either role—or, if necessary, both at the same time. My ERA was right around 3.00 for the spring, and my control was the best it had been in years. Within a couple days of the trade, I found out I had made the club.

The problem was there were no games to play. The player's union had been fighting all winter with MLB owners over pension benefits, and when the owners refused to meet union demands the first strike in big-league history became official on April 1. All remaining exhibition games were canceled, and the owners pushed back by cutting off our meal money, our hotel rooms, and making us clean out our Winter Haven lockers. The Red Sox paid for our transportation back to Boston, but some guys headed home instead to save money on rent.

Boston player representatives Gary Peters and Ray Culp joined reps from the other twenty-three teams and union chief Marvin Miller in negotiations with owners, and a bunch of us including Harper, Reggie Smith, Bob Montgomery, and I stayed sharp by working out at the Harvard College batting cage. All the guys were worried about how they were going to make their mortgages and car payments if the paychecks stopped coming; I was just glad Maria and the kids were down in Mexico City where the cost of living was cheaper.

Like always, I tried to make light of the situation. I joked with reporters that the "billions served" signs in front of all the McDonald's were going to have to be changed if the lockout continued more than a few days. Then I asked if anybody knew where I could find a job. But inside, I was worried just like everybody else. I never thought a move like that against the owners would actually happen. In Cuba they shot you for taking a stand like that.

Luckily the two sides came to an agreement pretty quickly, and the strike ended on April 13. We were happy to be getting back to playing—and getting paid—but the early part of the season turned out to be very frustrating. I began it in the bullpen, and after one strong relief appearance had a couple of spot starts ten days apart—not getting past the sixth inning either time. That old problem of needing steady work to be my best was creeping in again; ten-day breaks was *not* what I called steady.

Still, I did my best to stay patient, ready, and in shape. I'd played long enough to know that things always happen to a pitching staff. Some guys get injured, and others underperform. My chance would come.

Besides, Kasko had enough problems without me bothering him. The team had gotten off to a terrible start. We lost seven of our first ten games and were still under .500 as May 15 neared. This was the final date for teams to cut a player without having to pay him his whole year's salary, and I figured my 4.91 ERA in just five appearances made me a prime candidate for the chopping block.

I was wrong; somehow I survived again. Maybe it was because Kasko knew he could always turn to me at the last moment to start a game, and I'd be ready. That's what happened June 7. Lew Krausse, one of our new pitchers, came down with a virus and couldn't go against the White Sox in Chicago. Kasko gave me the ball, and I gave him five innings. They weren't pretty—I walked six and struck out four—but I only let up two runs and kept us in the ballgame. Lee pitched three scoreless innings after me, but we lost 2–1.

That was the single biggest problem with the Red Sox during the first half of 1972: our pitching was solid, we just couldn't hit. Harper and shortstop Luis Aparicio were doing their job atop the order, getting on base and each hitting around .280, but Reggie Smith, Rico, and especially Cater were all performing way below their norms. It didn't help that Yaz, already coming off his worst season in '71, missed most of May with a knee injury.

We all knew we were too talented a ballclub to stay in such a bad slump, and in time things turned. Yaz came back from the DL on June 9 and immediately started line-driving the ball to death, batting .377 over the next month to raise his average up to .300. He still wasn't hitting homers—he wouldn't hit his first until July 22, in his fifty-eighth game—but he was driving in runs because Harper and Aparicio kept getting on. Tommy was the fastest base runner Red Sox fans had seen in a generation, a big change from the home run or nothing mentality of most Boston teams. He could steal second or take the extra base, and fans loved it. Yaz's hot streak sparked the team, too, and other guys in the lineup like Rico and Reggie picked up the power slack.

But the biggest surprise on the Red Sox—and maybe in the entire American League in 1972—was our rookie catcher. Carlton Fisk was a farm boy from New Hampshire who grew up cheering for the Red Sox and came into the season as the third-string catcher behind Montgomery and Duane Josephson. Then Josephson went on the DL, Monty had trouble throwing out base runners, and Fisk got his shot. He ran with it, showed himself to be a great clutch hitter with twenty-homer potential, a quick, smart receiver, and a real take-charge guy on the field.

None of it surprised me. I met Fisk the previous summer in Louisville when both of us were working to get a call-up and could tell right away he had the determination, intelligence, maturity, and athleticism to make his mark on the game. He didn't take shit from anybody, even veteran pitchers, and he could *play*. Now the rest of the baseball world was finding it out.

One of my favorite pictures from that season shows Fisk and me celebrating a key win in the Fenway clubhouse; he has a big smile on his face, and I've got a big cigar in my mouth. This was nothing new; I've been smoking them since I was seventeen, and back in Cuba nobody thought anything of it. In the states, as soon as I got to the big leagues, they became my trademark. I've always liked a good cigar when I wanted to relax, and after a ballgame was of course the perfect time—win or lose. So the sportswriters and photographers always saw me with one, and they started mentioning them in their game stories.

Boston baseball fans really got familiar with seeing my cigars in 1972 because I had one in my mouth in practically every post-game photograph. I took my cigar with me to the whirlpool, the toilet, and the shower. Guys thought that was the funniest thing, especially when the cigar always seemed to stay lit. But to me that was just good sense; my matches were in my locker.

One thing people *didn't* make a big deal about when I first came to Boston was my windup and delivery. That's because for the first year I was with the Red Sox, I wasn't using most of the head bobs, shakes, and body swivels that I had in Cleveland—and in Minnesota before my injuries. I'd pull a little funny stuff out sometimes, but not too much.

When a young Peter Gammons of the *Boston Globe*, asked me about this in the spring of '72, I told him it was because I was still working my way back from my shoulder problems.

"Hitters will come up to me and tell me they haven't forgotten that stuff," I told Gammons. "They say it was really effective, that they couldn't pick up the ball too good. They ask me why I don't use it more now. But I'm still trying to come back. My control still isn't as good as I like. That can throw me off. But by July or August, who knows?"

Then I smiled at him.

"If I do good, maybe I'll start my act again sooner than I think."

My prediction wasn't too far off. On June 29, a Wednesday night at Fenway, Sonny Siebert started against the Tigers. They were leading the East, two games ahead of the Orioles, and we were eight out and trying to gain some ground. Sonny was having a real strong first half of the season, which made me feel good. Right at the end of spring training, I had noticed he wasn't popping his wrist as he released the ball during his delivery. He had corrected the problem when I mentioned it to him, and heading to the mound that night, he was 7–4 with a 3.14 ERA.

The Tigers were a veteran, hard-hitting team, and they got to Sonny for three runs early. In the fourth, with Detroit up 3–1, Kasko pinch-hit for Siebert with two out and two on. The designated hitter was still a season away—if there was one in '72, Sonny probably would have stayed in—and we needed to get a run when we could against Tigers pitcher Joe Coleman, a real tough right-hander. The gamble didn't work; Ben Oglivie, our top pinch-hitter, popped out.

So the call came down from manager Kasko to the bullpen: send Tiant in.

I was feeling strong and got through the fifth inning easily. Then our bats got going in the bottom of the fifth, and we took the lead 4–3 on RBI hits by Yaz, Reggie, and rookie Juan Beniquez. That chased Coleman, but I was probably too pumped up to start the sixth; Mickey Stanley led off with a double, and Dick McAuliffe walked with two outs. That brought up Aurelio Rodriguez, a right-handed batter who already had two run-scoring hits off Siebert earlier in the game.

I had Rodriguez two strikes and no balls when suddenly a thought popped into my mind: *I'm going to try something different—something I have never* even practiced—and see what happens. Switching to an overhand windup, I turned my body so I was looking directly into centerfield. Then I looked into the sky, spun back toward the plate, and followed through.

Rodriguez's eyes looked as big as saucers! He jumped away from home plate, and the ball just went—POOF!—into Fisk's mitt, right down the middle. I knew he had no chance to hit it because he had moved so far away.

Strike three.

Fisk started laughing. So did everyone in our dugout. Then Rodriguez turned around and asked Fisk, "What was that?!"

"Oh, that's a new pitch."

(God bless Fisk. He also had no idea but was covering for me.)

"Goddamn!" Rodriguez said. "He's going to come at me with THAT shit now?! How are we supposed to hit *that*?!"

They weren't—that was the idea.

Rico was playing behind me at third base when it happened. He was surprised too.

"We thought he was going to throw to second base—that's how far around he went," he remembers. "But he kept his right foot on the rubber, and after he looked over at second, he turned back around the other way and threw! We were like "WHOA! What the heck was THAT!?"

Later, in the dugout, I told Rico and everyone else the new pitch was something I came up with on the spot. I had always shown the batter my number [on my back] by turning around during my windup, but turning completely around, looking up at the sky, and hesitating before whipping back around? That was all new. And for the rest of the night, I stuck with it.

Detroit couldn't do anything with me after that. Right-handed hitters? They prayed. They had no chance, and by the top of the ninth it was 5–3. I got big Willie Horton—always a home-run threat—to ground out to first, but then walked McAuliffe (again) on four pitches. Next came Rodriguez, and I missed with my first three to him. I was probably pressing, and Kasko said after the game that he planned to take me out if I walked Rodriguez.

I didn't. Figuring that my sinker was dipping too low. I went into my full overhand windup, twist and all, and struck him out with three straight not-too-low sinkers. Then I got Al Kaline swinging on a slider to end it. My final line: five innings, one hit, five strikeouts, two walks, and one big boost of confidence.

In the clubhouse after the game, Reggie Smith was joking around for the writers, pretending to be a pitcher going through a crazy windup that included shaking his head up and down, kicking out his leg, checking the runner at first, and then throwing a ball from behind his back.

"That," he said with a laugh, "is the only pitch I've never seen Luis Tiant throw."

Puffing on a victory cigar, I laughed too. Then I explained what everyone had just seen:

"I was back to my old motion tonight. My arm felt good. I'm ready to bring everything back. I give the batters my back and surprise them with my hesitation. I confused them tonight the way I used to before I got hurt."

It wasn't just the old motion and the hesitation; Fisk said he had never seen me pitch faster. He didn't catch me in Cleveland, where I could bring it in ninety-seven or ninety-eight miles per hour. But if I was only getting up to ninety-two or ninety-three now, that was OK. I was smarter than I was in 1968. I knew how to throw heat then. Now I knew how to *pitch*.

Kaline, a future Hall of Famer, was convinced too.

"He's as good as he was with Cleveland," he said.

That was it. For the rest of my career, I never went back to a conventional windup. And from that point on, I consistently worked on getting everything right: my delivery, my control, and my point of release. It's the same thing I tell all the young pitchers I work with—you need to know when to release the ball so it gets close to home plate. It takes practice and repetition. I only did the hesitation pitch about five or six times a game, just enough to make them wonder when it was coming.

Right after that Detroit game, everybody started talking about my windup again. The sportswriters all found different ways to describe it, like they did back in Cleveland. And, just like in Cleveland, some managers tried to get umpires to declare it illegal. They never did, at least not in the American League.

The whole thing drove hitters crazy. Players used to say to me, "Dammit! How can you pitch like that? How can you throw strikes?" That's something, I guess, that God gave to me and let me do. But He didn't give it to me free; don't think my load was easy to carry. It took a lot of hard work to get it right, and then a lot more hard work to get it *back*.

The key to everything was innings. The more consistent innings I got, the better my arm felt. The better my arm felt, the better I *did*—and the more confidence I had about going back to my special windup. What's great about that motion is you do most of the work with your body, so you don't put the strain on your arm that you do with a conventional delivery.

No sore arms meant I was ready when needed. So when Siebert had to be scratched because of shoulder tendinitis on July 3, I got another spot start and beat the Twins, 8–2, with help from Fisk's home run and my own two-run single. It was my first complete game in nearly a year, and I beat Bert Blyleven, the kid who took my rotation spot on the Twins.

"The name of the game is to win, you don't have to hate someone," I said about beating my old team. When one writer wanted to know why I was suddenly pitching better, I said the reason was simple: I was getting work.

The proof was in the numbers. During a two-month span starting May 21, I pitched in twenty games and had a 2.00 ERA over thirty-six innings. Included were two starts, four wins, two saves, and nine times that I was on the mound to finish a game. I wasn't the only one getting hot; by July 20, after a stretch of nineteen wins in twenty-five games, we were just five games out of first in a crowded AL East. Stars like Rico, Reggie, and Harper started catching fire, but everybody played a part.

When Aparicio got hurt, rookie Juan Beniquez—the other guy we picked up in the Lyle-for-Cater trade—came in to fill the hole at short. John Kennedy, who we called "Super Sub," played all over the infield and was also a terrific pinch-hitter. Two other rookies, Lynn McGlothen and John Curtis, gave our pitching a big shot in the arm when veterans like Culp went down. Marty Pattin, the key pitcher we got in the Brewers trade, rebounded from a 2–8 start to go 15–5 with a 2.22 ERA and four shutouts the rest of the way. And in September, after the minor league season ended, a twenty-year-old kid named Dwight Evans came up to play left field so Yaz could move to first. From his very first game with us, Evans was making diving catches and getting clutch hits. (He'd move from left field to right, where he'd win eight Gold Gloves, the next year.)

When Boston signed me after my release by the Braves, and I won my first game for Louisville, Red Sox farm director Ed Kenney said this about my chances of getting back to the big leagues: "He knows how to pitch, and if his arm stays sound, we'll have him available if a crisis arises."

I think August 5, 1972, was what he had in mind.

Siebert was scheduled to start that night against the Orioles at Fenway. His tendinitis was better, but now he was having dizzy spells. So about a half hour before the game, Kasko came up to me in the clubhouse.

"Luis, how do you feel?"

"Great."

"Think you can pitch tonight?"

"You're damn right I can! Give me the Goddamn ball, and I'll pitch it!"

I didn't have time to really get loose, and Baltimore scored twice before most people had sat down. Then I settled into a groove, and red-hot Rico took care of the rest with a double, grand slam, and six RBI in our 6–3 win. The best thing for me was that I went nine innings, struck out six, and didn't allow a single walk. That was a real big sign my control was coming back along with my velocity.

"Whether it's long or short relief," said Kasko after the game, "or whether it's on only an hour's notice, Tiant is always there!"

The manager wasn't the only one excited. Mr. Yawkey had been walking by Kasko's office when I offered to pitch in place of Siebert, and it made an impression.

"No complaints, no excuses, no alibis," Mr. Yawkey said later about my filling in. "He's a pro. I wish every player had his attitude."

It's not a bad idea to have the owner as your biggest fan, but Kasko didn't need convincing. He wanted to win, and it was clear I had a hot hand. That victory left us four-and-one-half games behind the Tigers, three behind the Orioles, and got me another start against Baltimore on the road a week later. I won that one, too, no-hitting them into the seventh before settling for a three-hitter. "Tiant was all kicks and twists, but the Orioles couldn't see him," Cliff Keane wrote in the *Globe*.

NBC put us on the nationally-televised Game of the Week the next Saturday afternoon at Chicago, and I imagined my parents secretly watching on the butcher's TV in Cuba. If they were, they saw me go into the seventh with a no-hitter *again* and wind up with a 3–0, two-hit shutout over the White Sox. The third-base ump, Art Frantz, told Rico that if a runner made it to third base, he was going to call a balk on me for using an illegal motion. That was a bunch of crap; I wasn't doing anything illegal. But it didn't matter in the end. No Chicago runner got to third.

After that win we were only three-and-a-half back, one of three teams (with Baltimore and New York) all bunched up right behind the Tigers in the AL East. It was going to be a dogfight, and Kasko announced after the White Sox game that I was now a regular member of the starting rotation. That took a huge weight off me; now I knew *what* I had to do and *when* I had to do it.

The next eight weeks was an incredible ride. Given all at stake, it was the best stretch of pitching I ever had—eleven wins, all of them complete games, in twelve decisions. Here it is by the numbers, starting with the first Orioles game:

DATE	OPPONENT	INN	H	R	ER	BB	K	FINAL	W–L, ERA
08.05	Baltimore	9.0	7	3	3	0	6	W, 6-3 (W)	5–4, 3.11
08.12	at Baltimore	9.0	3	3	2	3	8	W, 5-3 (W)	6–4, 2.99
08.16	at Texas	1.0	3	1	0	2	0	L, 8-9 (ND)	6–4, 2.95
08.19	at Chicago	9.0	2	0	0	1	9	W, 3-0 (W)	7–4, 2.67
08.25	Texas	9.0	4	0	0	1	9	W, 4-0 (W)	8–4, 2.44
08.30	Chicago	9.0	5	0	0	1	5	W, 3-0 (W)	9–4, 2.24
09.04	at Milwaukee	9.0	5	0	0	4	8	W, 2-0 (W)	10–4, 2.08
09.08	New York	9.0	4	2	2	4	2	W, 4-2 (W)	11–4, 2.07
09.12	at New York	5.1	8	3	3	4	0	L, 3-2 (L)	11–5, 2.19
09.16	Cleveland	9.0	3	0	0	2	5	W,10-0(W)	12–5, 2.05
09.20	Baltimore	9.0	4	0	0	4	7	W, 4-0 (W)	13–5, 1.93
09.24	Detroit	9.0	7	2	2	2	4	W, 7-2 (W)	14–5, 1.94
09.29	at Baltimore	10.0	5	2	1	2	8	W, 4-2 (W)	15–5, 1.88
Totals (13 games)		106.1	60	16	13	30	71	11-2 (team)	11–1, 1.10

Two things that really stand out for me are the four straight shutouts I pitched against Chicago, Texas, Chicago again, and Milwaukee, accompanied by a string of 40.1 straight scoreless innings. Both were broken up on September 12, when Celerino Sanchez of the Yankees singled in a run. The funny thing about that is I had been the best man at Celerino's wedding the year before in Mexico, which I could laugh about because we still won the game, 4–2. I also had forty-plus innings of shutout pitching for the Indians in 1968, so this made me and Hall of Famer Walter Johnson the only pitchers in big-league history with two such streaks in their careers. Not bad company.

The Yankees came back and beat me in my next start, the only loss I had during the stretch, but then I threw two more shutouts—giving me six shutouts in eight starts. "I think he's as good as any right-hander in the American League," White Sox manager Chuck Tanner said after I beat his club, 3–0. "He was a surgeon out there tonight."

Make that a stylish surgeon. A bunch of guys on the team were growing mustaches and beards that summer, and I started doing it too. I kept winning, so I didn't shave, figuring it was good luck. Someone said my beard looked like a cross between a Fu Manchu and a goatee, and after a while it became a trademark—how people recognized me, besides my cigars.

The more I won, the more articles started popping up about me in Boston and other cities. This was the first time a lot of baseball fans learned my full background, about how my father didn't want me to be a pitcher early on because of the racism he faced in baseball and how it had been eleven years since I saw him and all my other family back in Cuba. I think reading or hearing about that, and how hard I worked to come back from my injuries, made people look at me like an underdog—someone they could feel good getting behind.

"Things had evolved to where Luis was clearly the ace of the staff," says Kevin Vahey, the cabbie/college student. "The Red Sox still counted on a large walk-up crowd in those days, especially on weekdays. You'd meet your buddies at the bar around five-thirty, and somebody would say, 'Hey, Tiant is pitching tonight.' Then *boom*, off you'd go to Fenway. The crowd would be buzzing, standing up when he had two strikes on a guy with two outs. And, of course, everybody was chanting his name."

That was another great thing that happened in 1972. Fenway Park was small and loud and always packed. Those fans were wonderful to me, and I loved them. Once I started pitching really good that season, they started chanting "LOO-EEE! LOO-EEE!" for me. They did it every time I walked out to the bullpen to warm up before a game and again when I came back in. As soon as that bullpen door opened, they'd start it up, and if I had a good inning here or there during the game, they did it some more.

I loved it. I think fans like that make you work harder because you don't want to let them down. They are with you, pushing for you, and you want to do a good job. I appreciated how much they cared. It was good—man, it was *special*.

My teammates felt it too.

Even as a baby, Luis C. Tiant displayed
the confidence that would carry him
to the highest levels of his profession.
(Tiant family photo)

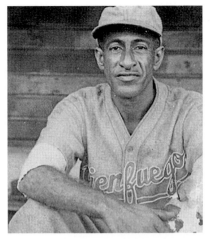

Father Luis E. Tiant—"Señor Skinny"—
in the latter stages of his playing career.
(Tiant family collection)

The first time Tiant saw Maria
del Refugio Navarro roaming
left field in a softball game, on
July 28, 1960, he was smitten.
(Tiant family photo)

Within a few years, while
Tiant was still working his
way up to the majors, he
and Maria had another
mouth to feed in Luis Jr.
(Tiant family photo)

On July 19, 1964, fans paying $2.50 for a mezzanine seat at Yankee Stadium saw Cleveland's "Cuban Cutie" etch his name into baseball history. Facing Whitey Ford in his big-league debut, Tiant pitched a 3-0 shutout. (Tiant family collection)

Luis wore a different number and no facial hair during his days with the Indians. His Fu Manchu and famous number 23 would both come in Boston, but Tiant enjoyed his Cleveland years—especially his fantastic 1968 season. (Courtesy of the National Baseball Hall of Fame)

Indians fans came to love Tiant, but he had no bigger fan than Little Luis. (Tiant family photo)

Tiant was an excellent all-around athlete with surprisingly quick reflexes on the mound. Even with his exaggerated windup, he was ready to pounce on any ball hit back to the box. (Courtesy of the National Baseball Hall of Fame)

When Tiant came north in the winter of 1969 to sign a new contract and pick up his "Man of the Year" award from local sportswriters, the Cleveland *Plain Dealer* had a fun photoshoot in which Maria and Luis fretted over the 21-degree temperature and admired the majesty of a snowball. (Tiant family photo)

Tiant preferred to spend his winters continuing to pitch in assorted warm-weather leagues. Here he toils for the Tiburones de La Guaira team of the Venezuela Winter League around 1970. (Tiant family photo)

During the stylish 1970s, two of the sharpest dressers in the Red Sox clubhouse were Tiant and outfielder Tommy Harper. (Tiant family photo)

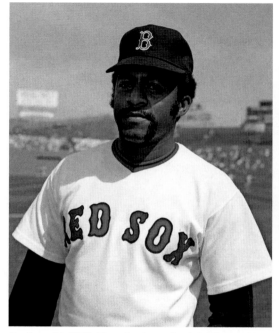

By the mid-1970s Tiant had acquired the look with which he would be most identified. This steely glare, which teammates and opponents saw on display during games, quickly melted away in the clubhouse—win or lose. (Courtesy of the Ray Sinibaldi Collection)

His early days in Boston were challenging, but Tiant never lost confidence that he could come back. In this shot from 1971 or '72, he appears to be measuring up his next victim for a practical joke. (Courtesy of the Ray Sinibaldi Collection)

A mouth full of chew, and a stylish two-tone cap on his head, Tiant is poised to begin the most famous windup in baseball. (Courtesy of the Ray Sinibaldi Collection)

Here is Tiant in mid-motion. . . . In the next moment, he will lift his left leg and begin the spinning-top swivel that left hitters staring at his back. (Courtesy of the Ray Sinibaldi Collection)

Here it comes—now see what you can do with it!
(Courtesy of the Ray Sinibaldi Collection)

Tiant has always had a sweet spot for men in blue. Even at the height of Boston's busing crisis and racial unrest in the mid-1970s, cops were happy to give Luis a light. (Courtesy of the Ray Sinibaldi Collection)

Tiant's regular clubhouse pose: towel around his waist, cigar in his mouth, lucky Santa Barbara medallion against his chest.
(Courtesy of the Ray Sinibaldi Collection)

Carlton Fisk lights a victory cigar for his batterymate in the Fenway clubhouse during the magical 1975 season. When Fisk came back that June after nearly a year on the disabled list, his first home run helped win a game for Tiant— and the best was yet to come.
(© Boston Red Sox)

In 1974, Tiant and fellow Latino pitching ace Juan Marichal were Red Sox teammates. Marichal's best days were behind him, but the "Dominican Dandy" did manage to go 5-1 for Boston—the last of his 243 big-league victories.
(© Boston Red Sox)

This scene was repeated many times over between 1972 and 1978: Luis Tiant has just retired the final batter of the ballgame and is about to embrace co-conspirator Carlton Fisk.
(© Boston Red Sox)

Danny Tiant, one-and-one-half, does not seem happy with the lineup for the August 1975 Father-Son-Daughter game at Fenway Park. (AP Photo/Peter Bregg)

In the end, young Danny had a great time.
(Tiant family photo)

When father and son embraced at Logan Airport on August 21, 1975, it was a hug fourteen years in the making. "Don't cry, the cameras will see you," Luis E. Tiant whispered. Luis C. Tiant did not care. (Courtesy of the Ray Sinibaldi Collection)

While son and starting pitcher Luis C. Tiant holds his jacket, 69-year-old Luis E. Tiant breaks in the Fenway rubber on August 26, 1975, with a ceremonial first pitch. Not happy with where his fastball crossed the plate, the former Negro League star asked for another toss and threw a knuckler down the middle. (Associated Press)

After the crowd erupts with Señor Tiant's second pitch, his son helps him back on with his jacket as Red Sox backup catcher Tim Blackwell comes out to congratulate him. (Courtesy of the Ray Sinibaldi Collection)

Señora Tiant, seated beside her granddaughter (and namesake) Isabel, grandson Luis, and daughter-in-law Maria, beams with pride as applause rains down on her husband and son. She had gone seven years since last seeing her only child and had never seen him pitch in person since high school. (AP Photo/J. Walter Green)

Before he died, Luis E. Tiant inscribed the ball he used for his ceremonial first pitches that night and gave it to his younger grandson Danny, who has carried it ever since as a good-luck charm. (Tiant family photo)

During their four-plus seasons together in Boston (1974–78), Jim Rice and Luis Tiant won many big games for the Red Sox. (Courtesy of the Ray Sinibaldi Collection)

In 1979, after his acrimonious parting from the Red Sox, Tiant donned pinstripes for an owner (George Steinbrenner) he felt showed him the respect he deserved. (Courtesy of the National Baseball Hall of Fame)

Thrilled to be back in uniform at Fenway, Tiant doffs his cap as he heads onto the field for a Red Sox Old-Timer's Game in the mid-1980s. Among the players laughing behind him are former teammates Bob Stanley (bottom, center) and Jerry Remy (bottom, right).
(Courtesy of the Ray Sinibaldi Collection)

Tiant's pride is evident as he poses with his family shortly after his playing career ended: Maria, sons Luis Jr. (with mustache) and Danny, and daughter Isabel. (Tiant family photo)

John Papile (in white) was lovingly welcomed into the Tiant family after his mother's death. Here, Johnny and Dora Papile celebrate their nuptials with bridesmaids including Isabel Tiant (to Johnny's left). (Tiant family photo)

When professional coaching jobs dried up, Tiant took a position as head coach at the Savannah College of Art & Design (SCAD), a fledgling Division III baseball program set on a beautiful Georgia campus. With Luis Jr. as his assistant, "Coach Tiant" won the love of players like Bees captain Tony Blankenship with his knowledge of the game and his zest for life. (Tony Blankenship photo)

Golf and charity are two of Tiant's favorite things, and he did both when he linked up on the links with "President 41" at the George H.W. Bush Celebrity Golf Classic at Cape Arundel. (Tiant family photo)

Family always comes first for Tiant. Celebrating the confirmation celebration for Luis Tiant V (in white) are (left to right) Luis Jr. (the IV), Maria, Johnny Papile, El Tiante (Luis III), Danny, and Isabel.
(Tiant family photo)

Twenty-five Octobers after their last game as batterymates, Carlton Fisk and Luis Tiant pose before the start of Game Four of the 2003 ALCS between the Red Sox and Yankees at Fenway.
(AP Photo/Elise Amendola)

In 2007, Tiant returned to his native Cuba for the first time in forty-six years while making the documentary *Lost Son of Havana.* He was able to see old family and friends, coach in a ballpark where he once starred as a young man, and make peace with his past. He would return again nine years later with President Barack Obama. (Courtesy of Hock Films)

The statue below once sat outside the Ted Williams Museum in Florida—where Tiant is enshrined in the pitchers' wing. Here Tiant and sons Danny (left) and Luis Jr. enjoy the museum's annual celebration in its current locale, Tropicana Field in St. Petersburg. (Tiant family photo)

Luis's love for cigars led him and his sons to start a business, El Tiante Cigars, after his playing days. Danny Tiant eventually assumed leadership of the company, which grew into Tiant Cigar Group and became very respected within the industry. (Tiant family photo)

Tiant poses with the statue, which depicts Williams placing a cap on the bald head of a young child with cancer. One of two identical statues (the other is at Fenway Park), it symbolizes Williams's efforts on behalf of the Jimmy Fund of Dana-Farber Cancer Institute, a charity to which Luis has also been devoted. (Courtesy of the Ray Sinibaldi Collection)

When the Red Sox celebrated the 100th anniversary of Fenway Park by having fans vote for an "All-Fenway Team" in 2012, both Tiant and fellow Latino ace Pedro Martinez made the pitching staff. As a Dodgers coach in the 1990s, Tiant had worked with Martinez's younger brother, Jesus. (Tiant family photos)

Tiant has advised Red Sox players since 2002, including pitcher Lenny DiNardo (above, around 2005) and current Gold Glove outfielder Andrew Benintendi (left, 2019). (DiNardo, Wisnia family photos)

Luis was clearly moved during the September 2012 memorial ceremony for fellow Red Sox legend Johnny Pesky at Fenway Park. As a coach, Pesky had been like a father to Tiant and hundreds of other Boston players since the 1970s. (© Billie Weiss/Boston Red Sox)

Still a hit each year at spring training, Tiant caught up with fellow big-game hero David Ortiz at Fenway South during February 2019. (Tiant family photo)

He may be nearing 80 years old, but El Tiante can clearly still bring the heat. (Tiant family photo)

"It's been forty-five years, and I still get emotional when I talk about this," infielder John Kennedy said shortly before he died in August 2018. "When Luis pitched, he'd be in the bullpen warming up, and when he got through, he'd start coming in. The fans would start to rise…LOO-EEE! LOO-EEE! By the time he got to the dugout, there were 30,000 people on their feet screaming LOO-EEE! LOO-EEE! It was just such an emotional thing, it sent chills up my spine—still does. You just couldn't believe it!"

Going into the final month of the season, it was still a four-team race in the AL East. Things were so tight that in the span of five days we went from fourth place all the way to first, and once we got there on September 7, we stayed within one game of the top—sometimes tied—for the rest of the month. Everybody in the lineup was doing his job, but nobody better than Yaz. After not hitting a home run for nearly a year, he started lifting his left elbow higher at the plate and hit eight in September. It seemed like every time we needed him to get a big hit, especially when I was pitching, he got it.

The Orioles came to Fenway for a five-game series on September 18. They were the three-time defending American League champs, and we didn't expect them to go down without a fight. After they won the first game, 5–2, we fell one-half game behind Detroit, and Baltimore was one-half game behind *us* heading into a Wednesday doubleheader. We swept it— Marty Pattin beat Palmer, 9–1, in the opener, and I topped Cuellar, 4–0, in the nightcap. It was my ninth win in ten decisions, and the crowd never cheered louder for me. They gave me a standing ovation when I came up to bat in the eighth, and another one all through the top of the ninth until I struck out Don Buford to end it.

Yaz had never heard anything like it. "Tiant deserved every bit of it," he said. I made sure he knew I never could have done it without him.

The sweep put us back in first by a game over the Tigers, with Baltimore two-and-a-half back. We finally put the Orioles and the Yankees away the final week. Yaz did it again, hitting our biggest homer of the year—a two-run shot off Palmer in the tenth inning at Baltimore to give me a 4–2 win on September 30.

In the loud visitor's clubhouse at Memorial Stadium, I pointed to Yaz as I soaked my pitching arm. "He's my magic genie."

We all hoped the magic would last a little bit longer. From Baltimore we headed to Detroit for the last series of the year, one-half game ahead of the Tigers; whoever took two out of three would win the East. We were not a real good road team and had lost five of six in Detroit earlier that year. But in September we had gone 7–4 away from Fenway and 20–9 overall, so I liked our chances.

Red Sox management did too; right after my win at Baltimore, they announced playoff tickets would go on sale at Fenway the next morning.

"I was in high school, and my brother, my friend George Papalandros, and me slept outside the ticket office on Jersey Street," remembers longtime Boston sportswriter Steve Buckley, who grew up a few miles from Fenway and now writes for *The Athletic.* "We were like 168th in line, so we thought we would get box seats behind home plate. We didn't know how things worked, with all the season-ticket holders getting first priority, and then a certain number of tickets going to the other team's fans, and then the celebrity requests. We wound up with seats in section three, way out in right field, but that was OK. It was the most excited Boston fans had been since '67."

The first game at Tiger Stadium was a battle of lefties: veteran Mickey Lolich of Detroit (21–11) versus our rookie John Curtis (11–7). Lolich, who won three times for the Tigers in the 1968 World Series, was a big-game guy again here—throwing a six-hitter with fifteen strikeouts. Curtis did a gutsy job for us, and we had a chance to get Lolich on the ropes early and quiet 51,500 fans. We just couldn't take advantage of it.

In the top of the third, with the Tigers up 1–0 on an Al Kaline homer, Harper and Aparicio both singled with one out. Then Yaz hit a deep drive over center fielder Mickey Stanley's head and took off like he might try for an inside-the-park homer. Harper scored easily from second, but Aparicio stumbled rounding the third-base bag and then, after righting himself, slipped on the grass trying to go home and fell straight down. He got up and scrambled back to third, just as Yaz was getting there. You can't have two guys on a base, and Yaz was tagged out. Aparicio was allowed to stay at third, but Reggie Smith struck out to end the inning.

So instead of being up 2–1 or 3–1, and still going for more, we were in a 1–1 game. Lolich never gave us another opening, and the Tigers got to Curtis and our relievers for three more runs—all driven in by Aurelio Rodriguez—to win 4–1. What's crazy is that even at thirty-eight years old, Aparicio was our best baserunner next to Harper. Earlier in his career, Luis led the American League nine straight years in stolen bases; he's in the Hall of Fame for his speed as much as his shortstop defense. But that's what makes baseball a great game: you never know what crazy stuff is going to happen. It's just not so great when it happens to *you*—especially as good a guy as Luis Aparicio.

This meant I had to win the next night or it was over, and I thought I could do it. I was pitching against Woodie Fryman, another tough lefty. Detroit had picked him up that summer from the Phillies, and he had been blowing teams away ever since—except for us. A couple weeks before I had beaten him, 7–2, at Fenway, so I was feeling pretty confident I could do it again.

There was another huge crowd at Tiger Stadium, and they were really loud and rowdy hoping they would get to celebrate a pennant. That didn't bother me either. I liked the challenge and had pitched well there. Plus we were due to break out offensively. Our bats had been quiet for a week, but we had pounded Fryman early in that Fenway game including a home run by Reggie.

We didn't do that this time, but things still looked good early when we scored an unearned run in the first on a botched double play. I held the fort into the middle innings and after five had only allowed four singles. It was 1–0.

Then we let the genie out of the bottle.

The Tigers tied it in the sixth on a walk, a sacrifice bunt, and an RBI single by Jim Northrup. In the seventh, with one out, McAuliffe doubled and Kaline came up. Later some sportswriters said that with first base open in a 1–1 game, we should have intentionally walked Kaline (a .313 hitter that year) and pitched to Duke Sims, a .239 career batter. I didn't want any of that. Kaline was a great ballplayer, especially in the clutch, but I had struck him out on three pitches his last time up. It was best against the best, which is how I liked it. I guess Kasko agreed because he didn't tell me to walk him.

This time Kaline got me roping a line-drive single to left to give the Tigers the lead. It was an inside pitch, on the bat handle, and I don't know how he hit it. But he did, so I give him credit. That's why he's a Hall of Famer. His hit knocked me out of the game, and we made a couple infield errors with Bill Lee on the mound later that inning to let in another run. It was now 3–1.

We had one last chance in the eighth. Yaz singled, and Rico hit a smash off Fryman to deep right. But Kaline caught it against the wall, and that was that. Chuck Seelbach came on in relief and shut us down in the ninth. That clinched the East for Detroit.

After the game, for the first time all year, I was too upset to talk. I'm not afraid to say I cried, and I wasn't the only one. That was my game to win, and I just couldn't get it done. Neither could our offense; in both of our last two losses, we had only gotten five hits and one run. Mr. Yawkey came into the clubhouse to console us, which I thought was a classy move; I'm sure he was frustrated, but he went around patting everyone on the back, thanking them for a great year.

When someone came over and told me that I had beaten Gaylord Perry for the AL ERA title, 1.9106 to 1.917, I said I didn't give a shit. I'd trade that for a pennant anytime. This is a team game. Maybe later I could appreciate that, and my 15-6 record, but not now.

It was a tough finish to a great season, especially when we won the next day and looked closely at the final standings. We had lost seven games from our schedule because of the strike, and Detroit lost six. The Tigers finished 86-70, and we were 85-70, so that one less game we didn't play could have been the difference. If we *had* played it and won, we would have been tied with the Tigers. Now we'd never know.

Still, looking back, there was a lot to be proud about. As a team, we went from playing lousy most of the first half to almost winning the division. As a pitcher, I went from not knowing my future with the Red Sox in spring training to being the key man on the staff during the pennant drive. The Boston fans embraced me, and I had a new lease on my baseball life. I planned to hang onto it as long as I could.

"Whatever fate awaits Tiant next year, Boston will never forget the image of this gallant Cuban with his trick deliveries and his sheer delight in pitching one great game after another," Larry Claflin wrote in the *Boston Herald*. "Thank you, Luis, for one of the most exciting stretches of pitching ever seen at Fenway Park."

I've hung onto one other thing from that year. Most of the guys shaved their beards and mustaches after the season, but Maria said she kind of liked my Fu Manchu-goatee combo. So I kept it. More than forty-five years later I've still got it, cut in the same style.

It's a little whiter now but a nice reminder of a very special time.

11

PUDGE AND ME

IT WAS IN 1971, DURING his summer of last chances, that Luis Tiant first got to know the catcher with whom he would soon be making headlines.

He and Carlton Fisk had briefly played against one another in spring training that year, when Tiant was still with the Twins and Fisk hoping to earn a roster spot with the Red Sox. Now they were teammates in Louisville, one young ball-player on the way up and one veteran trying to do whatever he could not to be released a third time in three months. Both, of course, had the same goal: promotion to Boston and the big leagues.

On the surface, they could not have been more opposite. Fisk was a stoic, outspoken farm boy from New Hampshire, a college graduate from a large family whose chiseled good looks seemed straight out of a turn-of-the-century base-ball card. His nickname of "Pudge," earned as a boy, had stuck long after his baby fat disappeared. He was a Red Sox fan from birth and a keen student of the game—which he believed should be played hard and well and without humor.

What did he think about the balding, fun-loving Cuban with the high-pitched laugh? Certainly Tiant was not what Fisk envisioned a ballplayer to look like; in fact, upon first seeing the team's newest pitcher stroll across the clubhouse with a towel across his barrel-chested waist and a big cigar in his mouth, Fisk might have thought his own nickname was better suited on the newcomer. Tiant's background did not offer much entryway for casual conversation; there were few, if any, Spanish-speaking men of color around Fisk's tiny hometown and no only children separated for a decade from their parents and other family members back in Cuba.

Tiant, however, had been what Fisk aspired to be: a major leaguer. Not just a guy on the roster, either, but a star. He had presence, confidence, and warmth that drew people to him. In their first days as a battery, Fisk also recognized in Tiant a level of baseball intelligence and will to win that matched his own. Neither took shit from anybody—even as a rookie, Fisk gave an earful to pitchers who didn't like his pitch selection—and the young catcher's own poise and leadership traits blossomed the more they played together.

By the fall of '71 they were doing so in Boston. And starting in 1972, when both were healthy, Carlton Fisk and Luis Tiant formed what was arguably the major league's best pitcher-catcher battery of the 1970s. When hot, each was capable of carrying a team on his back; together, they set a standard for excellence few could match.

In the end, they shared a sacred sixty-foot, six-inch bond through eight seasons and some of the most exciting games of the '70s or any decade. In time their families grew close as well, and today it is impossible for many Red Sox fans of a certain age to think of one without the other. That in itself is a great legacy.

More than forty years after "Tiant and Fisk" last appeared in a box score on the final day of the 1978 regular season, these two Red Sox legends are still linked together.

I THINK THE KEY for any pitcher is to get along with your catcher. Your catcher is like a spouse. You may get angry at me, but we understand each other. You have a mutual appreciation, and that's important. That way, you don't have to go too far. You just do what you have to do. By the time you've been pitching to him for a while, you really appreciate what he's trying to do. He's trying to help you; not let you make mistakes and lose the game. The more he does this, and does it *right*, the closer you get.

When I signed with the Red Sox and reported to Louisville, Carlton Fisk was already there. He was twenty-four and looked younger; I was thirty but felt older with my sore shoulder and not knowing what my future might be. I heard him talking about it once in an interview, and he said he appreciated it that I didn't come down to the minors like I was a king or anything because I had already pitched in the big leagues and did this and that. I was down there like a regular person who just wanted to pitch and make it back to the majors.

As Fisk remembers it:

"The rest of us we were all little minor leaguers, but he had been in the big leagues—he had experienced that big-league attention. The aura he gave off—the big-league aura—we could feel it. I mean, it wasn't like, 'I'm hurt, and you guys should understand that if I don't do good, it's because I'm hurt.' None of that. He'd be in the clubhouse smoking that big ole' cigar, and that was sort of the yardstick for being a big-leaguer. He was mature enough to smoke a cigar!"

Everybody called Fisk "Pudge," a nickname he picked up when he was chubby as a kid. But by the time we met, he definitely was not fat. He was six-foot-two, 210 pounds—solid, strong, and a great athlete. He had grown up in a big, sports-oriented family, and played basketball at the University of New Hampshire. That was his first dream; he wanted to play for the Boston *Celtics*, not the Red Sox, but settled on baseball when he stopped growing in college.

At the start, Fisk and I had one big thing in common: Darrell Johnson.

Pudge didn't have nearly as much catching experience as some guys when he got signed out of college in 1967. In New England, with the long winters, he played about fifteen games a season in high school. The kids in California, Florida, and Texas who he'd be competing with for jobs in the minors played year-round. His first few years in pro ball, he progressed through the ranks but didn't really stand out. At Double-A Pawtucket in 1970, he hit .229 with so-so power.

He went to spring training with the Red Sox in 1971, but manager Eddie Kasko wasn't impressed. "Fisk has a long road to go to make this club," Kasko said. "He can't do it on what he has shown this spring. He's got to go out and catch."

So he was sent to Triple-A Louisville. The manager there was Darrell Johnson—the same man who believed in me enough to encourage the Red Sox to sign me that spring with a goal of helping me get back to the majors. Fisk couldn't have gotten a better break.

Johnson spent nearly fifteen years as a journeyman catcher in the minors and the big leagues. He looked at Fisk's athleticism and determination and knew he could make a big leaguer out of him. The '71 season was his crash course, and Pudge picked up every ounce of information and expertise he could:

"I always worked hard, but I never knew what I was doing. He [John-son] taught me pitches, pitchers, sequences, and the difference between being a *catcher* and someone who goes behind the plate to catch and throw."

By the time I got to Louisville in mid-May, Johnson and Fisk had been together for a couple months. You could already see that Pudge was going to make it. He was the whole package, and *damn*, he was tough. He blocked the ball good, had a good arm, and hit the ball a long way.

But as talented as he was, he still understood how important it was to keep gaining as much knowledge as he could about every aspect of hitting and pitching. He saw me as someone else who could help him grow:

> "Luis had a lot of experience before he came to Boston, and I tried to learn from that. He had to learn how to pitch *again*. When he was with Cleveland, he was a power pitcher. When he came to Boston, he had to 'pitch pitch.' So that was what was so special about him. He had a passion for his half of the game, I had one for mine, and we blended well."

Fisk respected me and the way I played the game, and pretty quickly I came to respect him too. From the start, we got along beautifully. When you won, he'd come running to the mound and hug you. He wanted to knock you down, he was so excited. I liked that. We clicked really good.

Boston called me up in June of '71, before Fisk. I had been a starting pitcher nearly all my career, but when they brought me up and I lost a bunch of games they put me in the bullpen. It was different for me—a different way to think, a different way to prepare yourself. You've been mostly a starter, and your body gets used to it. Now when you try to do something different, it's hard to control your mind in that particular way.

Me, I still thought I could start. Kasko gave me some chances, but I didn't have much luck. I was throwing the ball good, I just couldn't get used to that reliever mentality. In September, when the Red Sox knew we couldn't catch the Orioles in the American League East, management brought up a bunch of young guys including Fisk. This was great because we got into games together and had a chance to get to know each other on the big stage.

Fisk agrees: "That little time we had together that first year really meant a lot to each of us. It just kind of blossomed at the big-league level."

Pudge made an impression right away, batting .313 in 14 games and hitting a couple home runs. His very first game was against the Yankees, who had a great young catcher of their own in Thurman Munson. Their names would be tied together an awful lot in the years to come, and I feel lucky that I was able to catch them both—in my opinion, the two best all-around catchers in the American League during the '70s.

By now Kasko could see Fisk was for real. His batting eye and his defense were both much improved after the summer with Johnson, and Kasko felt Pudge could be a team leader. That's what you need at that position. The two main Red Sox catchers in 1971 were Bob Montgomery and Duane Josephson; both were really solid, but neither was a guy who could stay healthy or consistent enough to play 120-plus games behind the plate. Boston had not had a "regular" catcher like that in a long time. They are always hard to find.

Like me, Fisk also had a big fan in the front office who thought he could do it. "He has a chance to be one of the best," Sox owner Tom Yawkey said after watching Fisk that September.

Not everyone was *that* confident, but it was thought that Fisk would get the starting catcher's job in 1972. During spring training in Winter Haven, he hit very poorly, but what I noticed most about him was how hard he worked to get and stay in shape. I'm sure Kasko noticed it too. Pudge was always stretching and doing all kind of exercises to keep his body limber and strong. I did plenty of stretching myself, and running, but most pitchers and catchers didn't back then. When they did, you noticed it.

Fisk made the team in '72, but his batting slump held him back when the regular season started. The Red Sox carried three catchers in April, and Pudge was third in line. Josephson was the starter, but he got hurt early on and Montgomery went in. Monty was a good hitter but had trouble throwing out runners. After the Indians stole a bunch of bases off him in one game, Kasko gave Pudge a start. He had a triple in his first game, and then two more hits in his second. After that the job was his, and Monty spent the rest of the 1970s doing a great job backing Fisk up.

Pudge was an excellent hitter from the start, and within a few months was leading the team in home runs and among the American League's top ten in batting, doubles, slugging, and triples. But what was always most important to him was his defense and controlling the game from behind the plate. Watching him emerge as a leader that year was an amazing thing. Here was a rookie—*a rookie*—who wasn't afraid to chew out star players if he didn't think they were hustling. Pudge only knew one way to play the game— HARD—and that earned him the respect of everyone.

Part of it was his intensity. He was such a fierce competitor that he didn't care if he was the rookie and you were a veteran. As a pitcher, if you made a mistake in the game, he'd rifle the ball back to you extra-hard or go out there and chew you out. That was different than other catchers I had who would just get a new ball from the umpire and toss it back to you. They wouldn't go out there and yell, "You better throw that ball where you're *supposed* to throw it!" He had guts.

One thing he did sometimes drove me nuts. He would throw the ball back at me so hard my hand would get red. I'd call him out and tell him, "You see my hand? Who's pitching, you or me?" He'd just cuss me out.

One day at Fenway, maybe our second or third year together, he did this a bunch of times in one game. My hand was stinging, and I decided I finally had enough.

"Next time you throw the ball back to me like that," I said, "I'm going to let it go through. I'm not going to catch it."

He wasn't buying it.

"You do that," he yelled back, "and I'll kick your big Black behind!"

This didn't scare me a bit.

"You're not going to do shit! You just get back there [behind the plate]— don't give me no bullcrap!"

Maybe he didn't *think* I would do it, but I did. He threw the ball back to me, and I let it go through—straight into centerfield. There was nobody on base, or I would never have done it. That didn't matter to him. He stomped out to the mound and chewed me out. He threw everything at me, really cussing me out good.

I waited for him to finish. Then I looked him right in the eye.

"Listen, I don't want to hear no more crap. I told you I'd let it go, and I did. The best thing you can do is go back to home plate, put your goddamn mask on, and catch. You take care of *your* business, and I'll take care of *mine!*"

Then I put a final stamp on the conversation.

"You mess with me, I'm going to cross you up and break all your goddamn fingers."

Fisk has his own version of that story:

"Oh sure, I remember that!

"Luis said 'AYE-TELL-AH-YOO!...AYE-TELL-AH-YOO!...I'm going to let it go!!'

"Ah, 'OK'," I said. I really didn't think he'd do it.

"Then I whipped it back hard a few more times, you know, daring him.

"If there were guys on base, or it was an intense part of the game, I knew he wouldn't do it. But that's the fun part about being out there with Tiant. I challenged him—'C'mon, Luis, just throw the F-ing ball! POW! POW!'

"He didn't like it very much, but then all of a sudden when you do that…I wouldn't call it waking him up, or whatever. But then he knows *I'm* serious about what I think of his game, and when he feels comfortable about me getting on his butt, *that's* when *he* feels comfortable letting the ball go through into centerfield.

"So he did—and I got out there fast.

"'You SON OF A BITCH!' I yelled. 'What did you just do?!'

"He just stared at me.

"'AYE-TELL-AH-YOO I would!…AYE-TELL-AH-YOO I would!'"

You see, we could talk like that. We never got to the point where we were going to really fight or anything. We went at it a little bit, but me and him, we got along great. He understood when to push me and when to lay off:

> "You know, that's part of the deal—part of me challenging Luis or any other pitcher on my pitching staff. You challenge them, and you ask them to do something maybe above what they *think* they can do. Then they *do* it, and all of a sudden their level of confidence rises. It's all part of the gamesmanship. The more he asks, the more you give, and the more he gives, the more you ask."

When you have a catcher like Fisk you can count on him to make almost all the calls. You know he's not trying to screw you. He's trying to protect you. He wants you to win more than *you* want to win. If I didn't want to throw a pitch, I didn't throw it. I'd shake him off. But I didn't do it too much. He knew me very well—and he knew what I could do.

We'd go after hitters and do certain things. He'd just put down those fingers, and I'd throw it. He knew me. We didn't even have to talk much in the dugout. He and I should have been twins; we think almost the same way. It was like we could read each other's minds.

One time I did surprise him was when I first decided in 1972—in the middle of a game!—to change my delivery and start turning myself all the way around, shaking my head and hands, and adding a hesitation pitch. He was a good sport about it, and he did a great job handling whatever I threw at him.

A few months later, after I had won ten of eleven games, Tim Horgan of the *Boston Herald* asked Pudge to tell him how we worked so well together. This is what he told him:

"Luis has only four basic pitches—fast ball, curve, slider, and change-up. Luis also has about four variations on each pitch. He might go straight over the top, or drop his arm down a little, or come in from the side. I just use the four standard signs for fast ball, curve, sinker, and change. Luis decides whether he'll come in overhand or sidearm, fast or slow. Oh, yes. He also has maybe six different speeds on his curveball and change-up. I never know how Luis will wind up. He decides on his own."

Forty-five years later, he looked back with the wisdom of age and explained it again:

"Luis's delivery was one of his weapons. We talked about all the pitches he had and how deception is the key to getting guys out. It's not power pitching, and it's not soft pitching. It's the back-and-forth, the little games you play with the hitter. And that was one of the games he played. I had never, ever seen anything like it before, and I was a young player then. I played a long time and never once came close to seeing it afterwards. It's kind of a lost art, to tell you the truth."

Fisk was the key to our late drive for the AL East title in 1972. Besides doing a great job with me and all the pitchers, he hit .293 with 22 home runs, a .538 slugging percentage, and won a Gold Glove for his defense. He even led the league with nine triples, which you don't expect from a catcher. It didn't surprise *me*—I knew how good he was—but a lot of people were caught off guard. He was better than they expected, and he won the American League Rookie of the Year. It was a unanimous vote, the first time that had ever happened. I was voted the Comeback Player of the Year, and both me and Pudge got a lot of MVP votes.

I think going through that experience together—from uncertainty one year to almost winning a division title—solidified our relationship. He had a lot of respect for me, I had a lot of respect for him, and we knew we made each other better. The way he commanded a game, and the way he pushed me, made me a winner:

> "We fed off each other; we understood each other. We demanded things from each other—and expected things from each other. When it comes to situations where the game is on the line, you know you can work as a team. You can get it done, knowing that whatever I feel in a situation that might work, he trusted me enough to go with it—or if he *didn't* like what I was doing, then I trusted *him* enough to know that *he* knew what he was doing. Obviously, he did."

Our managers, and our teammates, felt comfortable leaving much of the decision making of the game up to us. They knew us and knew we could handle it.

"They both had huge personalities and are really two dynamic dudes," says Fred Flynn, whose bat and amazing catches in centerfield helped us both. "That's what you want, really. You want those guys because they're controlling the flow of the game—they're controlling what's going on."

The fans saw it too.

"They had a bond, and that came through," says Kevin Vahey, a tremendous Red Sox fan and later a Fenway park cameraman. "There was love, and a lot of it was kind of comical. Carlton claimed that at times he couldn't understand a thing Luis was saying."

Even my ten-year-old son could see how special things were between me and Pudge from the beginning.

"They really seemed to hit it off, even in Louisville," says Luis Jr. "Their chemistry just came naturally. Fisk was probably one of the only guys who could tell my dad what to do on the mound. He knew how to call and control a game, and he knew when my dad was on and when he had to reach into his back pocket to come up with something to get a guy out."

Little Luis is right. It got to the point, over time, where Pudge knew my stuff so well that he could tell in the first inning if we were going to have to make adjustments.

> "There are three things involved with getting people out: velocity, ball movement, and location. If you've got two out of three, you've got a

chance to get guys out. Luis might have two of three things involved on a given day, and if he's got a couple of those things, then you try and work around everything else. I like to think that's my job, as his catcher, to try and use those two things to get people out.

"You kind of feel it around. First of all, you go out there expecting to get the same pitcher you always get. Then if you find out you *don't*, well then you have to work from there. Then sometimes as the game goes on, now you've got all three of them—or one goes away and another comes in.

"Some people thought he was just a trickster out there, but Luis was not just that. He was always thinking ahead, and so was I."

Another big part of our relationship was built around how we felt about each other off the field. I respected Pudge as a man who took care of his family—a good father, son, and husband. He respected those same things in me. I saw how hard he worked to come back when he was hurt, especially when he tore up his knee really bad in '74 and a lot of people said he might never play again. And he knew what *I* had to do to come back from my shoulder injury and to deal with racism and being separated from my family.

Over time, we got much closer. Our families got to know each other and our kids. A ballclub is like a family anyway, but I always felt a special connection with Pudge because we spent so much time in each other's heads. Sometimes it was like we were one person.

Pudge knows just what I mean:

"You would think it would end when baseball ends—or when you go your way and he goes his way. I went to a different team, and he went to a different team. And you would think that all of a sudden your teammate becomes your competitor. But that has never happened with him, or any of the guys I played with in Boston. Maybe it's because we're all in the same generation and because we played together so much. So you identify with those situations, and that identity never leaves. You always consider them your friends because they *were* your friends. Even if you only see them once or twice a year, it's like you're long lost buddies. That kind of thing never goes away, I think."

We really went to war together. We played during a time when there were some real super teams in baseball, and we took them all on—the Oakland A's of 1971-75, the Cincinnati Reds' "Big Red Machine" of 1970-76, and the Yankees of 1976-78. On paper people thought we couldn't match them, especially the Reds with all those Hall of Famers in their lineup. But we showed we belonged in their class:

> "It was a challenge, for sure, and that's the great part about Luis—he was up for a challenge and motivated by that challenge. And you see what happened. He was as good as anybody against the big guys in a big game. Even when he didn't have his good stuff, he wasn't going to give in or give up."

I was so happy when Pudge made the Hall of Fame in 2000, and the Red Sox retired his number, twenty-seven, that same summer. He deserved both honors because nobody worked harder or got more out of their ability. It was great to be invited back and be a part of the number retirement ceremony because those were the days when I was coaching in Georgia and wasn't around Fenway too much. I was also excited when the Red Sox asked me to "reverse roles" and be his catcher when Pudge threw out the ceremonial first pitch that day. I'd actually been thinking about suggesting it before they offered.

When I heard what Fisk said in his induction speech in Cooperstown, I was very grateful—and very honored.

"I played with Rico, and Yaz, and Dewey, and Freddie, and Spaceman, and Jim Ed, and Rooster," he said. "But the guy I had the most fun playing with, catching for, was Luis Tiant. The best and most colorful player I've ever caught, and the best and most colorful ever, I think, in a Red Sox uniform."

Later, he said it much more simply: "If I had one game I had to win, Luis Tiant would start it."

And he would most definitely catch it.

12

HEART AND SOUL

HIS 1972 COMEBACK HAD SHOCKED the sports world and earned him legions of fans throughout Boston and New England. Now Luis Tiant had to prove it wasn't a fluke.

Armed with a new contract and a spot atop the Red Sox rotation, Tiant set out to show his rehabilitated pitching arm could hold up to the rigors of a full season. The early results were mixed, but he had learned through all his trials not to let the good times or the slumps weigh too heavy on him. His teammates in Boston, as they had in Cleveland and Minnesota, admired Tiant's ability to not let himself be undone by a bad outing. They delighted in how he could make light of any situation and keep things loose. And they loved his determination.

"I think Luis never understood that he could not beat somebody, no matter what the possibilities were," says outfielder Bernie Carbo, a teammate starting in 1974. "He had the air about him that when he took that ball and went on that mound, you weren't going to beat him. Luis *expected* to win."

While they didn't share a clubhouse with Tiant, fans saw these same traits on display whether watching from the Fenway stands or their living rooms: the hunger, the humor, and the ease with which he moved from one game to another. Boston's past baseball icons had not usually fit this mold. Ted Williams made headlines for his tempestuousness as much as his hitting, and was often misunderstood or maligned by the sportswriters he scorned. Carl Yastrzemski, while admired for the unflappable, workmanlike way he approached each at-bat, felt largely unapproachable to the fans who idolized him. Tiant, in how he looked, talked, and acted, was a more refreshing, fun type of hero.

As one fan recalls, all you had to do was open the Sports page and see a photo of Tiant sitting in a whirlpool, with a cigar in his mouth, and you felt all was right with the world. The Fu Manchu mustache he first grew in 1972, combined with the scowl he gave batters, led legendary sportswriter Red Smith to describe Tiant's appearance as something akin to "Pancho Villa after a tough night of looting and burning."

Luis Tiant did no looting or burning for the Red Sox in 1973 and '74, but he did just about everything else—and the fans loved him for it.

LIKE I SAID BEFORE, being an only child, my friends were my brothers when I was growing up. We went through everything together—the good and the bad. Sure, life could be tough. Some of us were born poor, and things started tightening up for everyone when Castro first came in. There were times we got into fights. But no matter what shit we had to deal with, we always found a way to have fun. If one guy was down, the others picked him up.

To me, a baseball team should be the same thing. You are living and playing together day after day, traveling from one city to another. For more than half of the year, you're with each other more than you're with your family. It's a grind, and you need to keep things loose, so you don't forget why you're there. No matter what color you are, or where you come from, you all have one thing in common: *love for the game.* If you don't, you're in the wrong business.

Losing the pennant on the final weekend in 1972 hurt a lot, but it didn't take away from what we had accomplished. Not just that we were in the race until the finish, or that a bunch of us had good years. We could feel positive about the season because we had started bonding more and more as a team the further the summer went along. From being in last place in late June, and still under .500 in early August, we had played .635 baseball for two months to put ourselves in position to win.

We didn't get it done—*I* didn't get it done—but we gave it our best shot and felt really positive about the future.

What's the secret to good chemistry? I believe the key is not letting yourself or your teammates get too high when you're winning or too down when you're losing. Don't get too full of yourself, and don't get too down on yourself. If you remember that you're playing a game that is meant to be *fun,* and is not a matter of life and death, you can ride out the slumps and losing streaks a lot easier.

I never considered myself a leader in terms of being a rah-rah type of guy. Although I always played as hard as anyone *on* the field, I knew you also needed to find ways to ease the tension off of it. During my first year in the minor leagues, even when I couldn't understand most of what my teammates were saying, I learned I could make them laugh—and that broke the ice. It also helped me deal with all the racist bullshit going on around me and being separated from my family in Cuba. Laughing sure beat crying, and I noticed something else: the looser I was, the better I pitched.

In Cleveland we had a lot of funny guys on the club, but it was tough to joke around when things were so bad. The manager didn't like to see you laughing when you were in eighth place, not that I think there was any connection between the two. In Minnesota we had a great team *and* a lot of fun, so I knew it was possible to have both.

When I came to the Red Sox in '71, I figured they would be loose too. They always had big crowds, a competitive team, and an owner who paid them really well. But it wasn't like that. Things were kind of divided in the clubhouse; some guys hung out in one group, some guys in another, and the place was pretty quiet except for all the sportswriters asking questions. No loud music, no laughing, and no fooling around—especially when we lost. Nobody *likes* to lose, but what good does it do to let it eat you up? You got to get that shit out of your head so you can try and win the next day.

Once I was established in Boston, and especially once I started winning, I made it my mission to change the mood in and around the Red Sox clubhouse.

Nobody was safe. Tommy Harper, maybe because he was my oldest friend on the club, was my favorite guy to torture. Each day I would come into the clubhouse, wrap myself in a towel, grab a cigar and a newspaper, and head to the toilet to take a dump. When I was done, I'd get up, yell "Bye, bye, TOMMMMEEE!" so everyone could hear, and then flush it away. When I came out smiling, it broke up the room. Tommy always acted upset, which made it even funnier.

Then there was the time I got a dead fish, dressed it up in a little baseball uniform, and stuck a tongue depressor in its mouth so its lips curled upward in a smile. I propped the fish up in Harper's locker and had everybody wave "Hello, Tommy!" as they walked by it.

Yastrzemski was another regular victim. The two of us had already gone at it pretty good in the past—remember the three strikeouts in '67 and the extra BP I razzed him about?—but now he had me on his ass all the time. Yaz had this wrinkled old tan overcoat we called "The Columbo Coat" after the TV detective who wore one just like it. I told him it was a damn tragedy to see a superstar making $165,000 a year wearing a coat like that, and so I hid it every chance I could. One time I threw it out a bus window, but the damn thing found its way back; maybe he just got another one out of a dumpster somewhere.

Yaz and Harper were my main hits, but other guys would get hot feet or ice water over their heads whenever the time was right. Pretty soon I had to start watching my own back, and that was fine. Nobody ever got me with an exploding cigar in the big leagues—I learned my lesson back in the minors, but you can be sure I checked.

Nicknames were also always good for a laugh. They came natural to me, and I tried to be creative with them. I couldn't call Yastrzemski "Columbo" because that would have been too easy. When I saw him, it was always, "Hiya, Polack!"

Carlton Fisk was a big, handsome guy with a chiseled chin and broad shoulders, and he walked with kind of a swagger. So he was "Frankenstein."

Rick Miller was one pale dude, so he was "Walking Dead."

Doug Griffin, the thinnest guy on the team, was "Skeleton."

And if I couldn't think of something else, I just went with "Hey, Mullion!" That's good for anyone—it's baseball-ese for ugly.

"He called me that all the time," said John Kennedy, "and if you did something funny on the field, he would get on you. I struck out one time and had a really, really unbelievably awful swing. I came in to the dugout, and a lot of guys didn't want to say anything to me. Not Luis. He came right over.

"'Hey Mullion—that's the shortest stoke I've ever seen,' he said. 'You went from one shoulder to the other.' I just started laughing.

"Pitchers got it from him too. If a guy let up a huge home run, Luis might go up to him after the game or the next day and say, 'Hey, show me how you hold that pitch.' It would crack the guy up."

Cracking guys up *loosened* things up, and pretty soon everyone else was talking shit and pulling pranks. Guys were snipping each other's ties, nailing shoes to the floor, and waiting outside the showers with buckets of ice water. I'll never forget the time Luis Aparicio went to put on his $500 suit at the end of the season before flying home to Venezuela, and the arms and legs fell off. Yaz had paid a clubhouse boy to cut it up.

The important thing is this: with all that crazy shit going on, it was hard to get too wound up before a game—or too down after a loss. It kept things light and brought guys together.

"The Sox of my early years were somber clubs," Yaz later said. "Winning changed that, but Tiant helped make us nutty. I know that I became a different character in the locker room. When did it start? Maybe with the first hotfoot. Maybe with the first scissored tie. Come to think of it, some of the stuff we did was scary, maybe even dangerous. But it was great fun."

Sometimes I was funny even when I wasn't trying to be. This had been going on since my minor league days because of my high-pitched Cuban accent and the way I pronounced some words in English. Here is where the writers came in handy.

If I thought something was stupid, or wrong, it was "BOOL-CHEET!"

When I looked at myself in the mirror, and liked what I saw, I'd say I was, "One good-lookeen sonafabeech."

And if I was upset because another damn airplane was taking too long to get off the ground, I'd yell out my favorite Ray Charles line: "Heet Ze Road, Yack!"

Did it bother me when sportswriters quoted me in broken English or made fun in print of how I pronounced words? Not really. Once you've been called a monkey or a dumb Cuban nigger you get a thick skin, and I don't think they did it to make me sound stupid anyway. They were just trying to give the fans an idea of *how* I sounded, which I know could be pretty funny sometimes. (For the sake of my readers, and because I speak English much better now, I've fixed the broken English in my old quotes.)

One thing I will tell you; I might not have spoken the language as well as a lot of other guys, but I wasn't *dumb*. After I proved down the stretch drive that I could still be a big winner, I got myself a nice raise for 1973. My goal was to buy my family a house—a real house—in the Boston area. We were always living out of rented apartments, me by myself to start each season and then the four of us when Maria brought the kids up from Mexico City after school let out. I wanted someplace with a yard for Isa and Little Luis to play in and a big kitchen for Maria. Now those dreams were a little closer.

After another year of winter ball in Venezuela, I was set to prove that the second half of the '72 season had not been a fluke. It was the first time in four years I knew I had a set job in the starting rotation entering the year, and I was in no mood to give it up. I drove my new Cadillac nearly twenty hours straight, all the way from Monroe, Louisiana to Winter Haven, Florida, to make it to the first day of spring training. A few hours after pulling into the parking lot at Chain O' Lakes Park, I was in uniform and out on the field pitching to minor league catcher Vic Correll.

"He threw fast balls, curves, changes, and about everything," Correll told reporters that day. "He must have some kind of arm to do that."

You're damn right. I wasn't fooling around.

The big news in camp was our newest slugger, Orlando Cepeda. A former National League Rookie of the Year and MVP, "Cha-Cha" was a fantastic hitter with lots of experience in the outfield and first base. For us, though, he would be filling a new role: designated hitter. This was the first year of the DH, a move voted in by American League owners to generate more offense—and hopefully more fans—by adding another bat to the lineup in place of the pitcher's spot. Cepeda, who had 358 career home runs but two bad knees, was perfect for the role. The proud but beaten-up son of Ponce, Puerto Rico, would not have to play the field at all, just go up and take his swings.

Most pitchers were happy with the DH. They were glad to not have to worry about hitting anymore, or even taking batting practice, since they were so lousy at it. Me, I always liked being in the lineup; I was a better hitter than most pitchers, partly because I hit all winter in Venezuela, and I enjoyed the challenge of trying to help myself. But I also knew the change would help me conserve my legs for the long season and keep me in close games longer—since I wouldn't ever need to be lifted for a pinch-hitter. Plus there was less chance of getting injured by a beanball or while running the bases.

After Eddie Kasko named me the Opening Day starter, I became forever linked to the designated hitter. We started the season at home on a windy, damp afternoon against the Yankees, and Ron Blomberg came up in the top of the first inning as the first DH to bat in a regular season game. I was off to a lousy start and had already allowed two hits and two walks, but thanks to a double play it was still scoreless with the bases loaded. Then Blomberg also walked, forcing in a run.

The Yankees wound up scoring three in the inning, but Fisk took up right where he left off the year before with two home runs and six RBIs on the day, and I settled down to pick up a 15-5 victory. We beat New York big the next day too behind four hits and a homer from Yastrzemski, and after we won our first four games—all against the Yankees, including a walk-off victory on Cepeda's first shot over the Green Monster—fans figured they were in for a fun season.

Then we lost six straight.

That pretty much summed up 1973. We were up and down all year long, with several winning streaks keeping us close but bad stretches doing us in. Age had caught up to the Tigers, but the Orioles were back in their usual spot on top, and we only held first place a handful of times all season—never after mid-July. For the second straight year we played much better in the second half of the season than the first, but in the end, we just couldn't quite catch Baltimore. In late August, when we won ten of twelve games, we actually went from four to five games back since the Orioles were winning fourteen straight at the same time.

We finished 89-73, the best record by a Red Sox team since the '67 pennant-winners. A big reason was our much-improved offense. Cepeda never had to play even one inning in the field and was named the first "Designated Hitter of the Year" after batting .289 with 20 homers and 89 RBI. Fisk slumped at the plate in the later months but still hit 26 homers to lead the team and was great defensively. Yaz hit .296 with 95 runs batted in, Reggie Smith batted .303, and my old buddy Tommy Harper led the league with fifty-four stolen bases to set a new Boston record. Tommy also led the team in runs scored and hit *seventeen* homers, but I still got on his ass every chance I could.

Our pitching was decent, with a rotation that included me, Marty Pattin, John Curtis, and Bill Lee, but for much of the season we lacked an ace—a role expected to be mine. A groin injury dogged me during the first half of the year, and when I lost to Detroit on June 26 my record was 8-8. Willie Horton's homer off me that night was my twentieth allowed in seventeen starts, and my ERA was 4.09—more than twice my 1.91 mark from the year before. People were wondering whether I was on the downslide again.

Then my groin got better, and as the weather heated up, so did I.

Starting on July 1, I went 7-1 over my next nine games to help put us briefly into first place. Then, after losing three starts in which I allowed a combined seven runs, I ran off four more straight wins in September.

A year after I had come up with the new twists on my delivery, guys on other teams were still trying to figure out how to deal with it.

"His motion used to drive you crazy; you were never comfortable hitting off of him with the way he turned around," remembers Mike Andrews, who was on the White Sox then. "You never knew what he was going to do next."

Even the way I set myself before delivering frustrated batters.

"Normally, when a pitcher is in his stretch, he has to come to a set and then pitch—or step off the rubber," says Andrews. "He can't break his hands apart again or do anything else, or it's a balk. But Luis would set *three* times, keeping his hands together and drooping them down lower and lower each time. Because he did it the same way, every time, the umpires allowed it. I decided the best way to deal with it was to keep my bat on my shoulder until he got to his third set, and then pick it up and go.

"It didn't help much, but it was better than just freezing, ready to pull the trigger."

In the last few weeks of the season I had two shots to get my twentieth victory, something I had not done since 1968. Joe Coleman, the same guy who beat me in the AL East-clincher the year before, stopped us 3-0 on a one-hitter in my first try, at Detroit, but in my last start of the year I beat Milwaukee, 11-2, to get number twenty. I also recorded my two hundredth strikeout of the year during the game, making me just the fourth Red Sox pitcher to ever reach that mark (joining Cy Young, Smokey Joe Wood, and Jim Lonborg).

"I had brought this cigar with me to Detroit," I joked with reporters when I lit up after the game, "but I had to cart it home."

The fact I reached both milestones at Fenway Park was extra special. Ever since my rookie year with the Indians, I had loved pitching there; now that it was my home ballpark, I felt that way more than ever. In the five years between 1972 and '76, my Fenway records would be 10-1, 11-7, 13-5, 11-6, 11-6—a .690 winning percentage. Away from Boston, I felt I could compete with anybody; *in* Boston, I felt almost unbeatable.

A lot of pitchers have trouble with Fenway because of that left-field wall only three hundred and ten feet from home plate. I looked at it this way: The same chance I have, the other guy has. The same *he* has, *I* have. You make a mistake, you pay. If you *don't* make a mistake, you've got a chance. Thinking that way makes you a better pitcher. You know you can't make too many mistakes, and you have to make adjustments to your pitches and learn how to pitch here.

I found out when I came to the Red Sox that the best chance for a pitcher at Fenway was to pitch the hitters inside. Take advantage of the fact the ballpark has such little foul territory and the stands are so close. Let a guy hit the ball foul two miles, and then you go away, or you come back up and in. I started pitching much better that way. They tell you, "Don't throw a change-up inside to right-handed hitters," but I used to throw a change inside. They hit them two miles into the right corner, a foul ball WAYYYYYYYY over there to the right of the Pesky Pole. "OK," I'd say to myself, "that's just a strike. Now go back inside and get them out."

If you outthink the hitter, and don't pitch scared, you're already ahead of the game.

My final 1973 record of 20-13, with a 3.34 ERA and 206 strikeouts, sounded much more like an ace than 8-8. More importantly, with 272 innings and twenty-three complete games—fourth in the league—I had proven my arm was all the way back. It had been five years since my 21-9 year at Cleveland, and after all I had been through, twenty wins was much sweeter the second time around.

Unfortunately, it was not enough to save Eddie Kasko's job. In Boston fans were getting really hungry for a winner, and after four years of strong teams that couldn't quite do it, Kasko was fired. The only consolation was that his replacement as manager was Darrell Johnson, who like Kasko had encouraged the Red Sox to give me a shot back in '71. Johnson had been managing in Boston's minor-league system for the past three seasons, so a lot of the young guys on the team had played for him before. He knew them better than anybody, so it was a good choice.

For me, personally, it had been a greatly satisfying season—but I was also *very* tired. Combined with winter ball, I had thrown nearly four hundred innings in less than a year. For the first time since the Indians made me sit out during the winter of 1968-69, I decided to stay home and rest until spring training. Maria and the kids were happy to have me.

Just like the last off-season, when we picked up Cepeda, we added an aging superstar to our roster heading into the 1974 season. San Francisco Giants pitcher Juan Marichal, "the Dominican Dandy," was a six-time twenty-game winner who, like me, was a right-hander with a very distinctive windup in which he kicked his leg way up in the air. He had gone 6-16 and 11-15 the previous two seasons, but his stuff was better than his record. The hope was that, like Cepeda, he could have a bounce-back year in switching to a new team.

If he did, Cha-Cha wouldn't be around to see it. Right at the end of spring training, GM Dick O'Connell shocked everybody by releasing Cepeda and Luis Aparicio—two future Hall of Famers—on the same day. Even though Aparicio was about to turn forty, and Cepeda was thirty-six with those lousy knees, both had excellent seasons in '73 and were projected to be starters again. Bobby Bolin, our best relief pitcher the previous season with a 3-1 record and fifteen saves, was also let go. He was thirty-five.

I was sad to see all three of these classy veterans go, but I understood what was happening. Darrell Johnson had seen up close all the great talent in the

Boston farm system, and O'Connell was now giving him the opportunity to turn those young players into big leaguers by removing the guys blocking their way.

The place we loaded up on veterans for '74 was on the pitching staff. In addition to Marichal, we picked up two more well-seasoned National League starters—righties Rick Wise and Reggie Cleveland—in a pair of trades with the St. Louis Cardinals that cost us All-Star slugger Reggie Smith and *three* young pitchers: Lynn McGlothen, John Curtis, and Mike Garman.

Now in my fourth year with Boston, I was quickly becoming one of the most-seasoned members of the club. I wanted to set a good example for the new guys, but I had my second straight stinker of an Opening Day—letting up seven runs at Milwaukee. It took my Cuban countryman Diego Segui, another veteran we had picked up who could start or relieve, to bail me out with his amazing forkball in a 9-8 win. But that was just the start of my problems during the first month; we lost five of my first seven starts, and my ERA shot up near 6.00.

As was often the case, the home fans at Fenway boosted me up when I needed them. The Yankees were reemerging as one of the real powerhouses in the league, but I tamed them on May 9 with a three-hitter in which I retired the last fifteen men in a row and didn't allow a single runner to reach second base. The final score of 2-0 marked my first shutout in more than a year; even though I had twenty-three complete games in '73, and twenty wins, I somehow didn't have even one shutout. I made up for that in '74 with seven of them, my most since racking up nine with Cleveland in '68—and good enough to lead the AL for the third time.

It was that first one that really got me going. Starting with the win over the Yankees, I went 18-4 with five shutouts, seventeen complete games, and an ERA of 2.22 through the middle of August. More importantly, our team was in the thick of the pennant race, boosted by great play from some of the youngsters O'Connell was counting on when he released Cepeda and Aparicio.

Rookie Rick Burleson, who took over for Aparicio at short, had a fantastic glove and a fiery temper that sparked the team just like Fisk had two years before; I was the first to call Rick "Rooster" because of his aggressiveness and confidence, and it stuck. Dwight Evans, now the regular right fielder, was also outstanding defensively with great range and a tremendous throwing arm. He showed real promise as a right-handed hitter too, but the most complete player on the team next to Yaz was probably Fisk—tremendous at the plate and behind it. Cecil Cooper, Rick Miller, Juan Beniquez, and Bernie Carbo, all under twenty-seven, did their part while dividing up much of the outfield and DH load once filled by Cepeda and Smith.

Their contributions and their energy helped make up for what was not a very impressive team statistically.

The pitching, expected to be a strength, was more of a mixed bag. Left-hander Bill Lee had become an innings-eater who won seventeen games for the second straight year with his great sinker ball, but Cleveland was inconsistent, and Wise missed most of the season after injuring his triceps muscle in his very first start. Marichal showed flashes of his old brilliance, but his arm was running out of gas after nearly twenty years of pro ball. He pitched less than sixty innings and combined with Wise for just eight wins. Our team ERA of 3.72 was worse than the AL average, and Lee and I were the only regular starters with winning records. Segui led our relievers with ten saves.

The offense didn't jump out at you either. Yaz and Rico Petrocelli, the two holdovers from 1967, tied for the team high with fifteen home runs—the lowest number to lead a Red Sox club since World War II. Our 109 total homers was the least by a team calling tiny Fenway Park home in nearly twenty-five years and was a huge drop-off from the 147 we hit just one season before. One reason for the big letdown was also our biggest setback of the year: when Fisk tore ligaments in his left knee in a home plate collision on June 28. Pudge was out for the season, and many predicted his career—at least as a catcher—was over at age twenty-six.

It says something real positive about our team that even with our low power numbers, pitching problems, and with our best hitter and field general out of the lineup, we still managed to hold onto first place in the AL East most of the summer. In the case of Fisk's injury, two catchers stepped up to fill in: rookie Tim Blackwell and veteran backup Bob Montgomery. Neither hit much, but both did a great job defensively while holding the pitching staff together. That was how it went for most of the season; everyone on the roster contributed. Here's another example: although nobody in our lineup drove in even eighty runs, *as a team* we led the league in runs scored. It was a real group effort and beautiful to see.

Two games stand out for me from that season. The first was on June 14 against the California Angels in Anaheim. The Angels were not a strong offensive team, but with two outstanding young power pitchers in Nolan Ryan and Frank Tanana, they wound up in a lot of low-scoring contests. I was up against Ryan that night, and my arm felt great; I got the first nine men in order, and although I allowed three runs in the fourth inning—due in part to my own error throwing to second base—I locked things down after that.

Ryan, who had set a big-league record with 383 strikeouts the year before, was always overpowering but not always accurate. Through eight innings he had walked seven of our guys, struck out fifteen, and had a 3-1 lead. Yaz saved us with a two-run homer in the top of the ninth, and then I got a double-play grounder in the bottom of the frame to keep things tied and send it to extra innings at 3-3.

These days a manager will usually pull his starter after one hundred pitches no matter how well he's doing, but nobody worried about pitch counts then. The game stayed tied through the tenth, eleventh, twelve, thirteenth, and FOURTEENTH innings, and all Darrell Johnson did was ask me how I felt at the end of each one. I said I was fine, so he left me in.

Ryan was going through the same thing on his end. He was throwing a lot more pitches than me because of all the walks, and California manager Bob Winkles wanted to pull him after twelve innings. When Ryan asked if he could pitch one more "to get my record," Winkles thought he meant the mark for most strikeouts in an extra-inning game—Ryan had a career-high nineteen, and the major-league record was twenty-one. But Ryan was talking about his own high for most *pitches* in a game, and he knew he was closing in on the two hundred and forty-two he had thrown against Detroit the previous year.

Somehow Ryan talked Winkles into one more inning, but he wound up getting neither record: he didn't strike out another batter, and he "only" reached two hundred and thirty-five pitches. Barry Raziano came in to start the fourteenth for California, and he was perfect for two innings: six men up, six men down. That left it to me, still out there in the bottom of the fifteenth, to keep it at 3-3.

Most people back in Boston had gone to sleep when I got the leadoff man, Bobby Valentine, to fly out. But then Micky Rivers singled to center, and Denny Doyle—who already had two hits off me—drove him home with a game-winning, opposite-field double past Yaz in left. A loss was a loss, but my arm and my whole body had held up. That was important.

"I felt good and strong all the way," I told reporters afterwards. "I might have been out there yet if he [Doyle] hadn't decided to hit what I thought was a bad pitch—a ball. It was high and outside, and he reached up and slapped into the opposite field and that was it."

I guess Dick O'Connell didn't hold it against Denny; we traded for him the following June, and he wound up doing a great job for us at second base. He was just wearing the wrong uniform that night in Anaheim.

You know what's really funny about that game? Not only did I not feel tired afterwards, but I was back out there on my normal three days' rest later that week against lefty ace Vida Blue and the Oakland A's. Johnson didn't bring me back slowly, either; I went ten innings and picked up a 2-1 victory against the two-time defending World Series champs.

I figure in those two games combined, I probably threw close to four hundred pitches. That's more than a lot of guys make in *five* starts today, but we really didn't think anything of it. We just wanted the ball, and when we got in trouble the manager let us try and pitch out of it.

That's one of the big problems with young pitchers today; as soon as they give up two straight hits or walks in the middle innings, the bullpen is warming up. Then, if they allow a *third*, it's time for the hook. How can a guy learn to pitch in adversity under those conditions? He can't, and so he doesn't. Then when the playoffs come around, people wonder why guys melt down.

Sure, some of it might be pressure, but pitchers can also be left in longer in the postseason—or bought into situations that they've not been adequately prepared to handle. Back then we took real pride in getting out of jams and in going the distance. We learned through trial and error so that when it really mattered, we *had* the experience—and the confidence—to make the right decisions.

That was how I felt on August 23 when I faced the A's and Vida Blue again at Fenway. By this point I was 19-8, one step away from being the first twenty-game winner in the majors. Our lead in the East was six games and had been building even though we had hit only three home runs in twenty-one August games. The electricity in the ballpark was amazing, and there were 35,866 fans packed into Fenway—the biggest crowd for a game there since 1956.

Four people among them were extra special to me: Maria, Luis Jr., Isabel, and our brand new baby son Daniel. They had flown in from Mexico City just a few hours before, and I had a friend meet them at Logan Airport to rush them over to the ballpark. By the time they got there we were already winning, thanks to a leadoff homer from my man Tommy Harper. It was 1-0 until the sixth, when we added two more on a Yastrzemski single and a sac fly by a terrific-looking young hitter just up from the minors, Jim Rice. At several points during the last two innings, the crowd was on its feet chanting my name.

I felt tremendous pride surging through me, and it peaked when Yaz squeezed the throw at first base for the final out of my 3-0 shutout. Not only was my family there to see me win a big game, but afterwards the five of us would be driving to nearby Milton to spend our first night together in our new home—the first house Maria and I had ever owned in the United States.

"I think, without any reservation, that he [Tiant] should be the Most Valuable Player in the American League, as well as the Cy Young Award winner," Darrell Johnson said after the game. "Just look at the record on what he has done. There's no way a man can do more for his team than what he has done for us."

It was great to hear words like that, but I felt it right to spread the praise around.

"Naturally, I'm happy," I told reporters in the clubhouse. "You have to be happy to win twenty games. However, everybody deserves credit. All the guys play good behind me. That's the difference."

After I had a cigar, showered, and got dressed, I met up with Maria and the kids, and we headed to Milton. If I could have frozen time right there, with my family in our new house with the swimming pool and big yard out back for the kids, and the kitchen for Maria, and the Red Sox heading for the playoffs, it would have been perfect. But time never stands still, and our fortunes as a ballclub were about to change faster than I ever thought possible.

Starting with a 4-1 loss to the A's the next day, we stopped hitting overnight. All the clutch extra-base shots we had been getting all year long—we led the league in doubles and triples for the season—dried up. Home runs? Forget it. We could barely scrape together a few scattered singles. One thing I learned playing in Cleveland all those years was that it doesn't matter how good your pitching is if your hitters can't hit. Now it was happening to a Red Sox team that had been on fire for months, right when we could least afford it.

After my win on August 23, we had led the AL East by seven games. During the next month, while the two teams trailing us—Baltimore and New York—got red hot, we lost twenty of twenty-eight to drop into third, five games back. In one stretch we went *thirty-four straight innings without scoring*, and we were shutout in four of five games.

I had been the "stopper" for us all year, with eleven of my first twenty wins coming after Red Sox losses, but even at my best I couldn't stop this slump. In my first three starts after winning my twentieth, I lost 3-0, 1-0, and 2-0. All were complete games, and I pitched well, but my support consisted of eleven singles and zero extra-base hits *combined* over twenty-seven innings. You don't have much chance to win under those conditions, and all talk of big-time awards coming my way quickly stopped.

For some of us the bad luck spread *off* the field too. While we were in Baltimore over Labor Day weekend, getting shutout in three straight games by the Orioles, someone broke into my hotel room and stole all my credit cards and cigars. The thief was so sure he wouldn't get caught that he took a few minutes to enjoy one of my stogies before putting it out in an ashtray. Bill Lee was robbed too, losing his portable stereo, but we didn't know if it was the same guy because he didn't leave any cigars in Bill's room.

I'd like to say I laughed my way through the whole thing, but this slump was so bad it was tough to joke about. Instead I tried to keep everybody's spirits up, saying how there was still time for us to get hot again and for the other teams to go cold. We won six of eight in late September, capped by a 7-2 win at Detroit in which I picked up my twenty-second and last victory, but the Orioles and Yankees didn't start losing. Our final record of 84-78 left us in third, seven games behind first-place Baltimore. New York finished two back.

For the second time in three years, we had gone into the final month of the season looking like a playoff team. For the second time in three years, the Red Sox ticket office made American League playoff tickets that wouldn't be used. And, for the third straight year, my selection as the Red Sox "Most Valuable Pitcher" by sportswriters covering the team left me feeling proud but also frustrated. How valuable could I be if I couldn't pitch us to a pennant? What good was a 22-13 record and a 2.92 ERA if all it got you was third place?

Watching Oakland, the AL West champ, beat the Orioles in the playoffs and then the Dodgers in the World Series—the A's third straight championship—was also tough to swallow. We had Oakland's number; we had beaten them in eight of twelve games during the regular season. If we ever had an opportunity to face them in the postseason, I liked our chances.

As I sat in my beautiful new home, I tried to focus on the positive. It was sad to see old pros like Cepeda and Aparicio and Marichal come and go, but the great young players who had come up to the Red Sox in the last couple years had me really excited about the future. Guys like Evans and Burleson and Beniquez and Cooper made an immediate impact in the big leagues, and they were improving all the time. Lost a bit in our September collapse was the arrival of two more kids who looked like they were going to be something special: outfielders Rice and Fred Lynn. We needed more power, and they had it.

If this group continued to develop, and we got Reggie Cleveland and Rick Wise healthy, *and* Pudge somehow found a way to get back on the field and behind the plate, maybe 1975 would be the year it all came together for us.

13

RACE AND REUNION

TWO TOPICS DOMINATED THE BOSTON headlines, airwaves, and just about every water cooler and worksite conversation in the city during 1975: Busing and baseball.

The first was a byproduct of the court-ordered desegregation of Boston's public schools a year earlier and threatened to tear the city apart along racial lines. The second was the result of a fantastic season by the hometown Red Sox—led down the stretch by a pitcher whose own status as a man of color seemed to have no bearing on the respect and adulation fans of all backgrounds held for him.

How could these two situations coexist? Such was the magic of Luis C. Tiant.

At the same time that Tiant was getting the '75 season underway with an Opening Day start against the Milwaukee Brewers at Fenway Park, Boston was nearing the end of a school year in which the city had dramatically addressed decades of discrimination in educational opportunities for minorities. Thousands of children across the city, by court order, were now required to board buses and travel to schools miles away from their own neighborhoods to create more racially-balanced classrooms. This did not sit well with some residents. In white, largely Irish-Catholic South Boston, angry teens and parents met incoming buses from predominantly Black Roxbury with racial epithets and rocks.

By September, as Tiant and the Red Sox were routinely filling Fenway Park during a stretch-run battle with Baltimore for the American League East title, the second year of the busing crisis was underway. Many high school classrooms in South Boston and Charlestown remained empty due to student boycotts, and there was backlash against Black and Latino residents of all ages—even those far from the front lines. Fenway, meanwhile, rocked with chants of "LOO-EEE!

LOO-EEE!" as advocates for and against busing found one subject they agreed upon: their love for the darkest man on the diamond.

Playing minor league baseball in the Deep South of the early 1960s as a man with Black skin and limited English, Tiant had experienced racism and isolation on a grand scale. His father had encountered the same challenges while traveling the dusty Jim Crow roads of the Negro Leagues a generation before, which is why he attempted to dissuade his son from following in his footsteps as a ballplayer.

Thankfully, Luis did not listen.

A decade later, when he emerged as a pitching ace with the Red Sox, he was embraced by the city at a level afforded few athletic heroes before or since. Everybody seemed to love Luis, from Southie to Roxbury and all the spots between and beyond. One of the most popular players in team history, Tiant also served as a role model and inspiration to non-white fans who had long felt the occupants of Fenway Park were not really *their* team.

And as *all* fans—and teammates—learned more about the years of forced separation between Tiant and his aging parents in Cuba, it further bonded him with the public. Diplomatic intervention in 1975 opened the possibility of the family being reunited, and progress in the situation began sharing headlines with busing and the ballclub as summer wore on. Through the dog days of July and August, as Red Sox die-hards hoped for that elusive AL East title, and a resolution to the racial conflicts besetting their neighborhoods, they also yearned for Boston's best pitcher to be together again with his mother and father.

If the Tiants could have a happy ending, maybe—just maybe—their city and their team could as well.

BACK IN MY HOME country, I grew up with Black kids and white kids, and we all played together. It was the same when I started playing ball, in Cuba and later in the United States. I never had any trouble with teammates because of color—it was always the people *outside* the clubhouse who had the problem.

For a while I thought I left the worst racist crap down south, but things got pretty rough in Boston during the mid-seventies. There was a lot of anger, on both sides, about Black and white kids being bused miles away from their own neighborhoods for school. The idea of giving everybody a decent education was good, but people didn't want someone else telling them where they or their children had to go to school—especially if it was putting

kids in danger. Those who could afford it were leaving Boston for the sub-
urbs where the schools were in better shape overall and busing wasn't an
issue.

Maria and I had three children now, and two of them—Isabel and Luis
Jr.—were in school full-time. We wanted to be together in one place all year
round, not separated with me living alone in Boston and the rest of the
family in Mexico City for the school year. I had a better contract and more
stability by 1974, so I felt the time was right. I started going out looking for
houses in the afternoons and on off-days, and as I told you already, I found
a real nice one in the small town of Milton about fifteen miles from Fenway
Park.

But that's not the end of the story. After I had found the house, and asked
the real estate agent for a price, she said it was no longer available. The
owner had decided not to sell. The truth, I found out, was that some people
in the neighborhood didn't want any more Black people living there. They
already had one a block and a half away from this house; one was enough.

But I fooled them. I went to the house myself, knocked on the door, and
a lady answered. She was Puerto Rican, and it turns out she and her husband—who was white—were the owners. When I told her how much I liked
their home, she made sure that we were able to buy it. I guess she
understood.

Maria, me, and the kids all loved the house, and we were very happy
there. Most neighbors were nice to us, and we made some great friends in
Milton. Luis Jr. was a teenager by this point, and really enjoyed himself.

"People used to just knock on the door to say hello, and after a game my
dad won, people would come back to the house and my mom would cook
up a heck of a meal," he remembers. "Before you knew it the whole street
would be filled up with cars. Everybody would eat and drink. It was mostly
mom cooking; she and a couple friends would take over the kitchen. We had
a pool too. There were lots of cigars, lots of music—salsa, merengue, old
school funk, and disco. Some of my friends would come and hang out.
Sometimes guys from the Red Sox or the visiting team would come over—or
a guy Dad knew from Cuba or winter ball. We had a good-size basement, a
bar, and a pool table, and he had a custom-built trophy case in there, too."

We did have some great times in Milton, but we could never forget, even
if we wanted to, that we still looked like outsiders to a lot of people.

One day not too long after we moved in, I was raking the leaves in the
front yard when a lady stopped her car near me. Then she rolled down her

window and asked—assuming I was the gardener—if I might be interested in picking up some extra lawn work at her place.

"Raking my own yard is enough for me," I said with a smile, "but thank you for the offer."

Besides, I could have told her, I already had a pretty good job playing baseball.

In February 1975, when the Red Sox reported to Florida for spring training, there was little moping around about our collapse the previous September. We knew we had a great mix of veterans and younger players who had already been through a pennant race together. Burleson at short, Evans in right, Cooper at DH, and rookie outfielders Rice and Lynn—both of whom looked real good when called up for the last month of the '74 season—were all twenty-five or younger. Yastrzemski at first and Petrocelli at third were the "old men" on the team, clutch hitters who were smart and steady in the field after a decade-plus in the majors. There were really only two uncertainties: Doug Griffin, a great glove man at second, had a bad back; and Fisk, still recovering from his knee injury suffered the previous June, was limping early in camp. Pudge insisted he would be ready by Opening Day, and knowing his toughness, we didn't doubt it.

The problem with all this talent was that it left no room on the roster for one of my best friends on the team. So in December 1974, outfielder Tommy Harper was traded to Oakland, ending our second long stint as teammates. I'd no longer have anyone to "flush away" each day in the clubhouse.

Before getting to the '75 season, I have to share one of my favorites of the many adventures I enjoyed with Tommy. Both of us loved dog racing, and one time while in spring training with Boston, we were coming back from a day at the track when a cop pulled us over for speeding. I was driving, and so the officer came up to my window, lifted his dark sunglasses, and leaned in.

"What were you doing going so fast back there?"

I looked at him, paused, and then said the first thing that came to my mind:

"I was bringing some HEEEEEEEEEEAT!"

As one old friend left the club, another came aboard. Stan Williams, teammates with me and Harper on the Indians, and then with me again in Minnesota *and* Boston, was back in a Red Sox uniform for 1975—this time as our pitching coach. Stan was a master of his craft, with pro experience stretching back nearly twenty years, and like me had reinvented himself mid-career after a major injury robbed him of his fastball. His wisdom would definitely be welcomed because outside of me and Lee, the area where we had the most question marks entering '75 was starting pitching. Wise and Cleveland were coming off disappointing first seasons with Boston, and Rogelio Moret was a great young talent who lacked consistency and maturity.

Stan was more than just a teammate. He was my dear friend, my supporter, and, when necessary, my defender. I'll let him tell this story, another one from spring training:

"Luis resented the feelings they had about Black folks in some parts of Florida, as did I," Williams remembers. "One time we were in a restaurant, and the people were all pointing and mumbling and cussing because a Black man was in there having dinner. So I got up and said, 'You people really know how to treat a guy, don't ya? If you've got anything more to say, say it to me outside. Two at a time—no, make that *three* at a time because I want somebody to catch the other two.'"

Stan was six-foot-five and 230 pounds in those days. Nobody took him up on the offer.

We had a real solid pitching staff for Stan to work with, but it could have been even better. Early in the 1974-75 off-season, we were rumored to be the favorites to sign reigning Cy Young winner Catfish Hunter, who was declared a free agent when his contract with the A's was voided by an arbitrator. The Yankees outbid several other teams and signed Hunter, who had led the American League in wins (at 25-12) and ERA (2.49) in '74, to a five-year, $3.2 million contract. It was the biggest deal in baseball history; Dick Allen, the highest-paid player in the majors the previous season, had made $250,000, and the average big-league salary in 1975 would be $44,676.

Our general manager, Dick O'Connell, refused to even try and match New York's offer to Hunter, even though Catfish was on the record as saying he hoped to play for the Red Sox. Dick told reporters that "the unlimited bidding process is inconsistent with the best interests of the Boston club," but I think all of us in the clubhouse would have been *very* interested to have Hunter on our club. The move instantly made the Yankees contenders in the AL East, along with us and Baltimore, and made the rest of us players start thinking more about our contracts.

The other new coach we had for the '75 season was Johnny Pesky at first base. Johnny was a beautiful man who became like a father to me and so many other guys on the team over the next thirty years. He had been a great player with the Red Sox in the 1940s and early '50s, a terrific shortstop and third baseman who hit .300 setting the table at the top of the order for Ted

Williams and Bobby Doerr. Later he managed the Sox for a couple seasons, and after a stint coaching and managing in the Pirates system, he was back where he belonged in a Boston uniform. Nobody loved wearing one—or was more proud of doing so—than Pesky. Especially when it came to working with young ballplayers, he was one of a kind, and he would still be hitting ground balls and fungos well into his eighties.

Even with Stan and Johnny coming on board, the biggest news for the Red Sox in spring training was bad: Fisk, catching in just his second game since coming back from his knee injury, was hit by a pitch in an exhibition game on March 12 and broke his right forearm. He was expected to be out until midseason, once again leaving us without our cleanup hitter and starting catcher. The catching would now be handled mostly by Bob Montgomery, a solid defensive player but a .250 hitter with little power. Sportswriters warned of a big drop-off in offense, but Monty rose to the occasion—coming through in the early weeks of the regular season with several clutch hits including a two-run double to help beat the Milwaukee Brewers at Fenway Park on Opening Day.

I started the opener and earned the 5-2 win, but most of the attention was on the designated hitters: Tony Conigliaro for the Red Sox and Hank Aaron for the Brewers. Tony C, making his latest of many comebacks since he was almost killed by a pitch in 1967, singled in his first at-bat—which got him a long standing ovation. Aaron, making his American League debut after twenty-one seasons in the NL, got one too, with the fans saluting his status as baseball's new home run king. He had passed Babe Ruth's famous 714 mark the previous year with the Atlanta Braves and now had 733.

Me? I got booed—for walking Aaron in his first at-bat. I understood; if I was a fan, I would have booed me too. Everybody wanted to see Hank hit his first American League home run, but I made sure it wouldn't be on that day.

Aaron would wind up playing two full years in Milwaukee, finishing with 755 homers. Conigliaro hit *our* first home run of the season three days later but then pulled a groin muscle and never got back on track. He was sent down to Triple-A Pawtucket when his average fell to .123, with the hope that things would improve and he'd be back up. They didn't, and after dealing with back spasms and hitting .220 in the minors, Tony C retired for good in August. He was just thirty. "My body," he said, "is falling apart."

It was sad to see a guy with his guts and determination have to walk away from the game when still young and strong. I could appreciate some of what

Tony had been through because I was thirty when I made my comeback with Boston. Now, like everyone else, I would always wonder what could have been. Tony is still the youngest player to ever lead the AL in home runs, when he hit thirty-two in 1965 at age twenty, and he might have hit 500 homers if he had the long, full career at Fenway Park that he looked to be heading toward.

Just as Conigliaro had surprised everyone by becoming a star almost overnight in the 1960s, we had *two* guys who did the same thing for us in '75: Jim Rice and Fred Lynn. Both won starting jobs in the outfield early in the year, and they went on to have the two best rookie seasons I've ever seen.

Rice, six-foot-two and all muscle, started out as a DH when Tony C got hurt. Then, to get Cecil Cooper into the lineup, Rice took over in left to continue the great Red Sox tradition of Hall of Fame players at the position: from Ted Williams to Carl Yastrzemski and now to him. Jim Ed was a soft-spoken gentleman from South Carolina and a great all-around athlete with unbelievable strength. He broke bats with check-swings and could hit a golf ball further than some pro golfers.

That summer Rice, a right-handed hitter, smashed a line-drive home run at Fenway that went over the old center-field wall to the right of the flagpole and completely out of the ballpark. Tom Yawkey and several sportswriters, all of whom went back to the days of Jimmie Foxx and Babe Ruth in the mid-1930s, agreed it was the longest homer they had ever seen hit there. Peter Gammons had a great line when he wrote in the *Boston Globe* that the July 17 shot off Kansas City's Steve Busby, which left Fenway heading north, would be "stopped only by Canadian customs."

Aaron took one look at Rice in action and predicted he would break his record for career home runs. For the next several years, it looked like a good bet. Nobody had a fiercer work ethic than Jim Ed, who gave one hundred and ten percent and played almost every day despite numerous nagging injuries. He had a reputation with fans and sportswriters for being moody, but he was really just a shy guy who didn't like the constant media attention you get playing in Boston. And although most fans loved him, he also dealt with a lot of racist crap yelled at him by assholes sitting in the Fenway bleachers. Few people knew about it because he didn't complain.

Rice's .309 average, 22 home runs, and 102 RBI in '75 would have made him an easy Rookie of the Year pick any other year. But we also had Lynn—who hit .331 with 21 homers, 105 RBI, and a league-leading 47 doubles, 103 runs scored, and .566 slugging percentage. Lynn had less pure power than

Rice, but he could crush the ball too. In one game at Detroit that June, Freddie had three homers, a double, and *ten* runs batted in. That's the kind of support a starting pitcher (me that night) only expects from a guy wearing an "S" on his chest.

I got on Lynn all the time his first year for being a clean-cut Southern California boy, but he really was a good kid and already the most complete ballplayer in the league at age twenty-three. He had a great batting eye, could run like a deer, and never made a mistake in the field or on the bases. His sweet, left-handed swing was made for Fenway Park; in seventy-six home games that year, he batted .368 with a .451 on-base percentage. Lifetime, he would have a .347 average, .601 slugging percentage, and .420 on-base percentage in 440 games at Fenway.

The problem with Freddie was keeping him healthy. Lynn was fearless in the outfield, diving across the grass for line drives and jumping against and above walls for long flies. He wasn't as big or muscular as Rice but had tremendous leaping ability and caught anything hit near him. Great defense is a pitcher's best friend, so I was very happy to have Lynn behind me for five years. The same goes for Rice, who worked harder on his fielding than fans ever knew and over time became very good defensively—especially at playing the Green Monster. Johnny Pesky hit hundreds and hundreds of fly balls to Rice, many of them off the Monster, and it paid off. As a rookie, Jim Ed didn't make a single error in left.

Lynn and Rice were dubbed "The Gold Dust Twins," and they were the talk of the league by midseason. Their great performance that summer took some of the pressure off of Yastrzemski, who was now a fifteen-year veteran and still an excellent player at thirty-five years old. Yaz moved to first base full-time so Rice could play left and Cooper DH, and fans no longer booed Carl if he went through a dry spell at the plate. Jim Ed and Freddie also helped us get through the period until Fisk's return in late June. When Pudge did come back, after nearly a full year out with his knee and arm injuries, he was better than ever—hitting .331 with 10 homers and 52 RBI in just seventy-nine games. The man was simply amazing.

The rest of the team was also rock solid. Burleson was an excellent defensive shortstop, a .280 hitter, and the type of intense, driven guy everybody wanted on their team—kind of like Dustin Pedroia would become later on for Boston. Evans continued his development into an All-Star-caliber ballplayer and combined with Lynn and Rice to give the Red Sox their best all-around outfield since World War I. Cooper found a regular lineup spot as a .300-hitting DH, and to add some more depth at second base, we picked up Denny Doyle from Philadelphia—who surprised everyone with a .310 average and twenty-two-game hitting streak after becoming a regular in the second half of the season.

Having the league's best all-around offense was a big plus, but it was our deep pitching staff that helped us move into first place in the AL East and hold it through the summer. Wise—who I called "Owl Man"—bounced back from his injury-wracked first Boston season to lead the team in wins with a 19-12 mark. Lee won seventeen for the third straight year, going 17-9, while Cleveland was a much-improved 13-9. Moret went 14-3 as a swingman and became a key fifth starter down the stretch. Dick Drago and Jim Willoughby were strong performers out of the bullpen, with Drago carrying the load in the first half and Willoughby giving us a big boost with his sinkerball when picked up in midseason.

Lee may have been known as "Spaceman" for the wacky stuff he said, but I saw him as really more of a deep thinker. When it came to a true spaceman, the wildest cat of all in our clubhouse was probably Bernie Carbo. He was a great pinch-hitter and fourth outfielder who, like Jackie Bradley Jr. on the 2018 Red Sox, could hit the longball and carry a team by himself when hot. Bernie came to us in a trade from St. Louis and brought to Boston a stuffed gorilla he named "Mighty Joe Young." He carried that thing everywhere, and like with Yaz's Columbo Coat, I made a point of threatening to do away with Carbo's monkey.

As for me, it was a season of ups and downs. I was 2-3 in April with a real bad ERA, and for once I had a hard time separating the game from the other things going on in my life. My parents were not getting any younger, and more than anything I wanted them to finally get the chance to visit me in the United States. I had tried to make arrangements for them to come in 1972 and in '74 when it looked like we might make the World Series. But Fidel Castro was still not letting anybody out of Cuba, even just for a few weeks, no matter how old they were.

"How much longer?" I asked *Boston Herald* sportswriter Joe Fitzgerald during a 1975 interview at my new house. "It's been fifteen years [actually fourteen] since I've seen them. All my life they gave me the best they could, and all they ever wanted was what was good for me. My father's seventy now, and he's not well. Yet he still works in a garage down there, and here I am, living like this, and I can't even send him a dime for a cup of coffee. He doesn't know my wife. He doesn't know my children."

It looked like a hopeless situation. Then, in May of '75, came a new opportunity.

I had known Senator Edward Brooke of Massachusetts for a long time, and a friend of mine, our family doctor Nathan Shapiro, was especially close with him. Dr. Shapiro found out that another senator, George McGovern of South Dakota, was going to Cuba to meet with Castro on a sort of unofficial diplomatic mission. So Dr. Shapiro talked to Senator Brooke about my situation, and he agreed to write this letter and give it Senator McGovern to share with Castro:

May 2, 1975

Prime Minister Fidel Castro
Republic of Cuba
Havana, Cuba

Mr. Prime Minister:

I am hopeful that Senator McGovern's visit to your country will prove beneficial to the efforts to normalize relations between our countries. While achievement of normalization will be difficult, it is an objective that merits the attention of both our governments.

My specific interest in writing you is to seek your assistance on a matter of deep concern to myself and one of my constituents, Mr. Luis Tiant. I am sure you know Luis as a star pitcher for the Boston Red Sox.

Luis's parents, Luis Eleuterio Tiant and Isabel Rovina Vega Tiant, reside at Calle 30 3312, Apt. 9, Mariano, Havana, Cuba. He has not had the chance to spend any significant time with them for many years. Naturally, he has a great desire to do so.

Luis's career as a major league pitcher is in its latter years. It is impossible to predict how much longer he will be able to pitch. Therefore, it is hopeful that his parents will be able to visit him in Boston during this current baseball season to see their son unembolden.

I have contacted the State Department and have been assured that the granting of visas to enter the United States will be no problem. Therefore, with your help, I am confident that a reunion of Luis and his parents is possible this summer. Such a reunion would be a significant indication that better understanding between our peoples is achievable.

I look forward to receiving your response.

Sincerely,

Edward W. Brooke

It was a long shot, but I had a couple things working in my favor. Castro had been an amateur pitcher himself when he was younger, and I knew he loved the game. When I played in the Cuban winter league in 1960 and '61, he used to come in the clubhouse to talk with all the players. Even if he didn't remember me, I'm sure he knew about my father. What I *didn't* know was if my family's baseball background would be enough to get him to grant our request.

Senator McGovern took Senator Brooke's letter to Cuba. He was going to give it to Castro at their first meeting, but Castro was not in a good mood. It turned out to actually be a positive sign because of what had made him upset.

"He [Castro] was late for the meeting with my wife and me, and he apologized," McGovern recalled later. "He said kind of sheepishly, 'I've been to a baseball game. We're having what is the counterpart to your World Series.' Then he said with a real sadness, 'My team lost, and I've been kind of down about that since.' I knew the minute he talked with such sorrow that I was halfway home on anything pertaining to baseball."

Later that night, as Castro's mood improved, the senator took out the letter and handed it to him. Then he asked a question:

"Do you know who Luis Tiant is?"

"The father or the son?" Castro replied. "I know about them both."

"The one pitching for Boston in the big leagues. He wants to bring his mother and father to Boston to see him pitch."

Looking closely at the letter, and then putting it into his pocket, Castro said he would see what he could do about the request. And when McGovern came back the next day, he got the best news possible.

"Luis Tiant will be able to see his parents," Castro told him. "They can go to Boston, and they don't have to stay just for the games, or for the World Series if they are in the World Series. They can stay there as long as they wish."

Decades later, McGovern called it "a remarkable feat," adding that, "I don't know of any [other] time Castro personally intervened and said, 'It's OK for you to leave.'"

Call it the magic of baseball.

I was in California with the Red Sox to face the Angels when a reporter called on May 8 and gave me the details. My parents, he said, were scheduled to come in August—flying from Havana to Mexico City and then on to Boston. It was still a long time away, and I kept hoping and praying they would be alright until then. But after fourteen years, I could wait three months longer. My dream appeared to finally be coming true.

In the meantime, I focused my energy on doing what I could to help the Red Sox achieve *their* dream of making the playoffs for the first time since 1967. Two days after learning about my parents, I pitched a four-hitter against the Angels. Even though I lost, 2-0, I considered it a victory of sorts after my poor April. I was shutout in my next start, too, dropping my record to 3-5, but again pitched well enough to win.

I felt it was only a matter of time before the great offense our team was generating for other pitchers would start clicking for me. Later in May, that happened. Backed in consecutive starts by ten, six, eleven, and thirteen runs, I won all four—starting me off on a 10-3 midseason stretch. It wasn't like my hot streaks in '72 and '74—my ERA during this run was still over 4.00—but my arm felt so good that I wasn't that concerned about allowing a few extra runs in lopsided games. If the situation demanded it, I felt sure I could bear down in the lower-scoring ones too.

The important thing, as I always said, was to pitch good enough with the stuff you have on any given day. Look at June 26, just the fourth game Fisk had played since his year-long layoff. We were facing the Yankees at Fenway, where I had beaten them seven straight times, and the place was packed with the biggest crowd of the year. It was the start of a four-game series, and New York had a one-and-a-half game lead in the East. If we could win three of four, we'd take over first heading toward the All-Star break.

The fans were into it, starting with the "LOO-EEE! LOO-EEE!" chants as I made my walk in from the bullpen. New York took a 1-0 lead in the top of the first, and I realized pretty early that I didn't have my good fastball. So I had to go to Plan B and really mix things up, throwing more curves and sliders and sneaking in fastballs here and there.

We came back with three in the fourth, and it was still a tight 3-1 game in the seventh when Fisk hit his first home run of the year. After seeing how excited he was skipping around the bases, I just *couldn't* let us lose. The Yanks got a bunch of runners on in the late innings but didn't score again after the first.

"The rest of the night belonged to Tiant, whose pitches, twitches, and annoying gestures were enough to drive the Yankees to the nearest bar," Larry Whiteside wrote in the *Boston Globe*. "He teased them as only El Tiante can do, then closed the door with a quick fastball."

After the game, which we won 6-1, Yankees second baseman Sandy Alomar did a good job summing up how I always liked hitters to think when they came up against me.

"He's the kind of pitcher you can't say, 'I'm going to wait and look for a certain pitch,'" Alomar told reporters. "He's got so many pitches, so many motions, it's difficult to get set. He keeps you off balance."

That game gave us the momentum we needed. We *did* win three out of four in the series to move back into first, and we stayed in the top spot all the way until September.

As we continued to win and pack Fenway, our team became somewhat of an escape for people dealing with bigger issues outside the ballpark. For the second straight fall, the beginning of the school year was expected to include protests and violence around the busing crisis. Black and Latino fans told me later that my success gave them a reason to root again for a Red Sox club that many of them—or, in some cases, their parents—had turned against because it had been the last major league organization to have Black ballplayers and was labeled as racist.

"To me, Tiant represented a beacon of strength," says Jeff Anderson, an African-American who grew up a Red Sox fan in the Bromley Heath Housing Project in Boston's Jamaica Plain neighborhood. "He was a person of color who had otherworldly athleticism, and it made you gravitate towards him. He was somebody who led by example, just by his presence, and was a towering figure who let his pitches do all the speaking for him."

Anderson, who says he didn't even know there was such a thing as dark-skinned Latinos until "a Black kid in the Bromley-Heath playground started speaking Spanish to me," admired my ability to "display my Latin pride without angering the white establishment." This helped Anderson convert some of his older family members back to being Red Sox fans. They knew the stories about the Sox having chances to sign Jackie Robinson and Willie Mays before any other team, and remembered Black pitching ace Earl Wilson being traded from Boston after he "made waves" by telling sportswriters he had been denied service in a pub during spring training in Florida.

Watching on from afar, in Cleveland, I had learned too. I let it all hang out on the field and spoke my mind off it, but I also knew what I should and shouldn't talk about.

"Tiant had a swagger, but because of the climate, he had to be careful about it," says Anderson. "During this period, you couldn't have a Muhammad Ali-type athlete in Boston. So Tiant's humility spoke of an inner strength. He wasn't going to allow himself to be braggadocious, nor was he going to allow himself to be marginalized by mainstream Boston media. He was going to be who he was."

Latinos felt the same connection to me as African-Americans, and not just because of busing.

"When Luis Tiant came to Boston, he probably didn't realize what he was walking into, but it was a really tough time," recalled Jorge Quiroga, a longtime Boston newscaster. "A big backlash not only against [busing], but also against the growth of the Latino community and the beginning of the Latino community demanding its rights. He walked into this situation that was by all accounts—and history will verify—it was a nasty time in Boston. He [Tiant] became absolutely *adored* by the fans...and he softened the edges of the backlash.

"I can't tell you how proud we were. We all basked in his glory."

Hearing these sentiments now means a lot to me, but what I most cared about doing in July and August of 1975 was getting healthy. My back was acting up again, and in an attempt to compensate for the pain without telling anyone, I unknowingly changed my delivery. The change gave me tendinitis which led to arm weakness. Before I learned of the problem and how to fix it, I was getting lit up like a Christmas tree.

After a win over the Royals raised my record to 13-8, with a 3.51 ERA, I won just two of my next nine starts and allowed nearly six runs per outing. Opponents batted .312 with a .510 slugging percentage against me over sixty-plus innings, the kind of numbers that will put you in the Hall of Fame. But here's the great thing about my crisis: *it did not impact the team at all!* Fellow starters Wise, Lee, Cleveland, and Moret all stepped up to fill the void, so that during the five weeks I was struggling, the team actually *gained* a half-game in the standings—going 3-6 when I started and 18-9 in games started by everyone else.

While I was trying to work out my pitching problems, my parents were officially granted permission in mid-August to leave Havana and fly to Mexico City on the first leg of their journey to Boston. When it was confirmed that they were coming, Maria found out first and decided not to tell me right away because I was pitching that night. After she *did* tell me I almost hit the ceiling I was so excited.

They wound up having to stay in Mexico City four or five days because my father didn't feel too good; it's so high above sea level there that he said he couldn't breathe. I spoke to them every day during this time, and eventually his condition improved enough to travel. After they finally got their visa, they flew to Boston on Thursday, August 21. I was waiting for them at Logan Airport with Maria, our three kids, a few friends, and what seemed like every newspaper and television reporter in New England. There were cameras everywhere.

I thought I'd handle my emotions fine, but when my father caught my eye and smiled as he came toward the American Airlines gate, I broke down crying. Then I ran over and gave him a big bear hug.

"Why are you crying?" he said. "The cameras will see you!"

"I don't care," I told him. "This is how I feel. I thought I was never going to see you guys again."

It was the first time my kids ever saw me cry—but what could be a better reason?

Someone asked Dad, through a translator, if he was ready to pitch for the Red Sox. He said he was, but then my mother stepped forward to set the record straight.

"It's been a long time since he has thrown a ball," she said. "He'd have to go into training."

Because we figured my parents would be very tired from their trip, we did not plan a big family celebration around their arrival. We drove home to Milton, watched ourselves on the news, talked for a bit, and then went to bed. The next day our photos were all over the newspapers, including one of all of us together on the front page of the *Boston Globe* and another of me and my father hugging on the front of the *Boston Herald*. Over the next week, there were many more stories, interviews, and TV reports.

Dad loved the attention.

"You know," he said to me later, "that never happened to me in my life. All the years I played, people were never that nice to me."

"Yeah, the people are nice here," I agreed.

Then he gave me an example.

"You know what? I went to take a leak, and people came over and wanted me to sign an autograph while I did it!"

I laughed.

"I know. They do it to me too!"

At the time, even after what Castro told Senator McGovern, we were not sure if my parents would be allowed to stay in the United States indefinitely. Castro could always change his mind, we knew, and their visa was only for three months. We wanted to make the most of our time together, so every game I started at Fenway, I made sure they drove into the ballpark with Maria and the kids to watch. Dad came to most of the other home games too, and he was no longer hiding behind posts, like back in Cuba.

By now there was a third generation making his way in the family business. Luis Jr. was a right-handed starter for the Milton Little League All-Star team and had a pair of four-hit wins—including a 6–0 shutout—in a playoff tournament right around the time my parents came. I was very proud of him, as I have always been of all our kids.

The first major league game I pitched with my parents in the stands, and the first time they ever saw me play at *any* level since high school, was against the Angels on August 26, 1975. As Sherm Feller announced over the public-address system, *"Ladies and gentlemen...please welcome on the greatest pitchers from the New York Cubans..."* my father came out to the mound with me to throw out the ceremonial first pitch. The crowd gave him a huge standing ovation, this time chanting "LOO-EEE! LOO-EEE!" for the *first* Luis Tiant to play there.

We had learned that in 1945, Dad had pitched at Fenway while with the Cubans of the Negro National League. He could not remember how he did back then, but neither of us would ever forget *this* moment. I'm sure he was feeling proud, like he had finally made it to the white man's league after all these years, but he didn't say anything.

It was very emotional for me and for my teammates watching on from the dugout.

"Something like this," Rick Wise said, "it makes you realize what life is all about."

Handing me his jacket, Señor Skinny took the ball. Then he went into his windup and threw a fastball in to backup catcher Tim Blackwell. Dad didn't like where the ball went, a little low and outside, so he asked for it back. This time he threw a knuckler for a strike, right down the middle. The fans loved it.

As I handed him back his jacket, Dad whispered something in my ear: "Go get 'em. Don't worry about me being here."

Then, in the dugout, one more thing—for me to pass on to the manager:

"Tell 'em I'm ready to go five."

Maybe I should have taken Dad up on the offer. I got hit hard, was gone after six innings, and we lost 8-2 as my family watched on from the front row behind home plate. I wasn't nervous; I wanted to win for my parents, but I kept my emotions inside. As a pitcher, you have to do that. It was just too hard for me to throw my regular game. My back was still hurting, and that had a big impact on my mechanics and where the ball ended up.

The loss dropped my season record to 15-13 and raised my ERA for the year to 4.17. This was after allowing under three runs per nine innings (2.83) for the previous three seasons *combined*. Some wise guy in the press box that night said it was too bad my mother and father came "a year too late" when I was no longer a top-flight pitcher. I didn't let that bother me, and when a sportswriter asked how great it was to have my parents there to watch me, I shot back:

"It *is* great, but I hope they get another chance—at the World Series."

Those hopes took a hit in my next start when the Oakland A's knocked me around for six runs in less than three innings. If we won the AL East, we knew it would likely be the A's we faced in the playoffs with a World Series appearance on the line. They had won the Series the last three years and were going for four straight with a veteran lineup featuring Reggie Jackson, Sal Bando, and Joe Rudi—guys who really knew how to hit. I loved the challenge of beating them, but I just couldn't do it this time. My sore back made it hard to stretch or go into my windup. I could barely bend down.

That was August 30. For the next twelve days, Darrell Johnson wouldn't let me pitch in a game. We still had a six-and-a-half game lead over Baltimore after the Oakland loss, and Johnson probably figured there was enough breathing room to give me a nice rest. I wasn't happy with the long layoff, but I figured if I couldn't change his mind, at least I could use the time to try and figure out my problems.

Stan Williams had always helped me in the past, so now I turned to him again. We watched film of my delivery taken before and during my slump, and Stan noticed the unseen flaw in my delivery I had picked up while trying to protect my bad back: I was throwing my arm across my body like a tennis player instead of driving straight through. After working with him to fix this, and taking the twelve days rest between starts, I felt great.

What's more important—or so I hoped—was that my parents would now have a chance to see me perform at something closer to my best.

That chance came on September 11. When I took the mound that afternoon against Detroit at Fenway, we were still in first, but the Orioles were now just five games back. Earl Weaver was promising they'd catch and then overtake us, just like they did the year before by winning twenty-eight of thirty-four down the stretch.

I needed to shut the Earl of Baltimore up, and three-hitting the Tigers with ten strikeouts was a nice first step. I had a no-hitter into the eighth inning before Aurelio Rodriguez hit a ground-ball single up the middle, but I really didn't care about losing the no-hitter because we got the "W" and my back felt great. The Orioles also won that day and were still within striking distance when they came to Fenway a week later for two games—our final series of the season against them. If they won both, they would close within two-and-a-half games. They had their hottest starters going in Jim Palmer and Mike Torrez.

"We've crawled out of more coffins than Bela Lugosi," Weaver said before Palmer's matchup with me on September 16. Earl was still sure his team would come back, but this year felt different. We were peaking, not slumping, down the stretch.

Palmer-Tiant on September 16 felt like the seventh game of the World Series. Fans knew it was Baltimore's last real chance to catch us, and Fenway Park was never louder. The official attendance was 34,724, but there had to be more than 40,000 people jamming the aisles and every little corner of the ballpark. Fire marshals looked the other way, and fans with more guts than cash to scalp a ticket climbed the billboards high above Kenmore Square to watch for free.

"When my dad pitched, everyone got along," recalls Luis Jr. "There would be guys hanging from the billboards outside the park—Black guys, white guys, Latin guys. As you get older, you start to appreciate everything he did for the city, and how much he impacted people. But at the time, you're just proud of your dad."

A wonderful atmosphere, and the kind I liked best.

"Luis pitched better in big games," says Fred Lynn, who was behind me in center field for plenty of them. "I think it was that bulldog in him saying 'I'm not going to lose. I'm not going to be the reason my team loses.'"

Palmer had twenty-one wins for the year and had proven to be at his best when the chips were down. My goal was to keep Baltimore off the scoreboard as long as I could and hope we could break through against him. My general feeling about pitching was if you get me in the first three innings, I'm done—finished for that day. But if you *don't* get me, then that's my game.

My teammates did their job, getting me the lead. Petrocelli, like Yaz a holdover from Boston's last playoff team in 1967, led off the third with a homer into the left-field screen to make it 1-0. Then Fisk knocked one to the same spot in the fourth. Pudge had been unbelievable since coming back from his broken arm, heating up in the last two months just when other guys on the club were wearing down. Montgomery had done a great job when Fisk was out and deserves a lot of credit for what we did that year, but it was crucial for us to have Pudge's bat in the lineup for the stretch drive.

My back held up, Palmer settled down, and the score was still 2–0 heading into the late innings. We had help available in the bullpen, but Darrell Johnson knew I took pride in finishing what I started—like my father, watching from the stands, had always told me to do. Johnson kept me in, and I got the last eight straight to preserve the shutout. After the final out, Fisk ran over and hugged me like we had won the East already.

"Tiant was as good as we've ever seen him," Weaver admitted afterwards. His bragging was suddenly all but absent.

In the summer of 2018, sitting high above the Fenway diamond where we had battled, Palmer—now an Orioles broadcaster—reflected on his and my rivalry.

"The thing about pitching is that it's a blank canvas. Every game is different, and you try and draw or paint the best picture you can paint on that particular day. Luis was very good at that—he had deception, he had flair, and he was a money pitcher. He had a good slider and a good curveball and a fastball he could command. So he had quality pitches, and when you take the deception and the fact you really couldn't sit on any one pitch, he could get you out three or four different ways and do it three or four different times.

"When you faced Luis Tiant, you knew you were facing an artist."

By now another school year had started, and in Boston that meant more problems around busing. The boycotts and protests were still going on, and it wasn't even just in the city; my son and daughter were having problems with other kids in Milton. But somehow the fans felt different when it came to me. I still don't fully understand it all these years later.

Maybe it's because they read about what I had gone through with my family and saw how I tried always to be upbeat rather than angry out on the field. I could be as mad as the next guy, believe me, but I didn't think the ballpark was the place for that. The ballpark was where you went to *forget* your problems, not dwell on them.

Whatever the reason, the special connection I had with the people of Boston was a beautiful thing I will never forget.

"At the height of the busing crisis, the most popular person in Boston was a Black man who smoked a cigar in the shower," says Dick Johnson, curator of The Sports Museum and a leading Red Sox historian. "He wasn't overly glib or anything; he just took care of business and led by example. But I'm hoping what he also did was to make people think twice about their feelings on race, when their most popular player—the one who got the loudest ovations at Fenway Park—was a gentleman of color."

The biggest ovations for all of us were still to come. Baltimore never got closer than three-and-a-half games in the final two weeks, and we clinched the East on September 27, one day after Reggie Cleveland and I pitched back-to-back 4-0 shutouts against the Indians in a doubleheader sweep at Fenway. In the end, we had the Yankees to thank; we lost, 5-2, to the Indians on the 27th, leaving our magic number at two, but that night New York swept two games from the Orioles to give us the title.

We had all already left the ballpark to go home after our game when Baltimore's second loss made it official, so most of the guys celebrated by going to dinner with a few teammates and their wives. Nothing too crazy, which was fine. There was still plenty of work to do. If we wanted to reach the World Series, we would have to win a best-of-five playoff against the three-time defending world champion A's to get there.

The next day, a Sunday, was our last regular-season game. As guys started coming into the Fenway clubhouse to get ready, Mr. Yawkey was waiting to congratulate each of them one by one.

"Thank you, Mr. Yawkey," I said, thinking of the opportunity he and the team gave me back in 1971. We had a quick hug, and then he said something that stuck with me.

"Thank *you*, Luis. You were the man who did it."

14

THE WORLD IS WATCHING

A BANNER IN THE FENWAY grandstand read "Loo-Eee for President!" while "El Tiante" T-shirts sold briskly on streets outside the ballpark. Scalpers were getting $100 for $10 seats, fans clamoring to get a look at one of the most improbable comeback stories in sports history as it reached its zenith.

Never was Luis Tiant's pull on New England's heart stronger than in the fall of 1975. After leading the Red Sox to the AL East championship with a string of clutch September pitching performances, the team's Cuban ace was determined to keep them winning deep into the postseason. Doing so would eventually require beating two of the best major-league teams of the last half-century, but Tiant seemed up for the task. As much as any seasoned CEO or spy, he possessed both courage and craftiness in abundance.

Everywhere he went that October, Tiant was a balding, cigar-chomping leading man. Playoff broadcasters latched onto his story as pure theater—his parents' August voyage from Havana to Boston, ending a fourteen-year separation between father and son; his use of a wildly entertaining (and wildly effective) whirling dervish pitching delivery; and his incredible ability, time and again, to perform his best in the biggest games. Once, as casual fans learned in the many biographical sketches popping up in Sports sections daily, Tiant had been a rising young star who blew batters away with a fastball nearing triple digits; now, after a mid-career injury, he had reinvented himself as a purveyor of screwballs, hesitation pitches, and other wizardry that laughed in the face of normal baseball convention—and bats.

Tiant's loved ones, also flashed across millions of TV screens from their spot in the stands, were colorful in their own right. His bride, Maria, supportive as ever, led a contingent of family, friends, and fellow Red Sox wives in spinning matracas—handmade noisemakers brought in from Mexico for the postseason. Then there was Tiant's aging father, Luis Sr. The former lefty pitching ace in the Negro Leagues watched with pride from the stands, clad in a fedora and perpetual grin, as his namesake did him proud. Racism had denied the elder Tiant a shot at the majors, so now his son was winning for them both in a city embroiled in its own racial strife.

Finally, looming over the entire tableau was Fidel Castro. Tiant still did not know just how long the Cuban dictator would be willing to allow his parents to stay in the United States—three months? Forever?—and this too was never far from his mind. He didn't know if he could go through losing them again, but he might have no choice.

Boston's most popular athlete did not feign an interest in politics. All he wanted was to be the best ballplayer, teammate, family man, and friend possible. And, in the end, it really didn't matter if the Red Sox beat out the heavily-favored Oakland A's in the American League Championship Series, or the All-Star lineup of the Cincinnati Reds in the World Series that lay beyond that hurdle.

In all four areas, as judged by the world watching him in the fall of '75, Luis Clemente Tiant would come out a champion.

I KNEW MR. YAWKEY was just being nice with what he told me in the clubhouse; winning the AL East had definitely been a team effort. But I had been our most dependable starting pitcher in September with a 1.47 ERA and three complete-game wins—including two shutouts—as we held off the Orioles down the stretch. The 1975 season was not my best; not even close. When it mattered *most*, though, I had come through, just like I dreamed I would during those lean years in Cleveland.

So while Rick Wise led the team in wins with nineteen, and had a better ERA on the season that I did, Darrell Johnson felt I had earned the right to start Game One against the A's in the American League playoffs. I was the hot hand, especially at Fenway where the first two games would be played. I had allowed just one run at home in twenty-seven innings and had beaten Oakland five times in a row going back to 1973.

Since we had home-field advantage for the playoffs (with Games One, Two, and Five slated for Fenway), and had split the twelve games we played against Oakland during the regular season, we felt good about our chances going into the series. Most everybody outside Boston, though, felt we had *no* chance. The experts all talked about how the A's had shown they could turn up the intensity when it was necessary in the postseason. Their roster was filled with guys—Reggie Jackson, Sal Bando, Joe Rudi, Bert Campaneris, Ken Holtzman, Vida Blue, Rollie Fingers—who had played on all of their three straight world championship teams. They were used to the spotlight shining on them in October and didn't let it bother them.

Another reason Oakland was favored was that we were missing one of our best players. Late in September, just a week before the end of the regular season, Jim Rice was hit by a pitch that broke his left hand. Our leading home run hitter and number-two RBI man would be out the entire postseason, and his injury forced Darrell Johnson to make several changes. He moved Yaz from first base back to his old spot in left field to take over for Rice. Cecil Cooper, normally the DH, replaced Yaz at first. Juan Beniquez, normally the fourth outfielder, would now DH.

I tried hard not to think about those moves or anything else going into Game One; all I concerned myself with was the task at hand. I wouldn't be surprising Oakland with my stuff—they had seen me enough over the years—but I felt that my fastball was moving better than it had all season and hoped to use this to my advantage.

Mostly, I just felt confident—and relaxed.

"Luis knows how big the game is to all of us," Yastrzemski said before the opener. "But he will be the calmest person on the field. Nothing bothers him."

Just as they had down the stretch of the regular season in 1972, '74, and again in '75, the crowd gave me a special salute before this and every home playoff game I pitched, that pumped up the whole team. I'd finish my warmups in the bullpen, and then, as Dwight Evans later described, "...that lever came up from that gate, there was dead silence, and as soon as that latch opened he [Tiant] got a standing ovation all the way to the mound. It was exciting for us to see that, and it got us going, too. It was a tremendous thing."

All that electricity from another overpacked house of 35,578 at Fenway for Game One must have affected our opponents. How could you hear that and not be a little intimidated, even if you were the defending champs? Oakland would never admit it, but look what happened at the start of the opener:

I got the A's in order in the top of the first, and their starter, veteran lefty Ken Holtzman, got two quick outs in our half. Then the fun started. After Yaz singled to center, Fisk hit a hard grounder right to third baseman Bando. The inning looked over, but the ball got by the usually sure-handed Bando (error No. 1). Yaz never stopped running and came all the way around to score when Claudell Washington—backing up Bando in left field—threw the ball wildly trying to get it back in (error No. 2). That made it 1-0, and then a second run scored on the next play when Phil Garner booted Lynn's easy grounder to second (error No. 3).

So much for the cool-headed champs.

The A's strategy against me seemed to be to swing hard and knock the ball all over the park, which made sense since they had rocked me for six runs in less than three innings when they faced me on August 30. But I wasn't the same pitcher I had been then; my back was better, my control was better, and I was able to place my fastball right where they couldn't get good wood on it. They *did* get plenty of balls in the air—they only hit two grounders the whole game—but none went out. They didn't even get their first base hit until the fifth, and we kept our 2-0 lead through the middle innings.

Then, in the seventh, we broke things open thanks to more bad Oakland defense. The biggest mistake came on Lynn's liner to left field that Washington should have caught. He misjudged it, thinking it was going to bounce high off the Green Monster, and then watched as it scraped the wall just a few feet up to give Lynn a gift double and two RBI. Center fielder Bill North also dropped a fly ball that inning, leading to another run.

The A's got one back in the eighth, but that was all; I wound up with a three-hitter and a 7-1 win. Holtzman definitely didn't pitch as bad as it sounds, and only two of our runs were earned, but they all count the same on the scoreboard.

After the game, the reviews of my first career postseason start came in.

"A man can't pitch any better than that," said Darrell Johnson. "Today was no different than the last two years. Luis has done the job over and over for us."

"The way he has been these last few starts," said Fisk, "give him a couple of runs, and that's it." Pudge did his part to help, scoring twice and diving into the stands to make a great catch on a foul pop.

"This is Louie's palace," said Yaz. "In here he can do no wrong. I've never seen people react to a ballplayer the way they do with Louie here. It's beautiful."

Then there was Reggie Jackson, Oakland's top slugger. He was held to one single in four at-bats and must have been impressed by my moves on the mound.

"Luis Tiant," he said, "is the Fred Astaire of baseball."

It felt so good to win for my parents, for my wife and kids, for my team-mates, and for all the fans. We had a sign up on the bulletin board in our clubhouse that said, "SEVEN WINS IN OCTOBER!" and it was important to us that we got that first one quick. It gave us a lot of confidence that we hoped would carry over to the rest of the series.

One other extra-special thing about Game One was the manager watching it from the visitor's dugout: Alvin Dark. Remember him? The guy who when we were both with Cleveland was convinced my injuries in 1969 were caused by my delivery? He predicted I would never last in the majors pitching that way, and as soon as he was able to trade me that winter, he did.

After Game One, they brought me into the interview room to meet with the press. Dark was there already, up at the microphone, so I went and sat down behind him. When he saw me, he leaned over and patted me on the head.

"Luis," he said loud enough for everyone to hear, "you were beautiful out there today."

I was glad he noticed, but I didn't say so.

Johnson had me set to pitch the fourth game if the series got that far. It didn't. We were down 3-0 early in Game Two against another lefty, Vida Blue, when Yaz started our comeback with a homer in the fourth. Then, after we had tied it, Captain Carl kept it at 3-3 with several great defensive plays in left field—performing like he had never given up his job out there.

"I can play left field in my sleep," Yaz said after the game, in which he also doubled and scored the game-winner in a 6-3 victory.

Game Three was in Oakland, and we expected the A's to put up a big fight at home and try to avoid the sweep. Rick Wise had other ideas. After just missing his twentieth win in his last start of the regular season, he got it here—where it meant much more—by pitching into the eighth and holding the champs down after we built up a 4-0 lead. Oakland's pride was still there, and they put a late-game scare into us, but Yaz made some more great plays in left and Drago shut the door again. We clinched the pennant with a 5-3 victory.

This time we had a true celebration, partying and pouring champagne on each other's heads in the visitor's clubhouse. Sal Bando, captain of the losing team, stopped by and told me to "shake and bake those National Leaguers." That was a class move and advice I planned to follow.

At that moment, right in the middle of all the yelling, I realized that the two biggest dreams for my life had come true at the same time:

1. After fourteen years, I was reunited with both my parents.
2. After *seventeen* years of pitching professionally. I was finally going to the World Series.

Our opponents for the series were the Cincinnati Reds, a team I remembered well from when I was a teenager back in Cuba. The Havana Sugar Kings of the International League were the Reds' top farm club from 1954 to 1960, and Cincinnati signed up a lot of the best Cuban players before Castro took over and outlawed pro ball. Among them was my friend Tony Perez, now Cincinnati's star first baseman.

I played for the Sugar Kings' team in the Cuban Winter League but didn't get signed by the Reds. The club's management reportedly thought I was "awkward and not coordinated and very young" when they checked me out as an eighteen-year-old, so they passed on me. Hopefully I could make them regret it.

When it came to the oddsmakers, even our sweeping the defending champion A's wasn't enough to change our underdog status. The Reds, who had beaten the Pittsburgh Pirates three in a row in the National League playoffs, were a powerhouse team that is today considered one of baseball's greatest all-time clubs. Manager Sparky Anderson's crew led the majors with a 108–54 record, more wins than any other team in 1975 and thirteen games ahead of our 95–65 total. They were known as "The Big Red Machine" for how they rolled over opponents with speed, power, defense, and pitching depth.

Cincinnati's starting lineup read like an All-Star roster: Pete Rose, 3B; Joe Morgan, 2B; Johnny Bench, C; Tony Perez, 1B; George Foster, LF; Dave Concepción, SS; Ken Griffey, RF; Cesar Geronimo, CF. That's the all-time hit king leading off, followed by three Hall of Famers and four more guys who would make anybody's team better. Lefty fireballer Don Gullett was the only really big name on the Reds pitching staff, with a 15–4 record despite missing two months with injuries, but Anderson had five other very dependable starters and several relievers he wasn't afraid to put in at the first sign of trouble.

Sparky was ahead of his time in how he handled pitchers. He pulled starters after five or six innings, even if they were doing good, and then quickly started swapping relievers in and out—sometimes letting a guy face just one batter. This is how most teams do things now, but back then it was so unusual it earned Sparky the nickname "Captain Hook." It probably also pissed his pitchers off, but it got results: six guys with double-figure wins, a terrific 3.37 team ERA, and a league-leading fifty saves.

Still just forty-one years old, Anderson was in his sixth season as Reds manager and had already won two NL championships—in 1970 and '72—before this one. Eventually Sparky would win three World Series in his career including one with the Detroit Tigers, and join many of his former players in the Hall of Fame. But at this point he had yet to win any. He was looking for any edge he could get, and before the series started he began telling reporters, umpires, and anybody else who would listen that he was convinced something in my delivery constituted a balk.

By its simplest definition, a balk occurs when a pitcher on the rubber goes into his regular wind-up or pickoff move but then doesn't throw the ball. A called balk, as ruled on by the umpires, allows all baserunners to advance one base. The Reds led the NL with 168 stolen bases in 204 attempts that year and had eleven more steals in three playoff games, so running was a huge part of their offense. Sparky wanted to make sure he and his baserunners knew exactly what I could and couldn't do.

Thanks to him, all or parts of this excerpt of rule 8.05 of the 1975 baseball rules appeared in newspapers across the country before and after Game One:

> "If there is a runner, or runners, it is a balk when the pitcher, while touching his plate [rubber]—
> (a) Makes any motion normally associated with his pitch and fails to make such delivery;
> (b) Feints a throw to first base and fails to complete the throw;
> (c) Fails to step directly toward a base before throwing to that base."

Even with my herky-jerky delivery, I had *never, ever* been called for a balk in eleven seasons of big-league baseball—all in the American League. I made sure every AL umpire knew that *all* the steps in my delivery, including my head shakes and body twists and the three-step drop with my hands holding the ball, were done at the same exact pace and with the same exact motion each time. They videotaped me to make sure, and I passed the slow-motion eye test. The consensus was that there was no intentional deception in my moves.

The potential problem was that AL *and* NL umpires would be working the World Series, and the NL umps had only seen me pitch a couple times in All-Star games and during spring training. According to Sparky, they had a different view on what should be called a balk.

"He couldn't play in the National League in 1975 with his no-step [pick-off move]," Sparky told reporters before the series. "There are two no-nos that we'll be watching for: any dip of the hands after he gets them down to his belt, and any throw to first base without stepping in that direction."

The afternoon of October 11, 1975 was gray and damp. It was sixty degrees, with a little rain falling, as I took the mound for Game One of the World Series. When I saw Sparky talking to the umps, I figured he was suggesting to them that as soon as a runner got on first for the Reds, they should try and catch me in the act and call a balk. But if that was the plan, they would have to wait a while.

My family—and the world—was watching. This was my chance to show *all* of them what I could do.

I was perfect over the first three innings, while we left four men on (including one thrown out at home) against Gullet. Then, with one out in the fourth, Morgan singled to center to become the first Cincinnati baserunner. He was among the top base stealers in baseball with sixty-seven during the regular season, so I was pretty sure he would be running here. I also knew that the umps would have their eyes on me, but I wasn't worried—I had a real good pickoff move, and Fisk had a terrific arm.

"Now the drama starts," broadcaster Curt Gowdy told the forty million fans watching the national broadcast on NBC—plus a few more tuned in illegally down in Cuba. "Will Joe Morgan run on Carlton Fisk? Tiant—does he balk? Some say he does, some say he doesn't."

Before making my first pitch to Bench, I looked over and saw Morgan taking a big lead. I stepped off the rubber, keeping him honest, and he hurried back. Then, after Bench fouled one off, Morgan took the same bunch of steps toward second—so I threw over to Cooper, and Morgan dove back.

I knew he'd keep taking that big lead, and I felt I could get him, so I kept throwing over. The third time, it was REALLLLL close, with Cooper sweeping his glove hand onto Morgan's arm at almost the same instant it touched the bag. Cooper, our bench, and most of the fans seemed to think he was out, but first base ump Nick Colosi's safe call was all that mattered.

Man, I thought, I almost had him there. Was it worth one more shot? Why not?

So I gunned it over again, and this time Morgan yelled, "Balk!" Colosi agreed, sending Morgan to second base. I couldn't believe it—I *know* I stepped toward first before I threw, which is the rule to keep it from being a balk. Gowdy and his partners Dick Stockton and Tony Kubek on the NBC telecast watched the replays with the rest of the country, and they thought my move was legit. But it didn't matter what they, me, Darrell Johnson, the fans, or my teammates thought. Just the man in blue.

I was steamed and ran over to try and find out from Colosi what he was thinking.

"What's the matter with you?" I said. "I've been here a long, long time— since '64," I said to him. "This is 1975. Nobody has ever called me for a balk, and now you're going to come in here to an American League town and you're going to call me for a balk? What's the matter with you—do you need glasses?"

"You double-dipped your knee, and that's a balk," he replied. "By National League rules, it's a balk."

I had a few more things to say after that, including a couple of *bad* things, but nothing I felt should really offend him. He let me yell a bit, bull-this, and bull-that, and then he said his final piece:

"You better go back over there (to the mound), or I'm going to throw your Black ass out!"

My Black ass? If he tried to say that shit now, they'd throw *his* ass out of baseball. But back then, I just did what I was told and got out of there as quickly as I could.

"OK, thank you very much. Nice speaking with you!"

When you've been working all your life to get there, you've got to be stupid to get yourself thrown out of a game that big.

So now I had Morgan at second, Bench at the plate, and Perez on deck. Kubek had asked me the day before if a balk call would throw me off my game, and I said no. Now I had to prove it. It took *thirteen* pitches, including seven foul balls, before Bench popped one up behind home plate that Pudge caught by the screen. Two outs. Then I climbed the ladder with Perez, got him to one-and-two, and froze him with one on the outside corner for strike three. As I ran to the dugout, and my teammates slapped me on the back, I felt a huge rush of energy.

The Big Red Machine had not squashed me, and the balk call had not rattled me. I kept pitching the same way, and they never called another balk on me the whole series.

The funny thing was I really didn't have a strong fastball that day like I did against Oakland. I had just enough of one to use it when I had to, and my control was so good on my curveball, slider, hesitation pitch, and everything else that I could stay in command. Cincinnati had seen video from the Oakland game and was expecting lots of fastballs they could try and slam off and over the Green Monster. They didn't get them.

The game was still scoreless into the bottom of the seventh when I led off. Since we had added the designated hitter in the AL in 1973, I had only batted once in three years entering this game. The NL was so anti-DH that they wouldn't even agree to allow it in the World Series until 1976—so all us rusty AL pitchers were at a big disadvantage.

I had already struck out once against Gullett, and I figured he would try to get me again with his great fastball. When he fed me a slow curve instead, I waited it out and pulled it on the ground into the hole between third and short for a base hit. I'm still not sure why he didn't just blow me away again.

The crowd gave me a standing ovation, and I could hear Maria up in the stands spinning the two-foot-long matraca noisemaker our friend Mario had brought her from Mexico City. Coach Johnny Pesky gave me my big blue warm-up jacket at first base, which made me look and run even slower than normal. Then, when Evans bunted to the mound on Gullett's next pitch, I figured I was dead meat at second—until Gullett bounced his throw wild past Concepción covering the bag. I slid a little early (OK, a *lot* early), jumped up, rounded the bag, and then took a few big strides toward third before realizing I'd never make it.

High-tailing it back to second, slipping along the way, I was just in time to beat Geronimo's throw in as Curt Gowdy on NBC and a good chunk of the sellout crowd laughed. Watching the highlights later, I have to admit it *was* pretty funny. My helmet went one way, my upper body the other, and my lower body someplace else! But all that mattered was how I ended up: *safe.*

Now the fans were really into it, and you could see Gullett was rattled. Doyle tried to bunt, fouled it off, and then grounded a single into the same shortstop hole I had found. This got me to third, loading the bases with nobody out.

Who was up next? Who else? Yaz.

Those were the situations Captain Carl loved most, and he came through as usual—lining one to right field that landed just in front of Griffey. I had to stay at third, ready to tag up, in case Griffey caught it, but I still ran (and slightly stumbled) home easily. My momentum carried me to the on-deck circle where I high-fived Fisk.

There was just one problem…

I missed home plate.

It was only by about a half-inch, and hoping nobody had noticed, I started sneaking back to tap it. Pudge, who was in the on-deck circle, *did* notice but didn't want to yell and draw Bench's attention to the situation.

Bench knew too, and so did Concepción at short. They both started screaming for Perez—who had taken the cut-off throw from Griffey—to throw the ball home from first. *I* could hear Bench, who was right near me, but the crowd was so loud that *Perez* never heard either of them. My mistake cost us nothing.

I tapped the plate, we took a 1-0 lead, and my teammates, the fans, and my family and friends got one more big laugh.

"You forget how to do things when you don't do them for a long time," I recalled for a reporter years later. "The main thing is I didn't get hurt, and I can come back and continue to pitch."

That play got Captain Hook out of the dugout. Sparky pulled Gullett and brought in Clay Carroll, but the move backfired. Carroll walked Fisk to bring in *another* run and *another* trip to the mound by Sparky. This time he called for Will McEnaney, and things only got worse for the Reds. While I was sniffing smelling salts on the bench after my big trip around the bases, we quickly added two singles and a sac fly to make it 6-0.

They say a big lead is never safe at Fenway, but with the wind blowing in and the crowd yelling, "Hang in there, Luis!" I was determined to not let this one get close. Getting the last six men in order in the eighth and ninth, I preserved the shutout and earned myself hugs from my teammates on the field and from my father later in the clubhouse.

Having Dad there with us after the game, with all the press around, was great. I knew it was one more way to make him feel like a real big leaguer—and a real teammate—again. He was even good for a quote; when I told reporters that day had been my greatest ever in baseball, both because of what it meant to my family and what it meant to my teammates and our fans, he said through an interpreter that it was *his* greatest, too.

"One of the things that I admired about Luis was all the love that you could see between him and his father after the years and years they had been apart," Bernie Carbo recalls. "They were really proud of each other, and that was something that I think we all, as players, looked to when Luis brought him into the clubhouse—seeing how much fun they had.

"I wish I would have had the relationship with my father that Luis had with his father. Luis said, 'Dad, I'm going to take care of you. I'm going to show you how much I love you.' Then he did."

Bernie was right. It was wonderful to share that moment with my father, my mother, and the rest of my family. I had been waiting for it all of my life.

Among those who felt strongest about my win were those Black and Latino Red Sox fans for whom my presence on the field had special meaning—like Jeff Anderson in Jamaica Plain. Bob Parajon, whose parents had managed to get their family out of Cuba in 1965, was another one.

"Every time Tiant took the mound, it became a family affair; everyone crowded around the TV," remembers Parajon. "We would all enjoy Luis as a family, and knowing that his parents had come over from Cuba too gave it all more meaning because of the political climate at the time. It was a sense of pride."

Sportswriters had fun with me too, as usual, but now there were more of them than ever from across the country focusing on my delivery. Some of their descriptions were really funny, like this one from Phil Pepe of the *New York Daily News*:

"On one pitch, he checked the position of his centerfielder, counted the house, looked up to see if it was raining, and then ordered three hot dogs from a vendor behind third base before striking Tony Perez out with a side-arm curveball."

Then there was Roger Angell of *the New Yorker,* who gave my pitches new names like "The Slipper Kick," "Falling Off the Fence," "The Runaway Taxi," and "Call the Osteopath" during which "in midpitch, the man suffers an agonizing seizure in the central cervical region, which he attempts to fight off with a sharp backward twist of the head." All you have to do is read those to me out loud, and I start laughing.

The Reds, I can guarantee you, were not laughing after Game One. They realized now that we weren't going to roll over for them. We might have only had three guys with World Series experience (Yaz, Rico, and Carbo) to their fifteen, but we never felt like underdogs. After sweeping the A's and now beating Cincinnati in the opener, we had proven we could play with anyone.

Pete Rose wasn't convinced. Even after a zero-for-four day, and a 6-0 loss, he didn't think too much of my pitching.

"We must have had fifteen line drives, but everything was right at somebody," he told reporters inside the quiet Reds clubhouse. "I couldn't have hit the ball any harder."

In one at-bat during the game, Rose had held up his thumb and forefinger—forming a zero—so Pudge could see it.

"Nothing," Rose said. "The guy has nothing."

So did the Reds, and over my last six starts—including two in the postseason—I had now gone 5-1 with a 0.92 ERA and three shutouts. Not bad for a guy with nothing.

That night, like every night we were home during the postseason, my family partied deep into the night at our house in Milton. Friends, teammates—everybody was welcome. We had soul and disco on the stereo, dancing by the pool, and plenty of food and drinks. I remember three guys and two women showed up who I had never met before, but since they brought along some booze, and were friendly, I just said, "Come on in." The next morning when the sun came up, they were still there, talking away. We never did figure out who they were.

In the middle of it all was my dad, sitting quietly in the corner of my basement rec room with a smile on his face. The last few months had been so special for all of us, but I imagine they were most special for him. He had seen me live out my dreams and *his* dreams at the same time, and his was a look of pure contentment. There were no words to describe it, but no words were necessary.

The miles between us, and the years, had melted away.

If Pete Rose or anybody on Cincinnati still doubted that we were for real, we changed their minds the next day. Bill Lee started Game Two for us and delivered his best performance of the year. He really had his sinkerball going, even after a twenty-seven-minute rain delay, and held a 2-1 lead through eight innings.

So much was riding on the game that Lee must have figured Darrell Johnson had him on a short leash. Sure enough, after Bill let up a leadoff double to Johnny Bench in the ninth, Johnson called on Dick Drago to close things out. Drago had been terrific against Oakland in the AL playoffs, but here he let up a single by Concepción to tie the game and a double by Griffey to give Cincinnati a 3-2 lead. Rawly Eastwick, the Reds' nasty right-handed bullpen ace, got us one-two-three in the bottom of the ninth.

Moments earlier, we had been one out away from a two-zero lead in the series. Now, just like that, it was tied heading to Cincinnati.

Game Three, played in front of more than 55,000 at the Reds' huge Riverfront Stadium, was a back-and-forth battle. Fisk gave us a 1-0 lead early with a homer off Gary Nolan to start the second inning, but then the Reds scored five unanswered runs against Wise in the middle innings. The Owl Man was the moon man that night, letting up home runs to Bench, Concepción, and Geronimo before being pulled midway through the fifth.

Jim Willoughby settled things down for us in relief, and Fred Lynn got us a bit closer with a sacrifice fly in the sixth. Then it was our turn to hit the long ball again. Bernie Carbo did what he did best, knocking a pinch-hit homer off Carroll in the seventh, to make it 5-3. Then Dwight Evans smashed a two-out, two-run bomb in the ninth to tie the score and force extra innings.

What happened next will always be known in Boston as "The Armbrister Play." In the bottom of the tenth, with the game still tied 5-5, Geronimo led off with a single, and light-hitting Ed Armbrister came to bat in the pitcher's spot. Everyone expected a bunt to get Geronimo into scoring position, and that's what Armbrister did—but after getting the bunt down he seemed to freeze in place as the ball bounced up in front of the plate. Fisk leaped forward to grab it and try for the lead runner at second base, but he had to literally push Armbrister away to get to the ball. Pudge wound up rushing a throw that sailed past Burleson at second, and as the ball rolled into center field Geronimo rounded the bag and headed safely to third.

After a long argument in which Fisk and Darrell Johnson insisted to home plate umpire Larry Barnett that Armbrister had interfered with Pudge's path to the ball—claims that the TV replays strongly supported— the play stood. The Reds now had the winning run ninety feet away, and three batters later Geronimo scored easily on a single by Joe Morgan over a drawn-in outfield. Cincinnati had a 6-5 win, but none of us in the visitor's dugout or the majority of fans watching the game felt they deserved it that way.

"Of course he interfered with me; you all saw it," Pudge told reporters after the game. "He stood right under the ball."

Roger Angell of the *New Yorker* called the play "mind-calcifying," but Darrell Johnson might have had the best line about Barnett's decision:

"Collision? I thought it was collusion."

During the course of the next week, Barnett received more mail than anybody on either team—most of it negative. He also got at least one death threat. Meanwhile, we were down two-games-to-one, making Game Four a must-win for us. If we lost, Cincinnati would only need to take one of the last three contests to clinch the World Series; if *they* lost, it guaranteed the series would come back to Boston for at least one more game—the sixth.

I got the start for us in Game Four, and right away I could tell my stuff wasn't nearly as sharp as in the opener. In the first game they barely touched me; this time they hit me early and often.

Leadoff man Rose worked the count to three-and-two, fouled off three pitches, and then grounded one past me into centerfield for a single. Griffey followed this with a first-pitch smash to deep left-center field, scoring Rose, but I got lucky when a beautiful relay play from Lynn to Burleson to Petrocelli at third nabbed Griffey trying to leg out a triple. The luck was because of what happened next: a walk to Morgan and, after a groundout by Perez, *another* run-scoring hit—this one a booming double by Bench to the center-field fence just between Lynn and Evans.

It was 2-0 already, but it could have been much worse were it not for that great relay. I managed to stop the bleeding for a while, getting the next seven men out, and we were still down two when we came up in the top of the fourth. Big innings were becoming our specialty in this series, and now we had another one just when we needed it.

Fisk and Lynn singled off Reds starter Fred Norman, and after Petrocelli popped up, Evans had his second huge clutch hit in as many games—a triple off the center-field fence that scored Pudge and Freddie to tie the game. Burleson then doubled in Evans, knocking out Norman, and after Pedro Borbon came on in relief, I singled up the middle to move Burleson to third. That kept the string going, and Rooster and me both soon scored on singles by Beniquez—who played left field in the games at Cincinnati—and Yaz. That made it 5-2.

If I had my Game One stuff, that lead would have felt really safe. But on this night, it took all I had to keep the Reds from tying things back up. Maybe it was because the mound was a little higher at Riverfront than Fenway, and my control was a little off as a result. Whatever the reason, it was a struggle all the way.

I got the first two outs in the bottom of the fourth, but Foster got an in-field hit and reached second when Doyle's off-balance throw got by Yastrzemski at first. Concepción brought in the runner from scoring position again with a bloop double that landed between three guys, and then *he* scored on Geronimo's bloop triple to right—cutting the lead to 5-4.

Darrell Johnson could have pulled me right then, but he didn't. He probably realized that we should have caught one of those ugly bloopers and wanted to give me a chance to get out of the jam. I did, striking out pinch-hitter Terry Crowley, batting for Borbon. Geronimo was stranded on third, and we were still on top.

"In that game at Cincinnati, the big thing about Luis was he would battle out of any situation," Petrocelli remembers. "He would give up a couple hits, and then he would really start to bear down against the next man and get the big outs. On one of those bloop hits, he got a little upset at one of the young outfielders—Juan Beniquez—who had started after the ball, and then hesitated. Luis felt that if he would have kept going, he could have caught it before it fell in. But he got over it fast."

Rico's right. It's easy to lose your cool in a tight ballgame like that, and it happened to me again the next inning. I walked Rose leading off the fifth, and after a deep flyout by Griffey, a couple guys started warming up in our bullpen. Now I figured I was probably one more baserunner from being pulled, and after three straight balls to Morgan—the first two of which looked pretty good to me—I went crazy. Pudge and Stan Williams saw me stomping around the mound cursing to myself about the calls and ran out to settle me down. Morgan still walked, but I came back to get Perez and Bench.

From that point on, I protected that one-run lead like it was my fourth child. A lot of my pitches weren't doing what I wanted, and between the fifth and the eighth the Reds got two hits, two walks, some loud lineouts, and smashed two balls to the deepest parts of the ballpark. All they had to show for it was four more zeros on the scoreboard, and with Clay Carroll and Rawly Eastwick shutting us down, it stayed 5-4 heading into the last of the ninth.

By now I was nearing one hundred and fifty pitches for the game, not that I was keeping count. Was I tired? Sure. But here is how I looked at the situation. When you come to this time of the season, you've played for five and a half months—plus another one and a half months of spring training. Your *whole body* is tired. At that point, everything is mental; you've worked all year to get to this situation, and you're not going to mess around. You *want* to be there, and you don't want nobody taking your spot.

In his autobiography, Don Zimmer—then our third-base coach—wrote that, "Once you got to the ninth inning, you could sit your bullpen down. Tiant was his own closer."

That's just how I felt about it. I'd kill somebody before coming out of a game like that. Other players may feel differently, but *me*, I *had* to be in there pitching. As long as my arm was OK, I was going to do whatever it took to win. Rest? That was for winter.

So even when Geronimo singled leading off the ninth, and Armbrister bunted him to second, I was determined to keep going. Rose was up next, and he had already singled, walked, and hit a wicked liner to second. I didn't *want* to walk him, but I had to be careful because he was heating up and could tie the game with another single. So I gave him five straight outside fastballs, and he took them all to work a walk.

Rookie Jim Burton, a lefty, was warming up in our bullpen. Ken Griffey, a left-handed batter, was due next. Managers always like a lefty-on-lefty pitching matchup, but there was no way I was coming out of that game. I knew it, my teammates knew it, and the manager knew it.

Or did he?

I looked over at our dugout. Stan Williams was on his feet, clapping for me as always, but Darrell Johnson was walking out to the mound. I couldn't believe it.

"What the fuck is he doing?" I yelled to no one in particular.

Fisk started coming out, too; he heard me, and yelled back: "What the fuck *is* he doing? He knows he's not going to take you out."

Now I turned to Fisk.

"I don't know what shit he's going to tell me. But he better do it quick."

By now Johnson had reached the dirt by the edge of the mound. I looked at him.

"What the fuck are you doing here?"

"What do you guys think? I got a left-hander down here, Luis."

He meant Burton, in the bullpen.

"Get the fuck out of here! I don't want to hear any more shit. I don't want to talk to you!"

Fisk was laughing and looking over to Yaz at first base. He was laughing too.

Then Johnson asked me about Griffey.

"Can you get him?"

"Sure I can. Now get the fuck out of here. I don't want to talk to you—I don't want to talk to *nobody!*"

The funny thing is that Johnson had a microphone in his pocket, which was recording our whole conversation. NBC was getting audio of both managers talking to their players to use in the World Series highlights video coming out later. Whatever sound they got from Johnson and Sparky would be used in the video, but not heard live during the game.

If you watch the video—you can find it on YouTube—you'll see that every time I open my mouth, they drown out what I'm saying to keep it clean. It's pretty funny.

When Johnson finally left, Ken Griffey stepped in. He worked the count full and then smashed a line drive to center; Lynn turned his back to the plate, ran straight toward the fence, and caught the ball over his shoulder at the edge of the track. It was an incredible play at the most crucial moment— if he doesn't catch it, we lose—but it was no surprise to anybody on the Red Sox. Freddie had been doing that for us all year.

"Luis absolutely loved his defense," Lynn remembers today. "Pitchers back then, unless they were Nolan Ryan, didn't try and strike everybody out. They wanted you to hit the ball and let the defense do what they do. Their job was to put the ball where we wanted it to be put, so the defense could make the plays for them. Luis did that as well as anyone."

Now, with two outs, it was up to Joe Morgan. He took ball one, then swung at my 163rd pitch and popped it up sky-high to first. Yaz caught it, my teammates all mobbed me on the mound, and we had tied up the series— guaranteeing at least one more game in Boston.

"The pitch I hit for the last out was the best one Tiant threw me all night," Morgan said, "and that's what was bad about it."

Before we even left the dugout, I was already giving my first postgame interview—to a sportscaster for a Providence, Rhode Island television station. It was Tony Conigliaro, covering the series as part of his first post-playing job. It was great to see Tony C, even if he couldn't be in uniform.

Then it was on to the clubhouse, where I found out just how many pitches I had thrown. A reporter asked if I was tired after throwing that many.

"I don't care if it's 3,000," I said, puffing on my victory cigar, "as long as I win."

I wasn't just blowing smoke; the number really was not a big deal to me. The year before, when I had that fifteen-inning game against Nolan Ryan, I figured I threw about two hundred pitches—and that wasn't the World Series.

"Guts, guts, guts," Yastrzemski said about my performance. "I'll tell you, I'd let him pitch to the whole world the way he battles."

Yaz was a pretty good battler himself; he had barely hit .200 the second half of the regular season after severely pulling ligaments in his shoulder, but now that the chips were down he was pushing past the pain—hitting well over .300 and making one great defensive play after another in the postseason. *That's guts.*

Darrell Johnson, who had already told writers that I averaged 133 pitches a game, was asked if he ever thought about taking me out after I went way past that total.

"I went out to talk to Luis, discussed the situation with my catcher, and saw no reason not to let him finish what he started. Luis is a very strong man."

Then the big question, again to me: Would I be able to come back and pitch a seventh game?

"You better believe it."

The importance of our pulling out Game Four was made clear the next day when the Reds beat us 6-2 at Riverfront behind a great performance from Don Gullett. The big blows were two home runs off our starter, Reggie Cleveland, by Tony Perez—the second one a three-run job in the sixth to knock out Cleveland. Perez's first hits of the series broke his zero-for-fifteen slump, and Gullett cruised from there. Of the five hits he allowed, three came with two outs in the ninth.

We were now down 3-2 in the series but still felt good about our chances with the last two games at Fenway. Bill Lee was set to pitch Game Six and me the finale if it got that far. But when more rain postponed the series for two days, Darrell Johnson decided to make a switch. He called me into his office and looked at me across the desk.

"You're going to pitch the sixth game."

"Why?"

"I want you in there."

"Goddamn it, it's supposed to be Bill Lee's turn. I threw all those pitches the other day."

"I know, but I want you to pitch."

"OK, I'll pitch."

That's his job as manager; I'm not the one who is going to decide. But I felt bad for Spaceman, who was a great competitor, had pitched terrific in Game Two, and I figured would take it hard. I was right; Lee was pissed then, and he's *still* pissed now.

"Johnson should have let me pitch Game Six and Luis Game Seven," Lee says today. "Luis could have used the extra rest, and that's all I wanted for him. Besides, how could you not want Luis Tiant pitching the seventh game of the World Series?"

I appreciated the compliment, but it went both ways; I was confident that *he* would do a great job in the seventh game. Starting Game Six was fine with me, even more so after a third straight rainout got me that extra rest Bill was so worried about.

In the end, the game I *did* pitch in turned out to be one of the best in World Series history.

We got off to a fast start; after I got the Reds out in the top of the first, Lynn hit a three-run homer off Gary Nolan deep into the right-field bleachers in our half of the inning. There was a lot of pregame talk about how far I could go after my heavy workload during the past month, but I felt *strong*— and had much better and faster stuff than in Game Four. I allowed two hits and no runs over the first four innings, making it forty straight innings at Fenway Park since I had allowed an earned run. My ERA in my last six home games, covering forty-nine innings, was now 0.18.

I knew streaks like that couldn't go on forever, especially against the Reds. In the fifth, they broke it. Armbrister walked, Rose singled him to third, and then Griffey hit a ball to dead-center that Lynn leaped for and *just* missed— slamming off the concrete wall and falling to the ground as Griffey reached third with a two-run triple. The whole park went silent as everyone waited to see if Freddie would be okay. He didn't move for a while, but then he got up, stretched a bit, and stayed in the game. Tough kid.

It seemed like every time I was in a jam during this series, Morgan and Bench were coming up. Now here they were again. I got Morgan to pop to third, but Bench slammed a single over Yaz's head in left field—the first hit anyone had off the Green Monster in three games. It was now 3-3, and with us doing nothing against four Reds relievers, it stayed that way until the seventh.

Now my magic was running out. Griffey and Morgan led off the Cincinnati seventh with singles, and after Bench and Perez flew out, Foster hit a two-run double to center that made it 5-3. That was the Reds' tenth hit, and when Geronimo led off the eighth inning with a first-pitch homer on a hanging slider—the one real bad mistake I made that game—I had no reason to argue when Darrell Johnson came to take the ball from me.

The crowd gave me a standing ovation as I walked off, but I knew it was more for what I had done over the past several weeks than on this night.

It looked like the World Series was over, with the score 6-3 and Rawly Eastwick now into the game for Cincinnati, but we still had one more comeback in us. We put two men on with two outs in the eighth, and Johnson sent Bernie Carbo to the plate to pinch-hit. Carbo, a former NL Rookie of the Year with the Reds, had already hit a big pinch-homer against his old teammates in Game Three. Now, after a few real ugly swings, he did it again—stunning Eastwick and the whole ballpark with a shot into the center-field bleachers. That tied it at 6-6, and Fenway shook as loud as it ever did. Mighty Joe Young's papa had come through.

That's where the score stayed until the twelfth inning, thanks largely to another incredible defensive play. In the Cincinnati eleventh, with one out and Griffey on first, Joe Morgan hit a fly ball that Evans tracked to the right-field corner and then leaped and caught one-handed just before it reached the seats. Dewey hit the fence, spun around, and threw the ball back in to double-up Griffey—already well on his way to third with what he figured was the go-ahead run.

I saw that play on TV, from our team whirlpool where I had gone during extra innings for a good soak and a cigar after my long night's work. I was still in there around 12:30 a.m. when Pudge led off the bottom of the twelfth, and when he hit Pat Darcy's second pitch off the left-field foul pole for a game-winning homer, I jumped out of the water and started running down the hall to get onto the field and celebrate with my teammates.

Then, when I got into the dugout, I suddenly realized something—and stopped just in time.

"Goddamn!" I yelled. "Somebody get me a towel!"

I was so excited, I had almost run out onto the field in just my jock strap! It's a good thing they didn't have the camera zoomed in on the dugout like they do today. The TV fans would have had SOMMMMMMME treat.

In the next morning's papers, more than one sportswriter half-joked that rather than try and top Game Six, they should cancel the finale of the World Series and declare it a tie. Of course that couldn't happen, and so Bill Lee took the mound against Game Five hero Gullett to decide a winner at Fenway. Sixty-nine million people watched on NBC, the largest television audience ever for a sporting event.

Just like the night before, we took an early 3-0 lead, but we also blew chances to score more runs and left a bunch of men on base. You can't get away with that against a team like the Reds, and eventually they made us pay. In the sixth, with Lee still cruising along with a shutout, Rose singled and then made one of those key plays that can make or break a series. With one out, Bench grounded what looked like a double-play ball to short. Burleson threw to Doyle to get Rose at second, but Pete's hard slide into Denny forced him to throw wildly to first for a two-base error.

Lee should have been out of the inning but now had to face Perez. He had held Tony hitless through almost two games, and as a pitcher when you've got a guy in your pocket like that you don't want to try anything different. But the Spaceman has his own way of doing things, and so he threw a big slow curve to Perez that he called the "Leephus" pitch. He had thrown it to Perez once before, for a strike, and he thought he could get it by him again. But this time Tony had a better feel for it as it came in and crushed the hell out of it for a homer over the Green Monster. Now it was 3-2.

Still, Lee had a chance to be the hero. Then he developed a blister on the thumb of his pitching hand in the seventh inning and had to leave. Rogelio Moret relieved and gave up a game-tying single to Rose, but Jim Willoughby came in to get Bench with the bases loaded. The score was 3-3, and it stayed that way as Willoughby retired all four men to face him.

Then Johnson made a decision that fans would second-guess all winter. With two outs and nobody on in the bottom of the eighth, he pinch-hit for Willoughby with Cecil Cooper—who had been struggling badly with a .056 average in the series. Coop stayed in his rut, fouling out to third, which now left the ninth inning in the hands of rookie lefty Jim Burton. Two walks and two groundouts later, Morgan just got his bat on a good two-strike, low-and-outside slider from Burton and slapped a soft, sinking liner into center that landed in front of a charging Lynn for a single as Griffey scored.

That was it. We went in order, with Yaz making the last out on a fly ball to Geronimo in center; the Reds won the game, and the series, 4-3.

The cumulative totals show just how close the series was. We had sixty hits, the Reds fifty-nine. We scored thirty runs, the Reds twenty-nine. A record-tying five games were decided by one run, two in extra innings and two in the ninth. In the end the Reds were just one bloop hit better. Give us a healthy Jim Rice, and I bet things would have ended differently.

The day after Game Seven, the *Boston Globe* ran a tribute on its editorial page—a place you almost never see sports stories. Here is how it described the two teams:

"It was a contest between middle America with the glittering 56,000-seat Astroturfed Riverfront Stadium and Sparky Anderson running his clean-cut short-haired pitchers in relays from the bullpen and New England with its feisty old Fenway Park, misshapen but cozy as a living room with real grass and seating for 35,000 (not counting the fans on the billboards), and stoical Darrell Johnson waiting and watching as an ageless Cuban showed what it means to pitch from the heart."

I liked that image of me pitching from the heart. It was true because at that time I felt I had so much in my heart to give—so much to be thankful for. That's why that was my happiest time in baseball. Not just our making the postseason, but finally having my family all together.

That was my World Series trophy.

15

DAMN YANKEES

ON NOVEMBER 2, 1975, MILTON, Massachusetts held a parade for its favorite adopted son.

As he and his family drove slowly through town in an antique touring bus, Luis Tiant looked out at the throng of neighbors cheering him along the three-mile route. There were parents holding up children, older folks who probably saw Babe Ruth pitch for the Red Sox, even cheerleaders and marching bands. One family plastered the front of their house with banners including the very effective, "Honk if you love Luis!"

In a ceremony held after the parade, there were bouquets for the Tiant ladies and a Paul Revere bowl for the man of the hour. Sharply dressed in a green leisure suit, orange-tinted sunglasses, and his ever-present cigar, Luis laughed upon receiving a gift from the Milton Little League: his very own home plate. It was a reminder, of course, of the one Tiant initially missed, then sneaked back to tap, when scoring the first run of the World Series. Always a prankster, he appreciated the good-natured dig.

"Heavenly Father, we ask you to especially bless our favorite right-hander," the monsignor of a local parish offered in the day's benediction. "Prevent his curveball from hanging, his fastball from rising, and always have the wind at his back when he throws another eephus ball, especially at Fenway Park."

Boston had fallen just short to Cincinnati in the '75 Series, but two weeks later, Tiant was being celebrated as a hero—and not just in Milton. The New York City chapter of the Baseball Writers Association of America selected him to receive the Babe Ruth Award as World Series MVP, the first time since its 1949 inception that the honor went to a member of the losing team. It was a fitting choice; after the stretch of baseball they had just played, Tiant and his team-mates did not seem like losers.

Most experts agreed that even in defeat, the Red Sox were on the verge of becoming baseball's next dominant club. Their young, talented core of mostly homegrown position players—Fred Lynn, Dwight Evans, Carlton Fisk, Rick Burleson—had pushed a far more seasoned Reds team to the ninth inning of Game Seven. Add to this a healthy Jim Rice, the ageless Carl Yastrzemski, and a strong pitching staff anchored by Tiant, and additional playoff appearances seemed a certainty.

Injuries, infighting, and contract disputes, however, all impacted the Boston club in its attempt to stay on top, as did the rise of a powerful new adversary within its division. The once-mighty Yankees had spent the previous decade steeped in mediocrity, chasing the likes of the Orioles and Red Sox in the American League East. Then, in 1976, they bounced back with a vengeance. Led by gritty catcher Thurman Munson—whose feuds with Boston backstop Fisk, real and imagined, made for great ballpark theatre—and brilliant but oft-unstable manager Billy Martin, New York supplanted Baltimore as Boston's staunchest inter-division foe and revised a rivalry that had been largely dormant for twenty-five years.

The Red Sox and Yankees battled each other with their bats, gloves, and sometimes their fists in the late 1970s, producing memorable ballgames and storylines. At the center of it all, poised on the mound like a matador facing a charging, pinstriped bull, was Boston's fearless Cuban warrior, who gave his all no matter what the stakes.

In the end, Tiant would have precious little time to reflect on past glory. Conqueror of obstacles on and off the field, he would face many more sooner than expected. He would be tested as a ballplayer and a son. Knocked down, he would pick himself back up. Heartbroken, he would find a way to go on.

The parade would not last long, but it would strengthen him for what lay ahead.

WHEN I WAS A KID thinking about what I wanted in life, I had said to God, "Here's what I want to do: have a nice house, all my family with me, and food on the table." Now, I had finally done it.

That off-season, we had a wonderful Christmas and New Year's—three generations of the Tiant family under one roof. Castro had extended my parents' visa indefinitely, meaning they could stay in the United States as long as they wanted. They no longer had to fear their time with us would end, and they moved in with us in Milton permanently. Maria took care of my mother, and I took care of my father. The kids had fun getting to know their grandparents.

Among the things I did for my dad during this time was take him out to buy all new clothes. He didn't want it; he said, "Don't spend all your money on me." But I knew he liked to dress well. During the years that he played, he would sometimes change his suit three times a day when walking around town so he would always look his best. And shoes—so shiny you can see your face when you look at them. I knew he liked that too.

One day during the winter, we were at home when my father suddenly said to me, "Give me your shoes."

"What do you want them for?" I asked. I didn't understand.

"Just give them to me."

So I did.

I left for a while, and when I came back later, he had shined them. All my shoes.

Those little moments are the ones I would not forget from that time. My father shining my shoes. Little Danny following him everywhere, and Dad playing catch with Luis Jr. in the backyard. Isabel spending time with Maria and my mom. I tell you, boy, that's a good feeling. Money don't beat that. Um-um. It's beautiful. I'm a family man; I just like *being* with my family, getting together and talking.

After all those years thinking I might never see my mom and dad again, I was lucky enough that God made it happen. But as quick as happiness comes along, there are always new challenges to face—on the field and off.

Now that I had two more family members to support, job security was more important to me than ever. For professional athletes, security comes from multiyear contracts that protect you in case you get injured. After what I had done for the team in the postseason, I felt I deserved that type of respect from management.

A year before, in the winter of '75, I had asked Dick O'Connell, our general manager, about a three-year contract. He said that almost nobody besides Yaz ever got them on the Red Sox. I was surprised because I knew the reputation owner Tom Yawkey had with his players for being generous. But I believed O'Connell and signed a two-year deal.

All that year, I kept wondering about it. Finally, I decided to find out for myself by asking other guys on the team what kind of deals they got. It turned out there were *plenty* of guys besides Yaz getting signed for three years, including pitchers like Rick Wise and Bill Lee. That got me ripped.

The start of spring training was delayed three weeks in 1976 when the owners all shut down their camps while negotiating a new labor agreement with the player's union. I stayed in shape by running and doing some throwing to a friend at Brookline High School, which had a big indoor gym and was just a mile from Fenway Park. When the camps reopened in late March, everybody on the Red Sox started flying down to Winter Haven.

Not me. I called O'Connell.

"You told me there were no guys on three-year deals but Yaz, and that was a lie—there are plenty of them," I said. "I'm talking to my sports attorney, and until we work this out, and I get three years, I'm not coming down to Florida. I'm staying in Boston."

I also told him if I didn't get what I felt—and *knew*—I deserved, I would consider quitting baseball for the year. I felt that strongly about it.

That night, I was sitting at home when the phone rang. It was Mr. Yawkey.

"Luis, what are you doing? Please come see me tomorrow, and we'll talk about it."

I said OK.

The next day, I stood across from Mr. Yawkey in his Fenway Park office. We had always gotten along good, and he looked at me like he was really concerned.

"So what's the matter, Luis? You know you can't do what you did."

"I can do what I *have* to do," I replied. "I don't *want* to do it, but I don't like people lying to me. I told Dick O'Connell I wanted three years, he said they don't want to give it to me, and then I found out all these other guys got three-year contracts. So that's why I'm staying home; I don't want to return to the team until I get the same thing."

"C'mon, sit down," he said. "Listen to me. You don't have to worry about anything. You go down to Florida, and I'll take care of you."

I believed him, so I did—and he did. He and club treasurer John Harrington met for three hours with my sports attorney, Bob Woolf, and then spoke to O'Connell. They wound up turning my existing two-year contract, which had one year left, into a two-year deal with an optional third year for 1978. My salary was about $180,000, and Mr. Yawkey said there would also be a nice bonus at the end of the '76 season if I did well.

You see, that's the way Tom Yawkey was; he respected me. During the season, he would come into the clubhouse and sit down next to me at my locker and we'd just talk. He loved baseball, and he liked me. He used to always say, "You know, I *like* the way you pitch!"

One guy everybody liked as a pitcher was the newest member of our staff: Ferguson Jenkins. "Fergie" was a six-foot-five right-hander from Canada who won at least twenty games six times in a row for the Cubs from 1967 to 72, and then after coming to the American League in 1974 went 25-12 for the Rangers. At age thirty-two he was still cranking out nearly three hundred quality innings per season, and all it took to get Fergie from Texas was $250,000 of Mr. Yawkey's money and a couple of promising ballplayers we didn't really need—outfielder Juan Beniquez, pitcher Steve Barr, and a minor leaguer to be named later (who turned out to be pitcher Craig Skok, 4-7 lifetime in the majors).

A rotation of me, Jenkins, Bill Lee, Rick Wise, and Reggie Cleveland, plus our powerful lineup and depth, made us the favorites to repeat as AL East champs in '76.

Darrell Johnson said he was worried I'd be out of shape when I got to Florida, but I surprised him just like I used to surprise Al Dark. I had the best spring training of my career and couldn't wait for the games to start counting. Knowing my *whole* family—including my mother and father—were all together and safe back in Boston was a huge weight off my shoulders, and I am sure that helped my pitching. So was knowing that my dad would be coming to see all of my starts at Fenway; I hoped to give him plenty to cheer about.

The good feelings I had in Winter Haven continued into the regular season. I usually started slow and heated up with the warmer weather, but by the middle of May I was already 5-2 with a 2.39 ERA. This was great except for one thing: the rest of the team was 6-14. Even though we had basically the same lineup that had won in '75, that magic feeling we had the year before seemed to be missing.

Three of our key guys—Fisk, Burleson, and Lynn—were playing with unsigned contracts as their agent tried to get them some of the real big money players on other teams were starting to get. There were rumors that one, two, or all three of them would be traded, and the constant headlines and questions from reporters made the clubhouse less fun. The fans had bigger expectations after '75, so when we started slow, we felt even more pressure than usual. We were playing tight, and in late April and early May we lost ten straight games.

On Friday, May 20, we went into New York to play for the first time at the "new" Yankee Stadium. The Yanks had played the two previous seasons at Shea Stadium, home of the Mets, while their ballpark was being completely redone. I always had special feelings for the old Yankee Stadium because it's where I won my first big-league game, and my dad had also pitched there, but the new version had a lot of the same elements. You still felt like you were someplace special and historic.

There was plenty of buzz around the ballpark that first game, not only because the defending AL champions were in town for the weekend but because the Yankees were in first place—six games ahead of us—with a 19–10 record. They were playing with a swagger under a new manager, Billy Martin, and I'm sure wanted to impress their fans and make a statement by beating us. We had finally put together a decent stretch after the long losing streak, winning eight of nine, and wanted to keep it going.

Even before that series, you could really feel a new rivalry building between the two teams. A lot of it revolved around Fisk and Yankees catcher Thurman Munson. Both were great players, tough as hell, and the papers liked to talk about how much they hated each other. A lot of that was overblown; Munson might have been a little jealous of all the publicity Fisk got, especially after his big homer in the World Series, but they had mutual respect for one another because they knew what it took to *be* a good catcher. Each used the other to push himself.

The guy on the Yankees who *really* hated Fisk was right fielder Lou Piniella. When he was catching, Fisk used to always talk to the batters when they came up to hit, trying to mess with their concentration. It drove Piniella crazy.

On May 20, a few hours before the first game of the big series, Piniella was in the batting cage. When he saw me, he yelled out:

"You tell that motherfucker Fisk to stop asking me how my mother is doing! I don't want to hear it! I'm tired of hearing that—'How's your mother? Is she OK?' If he says that to me again, we're going to fight!"

I told Fisk, but I guess it didn't do any good. In the bottom of the sixth, with New York up 1-0, Piniella singled off Bill Lee and went to second on another hit by Graig Nettles. When Otto Valez singled to right, with two outs, Piniella rounded third at full speed and headed home.

Evans made a great throw from right that beat Piniella to the plate, so he barreled into Fisk with his knees and cleats up—trying to knock the ball loose from Fisk's grasp. Pudge held on for the out, pushed Piniella off of him, and then they both started swinging. Fisk said Piniella's slide was "an act of violence and uncalled for;" Piniella claimed that Fisk tagged him "with both the ball and his fist."

Whoever started it, the next thing you know, everybody was out there fighting. When he ran over and tried to get into it with Nettles, Lee got punched to the ground, pushed around, and then punched some more. He wound up with torn ligaments in his left shoulder.

As Lee limped off the field with trainer Charlie Moss, holding his arm, the Yankees fans went wild.

It was great for the rivalry, and the newspapers, but any chance we had to get back to the playoffs went out the door right there. Although we won that night, New York beat us in the next two games on walk-off hits—then came to Boston a week later and took two of three at Fenway. Lee, who had a better record against the Yankees than just about any pitcher in baseball, was out for two months. We were never able to replace him.

Dick O'Connell still must have thought we could turn things around because right at the June 15 trade deadline he made a huge deal. Oakland owner Charlie Finley decided to sell off all his best players before they could become free agents, and O'Connell got A's All-Stars Joe Rudi and Rollie Fingers for $1 million each plus a couple back-ups. They joined our club and were given Red Sox uniforms, but before either one got into a game, commissioner Bowie Kuhn negated the deals (and one by the Yankees, who had bought Vida Blue from Finley for $1.5 million) as "not in the best interests of baseball."

It seemed like nothing was going right for us, and it only got worse a few weeks later. Tom Yawkey, who had been battling leukemia and pneumonia, died at age seventy-three on July 9, 1976. Like everyone else, I felt bad that in his forty-three years of owning the Red Sox, Mr. Yawkey had never won a World Series. We all had really wanted to win it for him in '75 because he was already sick and we didn't know how much longer he had.

Some of the stories that came out after he died mentioned the Red Sox being the last MLB team to integrate. Ever since then, people have debated whether Tom Yawkey was a racist. I don't like talking about it myself, but here's what I think.

From all I've heard, there were racists working for the Red Sox at the highest levels under Yawkey. The team developed a terrible reputation by passing on players like Jackie Robinson and Willie Mays, and that set the club back for a long, long time. By the 1970s, Black and Latino players didn't want to sign or be traded here.

As the owner, Yawkey could have—and *should* have—used his power to change that culture. If he did, maybe he would have won more.

But deep in my heart, I don't believe that Yawkey himself was racist. He never looked at me any differently because of my color; he always treated me like a man. I can tell when someone is not being sincere, and I never felt that from Tom Yawkey. If you talk to other Black and Latino players, they will say the same thing. He was fair and good to them.

So when people ask me about him now, I focus on the positive. Drive around Boston, I tell them, and you'll see the Yawkey name on many hospital and college buildings. He was also chairman of the Jimmy Fund at Dana-Farber Cancer Institute and made it an official charity of the Red Sox—which it remains to this day.

Yawkey didn't just talk the talk either. He and his wife, Jean, put plenty of their own money and time toward supporting cancer research and treatment through the Jimmy Fund, and that set an example for generations of Red Sox players to get involved. Today, from the time they are rookies, guys on the team are taught to support the Jimmy Fund by going to fundraising events and visiting with children and adults battling cancer at Dana-Farber—which is right down the street from the ballpark.

That should be his legacy in Boston.

Mr. Yawkey died right before the All-Star game, which was at Philadelphia. I was proud to be selected to represent the American League for the third time and pitched two shutout innings in a 7-1 AL loss. It was funny; in my first inning, with Fisk catching, Yaz behind me in left, and Pete Rose, Joe Morgan, and George Foster all batting for the NL, it was like a replay of the World Series. Rose led off with a triple—he never did that against me in the series—but then I got Steve Garvey, Morgan, and Foster to leave Pete stranded at third.

At this point the Red Sox were 40-40, already nine-and-a-half games behind the Yankees, and right after the All-Star break, we had a thirteen-game road trip that we figured would make or break our season. When we lost six of seven to start the trip, O'Connell decided he had to do something. So just a half-season after winning the pennant, Darrell Johnson was fired, and third base coach Don Zimmer took over as manager.

I felt bad for Darrell and will always appreciate how he had believed in my ability to come back from my injuries. Sometimes a team just gets into a funk and needs a change. Most of the guys on the club had slipped from their 1975 performances, and injuries really hurt the pitching staff: first Lee, whose shoulder got messed up in the Yankees fight; and then Jenkins, who had a torn Achilles tendon that he played with for half a season before having surgery in September. Guys were frustrated, and some had started to tune Darrell out.

Zim was an aggressive, hustling-type of ballplayer as a utility infielder in the 1950s and '60s, and he wanted the Red Sox to play that way under him. It took a while, but we finally started putting it together down the stretch and won fifteen of our last eighteen. Unfortunately, we were already way out of it by then, and we finished third in the AL East behind the Yankees and Orioles with an 83-79 record.

There wasn't much to play for as a team in August and September, but I had something very important driving me—my father.

That winter, Dad had first started complaining that he wasn't feeling well. We took him to the doctor and had them check everything out, and it turned out to be cancer. I started taking him to chemotherapy treatments, but every time he went, he was messed up afterwards; he would throw up and just not feel good.

This went on a for a while, and then one time he told me, "Nah, don't take me no more. I don't want to go no more." It was his decision, and I respected it even though we both knew it meant he would probably get worse soon. He wanted the quality of his life to be good, or it wasn't worth living.

It's funny, but during this time my father actually started missing Cuba. One day he told me he wanted to go home.

"What do you want to go home for? You've got your grandkids, you've got me, Mom, and Maria."

"I'm just homesick. I want to go home."

"Nah, you don't want to go home. Castro doesn't want you back."

We laughed about that, and he stayed—long enough to turn Luis Jr. into a pool hustler.

"Me and my grandfather became very close over time, and we spent a lot of time at that pool table," Luis Jr. remembers. "He was a shark, and he used to teach me. I used to come home from school, and he'd be downstairs waiting for me. He didn't like talking a whole lot about baseball or his career. I think he still had a sore spot about the way it had ended for him, and not being able to play bigleague ball. But I got to be pretty good at pool by playing with him. He and my dad were very serious with one another, but loving at the same time. He would give my dad advice, and if he didn't have a good game he would let him have it."

There were more good games than bad that summer. Dad kept coming to see me pitch at Fenway when he could and made it through the whole

1976 season. I slumped in July when Lee came back and Zimmer started using a five-man rotation, and at one point my record was 10–10. Then I convinced Zim to let me start pitching on three days' rest more, and I won nine of my next ten decisions.

On September 22, with Dad in the stands, I faced the Brewers at Fenway. I had a no-hitter going until my old buddy George Scott broke it up with a triple into the gap in the seventh, but I struck out Scott and Mike Hegan to end the game and get my twentieth win of the year. My final mark of 21-12 with a 3.06 ERA and nineteen complete games earned me a fifth-place finish in the AL Cy Young voting and made me the first Red Sox pitcher since Cy Young and Bill Dineen in 1903-04 to win twenty games three times.

The team fulfilled Mr. Yawkey's promise, too, giving me a $25,000 bonus in September for having the "good year" he and I had talked about in March.

Dad was excited by my season, but his health was getting worse. Since he and Mom came to Boston, we had played catch sometimes. Right up until that summer he could still pitch them in there pretty good, and he would give me advice like to keep my head down or how to throw a better knuckleball. We were still joking about which one of us was better, each saying it was the other one. Now he was too tired for catch.

I'll never forget that last day with him in the hospital. I was on the sofa, my father was in the bed, and my mother was on the couch on the other side of the room. She got up and went around to him, and my father started talking to her.

"Vieja—old lady—I'm going to go. You go with me, or you stay?"

"Don't worry, I'll go with you."

I didn't want to listen to that shit, you know? I didn't even want to look; I turned towards the TV and pretended I was listening to it. But I heard everything.

At nine o'clock I told her it was time to go home.

"No, I want to stay. He's going to die tonight."

"What are you going to do? See him die? I don't think that's a good move. Let's go, and whatever happens, happens."

So we went home, but she was mad. She wanted to stay. And about twenty minutes after we got home, maybe twenty-five, the doctor called and said, "You father just passed away." It was Friday, December 10, 1976. Luis E. Tiant was seventy-one.

I told my mother, and she cussed me out good.

"I told you! I told you!"

I didn't know what to say; what could I say? I just felt bad.

The newspapers had real nice write-ups on Dad, some with the photo of him and me hugging at the airport or my holding his coat while he made his first pitches. When the reporters asked me for a comment, I told them I believed my father died happy. "He was so glad to be here in the United States with us," I said. "And the people of Milton and the baseball fans of Boston were all so great to him and my mother."

The next day we had to go to the funeral home. Mom didn't want to go, but the doctor told me I couldn't leave her alone. So I took her with me. She went over to my dad's casket, and she stayed for maybe twenty-five minutes talking to him. Maria and I sat down in the other room, waiting, until she was done.

About 450 people came to the funeral home for the wake. Dwight Evans, Johnny Pesky, and Rico Petrocelli were there from the Red Sox, along with many friends and even some Red Sox fans we had never met before. The funeral home was in Brookline, about a mile from Fenway Park—where my father had spent the last year cheering me on.

At the end of the night we took my mom home. In the room where my parents stayed at our house, they used to sit and look out the window at the people outside. So when we got home, Mom told me she was going to go downstairs, get us some espresso, and then come back up to look out the window. Maybe ten or fifteen minutes later, around midnight, Maria went down to check on her.

Mom was on the floor, unconscious.

We called the ambulance, and they took her to Milton Hospital. As they worked on her I was looking into the operating room, and I saw them shaking their heads. She was gone; the doctors believed she must have had a heart attack.

It was 12:30 a.m. on Monday, December 13—just three days since my father died. Isabel Tiant, like her husband, was seventy-one.

I was so messed up that when they came out to give me her jewelry, I said, "I don't want it. I don't want NOTHING!" I had no brothers and sisters, and now both my parents had left me one after the other. It didn't seem fair.

Later, I admitted to a reporter that when my father passed away "I had a feeling something might happen to my mother. She felt it, too, but she didn't want to make me feel sad."

My father's funeral was supposed to be that morning, but we postponed it for one day. We had my mother's wake that night and then a double funeral the next day. Dick O'Connell came to the services, as did Carlton Fisk, Rick Burleson, and State Treasurer Robert Crane. Msgr. John Day of St. Elizabeth's Church in Milton led the service, delivering his eulogy in both Spanish and English.

When my parents came to Boston the year before, Msgr. Day said in his eulogy, they "did more for international peace and goodwill than all the diplomats put together." The cheers of the crowd as Dad threw out his first pitches at Fenway Park, Msgr. Day said, were "a sign of the love and respect for that man and his family, for his devotion and his love of family."

Bob Woolf, my agent, also had a very moving statement about my parents.

"It is a beautiful love story," Woolf said. "You know, thirty-six years ago they entered a church together to get married—and thirty-six years later they entered a church together to be buried."

That was true, I thought, looking at the bronze caskets side by side; they did everything as one, right up until the end.

We buried them in Milton Cemetery, about ten blocks from our home. And as long as I lived there, or nearby, I would go two or three times a week to visit them, bringing flowers and cleaning up around their graves. After being separated from them for so many years, I guess I wanted to make sure to keep them as close as I could. Today I still visit them whenever I'm back up in Boston.

The whole thing, them going like that one after the other, it almost killed me too. But you know what? I had fifteen months with them at the end, and they were the happiest months of my life. God answered my prayers and brought us back together. Taking them like that, it was His will.

For the next few months, people were wonderful in reaching out to me and my family with their condolences. Thurman Munson sent us a fruit basket. But as much as we appreciated everyone's concern, I was really looking forward to the baseball season so I could stop having to talk about my parents and could focus on something new.

Most Red Sox fans remember the 1977 season for two things: home runs and Bill Campbell. They saw plenty of both.

We sent balls flying out of Fenway and every other park we played in that summer. After hitting 134 homers as a team each of the previous two seasons, we had 213 in 1977 to set a new franchise record. Jim Rice led the AL with thirty-nine, while Yaz had twenty-eight, Fisk twenty-six, and Lynn eighteen. George Scott, who we had gotten back from Milwaukee with Bernie Carbo in a trade for Cecil Cooper, took over at first base and had thirty-three. Butch Hobson, our new third baseman with Rico's retirement, hit thirty. Hobson was also one of five players on the club with ninety-five or more RBI, even though he often batted ninth in our lineup. That tells you just what kind of offense we had.

At times we were hitting so many bombs that the games felt like batting practice. In beating the Yankees three straight at Fenway in June, we outhomered them sixteen to zero, part of a record ten-game stretch in which we hit thirty-three homers. We hit so many balls out that guys got sick of making curtain calls. One time, Scott hit one, and they kept yelling, "BOOMER! BOOMER!" for him to come out of the dugout. He wasn't budging, so I figured I'd go instead.

"Hey," I told the guys on the bench, "We all look the same anyway, right?"

So I ducked my head out, turned around to the stands, and waved. That's as close as I came to a home run since 1969!

That Yankees series featured another crazy moment in the growing Boston–New York rivalry. Reggie Jackson—New York's big free-agent signee that year—was pulled from right field by Billy Martin while everyone at Fenway and a national TV audience watched on. Billy was angry that Reggie had loafed after a Jim Rice bloop double, so he sent Paul Blair out to take his place mid-inning. Reggie had to run in as the crowd razzed him, and he was steamed. He had some words for Billy, who then went after him. They had to be separated in the dugout by coach Ellie Howard.

We were in first place in the AL East at that point and were either first or a close second the entire summer. During our best stretch we won sixteen out of seventeen games and built a three-and-one-half-game lead by mid-August. The problem was that our starting pitchers—including me—couldn't hold up our end. Every one of us—me, Wise, Jenkins, Reggie Cleveland, Lee—had down years. Our team ERA of 4.11 was the highest by a Boston staff in more than a decade, and because nobody emerged as a "stopper," we also had losing streaks of seven and nine games that kept us from widening our lead.

My twelve victories, 4.53 ERA, and three complete games (in thirty-two starts) represented my worst totals in seven full seasons with the Red Sox. I was the one regular member of the rotation not sent to the bullpen at least once by Zimmer, who kept trying to find the right formula but lacked the patience or confidence in our pitchers to let them work through their own problems. It got to the point where veterans like Jenkins—who had won his two hundredth big-league game for us the previous year—were barely talking to Zim.

The biggest reason that we stayed at or near the top all year—other than the homers—was Campbell. A right-handed reliever with a great screwball who we signed in the off-season as a free agent, "Soup" was a former Army radio operator in Vietnam who knew how to keep his cool in tight situations. We put him in plenty, and he was as good as it gets: a 13-9 record, 2.96 ERA, and thirty-one saves in sixty-nine games and 140 innings. He even led the team in wins, which is very unusual for a reliever but made sense that year because we played in so many contests that were decided late.

So Campbell did *his* part, but by September he was to the point where he was so overworked that Zim said he was worried his arm would fall off. We had to depend more on other guys, and in the end, we just weren't consistent enough or deep enough a staff to hold back the Yankees. We still had a great September, going 22-8, but they beat us two out of three in a key series at the Stadium that was our last real shot. New York finished 100-62 while we were tied with the Orioles, two-and-a-half games back, at 97-65.

The only teams with more victories than us that year were the four division winners, and no Red Sox club had won more games since the 1946 AL Champions. Those facts plus our 8-7 record against the Yankees—who went on to beat the Dodgers in the World Series—made us even more frustrated about the chance we let slip away.

The one real consolation for me was that I was again able to finish strong. After losing to Baltimore on July 1, I was 5-7; the rest of the season I went 7-1, and the team won fourteen of my last sixteen starts. In September, when every game was crucial, my ERA was 2.40. But I knew it wasn't enough. Big performances in September only really matter if they lead to big performances in October.

If we wanted a chance at more of *those*, it meant figuring out a way to beat out those damn Yankees.

16

OVER MY DEAD BODY

WALK PAST ANY LITTLE LEAGUE field in the Boston area during the mid-seventies, and there was a good chance you'd see at least one kid on the sidelines twisting his or her body and looking to the sky while pitching. Few dared to try baseball's most famous delivery in real games, other than the wiffle-ball variety, because they knew nobody but the great El Tiante could turn themselves into a human pretzel and still throw strikes. But it was always fun to try, chomping your imaginary tobacco and picturing yourself on the mound at Fenway Park—the game on the line and the crowd chanting your name.

Ninety-nine wins between 1972 and 1976, including three in the dramatic postseason run of '75, had helped make Luis Tiant the most popular pitcher in modern Red Sox history. But the death of his parents and Boston owner Tom Yawkey, who had supported him in salary disputes with management, weighed heavy on Tiant's mind. In 1977 he sat out much of spring training while haggling over another contract, and when he returned the magic seemed to be gone from his right arm. The head bobs and hand shakes and leg swivels that made up his wondrous windup were still there—but not the results.

For the first time since his 1-7 debut with the Red Sox six years earlier, Tiant's ability was openly being questioned in the summer of '77—in newspapers, on the radio, even occasionally in the stands. Luis's mysterious age had finally caught up with him, the skeptics said, or he was too concerned with his contract to focus on his job. His kids, already used to standing out as Black faces in a white neighborhood, were dealing with more challenges too. And even when Tiant rebounded to pitch strongly down the stretch in a three-way pennant race with New York and Baltimore, it was unclear whether the turnaround was a true return to form or a last gasp.

By the spring of 1978, while his Red Sox teammates and manager Don Zimmer still openly professed their confidence in Tiant, it was clear that the team's new executives no longer viewed him as Boston's ace. Big-name pitchers were acquired and slotted into the first and second spots in the rotation, and rubber-armed relievers were brought aboard as further insurance.

For the Red Sox to overtake the world champion New York Yankees in the American League East, the experts insisted, El Tiante would need to be a piece of the puzzle. How big a piece he *could* be was still unclear.

IT WASN'T JUST the Yankees causing me trouble.

Boston has the world's most passionate baseball fans, and they have always shown me love and respect. But some things I dealt with living in and around that city during the 1970s were not easy to handle, no matter how much people saw me smiling and joking. It wasn't always easy trying to bring up a family in the Boston area as a Black and Latino man then, even if your last name was Tiant.

Where we lived, in Milton, was almost all white. Most of the people were great to us, but some weren't—and the bad ones passed it down to the next generation. That was hard on my kids. Isabel used to come home crying from school because the other students made fun of her, saying things like "all you eat are beans and greasy stuff."

Luis Jr. was older, but he got it too.

"When we moved to Milton, I was about to turn twelve," he remembers. "Even though I had been traveling all around the majors with my dad in the summers, when he played in Cleveland, Minnesota, and then Boston, making a permanent move to the United States and going to school there was different. That's when you get hit with that racism, and I got it from both ends—because I was Hispanic and I was Black. I was prepared after hearing the stories about what my dad had been through, but it was still tough.

"The hardest thing was experiencing it in your own neighborhood. Guys would drive by and yell the 'N word' when we were out cutting the grass. I'm not sure if they knew who my dad was when they did it, but it probably would not have mattered. You grow up and get a wake-up call pretty early about that kind of stuff."

I always told my kids, if somebody makes fun of you because of who you are, you kick their ass! So, one time in middle school a bigger kid really got on Luis Jr., and he beat him up. Then he came home and told me what he did. I was sorry it happened, but I was proud of him for sticking up for himself—and told him so.

The next day I walked to the corner to meet Luis when the school bus dropped him off, but it went by without stopping. I thought something might be wrong, so I went to the school; it turned out they were punishing him because of the fight—keeping him after school. So I went to see the principal.

"What happened to my son?" I asked him.

"He got in a fight."

"Do you know why? Because I talked to my kid first, and he told me everything."

"Yes, we know why."

"Then why are you punishing *him*, but you're not also punishing the other kid? Because he's white?"

The principal didn't say anything, but I could tell I had caught him.

"If you permit that shit here, you're a racist," I said, raising my voice. "I tell you something right now. This is the last time you punish my kid like this. If you do it again, I'm going to come here and beat your ass. Then I'm going to bring in the television cameras and the newspaper reporters, and you're going to get fired."

That was one way being a pro athlete could help you out, but it didn't make me feel any better.

Sometimes, like Luis Jr. remembers, the trouble even came to our house. There used to be these kids who would pull down our driveway when we were inside, throw bottles at our house, and then take off. I'm sure they knew who we were, one of the only Black families in town.

One day I looked out the window and saw their car, so I decided to go after those motherfuckers. I jumped in my car, started chasing them, and when they turned into a little supermarket, I pulled in right beside them. Then I got out and went over to the driver's window.

"Get out of the car."

"What do you mean?"

"I mean get out of the fucking car. Why did you throw bottles at my house?"

"No, no, it wasn't us!"

"I saw your car, and now I'm going to kick all your asses."

There were four kids. At that time, I had a gun, a nine-millimeter, that I brought with me. They looked nervous and kept saying it wasn't them. They wouldn't get out, and I didn't want to force them, just scare them.

"I'm going to let you go *this* time, but if I see you again, I won't."

I knew all the police in town, so the next day I went to the station and explained to the chief what happened. Then I told him, "If I see these motherfuckers again, doing that shit, I'm going to shoot them."

The chief tried to calm me down and told me I'd get in trouble if I really went after the kids.

"I don't give a shit," I told him. "If they do that to me at my house, and to my family, I'm going to protect them."

In the end I did the smart thing. I got these big blocks and put them up at the top of my driveway. I painted them white, and those punks didn't come back again.

The crazy thing is, sometimes even *helping* someone could lead to problems. There was this old guy who lived across the street, and I'm guessing he was one of those people who didn't want us moving into the neighborhood four years before. Just before I left for spring training in 1978, New England was hit with the huge snowstorm everybody calls the Blizzard of '78. There were two to three feet of snow, lots of people lost power, and anyone who couldn't shovel was stuck inside their homes.

I got out my snowblower, cleaned up my driveway and everything, and then looked over at the old man's house. There was snow everywhere, real heavy stuff, and I knew he couldn't move any of it with a shovel. It was just him and his wife living there; their two daughters were grown up. So I went over with my snowblower and knocked on his door.

"I'm going to help you," I said.

"No, you don't have to do that."

"Look, I know you can't do it. You're going to have a heart attack if you try. Let me clean it."

So I cleaned it. Later on I looked out my window and saw the guy's garage door was open, so I went over to tell him. Nobody answered the front door this time, but I could see him looking out. Maybe he didn't recognize me, I don't know, but suddenly there were two police cruisers coming down the street—one from each side. Once they got close, the cops saw who it was and rolled down their windows. They knew me.

"What's the matter?" I asked one of them.

"Someone called and said a Black guy was knocking on their door."

"His garage door was open! I didn't want anybody to get inside his house, so I went over to tell him!"

"Don't worry about it. Just go home."

After that, I never spoke to the old guy again. But I did get a little revenge. When I went to sell my house, he and his wife wanted to buy it for one of their daughters. I said, "No way I'm selling it to *you*," and in the end I sold it to a dentist.

A *Black* dentist!

Eventually everyone got shoveled out and down to Florida. I was determined to show that I still had gas left in my tank after the 1977 season. It had been a bad year for me, and I won't make excuses for it. But there was a lot of stuff I was dealing with after the death of my parents, and now I felt like my mind was in a much better place.

"What's done is done," I told Joe Fitzgerald of the *Boston Herald*. "I'm going to spring training the way a rookie goes. I'm going down there to win a job. I'm not going down like a veteran who knows he's made the team. I'm going to work hard, and I'm going to show everybody that I can be the Luis Tiant I was two years ago."

Teammates like Fisk, Yaz, and Dwight Evans all told Fitzgerald and other sportswriters that they thought I would bounce back and have a good year. So did the manager, who really got my juices flowing when he said he was going to stick with a four-man rotation. I never felt right or pitched well on four days' rest, which I did for much of '77 when Zim used five starters.

"Luis is going to pitch winning ball this year for this club," Zimmer said shortly before the regular season. "I've been saying this since the end of last season, and if he doesn't do it, then a lot of people can laugh at me."

There were lot of reasons for Zim and the rest of us to be optimistic, besides coming off a ninety-seven-win year. About a year after Mr. Yawkey died, the Red Sox were sold to a group headed up by two of his closest advisors, team vice president Haywood Sullivan and team trainer Buddy LeRoux. Mr. Yawkey's widow, Jean, was the third senior partner, and since she had all the money, she had the final say. Mrs. Yawkey didn't like general manager Dick O'Connell, so he was fired, and Sullivan took over as GM. Originally a backup catcher for the Red Sox in the fifties, and later a big-league manager, Sully knew the game and didn't waste any time getting us just what we needed. By the time he was done, we'd have ten new players on our twenty-five-man roster, including six new pitchers on an eleven-man staff.

First was free agent starter Mike Torrez, a big, strong right-hander who had helped the Yankees to the championship the year before. He was good for at least fifteen wins and close to 250 innings every year, and had shown he could do it in the postseason with two wins (including the clincher) in the '77 World Series against the Dodgers. By signing Torrez we were also weakening the Yanks, which was a great bonus. Lefty Tom Burgmeier—a reliable veteran who could go long or short relief; and righty Dick Drago—our bullpen stopper back in '75, before we traded him to the Angels—were both brought in to lighten Campbell's load in the bullpen.

One player Zimmer had talked about getting for a while was Angels' second baseman Jerry Remy. Although mostly a singles hitter, Remy had a good glove, was a great bunter, and could steal you thirty to forty bases a season. Denny Doyle had done a real solid job for us at second the past three years, but he wasn't fast and turned thirty-four over the winter; Remy was only twenty-five. Zim figured having a young, scrappy guy at the top of the order who could get himself in scoring position with Rice, Yaz, Fisk, and the other big boys coming up would be a great fit. He also thought that because Remy grew up outside of Boston as a huge Red Sox fan, he'd be extra motivated to do well. Sully agreed, so we traded for Remy and released Doyle.

Our last move was the biggest. Just before Opening Day, Sully swung a deal with Cleveland that cost us Rick Wise and two top prospects but got us one of the league's best young guns: Dennis Eckersley. Eck was just twenty-three but had already thrown a no-hitter, made an All-Star team, and had a two-hundred-strikeout season. He was a tall, lean right-hander from California with a great fastball, tons of hair, and loads of self-confidence.

Fans loved Eck's energy on the mound, where he had a high leg-kick and liked to pump his fist after strikeouts. In the clubhouse he was a colorful guy with his own "baseball language" that reporters and fans quickly picked up on. Strikeouts were "punchouts," a pitcher with a good fastball had "cheese," and bad hitters were "lambs." If you punched out lots of lambs with your cheese you made more "iron"—money. He liked to have fun, but Eck earned our respect because he always told it like it was; if he made a horseshit pitch that cost us a game, he owned up to it.

I was excited to be part of a starting rotation with Eckersley, Torrez, and Lee, but that would have to wait. On March 17, two weeks before we swung the deal for Eck, I was hit on the index finger of my pitching hand by a line drive off the bat of Detroit's Steve Kemp. My finger hurt so bad at first, I thought it was broken, and if it was that could have been the end of my career. The index finger is crucial for pitchers because you need it for pressure when holding all your pitches. Luckily, it turned out to only be a dislocation, but I still needed to spend a month on the disabled list.

My first time pitching in the regular season, on April 18, was also my first relief appearance since 1972. The fans gave me a big hand when I came in to start the seventh inning at Fenway, with the Brewers beating us 6-5, and I pitched three hitless innings as we came back to win, 7-6, on a Fisk double in the ninth. It felt good to be out there, but I thought it would take me awhile to get up to my top form.

I was wrong. After pitching five decent innings in my first start, against the Indians, I went into Texas on April 28 and had a perfect game going into the sixth. I wasn't blowing guys away, but it was a seventy-degree night, and I always liked pitching in warm weather. Although I tired a bit in the later innings and left the game with the score 3-3, I felt good about my progress.

Then my luck went bad again. I was up 5-3 in my next start, against Minnesota, but after a thirty-eight-minute rain delay, I lost my control and blew the lead—although we did come back to win. My next time out, against Kansas City, I felt I had my best stuff of the season. But I pulled a muscle in my right hamstring fielding a bunt and had to come out in the third inning.

"I had felt something back there last week," I told reporters after the game, "but it wasn't until tonight that it popped. I've been trying to stretch it (the muscle) and now it's popped." Bill Campbell, our great reliever who was nursing a sore arm, walked by me in the clubhouse while I was talking about my hamstring. He looked like he felt bad for me, but I just laughed.

"Watch," I said to him. "Tomorrow I'll probably fall out of bed and bust my head."

Why was I joking around? First off, the doctor told me it wasn't serious and that I probably wouldn't even miss a start. Plus, even though all this stuff was happening to me, we were still winning. Somebody was always stepping up. That night, after I had to come out, Bob Stanley pitched the last seven innings to get the 8-4 win. It was our sixth straight victory and the fourth in the five games I had appeared in.

The doctor wasn't quite right about the timing. I wound up missing more than two weeks, and when I finally got back on the mound on May 22 at Detroit, I felt so strong I could throw the ball through a wall. That's not always a good thing; if your arm feels *too* strong, and you throw too powerfully, you can leave the ball up and have a hard time finding the strike zone. That's why I liked pitching every fourth day because you don't have time to get too well-rested.

I left plenty of balls up that night, walking six and letting up eight hits, but I gutted through. In the end, I got a 156-pitch, 9-3 win in front of a wild crowd of more than 52,000 at Tiger Stadium excited by their team's surprisingly good start. We had some injuries in our bullpen, especially Campbell, so Zim was happy to let me keep going until I asked out. The way I felt that night, he knew that wasn't ever going to happen.

So did my teammates.

"Luis was not going to go out there and try and go five innings; he was going to try and go out and complete the game," remembers Jim Rice. "Once he started a game, he had to be VERRRRRRRRY bad for you to take him out—because he wasn't going to *come* out."

That victory at Detroit put us in a first-place tie with the Tigers atop the American League East, one game ahead of the Yankees. It was only my second win of the year, but it got me rolling. I won my next four starts, two by shutout. I was really starting to feel good again.

"It's no longer a question of his coming back," Zimmer said after I beat the Mariners, 3-2, in early June, "only a matter of how many games he wins."

Pudge was more precise when I shutout the A's on a four-hitter my next time out: "He's as good now as he's ever been."

By the time I beat the Orioles on June 24, letting up three solo homers but getting the big outs when I needed them, I was 7-0 with a 2.84 ERA. The team had won my last nine starts, and my record put me in good company with the rest of our rotation: Torrez was 10-3, Eckersley 7-2, and Lee 8-3. Stanley, Drago, and Burgmeier were all doing a great job in relief, and with our lineup, we were in almost every game we played—and winning most of them. That's the night I first told reporters, "This is the best team I've ever played on," and I still feel that way. Just look at Zim's preferred batting order:

1. Rick Burleson (SS)
2. Jerry Remy (2B)
3. Jim Rice (DH)
4. Carl Yastrzemski (LF)
5. Carlton Fisk (C)
6. Fred Lynn (CF)
7. George Scott (1B)
8. Dwight Evans (RF)
9. Butch Hobson (3B)

All nine guys had been an All-Star at least once by '78 except Hobson, and he was a thirty-homer, one-hundred-ribbie guy batting ninth. Six of them won at least one Gold Glove in their careers, and a bunch had three or more. Rice, Yaz, and Fisk are all in the Hall of Fame. Lynn, Yaz, and Rice were MVPs. You get the idea; it wasn't quite the 1975 Cincinnati Reds, but it was damn close. We had everything—decent speed, great power, strong defense, and clutch hitters with postseason experience.

Our first series against the Yankees, from June 19 to 21 at Fenway, was the most hyped-up regular season series of 1978. My start against Ken Clay on the 19th drew a 14.3 rating and a 28 percent audience share on NBC's Monday Night Baseball, which means twenty-six million people watched at least part of the game. That was the most to watch a regular season baseball telecast in prime time since April 8, 1974, the night Henry Aaron hit his 715th home run to pass Babe Ruth. We were the hottest team in sports.

The only problem was that our manager wanted all his best guys out there every day. Don Zimmer was not big on resting players, and after coming up short in the '77 AL East race, he was determined to build such a big lead this year that we couldn't blow it. That's not a formula for success; during a long season, guys are going to need a break. Zim couldn't identify with that. He was a gamer, going back to his playing days with the old Brooklyn Dodgers when he had returned to the field after two serious beanings—including one that almost killed him. Guys who didn't want to come out, even when hurt, were his kind of players.

Jim Rice fit this type. Jim Ed *never* came out, playing through a bunch of nagging injuries and getting into all of our 163 games in '78. The reigning home run champion with thirty-nine the previous year, he was even better this time around—batting .315 and leading the majors in hits (213), home runs (46), RBI (139), triples (15), and slugging percentage (.600) to take home the MVP award. His 406 total bases that year made Rice the first player since Aaron in 1959 to top the four-hundred-mark, and it seemed like every one of them came at a big time. Jim Ed was quiet, reliable, and never complained; a "manager's dream" as Zimmer put it.

Rice was superhuman that summer, but most guys liked to take a breather now and then. Two of our best backups were fourth outfielder Bernie Carbo, who was still probably the top pinch-hitter in the game; and Bob Montgomery, an excellent backup catcher. Monty hardly played unless Pudge was on the disabled list because Zimmer wanted Pudge in there controlling the game, and he knew Fisk would never ask for a day off. In 1977 Fisk had been behind the plate for 151 games, and in '78 he would catch 154 more. Montgomery? He got into a combined twenty-seven games during the two seasons.

As for Carbo, he was a crazy character who never meshed with old-school guys like Zimmer. In fact, I think the only guy Zim had a tougher time with than Bernie was his close friend—original "Spaceman" Bill Lee. So as soon as Zim had a chance in '78, with us on top by a good margin in our division, he convinced Haywood to sell Carbo to Cleveland for next to nothing right at the June 15 tradeline. We didn't even get a player in return, just some small cash. That left Bob Bailey as our top power threat off the bench, and Bailey couldn't get around on a fastball anymore. Jack Brohamer, a reserve infielder with a decent bat, and Fred Kendall, a starting catcher the previous six seasons in San Diego and Cleveland, also rarely saw action.

For a while it didn't matter. The starting nine were going great, the pitchers were too, and we hit the All-Star break with a 57-26 record (34-6 at home) and a nine-game lead over second-place Milwaukee in the AL East. The Yanks were eleven-and-one-half games out, the Orioles thirteen back, and our .687 winning percentage translated out to 111-51 over a full season. Everybody figured we had the division all wrapped up.

Part of the reason for our great first half, I believe, was because so many guys on the team that were assembled the previous winter knew each other well. Since Scott had originally come up with the Red Sox in the sixties before we traded him to Milwaukee, the only guy in our starting nine who was *not* developed in our farm system was Remy. Many of the younger guys came up together in the minors, and us older dudes had played with and against each other for five or more years.

Overall, we had a lot of mutual respect for one another. We were not going to be the greatest friends, or go out on the town every night in one big group, but we were happy to play with each other and knew when we played as a unit that we could beat anybody. "Right now, this team is the closest I've ever seen a Red Sox team," said Yaz, then in his eighteenth season.

My job, as always, was to keep things loose. This extended from the clubhouse into the dugout where I was what they call a bench-jockey. I'd yell at guys on opposing teams, all in good fun, and would make sure our own guys got some ribbing too.

One day Yaz was at the plate, got jammed on a pitch, and broke his bat into three pieces. The bat boy went to put it in the back for scrap, but I said, "Give it to me!" Then I taped it up, got some string, and hung it up in the bat rack. Yaz could see his "fixed" bat from left field, and he cursed me out when he came in. But he was also laughing, which helped him get over getting jammed. The next time up, he got a hit.

Yaz and other guys on the team would do similar things to me. One time a batter took me real deep, and when I came into the dugout everybody moved away from me like I was contagious. I just put on my jacket, sat down in the corner, and drank a cup of water. Then one of them came over to me, holding a ball.

"How do you do it?" he asked, all serious. "Do you grip the ball with one or two fingers?" He really seemed to want to know how to give up a long bomb like me.

I told him what he could do with his ball.

We sent seven members of our starting lineup to the '78 All-Star game in San Diego—Burleson, Evans, Fisk, Lynn, Remy, Rice, and Yastrzemski—another sign of just how great a club we had. Then, when the regular season started back up, we quickly went on another winning streak to get our record up to 62-28 on July 19. The Brewers were still nine games back, the Orioles twelve and a half, and the Yankees *fourteen games back*. The only thing keeping New York from falling off the map altogether was their great young lefty pitcher, Ron Guidry. "Louisiana Lightening" was 14-1 with a 2.11 ERA after his win on July 20; without him, the Yanks were a .500 team.

Red Sox fans were probably thinking, "It can't get any better than this." They were right. Over the next two months, everything that went right the first half of the season began going wrong—starting with our health.

Injuries started hitting the team all at once in July; Burleson hurt his ankle, Remy cracked his wrist, Evans started having dizzy spells after a beaning, and Hobson developed problems with bone chips in his elbow. Fisk played with two broken ribs most of the second half and still caught 154 games. Yaz had back trouble that landed him in the hospital in August, along with wrist issues, and both greatly sapped his power; in a seven-week span from mid-July to early September, he hit just one home run.

The Yankees, meanwhile, had worked through their own injury problems and were starting to get healthy—and win. New York's hot-headed manager Billy Martin resigned in mid-July; under his successor, the much calmer Bob Lemon, the Yanks quickly turned their season around. Guidry kept doing his thing, raising his record to 20-2 by September 4, and other pitchers like Ed Figueroa and Catfish Hunter started winning consistently. New York's heavy hitters like Jackson, Graig Nettles, Lou Piniella, and Chris Chambliss were heating up too.

A major part of our problem was the same thing that happened when we blew our big September lead in 1974: we completely stopped hitting. Lynn (.332 average at the All-Star break), Evans (.286), and Yaz (.298) dropped way down in the second half as injuries and the lack of rest Zim gave them earlier in the season took its toll. It hit the whole lineup; seven of our regulars had their averages fall after the break, and as a team we hit only .250 in the second half compared to .283 in the first. Nobody felt it worse than George Scott, who went through a 2-for-42 slide at the plate in July and August and then a 2-for-43 dip in September.

The pitching slipped too, although not nearly as much. Our team ERA was 3.46 in the first half, 3.62 in the second, but because of the drop-off in run support we lost a lot of the games we had been winning earlier on. Torrez, 11-4 at the break, went 5-9 in the second half—including one stretch of eight straight winless starts. Lee, who like me started 6-0, went from 9-3 in the first half to 1-7 in the second before Zimmer pulled him from the rotation and then stopped pitching him altogether. That was a situation where Zim let his personal feelings override what was best for the team because Lee was still a strong veteran pitcher who we really could have used down the stretch.

Eck, our most consistent starter all year, was 10-2 at the break and 10-6 after it, but his ERA was actually much *better* in the second half—another sign it was our offense slumping the most. Me? I struggled like everyone else mid-year; 7-1 at the break, I lost six of my first eight decisions after the All-Star game. My ERA stayed respectably under 3.50, and one of my two wins was the two hundredth of my career—a 4-2, complete game six-hitter against Nolan Ryan and the Angels at Anaheim Stadium on August 16.

But nobody was paying much attention to *how* we were losing, only *how much* we were losing.

After reaching our high point of 62-28 on July 19, we lost eleven of fourteen games (including a 2-8 road trip) to let the Brewers surge back to within four-and-one-half games in early August. Then, after getting back on track for a few weeks, we went through another slump just before and after Labor Day. Only a rookie pitcher named Jim Wright, who earned a regular spot in the rotation when Lee was pulled and then went 5-1 in July and August, kept things from being even worse.

The Yankees, meanwhile, kept charging, and as they passed the Orioles and Brewers to move into second place, the sportswriters started letting us have it.

Boston was one of the first cities with a lot of sports talk on the radio. Most of the guys on the air then were former newspaper beat reporters and columnists who could say whatever they wanted since they no longer had to face players in the clubhouse. Zim got it the worst; I remember him telling me that his wife cried when she heard some of the shit they were saying about him in the car as they drove home from games.

With me, like always, it was mostly cracks about my age. It reminded me of back in '76 when I was 10-10 in July and the sportswriters were saying that I was over the hill—at thirty-five years old. Of course, they didn't *believe* I was thirty-five; they probably figured I was closer to *forty-five* and about to fall apart. Then when I was 15-10 in August, I heard the radio guys saying I was doing well "for a guy my age." I finished that year 21-12, so I guess they were right.

Now here I was two years later, slumping like the rest of the team, and again the "experts" figured it had to be my age. The *Boston Globe* published fan letters in the Sunday Sports pages, and one guy wrote in saying I should be pitching once a week to keep myself from wearing out. Even the *New York Times*, which was supposed to be the *serious* paper, had reporters writing crap like, "Tiant, who admits to being thirty-six years old."

I'll tell you something—*that* shit was getting old. I was doing just fine.

On September 6, after leaving my last start early with a pulled muscle, I was back on the mound to face the Orioles and red-hot Dennis Martinez at Baltimore. We both wound up pitching two-hitters, but I got the 2–0 win because I had Yaz—who hit a two-run shot in the seventh for his first home run since August 5. Yelling loud enough for all to hear, Fisk broke up the clubhouse by announcing that "a cripple and an old man" had been the difference-makers in the game.

"This was as big a lift as we could ask for," Yaz said as we hugged in the clubhouse.

"It was a big win for me, a big win for everybody," I replied. "The best I'd pitched all year."

What both of us were hoping was that the momentum from that game would carry over to the next four—which would be played against the Yankees at Fenway Park starting the next night.

It didn't.

The pressure was all on us; the Yankees were hot, we were struggling, and our lead was down to four games. We still felt like we could hold them off as some of our injured guys were healing up. But the Yanks were on some kind of a roll, and they whipped us in the first three games of the series by scores that still hurt to think about: 15-3, 13-2, and 7-0.

It was incredible; I never saw anything like it in baseball. Whatever could go wrong, *did* go wrong. We were outhit forty-nine to sixteen in the three games, committed eleven errors to their four, and none of our three starters (Torrez, Wright, and Eckersley) made it to the fifth inning.

On Friday night, after we made seven errors that led to seven unearned runs in the 13-2 game, I tried to spark some life into what was a very quiet clubhouse.

"All right, you guys, let's go. What the hell's going on here? Let's get some music on. Forget what happened tonight, and start thinking about tomorrow."

The speech seemed to help, at least for the night. Then when we lost the third game too, dropping our lead to just one game, I decided to take a more hands-on approach to picking up my teammates. I was scheduled to pitch Monday against Baltimore, as part of Zimmer's new five-man rotation, but I certainly didn't need the fourth day's rest. I wanted to do what I could to try and stop this horrible slide *now*.

So I went to Zim's office.

"Skip," I said, "I want to pitch tomorrow [Sunday]."

"No, we need you in Baltimore to face Jim Palmer Monday night; those games are just as important."

How could he say that? The fourth game with New York was as big as they got—a two-game swing in the standings and a chance to keep ourselves in first place with a victory. Zim, as I've said, was old-school all the way. He wanted to stick with our set rotation, and since he also refused to start Bill Lee—Yaz had tried unsuccessfully to sway him on that one, but Zim used Lee to mop up in the Friday blowout—he was going with a rookie, lefty Bobby Sprowl, to try and prevent a Yankees series sweep.

"He's got ice water in his veins," Zim supposedly said of Sprowl in defending his choice. But whatever coolness the kid may have felt didn't last long. He was gone after just six batters, having walked four and allowed an RBI base hit. Three runs were ultimately charged to Sprowl, who in bits of three more seasons never earned a single win in the major leagues.

Our fourteen-game lead was now completely gone, and we were tied for first with New York. It then took only six days and five more losses to fall *three-and-one-half* games *behind* the Yankees—with the last two of those losses coming in the Bronx during our last series there. We finally broke through with a win over New York on September 18, but we still needed to make up two-and-one-half games in the last two weeks of the season to catch them.

Many people have forgotten exactly what happened next, and they like to say we choked. We did not choke. While the Yankees went through the final two weeks with a solid 9-5 record, we went 12-2—including eight straight wins to close out the regular season.

I did my part. We had been beaten by the last-place Blue Jays, 5–4, on September 22, and when the Yankees won the same night, we were two games back with just eight to play. We could not afford to lose again, and heading into my start at Toronto, on September 23, I managed to say just what I felt:

"If we lose today, it will be over my dead body. They'll have to leave me face down on the mound."

No last rites were needed. I threw 142 pitches and kept twelve baserunners from scoring in a 3-1, complete-game win. "It was Tiant's game, vintage El Tiante, the fourth game of the 1975 World Series El Tiante," Peter Gammons wrote in the *Boston Globe*. "He was in more trouble than a Middle East border guard, but through one jam after another, Don Zimmer stood by him."

Jim Rice, who homered that day, says such games never surprised him.

"You knew when you went out there and got Luis two or three runs, you had a chance to win a ballgame," Rice recalls. "A lot of guys, you couldn't give them two or three runs and have that kind of confidence. With him, you could."

New York lost to Cleveland, so that win got us to within one game with seven to go. The final week of the season, as both us and the Yankees won every day and the Yanks clung to that one-game lead, the suspense grew.

On September 27, going against the Tigers at Fenway, I pitched six solid innings in a 5-2 win. It was a chilly night, and I had a good fastball that I used to get me out of some big jams. "This team has proven something," I told reporters after that game. "They've turned it around. Now we just have to see what happens."

For three days, what happened was three more wins by both the Red Sox and Yankees bringing us to the last day of the regular season. New York was playing Cleveland at Yankee Stadium that Sunday afternoon with red-hot

Catfish Hunter pitching. We were facing Toronto at Fenway Park with me on the mound. If the Yankees lost, and we won, there would be a one-game playoff for the AL East title at Fenway the next afternoon (we had won a coin flip to determine the venue). If *we* lost, or New York won, they would win the division.

I was confident I'd do my part. So were the fans.

"You wanted Tiant to have the ball in those big games," says Dan Shaughnessy, longtime *Boston Globe* sportswriter and columnist. "He was just a big-game guy, and he had a level of popularity that was very Pedro-esque in terms of what we saw later with Pedro Martinez. He was just such a joy to watch."

Like I did before every start, I took the Santa Barbara medallion I always wore and fastened its chain in between two buttons on my uniform top to keep it from banging around when I pitched. Saint Barbara of Cuba is the patron saint of artillerymen, and I was taking her with me to battle one more time.

There were really two games played at Fenway Park that day. Besides watching us and the Blue Jays, fans were constantly looking over at the left-field scoreboard for any updates from the Indians-Yankees matchup. Our bullpen pitchers were also helping out with audio reports from the Bronx.

"We had a radio in the bullpen and were listening to the Yankees game," reliever Tom Burgmeier remembers. "When the Indians got a few runs, Fenway just erupted."

It did not take long to see—and hear—that it wasn't Hunter's day. The Indians scored twice in the first on an Andre Thornton homer, and after the Yankees came right back with a pair in their half of the inning, Cleveland chased Hunter with four more runs in the second. By the fourth inning it was 7-2, and Indians starter Rick Waits made it hold up.

Our game took a while longer to take shape. It was scoreless into the bottom of the fifth when Butch Hobson singled, moved to third on an error, and then scored on a Jack Brohamer groundout. A little later that inning, Jerry Remy doubled Brohamer in to make it 2-0. The way I was going, I felt pretty good about that score, and after my teammates got me some breathing room with late homers by Burleson and Rice, it was 5-0, and the chances for a playoff game were looking really good.

I wound up with a two-hit shutout, and near the end it was pure fun. The New York-Cleveland game was going into its last innings around the same time as ours, so while I was pitching in the eighth and ninth, I started intentionally taking long peeks at the Yankees score when I twisted my body around during my windup. Some fans picked up on it, and in the ninth inning the Jumbotron scoreboard behind the centerfield bleachers flashed a message that sparked a loud ovation:

FINAL
CLEV 9-NY 2
THANK YOU RICK WAITS

The final Toronto batter of *our* game was Roy Howell. I jammed him with a rising fastball, and he sent it straight up and to the left of third base. Brohamer settled under it in foul ground and was already jumping for joy by the time he caught it.

When he did, we had finally caught New York.

There would now be one more game between the two teams with the best records in baseball. The winner would finish 100-63 and fly on to Kansas City to start the AL Playoffs. The loser would go home for the winter with a 99–64 mark.

A few fans were starting to rush the field, so I hugged Pudge and sprinted off the mound and into the dugout before things got too crazy. In the clubhouse, as I iced down my arm and had a cigar, I touched the Santa Barbara medallion, still around my neck. She had come through for me again.

"They would *not* lose that day," says Dick Johnson of the Sports Museum, who was at the finale. "It was one of the best-pitched games of Luis's career, and that was no surprise because it meant so much. Gosh, if only that had been the playoff game."

I wished so, too, and had already told Zimmer I'd be ready if he needed me against the Yankees. Who cares if I had no day's rest? I'd have the whole winter to rest.

Mike Torrez was going to have his hands full with 24-3 Ron Guidry. If we lost *that* game, I knew that many people—even after our eight straight wins, and our ninety-nine wins overall—would always see us as chokers.

Torrez had been slumping for six weeks, but he was very confident going into the playoff. He really wanted to beat his former teammates, and early on he was as sharp as I'd ever seen him. Sharper even than Guidry, who we got in front of 1-0 on Yaz's second-inning homer just inside the right-field foul pole. Gid had been almost unhittable all year, and would wind up with the lowest ERA in the league (1.74) since my 1.60 with the Indians ten years before. But on this day he seemed tired, and in the sixth inning we had him on the ropes.

Burleson led off with a double and was singled in by Rice. With two outs and men on first and second, Fred Lynn hit a line drive towards the right-field corner that Lou Piniella caught on the run just in front of the short fence out there. Baseball is a game of inches, and of preparation. Catcher Thurman Munson had told Piniella before the inning that because Guidry's slider—a sharp breaking pitch that cut across the plate—was moving slower than usual, the left-handed Lynn might be able to get his bat around quick enough to pull it to right. So, when Lynn came up, Piniella yelled over to center fielder Mickey Rivers, and the two of them each moved six steps to his left. That put Lou in perfect position to make the play when Lynn *did* pull the ball, just as Munson predicted. If Piniella had not moved, Lynn's hit would likely have rolled untouched to the corner and given us a 4–0 lead.

Instead, we let Guidry off the hook.

A game of inches. That's all Bucky Dent's home run in the seventh inning made it over the Green Monster wall by, but it was good enough to put the Yankees up, 3-2. Lynn called it a "fence-scraper." Dent, who hit five homers all year, got this one with one of Piniella's bats; Mickey Rivers gave it to him after noticing Bucky's was cracked on the previous pitch, which he fouled off his foot. Dent only swung the new bat once, but that's all he needed.

Why was that important? Well, if Rivers didn't notice the crack in Bucky's bat and switch it up, Dent might not have gotten as much on his swing. Plus, Rivers told me later that the bat was corked! I don't know if it's true, and when we were all interviewed for the "14 Back" documentary about the '78 season and the playoff game, Rivers smiled and said there was no cork. I guess we'll never know for sure.

Both teams scored two more runs, and in the bottom of the ninth, with New York up, 5-4, and two outs, everything came down to a few inches again. Yastrzemski was up with Burleson on third and Remy on first. Goose Gossage had come in for Guidry in the seventh, and we had hit him pretty hard. A single here would tie the game; a double could *win it*.

Gossage went to 1-and-0 on Yaz, then threw him a fastball that exploded at the last moment, rising up and in. A real sick pitch that fooled Yaz. He hit a high pop to third that Graig Nettles caught just off the bag in foul ground—the exact same play, in the exact same spot, that Brohamer made to end my win the day before. Nettles even jumped up just like Brohamer did, but this time the crowd was almost completely silent. The home team had lost.

The Goose got it right when he told someone that the American and National League playoffs that year, as well as the World Series, would soon be forgotten. "When people think back to the 1978 season," Gossage said, "the only thing they will remember is that Red Sox-Yankees playoff game."

They *do* still remember it, and in Boston, at least, I hope they also remember the one that came before it. The game that made it possible.

17

PINSTRIPES AND PLATANEROS

THE TV AND PRINT ADS ran throughout the 1979 baseball season, and each viewing was like another spike in the shin to Boston baseball fans.

There was Luis Tiant, who no less an authority than Carl Yastrzemski had dubbed "the heart and soul of the Red Sox," decked out in pinstripes and holding a hot dog that was most definitely *not* a Fenway Frank.

It was, in fact, a *Yankee* Frank, and this smiling spokesman was quick to remind consumers of its virtues as a dietary staple at home or the ballpark. After all, he told them in his thickest Cuban accent: "Eet's goood to bee veeth a WEEEENER."

An eye-roller of a punchline, for sure, but like most everything else he attempted on and off the field, it worked for El Tiante. Consumers could tell he was in on the joke and thought it as silly as anybody else, and this left them smiling—and no doubt hungry as well.

The newest Yankee pitcher had gotten the gig after the resignation of New York manager Billy Martin, a not-so-subtle reminder to New Englanders that their former ace was now with the enemy. But unlike other Red Sox ballplayers who would later make the Athens-to-Sparta switch—Wade Boggs, Roger Clemens, Johnny Damon, Jacoby Ellsbury—Tiant pulled it off with his reputation largely intact. When Luis returned to Fenway for the first time in Yankee gray, he was cheered, not jeered. Any other player who left town as a free agent seeking "security for my family" would get the same eye roll as the "weeener" joke; in Tiant's case, this excuse was respected as the honest feelings of a doting dad and husband.

Tiant enjoyed himself in New York and the several stops that followed—from the big leagues to the minors to Mexico and back. Each time it seemed he was

finished as a ballplayer, he showed he had something left. Each time the doubt-
ers pointed to his age and said it couldn't be done, he proved them wrong and
left smiles in his wake.

He never said he'd pitch forever—but when he stopped, he wanted it to be on
his clock.

AFTER THE PLAYOFF, in the clubhouse, everybody cried. Yaz, me, Fisk, Jim
Rice—we all cried. That was a tough one to lose. The way that year finished
was funny, you know? We were ahead for so many games, and then the
Yankees came all the way back and *passed* us, and then *we* came back and
tied them up. It was a great season, up and down, and both teams had fought
hard to the end. Then, to lose the way we did, that gave you a BADDDDD
feeling.

My record with the Red Sox in September and October, Peter Gammons
had reported in that morning's *Boston Globe*, was now 28-12—including a
3-0 mark in the '75 postseason. That's a .700 winning percentage in games
that mattered most, but now I wouldn't have the chance to add to it. The
only team in baseball with a better record than our 99-64 was the Yankees,
but that didn't matter. In the days before the wild card, second place meant
you went home.

So, with no more ballgames to play, I turned my attention to something
else: my expiring contract. Haywood Sullivan and Buddy LeRoux had been
unwilling to negotiate with me during the season; the one previous time I
talked to either one of them about my contract, in September, Buddy had
only said, "Before you think about becoming a free agent, Luis, think about
your age. I hope you have a lot of money in the bank."

I didn't like to be threatened like that, and I never forgot it.

Sullivan was willing to give me a one-year deal for $250,000 and then
renew it each year I made the club after that. He said that a multiyear contract, which was still what I was seeking, was out of the question. We had
been down this road before, but Mr. Yawkey was no longer there to support
me as my number-one fan. I made it clear that I was not willing to accept
anything less than a multiyear deal, and Sullivan repeated that he wasn't
going to grant it. So I contacted Marvin Miller and the Players Association
and filled out the paperwork to become a free agent.

This meant teams in both leagues could draft and make me offers starting fifteen days after the World Series. Most sportswriters, columnists, and

fans who spoke up at the time openly encouraged Boston management to do what was necessary to keep me in town.

"El Tiante is one of our institutions," wrote Tim Horgan in the *Boston Herald*. "The only way he should leave Fenway Park is on the shoulders of the populace, brandishing his stogie like a bull's ear. He should go out in style, not the fire escape."

Such support was encouraging, but it didn't sway the front office. Boston's best offer remained a one-year contract; I felt like I deserved *two* years, but Sullivan wouldn't budge. In my mind, it wasn't fair; after all I had done for them, not just pitching in but *winning* the big games, they should have given me more respect. I knew I could still pitch very well and had proven it by going 4-1 with a 3.09 ERA down the stretch that year. When we had to win every game, I won three of our last eight.

Now they were telling me that this was their offer, and I should "take it or leave it." I don't like being told what to do, but Sullivan tried everything to sway me. He even reminded me that it was the Red Sox who had given me a chance back in '71 when nobody else would. I told him I had certainly not forgotten but felt that I had paid them back *and then some.* I was named the team's most valuable pitcher for four straight years, led us down the stretch in four pennant races, and nearly won us a World Series title in 1975. I had won more games for the franchise—122—than anybody in history except Cy Young and Mel Parnell, and Mel only had me beat by one game!

"Isn't that type of success worth two years?" I asked Sullivan. "That type of *loyalty*?"

"Tell you what," he said. "We'll only give you the one year, but if you go to spring training in 1980 and make the club, we'll give you the second year."

"If you don't think I can even make the team in 1980," I shot back, "why would you want me here at all?"

The whole thing was going nowhere, and then a new option emerged. The Yankees selected me in the free agent draft, so my agent, Paul George, arranged for me to meet with their principal owner, George Steinbrenner, in New York.

The Yankees, Steinbrenner said, were ready to give me a *two*-year contract—plus another ten-year deal after I retired to do scouting and be a goodwill ambassador in Latin America. I had pitched well against New York and the rest of the American League East, so I'm sure that had something to do with their interest. They figured they could help their team and hurt the

Red Sox at the same time, the same thing the Red Sox did by signing Mike Torrez the winter before (and hopefully with a better end result).

Steinbrenner was very respectful and very careful. I know it sounds funny, given his reputation as a guy who went after what he wanted loudly and brashly, but he seemed really concerned over whether the Boston front office was okay with the Yankees possibly signing me.

"We don't want to cause any problems with the Red Sox, or anybody else," he said. "We *want* to sign you, but maybe you should go back to Boston and talk to them and see what happens. Then we can make an offer."

"I don't think that's necessary," I said, looking at my agent. "We've already talked with Red Sox management. I know what *they* want to do, and I know what *I* want to do. They don't want to give me a two-year contract, so there is nothing left for me and them to discuss."

Then I paused. Steinbrenner was right. This was a big decision, and it should not be made without both sides having all the facts. The thing is, I didn't want to have to go *back* to Boston, arrange another meeting with Haywood Sullivan, and go through all those steps again—just to (likely) reach the same point I was at now.

No more back and forth. It was time to settle this.

"If it's OK by you, Mr. Steinbrenner," I said, "I'd like to call the Red Sox right now."

He said sure.

So my agent called Haywood Sullivan from right there in Steinbrenner's office and put him on the speakerphone. When Sullivan came on the line, I spoke up.

"Look, Sully, I'm here with George Steinbrenner. He doesn't want to offer me any money yet. He wants me to go back to Boston and talk to you and see if I can get together with you guys."

"Well, we're still thinking along the same lines," Sullivan said. "We're going to give you just the one year."

"OK, that's fine," I said. "You know what? I'm thinking of signing *here*, with New York."

"Wherever you go," he said, trying to sound sincere, "good luck to you."

That almost put me over the edge.

"Why do you say that to me—'*Good luck wherever you go*'—when you won't help me work out a way to stay with you guys? That's bullshit, and you know it! But if that's what you *want*, that's what I'm going *to do*. I'm going to sign here."

I hung up from Sullivan, paused, and then called Maria to tell her that I wanted to sign with the Yankees. She said OK, and that was it.

The deal was for (at least) two years at $200,000 each, plus a $140,000 signing bonus. After I retired from playing, if I chose, I would move into my new role as Director of Latin Affairs at $20,000 a year for ten years. It was a contract that made me feel respected, not only as a pitcher but also as someone that the Yankees felt could help them find and evaluate talent in the future. Most importantly, it gave me long-term security for my family.

At the Yankee Stadium press conference announcing my signing, on November 13, the reporters started asking about my age—just like they did when I signed with Boston seven years before. I told them not to worry about it, that I could throw the ball to home plate no matter *how* old I was. When they kept asking, I just said, "My mother told me I was born on November 23, 1940." I figured if that was good enough for me, it was going to have to be good enough for them.

Besides, I added, Gaylord Perry is older than me. He just won twenty-one games and the National League Cy Young Award. Why not ask *him* about *his* age?

"Just like old wine," Yankees president Al Rosen joked, "Luis gets better with age."

During the press conference, I openly thanked the Red Sox for believing in me when nobody else did. What they were wrong about, I explained, was thinking that I was close to retirement.

"Nobody tells me when to retire," I said. "I'll know when to retire. I have pride."

Even with the way Haywood and the front office treated me at the end, it was hard to make that move. You've been in Boston all those years, and now you're going to the enemy. You start thinking about what's going to happen when you come back—how the fans at Fenway are going to react. A lot of people were mad at me, at least at first, but they didn't know it wasn't my fault. You have to go to wherever they want you.

My Red Sox teammates understood. They were very kind in their goodbyes.

"In my eighteen years with the Red Sox," Yaz said, "he was the best I'd ever seen. Nobody else even comes close. Maybe a few guys for a year or two. But nobody has done the things in my lifetime that he's done."

Pudge Fisk, who knew me better than anyone, couldn't believe it.

"How could they let that happen?" he asked when told the news. He talked about how I could "psychologically beat a team" just by going out to the mound, but it was really both of us. Pudge played mind games with batters all the time and always knew just which pitch to throw when. The two of us were great partners, and I'd miss working with him very much.

Then Pudge put in a good word for aging athletes everywhere.

"It doesn't matter how *old* you are," he said. "It's how *good* you are."

For the Yankees in 1979, I was pretty good—when I got the chance. I admitted in spring training that I felt "some kind of funny" in my new uniform, but that I appreciated the organization giving me a new chance, along with the security I had always wanted. There was a looseness around the club, a swagger, that I enjoyed. Reggie Jackson, Graig Nettles, Thurman Munson, Chris Chambliss—they all had supreme confidence in their abilities. They had earned the right to it after three pennants in a row and two straight World Series titles, and being around Yankee Stadium was like being around baseball royalty. You'd walk into the clubhouse and Joe DiMaggio, Whitey Ford, or Mickey Mantle would be standing there talking to Frank Sinatra.

There *were* some challenges for my kids, who were still loyal Red Sox fans.

"When I walked into the locker room at Yankee Stadium for the first time in 1979, and he was sitting right next to Bucky Dent, that was a tough one," Luis Jr. remembers with a laugh. "It was like a punch to the gut. His locker was next to Yogi and Bucky. I got to see Yogi every day, and he used to give me Yoo-Hoos.

"Sure, I got sh-- from my friends about Dad going to the Yankees. People didn't understand that he didn't choose to go over there. At that moment, it was tough. People were saying he betrayed the Red Sox. But over time, they got to understand what it was all about.

"New York was a whole different atmosphere—it was like walking into Hollywood every day. The fans liked Dad, but there were so many other great guys that dominated things, and he was toward the end of his career. He wasn't the focus."

On a club like that, I knew I needed to gain respect by pitching well right from the start. My new teammates were great to me, but in the early going I barely got any work—and was terrible when I *did*. I only pitched twice in April, was rocked both times, and when I got more starts in May they were often on five, six, or more days rest. Once, after a rainout, I got passed over completely, and I was averaging only around five innings per start.

It took me nearly two months—until May 21—to get my first win as a Yankee, over Mark Fidrych at Tiger Stadium.

Part of the problem was the other four pitchers in New York's starting rotation. Three were well-liked, established stars, and the fourth was another free agent getting more money than me to be a top-tier guy.

The ace, of course, was left-hander Ron Guidry. He was coming off a 25-3 season in which he had 248 strikeouts, a 1.73 ERA, and big wins in the playoffs and World Series. Gid had a tremendous fastball and slider, and the thing you noticed when you got up close to him was his size. You couldn't believe a guy that small could throw the ball that fast. I'd feel the same way about Pedro Martinez later on. Both were listed at five-foot-eleven, with Guidry at one hundred and sixty pounds and Pedro at one hundred and seventy, but they could whip it in as fast as anyone.

Guidry was twenty-eight and a product of the Yankee farm system, but the number-two starter was more like me: an old-timer and a free-agent signee. Tommy John, thirty-six, had gone 20-7 and 17-10 with the Dodgers the past two years. A left-hander with excellent control, a good curve, and a sinking fastball, he kept infielders busy by pitching down and getting lots of groundouts. Almost the direct opposite of Guidry, but nearly as effective.

Being on the same team with Tommy felt like coming full circle. He was the struggling young pitcher with the Indians whose roster spot I took after being called up from Portland in July of 1964, and shortly after that he was traded to the White Sox. A top starter in their rotation for several years, he was later traded to the Dodgers and helped them win three NL pennants. Both of us had gone through major injuries that nearly ended our careers and then returned stronger than ever. In my opinion Tommy John belongs in the Hall of Fame, not only for his 288 wins but also for undergoing the pioneering 1974 tendon and ligament surgery on his left elbow that now bears his name. Tommy John surgery has since helped many ballplayers at all levels get back on the field.

One time, Luis Jr. almost put Tommy *back* into surgery.

"The Yankees used to let me take ground balls at short before the games, until one Monday night," he remembers. "It was Monday Night Baseball, and I happened to overthrow the kid at first base. The ball went sailing over his head and I see someone drop to the ground. It was Tommy John, who was being interviewed by Howard Cosell! Needless to say I made it onto the telecast that night, and I almost cost Tommy John the start."

The Yanks were hoping Catfish Hunter, another of my old rivals from when he was with the A's, could continue the fine pitching he had shown during New York's great comeback in '78. But Cat had dealt with his own injury problems for much of the past two seasons, including arm fatigue brought on by averaging nearly 280 innings pitched a year all through his twenties. He announced that 1979 would be his last season, and he wanted to go out on top. But his arm could only handle three or four starts a month, and he was knocked around pretty good in a lot of them. It was tough to watch, but Cat was a battler who never gave up—and would always get credit from Steinbrenner later on for helping turn the Yankees back into winners after joining the team in 1975.

Catfish wound up 2-9, a big drop from his 12-6 mark in 1978. The other Yankees starter way off from his previous season was Ed Figueroa, who went from 20-9 to 4-6 due to arm trouble that would eventually end his career. On top of that, our ace reliever, Goose Gossage, would be out from mid-April to mid-July after injuring his hand in a fight with teammate Cliff Johnson. As Lemon tried to sort things out, we entered June in fourth place, just four-and-a-half games behind the Orioles.

If I had proven anything in my career, it was that I was much more effective when getting consistent innings. Lemon had been a Hall of Fame pitcher himself, so I went to talk to him about it. I told him my arm felt great, and I needed more work. His answer was frustrating—"I've got too many pitchers"—but he also told me not to worry; with the schedule getting busier as summer neared, there would be plenty of work for me soon.

There was nothing I could do but believe him, and things did get better. After entering June with a 6.03 ERA, I went 4-2 with a 2.49 ERA and three complete games that month—including one on June 30 in my first regular-season start against my former Red Sox teammates. Although there was a lot of kidding around and bullshit that Saturday afternoon at Yankee Stadium, I was trying to get them out and win the game, no question about that. My job was to beat them; they were still my friends, but they were now also the enemy.

The game was tied at two going into the ninth inning, me and Bob Stanley for Boston both going the distance. I had promised Yaz he would never see any fastballs, but in the ninth he got a great swing on one of my slow curves and lined it into the right-field bleachers—giving Boston the lead. It was the 399th home run of his career, three months before his fortieth birthday.

As he rounded the bases, I walked almost all the way over to third base yelling at him.

"You frigging Polack, you! You bastard!"

Yaz was laughing.

It was his third hit off me that day. So when he came out to play first base in the bottom of the ninth, I gave him a warning from the home dugout:

"Next time up, I'll hit you on your fucking wrist, you old Polack asshole!"

I wouldn't get the chance that day. Stanley got us out in order, and Boston won 3–2.

"It proves just one thing to me," Fred Lynn joked afterwards. "Fossils can hit fossils."

For a fossil, I did OK the rest of the season, although I ended it without the manager—or the catcher—I started it with.

I liked Bob Lemon as a manager; he was an easygoing guy who had the respect of his players. He had done a great job bringing the club back the year before, so even when we started June in fourth place, we felt we could still make a move. When he told me he would get me more work, he kept his word.

But even after you won a World Series for him, George Steinbrenner didn't have much patience, and on June 17, with our record at 34–31, eight games behind Baltimore, Lemon was fired and replaced with Billy Martin—who *he* had replaced the year before. This was the crazy way they did things in New York when "The Boss" was in charge; in thirteen years, Steinbrenner would hire, fire, and rehire Martin five times.

Billy was good to me. After Goose came back from his hand injury, Billy took me in his office and said, "All I want from you is to give me seven innings, and then I'll bring in Gossage." Billy was old-school. He liked old players because we played hard and hustled.

I joked much less around Billy than I did around Lemon, and we'd talk in his office a lot. He'd light a cigar, then light another one off of it and hand it to me. He had this country and western store, and one day in his office he said to me, "What shoe size are you? Do you like boots?" The next thing I know Billy is bringing me in a pair of ostrich boots and two Stetson hats.

Every fight Billy had, from what I could see, people were looking for it.

They would push him. He didn't go out of his way to bother anybody, but he didn't take any shit. He used to tell George Steinbrenner, "You're the boss upstairs, but I'm the boss down here."

As a manager, and a strategist, Billy was brilliant. If I wasn't pitching, and we were in the dugout, he'd say, "Come sit down next to me, and you watch. I'm going to get Weaver soon. I'm going to drive him crazy." Then he'd pull some wild move in the field or with the lineup and Earl Weaver wouldn't know what hit him.

After that talk with Billy, and after Goose came back, my days throwing complete games were mostly over. Gossage was a damn good weapon to have, and unlike today's closers, he often threw two or even three innings in a game. If I had a lead, and things were close, you could be pretty sure he was coming in.

A few days before Gossage's first game back, I went the distance for one of the last times. We were in Oakland, and I got the first nine A's out in order before their rookie center fielder lined a fastball to left-center leading off the fourth. He stole second, but then I got the next *eighteen* guys in a row, including the rook on a flyout to end the game. The 2-0, one-hit win was my forty-ninth shutout, and the kid who spoiled my perfect game—Rickey Henderson—would go on to get a few more hits and steals before he was done.

I only threw eighty-four pitches in the game and struck out four. By now I was throwing a lot more breaking stuff and slow curves than fastballs. This drove batters crazy, but young fireballers like Guidry enjoyed the show.

"If I threw ten breaking balls that slow, I'd give up nine hits," Guidry said after that game. "I'm past the stage of marveling at him [Tiant]. We get on him about how the outfielders have to run all over the place and the infielders have to dive all over, but he gets the outs."

After the game, of course, there were questions from the Oakland writers about how a guy "my age" could pitch so good—and just how old was I, anyway?

"I can pitch as long as I can get somebody out," I said, a cigar in my mouth and my fossil arm in a bucket of ice. "I'm getting tired of hearing that I'm fifty-five or sixty-five or ninety. What's the difference? I wish I was forty-five now. I could get my pension."

My catcher for that game, and most of my games those first months with the Yankees, was Thurman Munson. Like I said earlier, I feel very lucky that I was able to pitch to the two best catchers in the American League during the 1970s: Munson and Carlton Fisk.

Both led by example, always giving it their all on the field and often playing hurt. As catchers, I considered them equal in ability; both did a great job blocking the plate, calling a game, and throwing out runners. As hitters I'd give the edge in power to Pudge and in pure hitting to Thurman—he had a great stroke and almost never struck out.

They also didn't hate each other—they *respected* each other, and they were competitive with one another because each wanted to be number one. When their teams met up, they talked often about catching and how hurt they always were. By the time I got to the Yankees, Thurman was already starting to play some first, outfield, and DH because his knees were causing him so much pain. But he always hustled, just like Pudge.

Another thing they shared was a deep love for their families. This is one reason Thurman took up flying; when he got his pilot's license, he started flying his own plane to and from road trips. This gave him a chance to get out ahead of the team, stopover in Canton, Ohio, spend a few hours with his wife and kids there, and then meet up with us in New York or wherever we were headed. I guess because he was the captain, and such a beloved Yankee, Steinbrenner allowed him this special privilege. Thurman was proud of his plane and was always asking guys to go up in it with him. I was never a fan of flying even the biggest jumbo jets, so small prop planes were definitely not for me. A few teammates did fly with him, including his close friends Lou Piniella and Bobby Murcer, and they always said how happy he was up in the air.

Thurman was very excited when he bought a twin-engine jet during the 1979 season. The team was headed on a road trip to the west coast; while we were flying to Oakland, he flew his prop plane to Kansas City, picked up the jet, and flew that out to Oakland. He had an instructor with him as a copilot, because he was still logging his hours on the jet, and asked me and some other guys to fly from Oakland to Seattle with them. Jet or no jet, I still wasn't interested. I think Reggie, who seemed to get along much better with Thurman than I had read about, flew in the jet with him from Seattle to Anaheim later on that trip.

A few weeks later, on August 2, we had just gotten back to town from another road trip and were enjoying an off-day when some awful news broke and then spread through the team. Thurman had been practicing takeoffs and landings in the new jet when he crashed at the Akron-Canton Airport. He was dead at thirty-two.

There was talk of postponing our game the next night against Baltimore, but Thurman's wife, Diane, said she believed he would have wanted us to play—so we did. A bunch of the guys didn't feel up to being in the starting lineup, but it was my turn in the rotation, so I was out on the mound.

There was a service before the game. Every starter stood out at his position except catcher Jerry Narron; the spot behind the plate was left empty until the game started. There were some prayers, someone sang "America the Beautiful," and when they put Thurman's picture up on the big scoreboard…WOW. I was crying on the mound, and the fans stood and cheered for nearly ten minutes. At one point they all started chanting Thurman's name, and it felt like they were never going to stop.

Then I had to pitch!

I'm not sure how I got through that game; I wound up throwing a two-hitter, but one of the hits was a home run by John Lowenstein in the second inning. Scott McGregor, a very close friend of Thurman's who said he cried throughout the whole game, shut us out, 1-0, with ninth-inning help from Tippy Martinez. I wanted to win for Thurman so bad, but that's the thing with baseball. Even when you *should* win, sometimes you don't. But God gives you the strength to keep fighting.

When Thurman died, we were 58-48, in fourth place and fourteen games behind the Orioles. From that point until the end of the year we had the second-best record in the American League, but because Baltimore kept winning, we could never make up any ground on them. We wound up 89–71, still in fourth place.

My record was 13-8, the same as it was with Boston the year before, and I had definitely gotten better once I started pitching regularly. From June through September my ERA was 3.41, and I won six of my last eight decisions. The team also went 19-11 in my thirty starts, so I managed to keep us in games even when I didn't win.

It was hard to feel *good* about the season, especially because of Thurman, but there was one night that was very special to me. On September 11, I started against the Red Sox in my first game back at Fenway Park since signing with New York. Even in my Yankees uniform, I was shown the same love from the Boston fans that they had always given me, and I received a tremendous ovation in front of my family.

"It was a big deal at the time, but certainly he never felt the scorn that Boggs or Clemens did for going to the Yankees," says Dan Shaughnessy of the *Boston Globe*. "I think that people understood he was taking care of himself, and that he was near the end. It was never viewed in a very negative light here. [Today] it's largely forgotten that it ever happened."

Making that night in '79 even more dramatic was that Carl Yastrzemski came into the game with 2,999 hits—looking to become just the fifteenth player to reach 3,000 for his career. The place was packed. His family, friends, and the national media were all there to capture the big moment, but me, Ron Davis, and Goose held Yaz to zero-for-three with a walk (I got booed for that).

Like I always said, when I got on that mound, I had no friends. The big ugly Cuban won that duel, but I was glad I was there to see Yaz get number 3,000 the next night off my teammate, Jim Beattie. In a year when the Red Sox and Yankees were both going nowhere, and tragedy had touched our rivalry, it was great to be able to celebrate a great achievement by a true legend—no matter what uniform he was wearing.

George Steinbrenner was at it again in the off-season, firing Billy Martin and hiring another manager with longtime ties to the team. Dick Howser had been a coach with the Yankees for ten years before leaving to lead the team at Florida State University in 1978, so he knew most of the guys on the roster well. He was definitely no stranger to *me* because we had been team-mates on the Indians in the mid-sixties, and I later faced him when he played with the Yankees in 1967 and '68.

I came to spring training in 1980 feeling great, having spent the winter working on the new country home and farm that I was building for my family outside Mexico City. But before I retired to a life of chickens and cows, I wanted to win a few more ballgames. Howser said he had me slotted in as one of his five regular starters, which sounded good to me. I didn't enjoy those long gaps between appearances the year before. I was also really excited about our new pitching coach—Stan Williams, back with me once again; it was our fourth team together.

The season started out as a mixed bag. I was starting somewhat regularly, and winning, but it was more because the team was hitting good. Our of-fense, with Reggie, Nettles, Bob Watson, and our new catcher Rick Cerone, was really mashing the ball, but my ERA was hovering around 6.00 the first two months, and I had a slight groin pull that was bothering me. I needed one real good start to get me going.

Finally, on May 30, I got it. I was facing the Blue Jays at Yankee Stadium and got locked into a duel with Jim Clancy, Toronto's top right-handed starter. It was scoreless until the bottom of the seventh, when we scored four runs to chase Clancy. I took the mound in the top of the eighth with a 4–0 lead and six outs to go for my fiftieth career shutout—and first as a Yankee. I only pitched one complete game all of 1979, so I didn't know how many more chances I might get at it.

I got the first two men easily in the eighth, but then Barry Bonnell tripled, and Al Woods walked. It was only the third hit and first walk for Toronto all night, but I guess Howser didn't want to take any chances. Even though I had nine strikeouts in the game, and had struck out Pat Kelly, the next man up, twice, Howser came out to the mound called for Gossage to relieve me.

I was frustrated because I wanted the chance to get Kelly again and keep Toronto off the scoreboard. Sure, maybe I was thinking about the fiftieth shutout a little—less than twenty guys had that many—but mostly I just wanted that one more chance to finish what I started. Maybe Pudge could have helped talk Howser into it, or even Thurman, but Cerone and I were still getting to know each other. He wasn't going to stick his neck out for me yet.

Some fans were booing the manager for making the move, but it didn't matter. I knew this was a battle I wasn't going to win.

What happened next was a misunderstanding; his word against mine. Howser said I "threw" the ball at him as I left the mound. That's what the fans thought they saw, too, but here's what really happened: I meant to drop the ball into his hand, but because I was looking down, angry at myself and the situation, I didn't see he had his hands stuck in his jacket pockets. By the time the ball hit the ground, I was already headed off the field, not realizing my mistake.

If I really meant to *throw* the ball, I would have heaved it at his chest, the ground, or second base. It would have been obvious.

What everyone saw next was no mistake. Before stepping down into the dugout, I took my glove and flung it up into the first-base stands. That was a stupid move, and I shouldn't have done it. (A fan actually returned the glove to me later, which amazed me.)

I still got the win, but Howser didn't care. We had a shouting match in the clubhouse, and he fined me $500 for showing him up.

"That's the most I can fine him without going into the [grievance] courts," he told reporters after the game. "If I could have fined him $5,000, I would have. He has a lot of pride, sure. But sometimes that pride is overrated. He thinks he's pretty good, but I've got the best relief pitcher in baseball."

Afterwards Howser came by to try to talk to me, but I was too angry. He asked me into his office, but I wouldn't go. I needed to cool off, so took a long shower and sauna. Then I met with reporters.

"I don't want this to happen," I told them. "I don't want to be a trouble-maker. I've pitched twenty-one years; this has never happened before. Some-times you get mad and do things you don't want to do. I may be right, and I may be wrong. He's the manager, and I'm the player. What do you want me to do, punch him?"

The incident made big headlines, but we got past it. Howser didn't take me out of the rotation, saying I was pitching too good. But we also stayed with a five-man rotation, which didn't work to my strengths.

"Luis got upset with me in 1980," Stan Williams, still my great friend, remembers. "He said 'I thought you were my friend and my brother—how come you don't let me pitch every fourth day?' I told him first of all, it wasn't my decision. I took my orders from the manager. Second of all, 'You're not the man here. Ron Guidry is, and he likes to have four days of rest.'

"[Tiant] was a very proud man, and a tremendous competitor. Those were the things that really connected me with him. I loved the competitive spirit he had, and of course his ability."

The 1980 Yankees had plenty of ability. We wound up going 103-59, hold-ing off the Orioles—who won 100 games—to take the AL East title. I was one of our better pitchers down the stretch, even though my record didn't show it; at one point I lost six straight games in which the team scored a combined eight runs. Howser recognized I was pitching in bad luck, and even after I finished 8-9, he had me slated to start the fourth game of the playoffs against the Royals. But it never got that far; Kansas City swept us three straight, the first time they ever beat us in the postseason. They went on to the World Series, and we went home.

That didn't sit too well with George. In November, he replaced Howser as manager with Gene Michael; the story George told everyone was that Howser wanted to go back to living in Florida and working in real estate, so he resigned. He even had a press conference where Howser was sitting next to him as he told the story. But everybody knew the truth.

Then, after celebrating my fortieth birthday on November 23, I found out the Yankees were not renewing my two-year contract. They said I could come to spring training on a "look see" basis and try and make the club, or I could try and hook on with another team as a free agent.

My agent said the Yanks had "40-40 vision." They looked at my age, and their forty-man roster, and decided I was too old.

I said thanks but no thanks for the tryout offer; I wanted to go where I *knew* they wanted me.

That turned out to be Portland, Oregon, the same place my big-league career had launched from seventeen years before. I signed a one-year, six-figure contract to pitch for the Portland Beavers, now the Triple-A club of the Pittsburgh Pirates, with the understanding that I would also get a shot to make the Pirates in spring training. A lot of people in Portland still remembered me for going 15-1 back in 1964, and the club's management thought paying me a big-league salary to play minor-league ball would help them draw fans and get a good return on their investment. I thought if I showed what I could do there, then the Pirates—or another team—would give me a chance to pitch in the majors again.

It was a good deal for everyone. After being cut by Pittsburgh late in spring training, I went off to the Pacific Coast League and took up right where I left off in '64. In my second start for the Beavers, I pitched a seven-inning no-hitter against Spokane—striking out a former Red Sox teammate, Ted Cox, for the final out. That was my tenth strikeout, and Cox said it was the fastest he had seen me pitch in four years. I took that as a good sign.

Then, a week later, I came within one out of throwing *another* no-hitter, this time settling for a one-hit shutout. When the big leagues went on strike, the minors were suddenly more popular than ever. People wanted to see baseball, and we were the best there was out there. I enjoyed myself, riding the buses with teammates just a few years older than my son Luis, and everywhere I went in the league the fans came out—and were wonderful to me.

There was one guy on the team I already knew well; Willie Horton, the great Tigers slugger, was with the Beavers trying to make his own comeback at age 38. We had a lot of laughs, I got a lot of strikeouts, and he hit a lot of home runs. By August I was 13-7 with a 3.82 ERA and eleven complete games, and big-league scouts were coming to my starts. I was a little worried when the strike ended and some of the young kids on the team got called up instead of me, but I tried to stay calm.

This was my last chance, and I knew it.

Finally, on August 12, the Pirates purchased my contract for $25,000 and called me up. They were in a four-team race for the NL East title, and manager Chuck Tanner put me right into his rotation—starting me nine times the final six weeks of the season. The results were mixed; I only went 2-5, and we fell out of the playoff race, but I was in almost every game I pitched and had a very respectable 3.95 ERA. The Pirates' general manager, Harding Peterson, said I was the team's most effective pitcher down the stretch.

After the season, Pittsburgh released me, saying they were focused on a youth movement, but by then I had set another goal: Juan Marichal's record for most wins by a Latin American pitcher. The Dominican Dandy had 243, and I was at 225. I figured if I could make a club and stick for two full seasons, I might have a shot at it.

When no big-league teams showed interest, I decided to go back to where it all began: The Mexican League. Twenty-three years after my rookie season with the Mexico City Tigers, I was back to making thirteen-hour bus rides in sweltering heat, chasing the dream—this time as a member of the 1982 Tabasco, Veracruz Plantaneros (Banana Pickers). Tabasco was the worst team in the league, but my 2.01 ERA was good enough to get the attention of California Angels international scout Cookie Rojas. A Cuban countryman and former American League All-Star teammate, Rojas reported back to his bosses in Anaheim that my control was great and my fastball close to ninety miles an hour. "His arm was back, as good as it's been," he said.

The Angels liked what they heard. They purchased my contract from Tabasco on August 2 and announced that I would be starting three days later against the Twins. California was in a heated race for the AL West title, and I'd be reuniting with a bunch of former teammates including Rod Carew, Fred Lynn, Rick Burleson, and Juan Beniquez to hopefully provide some help for the stretch drive.

"I'm the happiest man on earth today," I said after hearing the news. "I figure I can still do the job."

I *could* still do the job. I lost my first start, against Minnesota, but struck out six over the first three innings to open lots of eyes. Then, in case anybody still wasn't sure I was for real, I won my next two starts. The first, 3-1 over the Twins on August 12, was a twenty-first anniversary gift for my lovely Maria. The second was special too, not because of the date but because of the opponent: the Boston Red Sox. I beat them, 10-2, at Anaheim, striking out eight and taking a shutout into the ninth inning.

Somewhere, I liked to think, Haywood Sullivan and Buddy LeRoux were watching the game and cursing to themselves.

My old pal Dwight Evans, who struck out three times for the Red Sox, told me he wished I had signed with *them* instead of the Angels; they were fighting to catch Baltimore and Milwaukee in the AL East. I smiled, then laughed. The thirteen-hour bus rides had been worth it to hear that.

I'd like to say that this was the beginning of another great run—that I pitched the Angels into the playoffs, helped them win the World Series, and then came back for one more season to pass Marichal with my 244th victory. The perfect win to retire on.

Things didn't quite work out that way.

The Angels *did* make the playoffs, but I was the last man cut from the postseason roster and watched as they lost a five-game series to the Brewers. I was released after the season, failed to catch on with another big-league club, pitched a little more in Mexico, and then finally called it quits. So that August 17 night in Anaheim, when I left in the ninth inning to a standing ovation and enjoyed postseason hugs with beloved friends on both teams, turned out to be my 229th and last major league win.

Come to think of it, it was pretty perfect.

18

FINALLY, BACK AT FENWAY

AFTER 295 VICTORIES, 746 GAMES, and nearly 4,300 innings spread out over twenty-three professional seasons—plus nearly that many years of winter ball—it was finally over. The world of pain-reducing whirlpools, shower-defying cigars, and good-natured clubhouse pranks was in the rear-view mirror.

There would be old-timer's contests, an old-timer's *league*, and numerous ceremonial first pitches to come, but the fiercely physical and ultra-competitive portion of Luis Tiant's baseball life was ending. Now he needed something to take its place—a way to channel all the energy and emotion that he once carried to the mound into another activity.

Tiant found plenty to do with the second half of his life. He added to his ever-growing circle of friends and admirers and showed that he was as adept at teaching baseball to others as he was at playing it. Graying gracefully alongside his beloved Maria, he watched with pride as his children grew and started lives of their own—including a "third son" who, while never officially given the Tiant name, was as beloved as anyone who did. Even talk of his age stopped; at fifty, and then sixty, Tiant maintained the bright-eyed, wrinkle-free appearance of a much younger man. He got the last laugh there, too.

Through it all, however, he never stopped loving or missing the city where his dreams as a pitcher and a family man came true. Where he built a home, and a life, that made his parents proud. Things were said and egos bruised as Tiant left the Red Sox, which made the possibility of his returning to the team as a coach or in another capacity highly unlikely under the same ownership group. So for twenty-plus years while the Yawkey name topped the letterhead at Fenway Park, Luis was a legend in exile. Loved, but at a distance.

Considering the limitless supply of baseball wisdom and wit that the franchise was denied during this period, and the pitchers from all skill levels and backgrounds who could have learned from his challenges and triumphs, it was an organizational grudge of epic proportions, the full costs of which cannot be measured. How, for instance, could Luis Tiant have helped Oil Can Boyd deal with the dual stresses of being a great young pitcher and a charismatic man of color, in a city where racial tensions still ran high? Could he have provided wise counsel to Bret Saberhagen on how to reinvent oneself after serious surgery?

We will never know, which is perhaps just as well. For in the time he *has* been given to make an impact on those wishing to ply their trade at Fenway Park, he has more than exceeded expectations.

YOU'VE BEEN DOING SOMETHING all your life, reach the top of your profession, and then come to a point when you can no longer meet the standards you set for yourself. What comes next? How do you move on—and how do you let go?

Some people never figure that out, but for me the answer felt obvious.

Since I was a little boy, throwing around homemade balls with my friends or watching my father from a dugout bench, baseball had been my life. My days and nights were always wrapped up in the next game, the next workout, the next season, the next pitch. When I wasn't playing or practicing baseball, I was thinking about it—sometimes too much. It was my profession and my salvation; it provided me with the freedom and courage to visit new lands, fight injustices, become a man, and find my voice. Through the game, I met many wonderful people and had many great experiences.

An inheritance from my father, baseball is what connected me to him as a boy and as a man. It sometimes seemed like a wedge between us, but in the end, it was a powerful force that kept us linked even when circumstances beyond our control forced us apart. My love for the game is what led my mother to advocate on my behalf and convince my father to let me pursue a career in pro ball. It also gave my parents the strength to make the most agonizing decision of their lives: telling me not to come home to Cuba. They sacrificed fifteen years with their only child so that I could achieve my goals.

Baseball, in large part, is what provided me with the opportunity to make their last months among the happiest of their lives. Through the game, and my success at it, I was able to show them that their sacrifice had been worth it. My dreams, and my father's dreams before mine, had all come true.

Because of baseball, I was able to raise my children in a beautiful home, give them a fine education, and teach them the meaning of hard work and dedication. The game brought me lifelong friendships, fame, and fortune (relatively speaking). And, most importantly, my love for just being around ballparks is what drew my eye one day to a beautiful left fielder in a softball game—and nearly sixty years of happiness with my wife and best friend, Maria Navarro Tiant.

All of this made my decision regarding the next stage of my life an obvious one. When I finally hung up my spikes as a professional ballplayer in 1983, after a 15–6 summer in the Mexican League, what I wanted to do next was clear: share with others all that the game had given to me.

In a way, I had already been doing this unofficially for years. I often took younger players aside to work with them on different things when I was in the majors, even if they were not on my team. Scott McGregor remembers one time when he was still establishing himself as a key member of Baltimore's great pitching staff, and I checked in after hearing he was having a tough time.

"We were playing the Yankees in Baltimore in '79," he recalls. "I had pitched a game, and my elbow must have been a little bit sore or something like that. It was written up in the paper, and the next day I'm out on the field during batting practice and Luis comes out and yells at me.

"'Hey amigo!' he shouts, then comes over.

"'Your elbow still sore?'

"'Yeah,' I say, 'it's still a little sore.'

"Then he immediately tells me what to do, how to fix it, where to ice it.

"'You're on the other team,' I say. 'What are you telling me this stuff for?'

"He just smiled.

"Here are the Orioles and the Yankees, battling it out for the AL East, he and I are not even close, and he's coming over and telling me what to do to help my arm. I already knew Luis's reputation, but I remember thinking at the time, 'This guy really *is* pretty special.' He just cared about people, and he cared about the fraternity of pitchers."

As much as moments like that made people like Scott feel good, they did even more for me. My first wish would have been to sign on after my playing days as a coach with the Red Sox, either at the major or minor league level. But the way things had ended between me and the team made that impossible. I still felt great love for the organization and its fans, but when I made it clear I was looking for a coaching job, they never called.

If I wanted to be involved with the game on an official basis, I would have to go elsewhere.

The Yankees were much more welcoming. The offer to scout for them in Latin America was still there, and I did it for a few years, but I found that I really liked working one-on-one with players more than evaluating or finding them. When the Yanks hired David Hirsch as their new farm director years later, I got my opportunity (or so I thought). Hirsch had been the general manager and owner of the Portland Beavers when I played there back in '81, and he remembered the job I had done sharing my twenty-plus years of experience with my Triple-A teammates.

"He was the best influence on young players we ever had there," Hirsch told Peter Gammons. "The job he did there was that of a pitching coach. His discipline and character were a tremendous influence."

Hirsch hired me to be pitching coach of the Class A Fort Lauderdale Yankees, working with manager and former big-league catcher Barry Foote. I made headlines before the season even started when I shaved off my famous Fu Manchu mustache and beard to comply with George Steinbrenner's rule that nobody in New York's minor league system have facial hair. I didn't mind doing it, but I knew Maria would be upset because she really liked me with the mustache.

The funny thing is, the Yankees decided to reassign me to Mexico as a scout less than two weeks later, so I shaved it for nothing. That's the last time I did *that*; the Fu Manchu, which has since turned gray, is here to stay.

I was sorry I *didn't* get to stay with Fort Lauderdale, but another opportunity to coach in Florida came up in 1984. In the past people were always bugging me about my age and my funny-looking body, but a lot of these new players I was working out with were older—and funnier looking—than me. These weren't minor leaguers; they were campers, aged thirty and up, who plunked down $2,550 in 1984 dollars to spend a week at the Sox Exchange Baseball Fantasy Camp in Winter Haven.

The camp took place just before Red Sox spring training got underway at Chain O' Lakes Park, and it was a blast teaching the game to lawyers, police officers, real estate executives, doctors, and industrial engineers, all of whom were excited to learn and loved hearing old-timers tell tall tales. Besides me, former teammates and rivals like Dick Radatz, Jim Lonborg, Mike Andrews, and George Scott were also instructors at the camp, where the highlight was the "Campers vs. Pros" game on Saturday—in which campers wearing home white Red Sox uniforms had a chance to hit against real big leaguers.

I had so much fun I've gone back almost every year since and was also involved with other Fantasy Camps in Reno and Los Angeles. I've developed great relationships with campers, many of whom also return again and again. Guys like Sox Exchange camper Paul Medici have become family friends through the decades.

"I have always been a Red Sox fan as long as I can remember but became a Luis Tiant fan during the 1975 World Series," says Medici. "I met Luis at my first Fantasy Camp in 1984. He was looking for someone to go to the dog track with him, and I said I'd go. That was the start of a thirty-five-year friendship in which I got to know Luis Tiant *the person*, not just the baseball player. Luis was so accommodating to all the campers—signing autographs, taking pictures, and talking about the Red Sox and baseball.

"He has a true passion for the game, and in all the years I've known him, including when we've gone out with our wives on numerous social occasions, he has *never* turned anyone away without an autograph. Luis is a loving husband, father, grandfather, and friend, and a person who always ends a conversation by saying, 'I love you.'"

Fans definitely don't want my autograph because of my acting skills, but I did get to play myself on the TV show *Cheers*—which was set at a Boston bar of that name about a mile from Fenway Park. The fictional owner and head bartender at *Cheers* was Sam "Mayday" Malone (played by Ted Danson), a former Red Sox relief pitcher from the 1970s who drank himself out of baseball. Although *Cheers* is fancier than a typical "sports bar," if you look carefully around the walls during the show, you might catch photos of me, Bill Campbell, Fred Lynn, and the 1978 Red Sox team photo.

In the episode I'm in, I play a former teammate of Sam's who is shooting a beer commercial with him. The ad starts with me talking about how great the beer is, but because of my Cuban accent I'm having trouble pronouncing the name. This goes on a while, and then a manager steps right in front of the camera.

"Bring in Malone!"

Then Sam comes in to "relieve me" and finish the ad.

I thought it was really funny, and I must have done OK because a couple years later I was asked to appear in one of those "Less filling! Tastes great!" ads for Miller Lite, and I have since been interviewed for a bunch of baseball documentaries, including *Lost Son of Havana*—a film about my life in the United States and Cuba (see the last chapter).

During the 1980s, when I was waiting for a coaching position to open up for me in pro ball—the Red Sox were still not calling—I kept myself busy. In 1986 I pitched some games in the Equitable Old Timer's Series, which raised funds for needy MLB veterans who had played in the pre-pension era. At Fenway, the first of the twenty-six big-league ballparks the series visited, I was happy to hear the LOO-EEE! LOO-EEE! chants again, even if just for a few hours.

Sometimes, after all those years of traveling by bus, train, and plane, it was nice just to hang around the house playing catch. During the mid-1980s, when our family was doing some major renovations on a new home outside Boston, I developed a friendship with Mike Dunn, the teenage son of our landscaper/contractor.

"I was on my father's crew, and I was so excited when I found out we were going to be working on Luis Tiant's house," Mike Dunn recalls. "I brought my glove with me that first day, and every day after that, Luis and I would play catch. He told me he had developed that funny twirl in his delivery because when he was younger, he had a shoulder injury, and he had to develop that delivery to relieve pressure and pain on the shoulder. At different times we would sit down, and he would cry about his parents. He was telling me stories about when he was younger and how it had been fifteen years that he couldn't see his mother and father; and even years later, it bothered him to talk about it. He was an only child but had a lot of cousins and uncles and aunts in Cuba that he had not physically seen for twenty years. That really, really took a toll on him.

"One of his sons, Danny, was about my age. Luis was so nice to him. Every time Danny would walk by, Luis would pat him on the head or on the back. You could tell there was a wonderful relationship between them. And even though Luis always gave me $100 to buy pizza or subs for the crew, his wife Maria would cook something for the guys too. Cakes or pies, or eggs and cheese and coffee."

There would be less time for catch starting in 1987 when I traded in my baseball jersey for a suit and tie and made the rounds regularly in Mattapan, Jamaica Plain, Dorchester, and other Boston neighborhoods as a personal assistant for Massachusetts State Treasurer Robert Q. Crane. I visited pharmacies, liquor stories, and supermarkets to publicize the Mass. Lottery, spoke Spanish in neighborhoods where residents felt more comfortable with it, and rode school buses with kids in Lowell to help soften some of the tension around desegregation in that city. Anything I could do to help Treasurer Crane better understand minority communities, and their needs, I did.

Everywhere I went people would wave, shout hello in Spanish or English, and ask for a handshake or an autograph. It seemed crazy that even though I was still very popular in the area, the team where I gained my fame didn't want me. If I thought about it too much, I would get really angry—so mostly I pushed those thoughts away and enjoyed the good feeling I got from meeting everybody in my travels.

Still, I never felt very comfortable making my living in a suit. I wanted to be back in uniform. And in 1989 there was one more chance to play ball on a regular basis, as part of the newly formed Senior Professional Baseball Association (SPBA). The thirty-five-and-older (thirty-two for catchers) league had eight teams based in Florida made up of former big leaguers, minor leaguers, and a few semi-pro players. Each team would play a seventy-two game, three-month schedule beginning right after the World Series and ending near the start of spring training. League owners hoped they could turn a profit and draw more baseball fans south for longer visits.

There were big names on every club, starting with Hall of Fame managers like Dick Williams and Earl Weaver and going down through sluggers like Dave Kingman and Graig Nettles and pitchers like Vida Blue and Rollie Fingers. I was selected to play for the Winter Haven Super Sox and told a reporter one of the reasons I was most excited about joining the league was that it was hard to give up the adrenaline rush you had with a game on the line and the crowd chanting your name.

"You never forget it; there's nothing like the big league," I told one reporter. "And after it's over, it's hard to adjust."

During my time in the SPBA, I was part of what might be one of the strangest deals in professional baseball history. When Winter Haven owner Mitchell Maxwell traded me to the Gold Coast Suns at my request, so I could play in Miami, it presented a problem: he and Suns owner Richard Berrie could not agree on a player that Maxwell needed or was willing to go to Winter Haven. Since Berrie was a novelty merchandiser, however, he had something else to offer—five hundred teddy bears. The bears were distributed to children at the Winter Haven ballpark that night.

I guess as much as fans like old-timer's games, having four of them every few days was overkill. The SPBA almost never drew well and folded early in its second season. By that time, however, I had finally drawn the interest of another MLB club looking for a minor league pitching coach: the Los Angeles Dodgers. Some of my friends in their organization spoke up for me—Lou Johnson, John Roseboro, and Reggie Smith—and that got the wheels moving.

The Dodgers assigned me for the 1992 season to their Class A team in the Gulf Coast League, in Kissimmee, Florida. It felt great to be putting on a real big-league uniform again—and not just for an old-timer's or senior league game. I was comfortable, like I was back where I belonged. The Dodgers were the classiest organization in baseball, the team that paved the way for integration to take hold, and they were still working hard to make their players good people—not just good ballplayers.

"They won't tolerate discrimination," I explained to sportswriter Gordon Edes about an incident that occurred during the Arizona Instructional League after I first joined the organization. "There was a fight between an Afro-American and a Spanish kid, and they sent them both home. Reggie Smith talked to the Afro-Americans, Chico Fernandez and I talked to the Spanish kid, somebody else spoke to the white kids, then we brought them all together into one room."

I wound up staying with the Dodgers organization for four seasons, eventually coaching pitchers for several different teams at the Class A and Double AA level.

Here's one funny story. Back when Tommy Lasorda was still managing the Dodgers in '95, we were at spring training at Vero Beach when he noticed something he did not like in relief pitcher Rich Linares's delivery. Tommy was one of the early managers to master Spanish, so he went out to the mound to pass on some instructions. He spoke for about a minute, en español, and Linares just kept looking at him all confused.

Finally, knowing Linares was a Los Angeles-area native, I spoke up.

"Tommy, I don't think he speaks Spanish."

One of my favorite pitching prospects who *was* a native Spanish speaker was a young left-hander from the Dominican Republic named Jesus Martinez, whose two twenty-game-winning older brothers, Ramon and Pedro, were also pitchers in the Dodgers system. Jesus was a great talent as well, a tall, thin left-hander and a terrific kid who worked very hard. He toiled in the minors for ten seasons, but I'm not sure he had the killer instinct that his brothers had out on the mound. Jesus never made it into a big-league game, although he was called up to the Dodgers in September 1996.

Sadly, he died of cardiac arrest in March 2018, just after his forty-fourth birthday.

"Jesus loved Luis dearly," says Pedro Martinez, looking back. "When Luis worked with Jesus, that's when I got to first meet him in person. Luis is a legend, someone we respect and someone we look up to. It's hard to imagine, when you look at him, so many things he did that were great for baseball, in his time."

By the time Jesus was joining his big brother Ramon on the '96 Dodgers, I was finishing up my latest challenge: serving as pitching coach for Team Nicaragua at the 1996 Summer Olympics in Atlanta. I got the position after meeting Nicaragua's minister of sports the previous December, when touring the country with a group of retired big leaguers. We hit it off, and the next thing you know he was offering me the job.

Coaching a national team was something totally new to me, but I enjoyed it a lot, and we made a lot of people take notice of us in Atlanta. We got all the way to the bronze medal game, which we lost to the United States. Two more wins and we could have had gold. Since my homeland of Cuba *did* win its second straight gold at the '96 Games, and my adopted home of USA took the bronze—I was proud even without winning a medal. But it would have been great!

The next year, 1997, was a big one for me and my family. I was inducted into the Boston Red Sox Hall of Fame along with my former teammates Carlton Fisk, Rico Petrocelli, and Dick Radatz (Dick and I were together in Cleveland after he left the Sox), former general manager Dick O'Connell, and the guy just ahead of me on Boston's all-time chart for pitching victories, Mel Parnell. It was a great honor to be enshrined, joining all-time greats like Ted Williams, Yaz, Cy Young, and Bobby Doerr, and I used the enshrinement ceremony as an opportunity to say how much I still wanted to work in the Red Sox organization.

The GM at the time, Dan Duquette, had grown up as a Red Sox fan and always said he was looking out for me and wanted to get me a job. But the Yawkey ownership was still in power at Fenway, and so there were no offers coming. I wasn't going to sit still waiting. My stint with the Dodgers was now up, so I took minor league coaching job in '97 with the Chicago White Sox at Sarasota.

Then I received a surprise phone call. The Savannah College of Art & Design (SCAD), the largest school of its kind in the country, was interested in building up its Division III baseball program. They were looking for a head coach, and the president, Richard Rowan, asked if I wanted to come up to visit and see their campus. We were living in Fort Lauderdale at the time.

At first it seemed strange to me; why would a school full of artists, not known for sports at all, try and beef up its baseball team? But when Maria and I drove up there and saw the SCAD campus, and met with President Rowan, we fell in love with the place. The president knew his baseball and was a fan of my career, so that was a big plus. It turns out he interviewed ten former major league players for the job before offering it to me.

President Rowan was a great man and really took care of us. We signed a four-year contract and set up our home in a beautiful complex right outside campus on a golf course. It's funny; some people thought I would have trouble coaching college players because I didn't go to college myself. But I wasn't teaching them how to go to college; I was teaching them how to play baseball. Plus, I had my son Luis Jr., who had been a shortstop at Boston College High School and then played in the Park League, with me as an assistant coach.

"You always want to play ball with your dad as a kid, and I never got the chance because my dad was in the majors," says Luis Jr., who had been a pitcher in middle school before hurting his arm. "So this was the next best thing—I got to *coach* with my dad. I left everything behind in Miami and went to coach the SCAD Bees with him for two years.

"We split duties; I took care of most of the administrative stuff and the recruiting. I used to have to remind my dad he was the coach and not a ballplayer. He wanted to make the experience as fun as possible for everybody. To this day, I keep in touch with a lot of the SCAD players. They were all great kids, and a lot of them graduated and have careers in graphic arts and architecture.

"You had the dynamics of college baseball and the student-athlete mentality and dealing with parents. It becomes a little stressful, but I wouldn't trade it for anything."

Luis Jr. and I went out and recruited kids from all over—California, Miami, everywhere. Not too many top ballplayers were also top artists and students, but we found them. Over time, we turned out to be a pretty good team. We beat a Division I school and we beat the shit out of Northeastern and MIT up in Boston. They never wanted us to come back up there!

After never going to college myself, it was great to be on a real college campus with my family. It had always been one of my dreams.

"Dad loved Savannah," says Danny Tiant, who played baseball at Canton High, Bridgewater State University, and Central Florida University. "When I came to visit them, it felt just like we were at Fenway Park. It was like he was the mayor. Everywhere we went it was 'Hey LOO-EEE!' and hugs and kisses and smiles or 'Hey Coach, how ya doing?' Everybody called him Coach."

Because the kids on the team were all too young to remember my career, I wasn't sure how much they would know about me as a player. I wanted them to respect me, but not just because I was a former big leaguer. In the end, things turned out pretty good. Sometimes I had to come down on them hard about staying out late or partying too much—we had this big field where Luis Jr. and I made them run laps until they puked for breaking team rules—but they were good kids, and I came to really love them.

"I played at SCAD for two years before Coach Tiant took the job, and I had not heard of him before," says Tony Blankenship, shortstop and captain of the Bees, and later a minor leaguer with the White Sox. "When I started researching him, I was blown away at his accomplishments. On paper, he was an amazing player. But after meeting him and working closely with him my junior and senior year, I learned that his character *as a person* dwarfs any on-field accomplishments he achieved.

"During this time, in my early twenties, I was trying to learn what being a man was all about. With my own father, who I was never close with anyway, in prison back in Ohio, my time with Coach Tiant was a godsend. You could tell that he came from a life of more serious consequences. Sometime when he'd come out to talk to a struggling pitcher, he'd tell them, 'Relax. OK? You're tight. For what? If you don't pitch good, they're not gonna drag you in the street and shoot you, right? So *fuck* it, throw strikes!' It broke the tension, it calmed everyone down, and put things in perspective.

"Coach was *hilarious!* He'd get on guys, talk trash, and laugh with us. He really enjoyed being around young guys who played the game because we loved it. We had some talented players, for a DIII college, but no big-league prospects. Just young men who wanted to play. Coach brought a genuine joy to the dugout. At any point during practice, you might catch him giving someone a powerful life lesson or ragging on them and chuckling as the rest of the guys fell over laughing. It was amazing to be a part of, and I never wanted practice to end."

Bradley Hesser, our third baseman, says the most important thing he learned playing for me and Luis Jr. was respect.

"Coach Tiant talked about it often and even talked about it last year when we met up with him at Fenway for my fortieth birthday," says Hesser. "If you give respect, you will *get* respect. He also constantly talked to us about getting our 'paper.' He said that baseball should be second to getting our degree as no matter where we go or what we do, no one can take it away from us. He took great pride in watching us develop into better men year after year."

I'm amazed how much these kids remember from some of our games. Here's a good story from Bradley:

"In the spring of 1998, in Coach Tiant's first year as our coach, we made a trip to Boston to play MIT. This was a big deal as it was his first trip back to Boston in a baseball capacity outside of the Red Sox. We were at the field going through warmups and had started taking batting practice. I was the number-three hitter, and as I was preparing to take my time at the plate, one of the TV stations told Coach Tiant he should throw BP for them to get some video. So as I enter the box to take BP, Coach Tiant goes to the mound to throw. I happen to hit one over the fence, and then he throws the next pitch at me.

"'Boy you knew it was coming!' he says, laughing. 'You hitting like that is making me look badddd!'

"All of this because of the cameras and because, well, Coach Tiant wanted to remind us of the fun we can have playing a game."

Maybe one reason I connected so well with the SCAD players is because Maria and I had raised two sons and then helped raise a third who has become as much our child as Luis, Danny, and Isabel.

Johnny Papile.

Danny likes to joke around, calling Johnny "my white brother from another mother." But there is no question, they *are* brothers, and he *is* our third son.

Johnny's father, Leo, was an MDC police officer who spent thirty-eight years on the force and lived in Quincy, the next town over from us when we were in Milton. I always got along great with cops, so I got to know Leo, and at one point I heard that his wife had passed away from cancer. Johnny was still a young kid and was a big fan of mine. So we arranged for me to meet him, and after that he became like a member of our family.

"The first time I ever saw a major league baseball game was in 1967," Johnny remembers. "I was nine years old, and my uncle took me to see the Red Sox play the Indians the last week of the season. Luis was pitching, and even though I was a Boston fan, I fell in love with that great motion of El

Tiante. He became my favorite non-Red Sox player, and when he joined the team in '71, I couldn't believe it. I went to watch him play as often as I could.

"When my mother passed away, in 1973, my dad got totally absorbed in his work. My brother was already out of the house, and I was often home alone. With my father's blessing, the Tiants started giving me meals, taking me to and from school, and basically adopted me as their fourth child. This was during busing, and my father was dealing with crazy stuff every day. One time he got hit with a brick in Southie, and he heard the 'N word' and everything else all the time. But here was his kid, in the middle of busing, sitting with the Tiant family at ballgames. The whole thing was incredible."

It gets better.

"One Christmas break during college, I went down to visit the Tiants in Mexico City," Johnny explains. "Luis and I were walking to the store one day, and I literally fell in love at first sight with a girl who was visiting the daughter of Luis and Maria's neighbors. Luis helped me to meet her, and we wound up getting married. Maria—who I call Mom—walked me down the aisle."

In the end, Johnny says only one bad thing has come out of his joining our family.

"After the Red Sox let Luis go to the Yankees, and would not give him the respect he deserved, I vowed to never root for them again. Since that point, I've been a Yankees fan."

We forgive Johnny for that, but we're sure to rub it in when we can.

In early 2002, after nearly eighty years of Yawkey family control, the Red Sox were sold to a new ownership group headed up by John Henry, Tom Warner, and Larry Lucchino. Almost overnight the entire feeling around the team and Fenway Park changed, and they began reaching out to a lot of former players about getting more involved again with the club.

I was one of them. Dan Duquette had promised me that when new folks came in, he would bring me back to the Red Sox family. As soon as Lucchino took over as team president, Dan kept his word. I'll always be thankful to him, and Larry, for that.

My first job with the organization was as a pitching coach with the Class A Lowell Spinners. Then I spent 2002 and '03 as a radio color commentator for Red Sox games on the team's Spanish Beisbol Network. For once I didn't have to worry about anybody understanding what I was saying, and I had a great time with my partners including Uri Berenguer, the youngest broadcaster in the major leagues at the time. Still in his early twenties, Uri was a Panama City native and a pediatric cancer survivor treated in the Jimmy Fund Clinic at Dana-Farber Cancer Institute—one of the official charities of the Red Sox. His uncle Juan Berenguer was a big-league pitcher whose career overlapped with mine, and Uri and I developed a special relationship.

"I was just starting my career, and El Tiante made it very easy to feel comfortable and confident," remembers Berenguer, who is still doing Red Sox games for the Spanish Beisbol Network. "Luis was always very nurturing and genuinely caring. He always made me feel important, and I marveled at his endless baseball and life experiences—some that made me wonder how he was able to overcome so much adversity."

Then he laughs.

"My one complaint about Luis as a broadcast partner is that he could never control his passion enough not to yell during home run calls. It got to the point where I had to learn to anticipate his joyous outbursts in time for me to mute his mic. Tiant's passion and love for baseball is second only to the love he has for his family."

After a couple summers yelling too loud for Uri, with whom I'm still close, I went back to doing what I love most—teaching. Over time, I've become more of a roving instructor for the Red Sox, both at spring training and throughout the season. My official title is now special assignment consultant. I meet with pitchers whenever I can at Fenway, and talk to them a lot on the phone as well.

"Luis Tiant is the personification of Cuban baseball, the epitome of old-school pitching, and a living, breathing icon of Red Sox baseball," says Lucchino, now president/CEO emeritus of the Red Sox, and chairman of both the Pawtucket Red Sox and the Jimmy Fund. "To have Luis with the Red Sox to offer his insights, instruction, personality, and to serve as an example to our young pitchers and players—particularly, but not exclusively, to the Red Sox players of Latino heritage—has been a priceless asset to the team and a factor in its success in the 21st century. He is a jewel."

It's been a fantastic experience for me. I love having the chance to be involved with so many great young men—pitchers as well as position players—and feel good when I can help them.

"The Red Sox do a good job of keeping the old faces around; I've heard it through the grapevine that not every organization is like that," says Lenny DiNardo, a Red Sox pitcher from 2004 to 2009. "When I was playing for the Sox, having guys like Dom DiMaggio, Bobby Doerr, Johnny Pesky, Jim

Rice, and Tiant around in the clubhouse was no big thing. They were a constant fixture, and that was not only a credit to them, it also gave us an idea of what we were playing for—and the hardships that the Red Sox went through in not winning the World Series in eighty-six years.

"These were guys who were extremely talented, with Hall of Fame careers, that didn't get a chance to get a ring. So to have them around to sort of mentor us and tell stories and basically just stay around like foster parents or foster grandparents in the clubhouse was really valuable. I always appreciated it."

I appreciated it, too, and when the Red Sox finally did win that World Series in 2004, they made us former ballplayers feel like we were part of it. I got a call shortly after the series asking me for my ring size, and that's when I realized they were going to be giving me a World Series ring—which was incredible. They also invited me to be on a duck boat during the World Series parade, not just that year but also in 2007 and 2013. Pudge and I have thrown out the first pitches before several playoff and World Series games. That never gets old, believe me.

Sometimes I make a special connection to a pitcher that develops over a season. In 2017, I worked a lot with Rick Porcello after he had a tough first year with the Red Sox. He's a good, good kid, and I told him he was *too* nice—he had to be meaner out on that mound.

"You've got the stuff to win twenty games," I told him. He looked at me like I was crazy, and I said it again. "With your fastball, and your breaking ball, you *have* to win twenty! But you've got to be willing to knock a guy down once in a while. You've got to have that killer instinct, really go after those hitters, and then once in a while come inside to them. *That's* how you become a good pitcher, not just by throwing hard."

He did what I told him, and he started winning more. We talked after every game he pitched that year, and I kept reminding him. He kept winning, and as he got closer to twenty wins I told him if he didn't get all the way there I was going to break his neck.

He *did* make it—and wound up going 22-4 and winning the 2017 Cy Young Award.

The first time he saw me after he won his twentieth, he came over and gave me a big hug.

"Thank you, Luis," he said.

"Hey," I told him, "You don't have to thank *me*. You did it yourself. I didn't pitch—*you* did. I'm just here to see if I can help you, or anybody else on the team who needs me."

That includes batting advice. I always try and remind guys on the team what a great hitter I was—.417 in 1970, look it up!—so I like to see position players lend an ear to my advice too.

"When he comes to Boston, he talks about hitters and how he would try to pitch to a hitter's weaknesses," says outfielder Andrew Benintendi, one of the wonderful young players on the 2018 World Series champs. "It's helpful, and it's fun to pick his brain. He has this way about him where he just lightens the mood. He likes to have a good time."

Because I still remember the challenges I faced learning a new culture and language when I first came to the United States, some of my most special connections on the current Red Sox are with Latino ballplayers dealing with similar issues.

"Since I had the opportunity to have met Luis in 2014, and especially now, he's been like a father to me," says righty pitcher Eduardo Rodriguez, 13-5 in '18 and just entering his prime. "He's in Boston most of the time, so before games and after games I have the opportunity to sit with him and chat. He's taught me everything. I always listen to him and what he has to say; it's been great to have the opportunity to have him on my side. I call him sometimes; I know if I need somebody to talk to, even in Spanish, I have him—and I have Pedro [Martinez]."

It's great to see Cuba once again making a name for itself in the major leagues. In the early 1980s, I believe, Tony Perez and I were the last two Cuban-born players in the majors from the pre-Castro days. Then there were almost no Cuban players for a long time, until in recent years a bunch, including stars like Jose Abreu and Aroldis Chapman, started to defect or get smuggled in—which of course was very dangerous. It was wonderful to see the deal the MLB signed with the Cuban Baseball Federation in 2018 that gives Cuban players a chance to sign with big-league clubs once they are twenty-five years old and have played six years in the Cuban Leagues. They are getting a chance to chase their dreams and help their families, just like we did, but now they can go back to Cuba without fear of being jailed or persecuted in any way.

Mike Lowell, 2007 World Series MVP for the Red Sox, is one of those guys who is old enough to remember hearing about me growing up, and I'm so glad that I helped to motivate and drive him as a man of color in the game.

"My father is the oldest of four boys, and his three brothers were all born in Cuba. So he grew up in Cuba from ages one to eleven, when he left," says

Lowell. "I knew a lot about Luis growing up, and I throw Tony Perez into that mix too. They not only came from Cuba and had success, but their color and the racial obstacles both of them had to deal with during that time was immense. So my eyes were opened to that fact.

"You kind of feel like there is a connection when you say 'Cuban.' Although I was raised in the states, my culture, my values, and everything I feel like I was raised with is based on a Latin family. I spoke Spanish before I spoke English, and I felt like I got the best of both worlds in that sense. So the talks about Luis and guys like that were pretty prevalent in my house."

Today, if parents are smart, they are telling their children to be like Mike Lowell.

Another wonderful development I've had since coming back to the Red Sox has been my reconnection with the fans at Fenway Park. When the new owners turned Yawkey Way—now Jersey Street—into a free-standing concourse area that fans can use during ballgames, one of the concession stands they put in was the El Tiante Grille. You can come pick up a Cuban sandwich or beer, and I'm often there to shake hands, sign autographs, or just talk baseball. I'm also one of the former players who rotates through the "Legends Suite" high above the first-base grandstands, which is a great way for me to really get to talk to fans for more than just a minute.

Fenway may be non-smoking now, but I still find time to enjoy my cigars. For a while I even made a living at it. Around the same time I came back to the Sox, I started a cigar company with my sons: El Tiante Cigars. At first, we had a hard time getting people to realize these were real good cigars, not novelty items, but over time we developed a reputation for making an excellent product. Luis Jr. got out after a while, but Danny studied the field and really built up the company—which he renamed Tiant Cigar Group—wonderfully.

Like my coaching with Luis Jr. at SCAD, traveling to different cigar events became my and Danny's father-and-son time for several years.

"I was sixteen when I had my first cigar at a high school party," remembers Danny. "I don't know where we got them—probably from my dad's stash—but I lit one up. And it's funny, I started to feel like my dad was inside me when I was smoking that cigar. My buddies were cracking up, saying, 'You look just like your father.' And I said, 'You know, it's funny, because I *feel* like him too.'

"That led to my love of cigars, and I think to the connection between him and me that we can still hang out and smoke them. I find it to be a great father-son bonding moment that we have. My mom smokes cigars once in a while. My brother got into it a little bit, but it's not really his thing. My sister can't stand it.

"My father always had a cigar in his mouth. That's one of the arguments he and my mom have all the time. He's not allowed to smoke cigars in the house anymore, and he always brings up how he was able to smoke them back in the day. She'll say, 'No you didn't,' and he'll say, 'Yes I did.' They always go back and forth on it. But I've come across pictures of my dad holding me in his lap, and he's got a cigar in his mouth. He was always smoking then. I'd say mom put that rule down in the last ten to fifteen years."

And I'm smart enough to follow it. Maria and I have been married nearly sixty years, which is a pretty good record. If there is a Hall of Fame for marriages, I'd put us in it. We have been blessed with wonderful children and grandchildren, and we spend as much time with all of them as we can. Family is everything,

Charity work is also very important to me. Like I mentioned, I've done a lot of appearances for the Jimmy Fund and Dana-Farber Cancer Institute through the years, visiting young cancer patients at the hospital or at Fenway and taking part in events like Jimmy Fund golf tournaments and the annual WEEI/NESN Jimmy Fund Radio-Telethon. Cancer is the disease that killed my father, and anything I can do to help fight it, I'll do. Sometimes I'll be out at an event, or just having dinner or something, and a mother or father will come up to me and thank me for visiting with their child in the hospital years ago. I enjoy hearing that, but what's even better is hearing what those kids are up to *today* if, God willing, they got better.

I've had my own health challenges in recent years. In 2003 I learned I had type 2 diabetes, a condition that affects more than thirty million Americans and can cause blindness, nerve damage, and death. I changed my diet to get healthier and started hosting Luis Tiant's Swing for Diabetes, a golf tournament that in its first three years raised $600,000 for the American Diabetes Association. Diabetes has had an especially big impact on the Latino community, which is at higher risk along with other minority groups. If I have a chance to make an appearance or play in a tournament to help raise awareness or money for the cause, I'm there.

And, of course, there is always time to watch or talk baseball—and always time to pass on what I've learned in a lifetime of observing the game.

What are the some of the most important things?

- As a pitcher, it's better to be smart and slow than fast and straight.
- Watch what umpires do—and learn from it. Don't show up the men (or women) in blue by glaring at the ball and kicking the dirt. If you can quietly approach umps about questionable calls without showing them up, it will likely benefit you greatly the rest of that game.
- Always have a Plan B…and C…and D.
- Be grateful for what you have—and cherish it. You may not have it tomorrow.

Jim Rice, my longtime teammate, friend, and golf partner, is one of those guys who says I'm funny even when I'm not trying to be. I'm not sure what to make of that.

"It's very hard to see this guy unhappy," says Rice. "He's always willing to make someone else happy or make someone else smile. A lot of times, you walk in a room, and some of the things he says, you just start laughing. Then again, sometimes you look at him like I'm looking at him right now, and I'm laughing."

One thing that would make a lot of people happy, based on what they tell me, is if I could get into the National Baseball Hall of Fame. I'm not going to say much about this except that I feel based on the numbers I put up that I belong. Plenty of other people do too, yet I never received more than 30.9 percent of the vote during my fifteen years of eligibility (75 percent is needed for enshrinement), and I have been nominated but not elected several times by the Veteran's Committee.

I can't explain it, and I know plenty of people don't agree with it.

"While it's always gamesmanship to compare this guy from this era to that guy in *that* era, Luis Tiant pitched in pretty much the same era as [Hall of Famers] Don Drysdale and Catfish Hunter, and the similarities in numbers are striking," says Steve Buckley, who has covered the Red Sox as a beat reporter and a columnist for more than forty years. "Pitching is so hard, and I know with guys who can last for a long time, they just call it 'putting up the numbers,' but it's hard to just put up the numbers as a pitcher. That's why I'm sympathetic to the plight of Jim Kaat and Tommy John and Luis Tiant."

I'm with Buck on that last part—Tommy John and Jim Kaat belong in the Hall of Fame too.

Rico Petrocelli played with and against me for fifteen years. Here's his view on the subject:

"To me, Luis is *absolutely* a Hall of Famer. They are always looking at the numbers, and he's got them. He got into the playoffs, and the World Series, and pitched great in both. He didn't win a Cy Young Award, but he was pretty close. There are other pitchers in there who didn't win Cy Young Awards, and remember he won 229 games—plus twenty or more four times. And how about those earned-run averages? They were just incredible. You throw those 1.60 and 1.91 ERAs up on a plaque—I mean, c'mon!"

One longtime Red Sox fan, college English professor Albert DeCiccio, feels so strongly about this subject that he's written a thesis that he calls *Prime: The Luis Tiant Story.*

Here's a portion of it:

prime
prīm/
adjective

1. of first importance; main.
2. of the best possible quality; excellent.
3. a state or time of greatest strength, vigor, or success in a person's life.

Luis Tiant is a prime example of a player who should be in the Hall of Fame. In two decades, Tiant won 229 games and compiled a 3.30 ERA. He struck out 2,416 in 3,486 1/3 innings. While he was named to just three All-Star teams, Tiant finished in the top six of Cy Young voting three times and in one season was fifth in MVP voting, because of an AL-best 1.60 ERA.

In 34 2/3 postseason innings, the lost son of Havana was 3-0 with a 2.86 ERA, helping the Red Sox make the 1975 World Series among the greatest of all time at precisely a time when baseball needed it most. In Game 4 of that fall classic, Tiant threw a remarkable 163 prime pitches in a complete game effort that helped the Red Sox tie the Series and that gave the team a belief it could beat the Big Red Machine that featured Hall of Famers Johnny Bench and Joe Morgan as well as the hit machine, Pete Rose.

On December 10, 2017, Tiant learned that, while he fulfilled the dream of his father, Luis Tiant Sr., he did not get into the Hall of Fame again. *Prime: The Luis Tiant Story* details the mistake Major League

Baseball continues to make in not enshrining Tiant in the Hall of Fame. Among other accomplishments in a premier pitching career, I detail the nine heroic innings Tiant hurled—yielding 9 hits and 4 runs—to win Game 4 of the 1975 World Series.

Just as his 2 wins in that World Series, his 163 pitches in Game 4, and 229 career wins are prime numbers, Luis Tiant, as a man and as a baseball pitcher, epitomizes the definition of prime. He is certainly "of the best quality"; he is "excellent." Yogi Berra said, "It ain't over till it's over," so Tiant still has hope. There is a place in Cooperstown for El Tiante, with a plaque bearing all his prime accomplishments and a clause stating, "Of first importance to Tiant was honoring his father's lesson by finishing what he started." When he finally enters the Hall of Fame, Tiant will have baseball immortality, and he will have finished what his father started."

I am deeply grateful for fans like Professor DeCiccio, media members like Steve Buckley, Peter Gammons, and Dan Shaughnessy, and the many, many teammates and opponents who have voiced their support for me over the years. Carlton Fisk called me the best pitcher he ever caught, and he was behind the plate for twenty-four years in the big leagues. That's a pretty good endorsement.

So it this one, from longtime pitching coach and teammate Stan Williams:

"It's a complete sin that Luis Tiant is not in the Hall of Fame. Luis was the best right-hand pitcher I ever saw, and I pitched in St. Louis one year [with Bob Gibson]."

I'm not sure what's going to happen with future voting, and I'm not going to get my hopes up. If it happens, it happens. It would be an honor to be enshrined beside teammates like Pudge, Yaz, Jim Ed, Catfish, Reggie Jackson, and the many other great players I suited up with and against.

But I do know this. Whether or not there is ever a bronze plaque with my face on it in a museum in Cooperstown, New York, I feel I have led a Hall of Fame life. I have been blessed beyond measure as a son, a husband, a father, and a grandfather. My friendships and my faith have taken me through very difficult days and helped me succeed when the odds were against me. I did not always win, but I always gave my best.

I fulfilled my father's dreams, and my own.

19

HOME TO HAVANA

IT STARTED WITH A CASUAL discussion and ended with the trip of a lifetime.

During the summer of 2004, the Red Sox were in the early stages of their historic run to a World Series title. By this point Luis Tiant was back at Fenway Park on a regular basis, greeting fans at the El Tiante Grille on then-Yawkey Way and schmoozing with them during ballgames in the luxury boxes above home plate. One day at the ballpark, Tiant struck up a conversation with Kris Meyer, a Quincy, Massachusetts, native working as a movie producer with the brother directing team of Bobby and Peter Farrelly. The Farrellys were at Fenway filming scenes for an upcoming film.

"Luis said he wanted to go home [to Cuba] before he died," Meyer recalled of their chat. "I asked, 'How long has it been?' He said, 'Forty-two years.'"

Much of Meyer's job with the Farrellys was finding those stories that might translate well to the big screen. Tiant's, he and the brothers agreed, was one. They all knew the pitcher's compelling background. What if they were to help Tiant return to Cuba and used that journey as the centerpiece for a film about his life?

There were significant obstacles to such a plan. Although in failing health, Fidel Castro was still very much in control of Cuba. Travel to and from the country remained heavily restricted for Americans. But in true Hollywood fashion, the Farrellys and Meyer, along with documentary filmmaker Jonathan Hock, found a way to make it work.

The film that resulted—*The Lost Son of Havana*—combined footage from their trip with old family photos, baseball clips, and interviews including Tiant's Red Sox teammates Carlton Fisk and Carl Yastrzemski. Premiering at the Tribeca Film Festival in April 2009, it went on to win numerous awards and shed new light on modern Cuban-US relations and the challenges faced by those living under Castro a half-century after his ascent to power.

Most importantly, *The Lost Son of Havana* enabled its star to return to the family and homeland he had yearned to see for forty-six years.

WHEN I GOT OUT of Cuba, I swore before God I didn't want to come back as long as Castro was there. But then the time goes by, goes by, goes by, and you start wondering—when am I going to come back? I'm not getting any younger.

Other than my parents, I had not seen my family—or my country—since 1961. That's a long time. Sometimes I'd think about it, and it hurt. I realized I had to go to Cuba before I died, even if Castro was still in power. That was going to complete my life.

As an American citizen, I couldn't travel to and from the island without a special license issued by both countries. I had applied for the license before and was turned down by both countries. My name didn't matter.

Then, in 2007, there was an opportunity. The movie directors Bobby and Peter Farrelly, famous for making comedies like *There's Something About Mary* and *Dumb and Dumber*, were big Red Sox fans who grew up in Rhode Island during the 1970s. They even made a movie about a guy obsessed with the Sox called *Fever Pitch* that came out right after Boston won the '04 World Series. The Farrellys knew my life story and wanted to produce a documentary about me that included my return home.

The Farrellys were used to making comedies, so they got Jonathan Hock, a documentary filmmaker from New York who did a lot of sports stuff, to sign on as director. Kris Meyer, a Boston native who had been with the Farrellys for years as a producer and worked at Fenway Park in college, filled out the film's senior staff.

There was a goodwill baseball game in Cuba each year between American amateurs and retired Cuban players that the documentary team heard about. All the American players had permission to travel to and from the country freely, and somehow they found a way to get their film crew onto the team. The crew's baseball experience was pretty shaky, but it didn't matter. The important thing was that by signing on as their coach, I could legally go with them to Cuba and be in the movie.

I packed for the trip on my sixty-seventh birthday: November 23, 2007. By this point I had not seen my Cuban relatives for forty-six years. I was not sure who was alive, who was dead, and whether my childhood home was even still there.

One of the things I took with me was an old black and white photograph of my father, in uniform, taken during his playing days. I thought if I came across anybody who knew of Dad as "Lefty" Tiant—the great Cuban and Negro League pitcher—they might enjoy seeing it.

Just before leaving, I visited with an old friend of my parents who remembered me from when I was a little boy. She made me some of her wonderful Cuban coffee, and I shared with her the story of the letter my father sent to me in Mexico City in 1961 telling me not to come home because Castro had outlawed all professional baseball on the island.

"You remember, I was their only child," I said to her. "They knew they might never see me again. I was all they had. But they wanted me to go pursue my dream. The dream that *he* had, to pitch in the major leagues someday."

Then she told me of *her* last trip to Cuba and how much it had pained her to see the conditions under which people lived.

"There's so much misery. You can tell the people are hungry!" she said. "They don't have anything to wear. The kids walk the streets barefoot. And even if you don't want to cry, tears come out of your eyes. Because what's there, Luis, it's so bad, so bad."

She said my family's house had still been there as of her visit, and then asked if my family there knew I was coming. I told her they didn't.

"What a surprise you're going to give them! And what a surprise you're going to get, my child!"

The film crew flew out of Miami together on a small plane, but I sat by myself. Plane rides had always bothered me during my playing days, and I used to fight my fears and crack my teammates up by yelling things like "C'mon, Get up! Get up!" during takeoff. But on this day, a strange sense of calmness came over me—like nothing I had ever felt before when flying. Looking down at the countryside as we flew in to Jose Marti Habana Airport, this was just one of many emotions I was feeling. I crossed myself as we landed, something I always did, and then the flight attendant came over the intercom:

"Ladies and gentlemen, welcome to Havana."

I had waited so long to hear those words. All the years I had been away.

The game against our Cuban hosts was held on the first day of our visit. It was in Pinar del Río, a small rural city west of Havana, and to get there we drove through villages that looked like they had not changed since I lived on the island. Almost all the cars we passed were from the 1950s and '60s because no one could afford anything newer. There were plenty of horse-drawn buggies and barefoot kids playing in the streets and very few stores or markets of any kind. It was like going back in time; it was like I never left.

"You know, I'm happy to come back," I said during the drive. "Good or bad, it's still my country."

The only thing that looked new to me was Estadio Capitán San Luis, the baseball stadium in Pinar del Río. It was actually nearly forty years old, but it was obviously kept up for the Cuban League team that played there. It was funny; this was my first time on a Cuban baseball diamond since I was pitching for the Sugar Kings in the winter of 1961. It was mostly younger fans in the stands, with kids running around, and nobody seemed to recognize me. That was fine. Our club was no match for the national team, but everyone had a lot of fun.

When we went back to the hotel, I met up with Juan Carlos Oliva, whose older brother Pedro was a Pinar del Río native and had been one of my teammates with the Twins. Like me, Pedro was not able to return to Cuba after Minnesota signed him and helped him get out in 1961 just before Castro locked things down. Pedro couldn't even use his real name in the United States; because he didn't have a birth certificate, he had used his older brother Antonio's name to get a passport.

Known from that point on as Tony Oliva, he became one of the best hitters in the major leagues. He won three batting titles, helped lead the Twins to the 1965 World Series, and later became a coach. If it wasn't for terrible knee injuries that cut his career short, he'd be in the Hall of Fame. He's still a hero in Minnesota, where his number is retired by the Twins and there is a bronze statue of him outside of Target Field.

Juan Carlos was just a little kid when Castro came to power. By the time he was seventeen and a great pitching prospect, it was too late. Cuban players could no longer sign with a big-league team and leave the island.

"You look just like your brother, same face," I told Juan Carlos as we shook hands and hugged hello. "I know you also played. He told me you were good."

"I represented the Cuban national team for ten years," he said proudly.

I responded with a smile.

"Tony said you were better than him," I replied, and now *he* smiled.

"No, that's not true. He lied about that. But you were great, and you're *still* great. You look young."

"It was time for me to return after forty-six years, that's what I was telling Tony. Years are easy to say, but those are days and nights."

"Years, thinking and suffering," he replied. "And in the name of all Cubans, we wish you the best time here. We want you to feel like a good Cuban, as you have always been."

It was nice of Juan Carlos to say that. Maybe he sensed the guilt I felt about having been away so long.

He drove us to his house that night for dinner. Juan Carlos worked for the government now, as a coach, and he lived comfortably. But seeing me surely brought up a lot of his own strong feelings about what could have been. Over drinks, he got very emotional.

"Tony Oliva, my brother"—that's what he calls Pedro, like everybody in the United States—"I hope he lives a million years. I think there's no one in the world like my brother. We used to live in the country. Tony was the head of our household. And one fine day, what came, came. He left for the United States, along with other athletes.

"Then the revolution came, and the counterrevolution at the Bay of Pigs, so they went and told him, 'If you go back to Cuba, you can't play professionally any more, but if you stay in the United States you have an open door—*if* you can make it.'

"So Tony said, 'Well I'm already here.' Many others came back. And honestly, Tony moved on. Our family suffered much when he left. But we also rejoiced...because he decided to seek out his future. He sought out his future, and he got it."

I took out the photo of my dad to show to Juan Carlos, and he started to cry. He was too young to have seen my father pitch, but he knew of his greatness and had grown close to him in later years.

"Your old man was my friend," he said as he continued studying the photo. "We hung out and went everywhere with our [Cuban national] teams in the '60s. We always talked about you. He'd tell me, 'My kid is playing really well over there. He's stepping into the major leagues and fighting for his chance.'

"He'd say you were coming home, that you wanted to come back. He always made excuses for you. 'It's not that he doesn't *want* to come,' he'd say. 'He wants to come!'"

"I *did* want to come," I said.

"But you couldn't. It's the same thing that happened to my brother Tony. You see?"

Then he looked again at the photo.

"This man [Luis Sr.] was out of this world. You see, we need to laugh. What a guy."

I tried to make him feel better.

"They say he was better than me," I said of my father. "That's what the old guys told me. 'You're good, but your dad was better.'"

Juan Carlos smiled.

"That's a lie. You were better. They said I was better than Tony. *That's* a lie. I was a crab next to him."

The next day I went to Havana to see my cousins and my aunts—my father's sisters—for the first time since leaving in '61. At first I didn't recognize anything, but as we drove closer to the area where my family had all lived, things started coming back to me. We went by the park where I skated as a kid, and then, a little further up, the narrow alley down which we had lived.

I couldn't believe how much it had changed; I remembered it being so nice, but now everything from the outside looked worn and old. I wasn't even sure my family was still living there, but my driver asked a man across the street who said yes, they were still in the area.

"Who was it?" I asked the driver.

"He says he knows you."

So we went over, and yes, I knew him. It was Fermin, a guy I had played ball with growing up.

"I defend this place…because I personally have missed you a lot," he said. He walked me over to where I used to live, knocked, and introduced me to the man who lived there now.

Fermin said he was angry with me, angry because he believed I had forgotten my family and the old neighborhood.

"You don't understand, that's not how it was…" I said softly. I explained that I had sent clothes and money and other things home through the years, but it had always been confiscated. My father never got it.

Fermin listened, but he didn't seem to believe it. Then he quickly got on me again.

"We were both right there as players," he said. "Damn, Luisito! I'm pissed as hell! Shit, you have no idea!"

I realized nothing I was going to say could make him feel better, so I just tried to be as nice as I could and pulled him in for a hug. That seemed to melt some of his anger away. He cried a bit and then saw some young guys and called them over.

"This is Luis Tiant," Fermin told the young guys, still near tears. "We played hardball as kids. My uncle was the one that signed him. When we used to practice he'd say, 'They are going to sign you for sure!' Everybody thought I'd sign first. But he signed. And me, well..."

I eventually broke away from Fermin by telling him the truth—I needed to go find my aunts. It turns out they had already heard I was there and were all together waiting.

"It's Luisito!" one of my aunts yelled. "Luisito! Look!" Then they all came over and hugged me; my aunts and my cousins. Everybody cried.

They lived in tiny apartments with old, beaten-up furniture. The government only gave them enough staple goods to last them half of each month, and things like toothpaste and soap and skin lotion were like gold. I brought them a suitcase full of such things, along with clothes for all of them. They seemed to appreciate it, but it didn't feel like nearly enough. I didn't know if I should cry for joy or for sadness; I ended up doing a little of both.

To lighten the mood, I joked around with them about my dad.

"When my father went there, to the United States, in '31, he threw so hard that he would knock the catchers down," I said. "So sometimes the catcher had to put a steak inside the glove on his hand. And when the game was over, the steak would be cooked!"

We laughed a lot, but we cried too. They told me how much my parents had missed me and how proud they were of my career.

"He left Cuba happy," my cousin said of my father, remembering when he and my mother went to Boston in 1975. "'I'm leaving,' he said, 'but I'll be back.' He was so pleased."

"He was pleased, eh?" I said. "He told me he wanted to go back to Cuba. I told him, 'No, you're not going back. Forget about that. Fidel says he doesn't want you back there anymore!'"

Everyone laughed again, but then I assured them that my father—and my mother—had really enjoyed their time in America before my father got sick. They tried to convince *me* that I should not feel bad about leaving for the United States in the first place. One aunt showed me a scrapbook she had made that was filled with newspaper clippings of my playing career, including when my parents moved to Boston.

"You can see that we're all very happy, right? Because you've come back, thank God," said my cousin. "And even if you didn't know it, here in this country, everybody, everybody in the neighborhood, would hear about you. About all the things Luisito would do.

"And with regard to your family, you've been away for a long time from Cuba. But what we know, and what I want *you* to know, too, is that *always, always, always,* we adore you, we miss you, and followed what you've done. And the love of your father and of your mother. They talked about you and how proud they were."

It was hard to take it all in. I still felt bad.

"Family is the most important," I said, "and because of that I've felt uncomfortable."

"You can't feel uncomfortable because you had your obligations and work. In any given moment, you have your obligations and work. And look, you're here *now!*"

"But too much time has passed that I shouldn't have let go by. I thought I would be able to see you again. I was going to come in '61, but my father sent me a letter saying not to come because there was no more professional baseball. You know, they gave their lives for me so that I could succeed—so that I could be someone. It's so hard. It's so hard."

"The time that needed to go by has gone by. And you can't beat yourself up about it because life is hard."

"But when you're talking about your family, that's something different," I said to her, "And the problem is that we're all going to die one day or another. And people that you left healthy and safe, and now you come back, and you run into all this."

Now another cousin spoke up.

"But don't worry about that, cousin, what we want is for you to be happy! It was their time, the ones who died. It was their time. You don't have to blame yourself for any of that."

It went back and forth like that throughout the trip.

Along with the film crew, I drove around the Havana area to point out what I remembered and see how much had changed. At one point we went to a place called *Esquina Caliente*—"The Hot Corner"—where baseball fans had been gathering every day for decades to talk and debate about their favorite teams, players, even lineups. While I stood off to the side, one of our guys got right in the middle of a big group of men and asked in Spanish who they thought was the best Cuban pitcher to play in the U.S. major leagues.

Immediately, men started screaming out their favorites:

"Jose Ariel Contreras!"

"El Duque! Orlando El Duque Hernández!"

"El Guajiro from Pinar del Río!"

"Livan Hernandez!"

When one man who looked much younger than the others quietly said "Luis Tiant," our guy told him, "Luis Tiant? He's right over there."

Within a few seconds everybody was crowding around me, shaking my hand. Most of the guys were probably born after I played my last game in the majors, but one elderly, white-haired man came up and said with a big smile that he had seen me pitch in Cuba during 1960 and '61.

They all started asking questions:

Who had I played for in Cuba?
Who did I play for in the majors besides Boston?
How long had I been away?
How fast could I throw now?

My answer to the last one got a big laugh: "Now I just throw myself in to the bath!"

One man said he had read an article about how there used to be more Cubans in the big leagues than any other Latino group—which is true.

"I think that if relations were normal with the United States," he said, "there would be more Cubans than Dominicans, Puerto Ricans, anyone, because Cubans are ballplayers from birth. Cubans are playing ball in their mother's bellies."

I shook my head in agreement. It was good to see this level of pride still existed, and that baseball was still the national pastime of Cuba even if nobody could play there as a paid professional. Then, when somebody asked if it was true that my father had been a great pitcher too, I passed around the same photo I had shown Juan Carlos Oliva. It was like I was bringing Lefty Tiant back to life after all these years.

After leaving *Esquina Caliente* we drove around some more. The gas station where my father worked after his playing days was still there. So was the Route 28 Field where he watched me pitch on Sundays while hiding behind the columns of the bus station across the street, thinking I didn't see him. The ballfield had been turned into a park, and there was a swing set where the mound used to be, but the bus station looked the same. The mound faced directly toward it, which is how I used to catch him sneaking peeks at me.

"Coming back and seeing all those things I used to do as a kid," I said, looking at the field, "to me, I feel like I am born again now."

While I was visiting with my family, some of my old teammates came by who heard I was there. We joked around about the old days, and the memories came rushing back. When I was at the airport, ready to go home, I thought about everything I had been through—and how I had finally gone full circle in my life.

This, Cuba, is my country. I don't know nothing about politics, and I don't care about politics. I was away too long from my family and my country—forty-six years—and that's crazy. I felt better; my heart was better; my *head* was better. I guess I could close my book now if I wanted. If I died, I would die happy. Now I was a free man. I felt free inside me; I felt good inside me.

"That was a feeling nobody could take away from me now."

Returning to my homeland once fulfilled a longtime dream. Going back *a second time* was an honor.

As part of ongoing diplomatic efforts to strengthen relations between the United States and Cuba, President Obama announced he was leading a delegation to the island in March 2016. In the group would be representatives from Major League Baseball, including the entire Tampa Bay Rays club, set to play an exhibition game against the Cuban National Team in Havana. Baseball had linked the two countries for more than 150 years, and I was invited to accompany them as a representative of the "old" Cuba—a ballplayer who had left the island in the early days of the Castro regime, made his way in the U.S. against the odds, and never forgotten where I came from. They also asked me to throw out one of the ceremonial first pitches before the game alongside Cuban National Team pitching great Pedro Luis Lazo, whose father I had played against in the Cuban League.

I did not say yes right away, because I knew that there were still Cuban-Americans who felt my going back even the first time had dishonored those living under Castro. The conditions were still bad now; the United States trade embargo with Cuba remained in place and very few people were ever able to leave the island. But in speaking with my family, and friends, I felt that this trip held the promise of better things for *all* Cubans. By going as a representative of both my country of origin, and my adopted land, I could hopefully play a small role in helping us reach that better place.

It had been nine years since my last time home, and three of the four aunts I visited when we were making *The Lost Son of Havana* documentary had died. I was not able to see the fourth aunt on this trip because we came in and out of the country so fast—the only things we did were go from the airport to the hotel, from the hotel to the ballpark for the game, and then back to the hotel. You could sense things had gotten a little better, though, because our delegation was allowed to invite Cuban family members to the hotel for dinner. I was able to have six cousins come, which was very nice. In 2007, none of them could visit me at my hotel.

The game was held at Estadio Latinoamericano, the same ballpark where I had pitched in the Cuban League in 1959 and '60. Once we got there, we lined up to meet the dignitaries. President Obama and the First Lady were very nice; the president asked, "What's happening?" and the First Lady said she was very pleased to meet me. This was actually my second time meeting an American president, as I had golfed and talked baseball with George H. W. Bush in the past.

Then, suddenly, I found myself standing in front of Raúl Castro, Fidel's younger brother. Fidel was nearing ninety years old, and no longer appeared much in public, so he had made Raúl the acting president.

Raúl stuck out his hand. Although I felt uncomfortable, I shook it. Tony Perez said later that he never would have shaken it, but I didn't see what else I *could* do. This was an official diplomatic event, with millions of people watching there and at home. I wanted things to be better between our two countries, and showing that level of disrespect, even if it was deserved, did not seem to me a way to make things better. I went with my gut, and did what I felt was right. That's how I have lived my whole life, and it's carried me to this point in good shape. If it offended anybody, I am sorry.

Less than a year later, in late November 2016, Luis Jr. texted me the news that Fidel Castro was dead. Even though we knew it was going to come at some point, it hit me hard.

A lot of emotions went through me. There was, of course, anger. Castro could die a million times, and he would never be able to pay for what he did—or what he *was*. Not just for me, but for all the Cubans over there and here in the United States. I never wish anybody to *die*. I think that's wrong, no matter how bad they are or how much you hate them. But that's what we expected; most of the Cubans expected him to die a long time before he did.

It had been hard, hard for all of us, during those first years under Castro. We don't know how many people died on rickety boats trying to cross the

Gulf of Mexico and escape—maybe one hundred thousand, maybe a million. We just don't know. Think of all the children, and all the separated families. I knew friends who lost loved ones that way, and their pain is what came back to me when I heard the news.

Then, once I had a little time to take it in, what I *really* thought about was what was to come next. How were things going to be for Cubans after Castro? It was unclear then, and it is still not clear now. Americans can visit Cuba freely, and I have talked with my family of bringing them there. None of them have seen my homeland, not even Maria. Maybe I could finally give her that honeymoon on the southern coast on Island de Pinos—the one she should have had in 1961.

It is true that Cuba is where my family and millions of others endured much hardship and pain, and where many still live in poverty. But it is also where I experienced great love. Where I saw my father treated as a hero, and where he and my mother worked long and hard to provide for our family. Where I laughed and broke bread with grandparents, uncles and aunts, and cousins who all helped each other in challenging times. We were poor, but we were happy.

It is where I formed the friendships that gave me strength and confidence, and brothers for life, even when time and distance separated us. And it is where I learned to play the game that gave me my livelihood, and led me to all the joy in my life—thanks to my parents and the sacrifice they made for me. I would like my family to meet their Cuban cousins, walk the streets I walked, and see the ballparks where I played and dreamed.

But whether or not they get there, they know where my *true* home lies. It is at the houses in Maine and in Florida where we gather together. It is at Fenway Park, and Fenway South, where I swap cigars and stories with old teammates and work to help today's Red Sox players forge their own dreams. It is in my heart, the heart of a man who has seen much and with God's help has reached a point of peace and contentment.

Home is not really a place. It is a feeling. A feeling you've lived a good life and done your best for yourself and those you love. That is what I've always done, on the field and off. It's been a good ride, and I'm still in there pitching.

ACKNOWLEDGMENTS

TWO OTHER PROJECTS served as initial inspiration for this one. The first was the book *El Tiante*, which Luis wrote with *Boston Herald* sportswriter Joe Fitzgerald in 1976. That volume, put out shortly after the 1975 World Series, provided wonderful insights into Luis's early life and seemed poised for a sequel that could bring readers up to date and go into more depth about various topics and individuals—teammates, family members, and more. Mr. Fitzgerald's obvious affection for Luis and the depth which with he covered his career before and after *El Tiante*'s publication provided us with excellent background for this book, and we are forever grateful.

Second on the inspiration list was *Lost Son of Havana*, the 2007 award-winning documentary film that Luis worked on with Jonathan Hock, Kris Meyer, and Peter and Bobby Farrelly. If you have not seen it, we could not recommend it more highly. The film serves as a lens into life in Cuba during the Castro regime and makes it clear that even in the twenty-first century many of the same hardships remain. The team behind the film was very generous in giving us permission to use any and all dialogue and insight from the production in the preparation of this manuscript, and the book was much the better for it.

Thank you, Keith Wallman and all the folks at Diversion Books, who have been tremendous to work with and very flexible when it became clear that the story would require more words than we originally thought. Keith understood that this was far more than a sports story and deserved the space to be told properly. Thanks also to Jake Elwell for initially championing the project.

The Red Sox were also very cooperative throughout, connecting us with several generations of players who touched on their experiences as teammates or students of Luis and also granting us access to some wonderful photos. Thank you to Sarah Coffin, Gordon Edes, Pam Kenn, Larry Lucchino, Abby Murphy, Brenna Peterson, Kathryn Quirk, Sheri Rosenberg, Fay Scheer, Dr. Charles Steinberg, and Billie Weiss.

Those players from the Sox and other teams, past and present, who granted us interviews include: Mike Andrews, Andrew Benintendi, Wade Boggs, Tom Burgmeier, Bernie Carbo, Lenny DiNardo, Carlton Fisk, Bill Lee, John Kennedy, Jim Lonborg, Fred Lynn, Mike Lowell, Pedro Martinez, Tippy Martinez, Scott McGregor, Jim Palmer, Rico Petrocelli, Jim Rice, Eduardo Rodriguez, Stan Williams, and Carl Yastrzemski. The wonderful reflections of minor league teammate Barry Levinson, whose interview Hock Films made available to us in its entirety, offered rare insight into the trials faced by Latino ballplayers in the Deep South during the early 1960s. Tony Blankenship and Bradley Hesser shared great tales of playing college ball for Luis. A special thank-you to Carl Yastrzemski for writing the Foreword and to Carlton Fisk for providing so much great detail into the marriage of pitcher and catcher—and why this union worked so well for he and Luis—for the "Pudge and Me" chapter.

Fans, friends, and media members provided additional sides of Luis's life. Thank you to those who shared their tales: Jeff Anderson, Steve Buckley, Prof. Albert DeCiccio, Alice and Dick Drew, Mike Dunn, Louis Galgano, Esq., Dr. Peter Hantzis, Dick Johnson, George Katis, Nancy Morrisoe, Bob Parajon, Dan Shaughnessy, and Kevin Vahey. The National Baseball Hall of Fame was helpful with article and photo files on both the left- and right-handed pitchers named Tiant. As was the wonderful writing of sportswriters from every era of Luis's career—especially Gordon Cobbledick and Russell Schneider in Cleveland, Sid Hartman and Mike Lamey in Minnesota, and Larry Claflin, Ray Fitzgerald, Peter Gammons, Tim Horgan, Clif Keane, Bill Liston, Leigh Montville, Bob Ryan, and Larry Whiteside in Boston.

Danny Tiant and Luis Tiant IV shared unforgettable memories of traveling, coaching with, and smoking cigars with their dad, and Johnny Papile shared the amazing story of how he came into the Tiant family—and how Maria and Luis helped him meet the girl next door. Isabel and Maria Tiant and Dora Papile were sources of support and comfort throughout, as were Michelle Alpert, Jason and Rachel Alpert-Wisnia, and the entire extended Tiant and Wisnia families. Jason Alpert-Wisnia also contributed photos and photo editing help to the project.

Finally, thank you to the 2018 Red Sox, who made for a wonderful diversion when we needed a break from interviews and writing. Their brilliance was an inspiration for us to reach as high as possible.

Luis Tiant and Saul Wisnia
March 2019

NOTES

CHAPTER 1: SHUTTING UP PETE ROSE

Red Sox underdogs in World Series, various sources including:
* Murray Chass, "Red Sox Appear Comfortable in Underdog Role for Series," New York Times, Oct. 10, 1975.
Reds as favorites (official odds):
* "Reds 3-2 favorites," Associated Press report from Harrah's Tahoe Racebook, many papers including San Bernardino County Sun, Oct. 9, 1975.
Pete Rose excited to face Tiant and Red Sox, many sources including:
* Hal Bock, "It'll be Gullet vs. Tiant," Associated Press, San Bernardino County Sun, Oct. 10, 1975.
Rose on Tiant's "spinning curve that never comes down":
* Peter Gammons, "El Tiante elegente, Red Machine pffft...6-0," Boston Globe, Oct. 12, 1975.
Details of Rose at-bat and atmosphere before game from NBC broadcast of Game One of 1975 World Series, YouTube.

CHAPTER 2: SEÑOR SKINNY

General sources for Luis E. Tiant's life and baseball career:
* Luis E. Tiant file, National Baseball Hall of Fame.
* Rory Costello, "Luis E. Tiant," Society of American Baseball Research (SABR) Bioproject, sabr.org/bioproject.
* Callum Hughson, "Luis Tiant Sr. Bio," Mop-Up Duty website, mopupduty.com.
* Cesar Brioso, "On this date: Luis Tiant—and not the one you're thinking of, was born," cubanbeisbol.com.
* Kyle McNary, "Luis Tiant Sr., Negro Leaguer of the Month," Pitch Black Baseball website, pitchblackbaseball.com.
* Baseball-Reference.com (statistics).
New York Cubans information culled from various sources including:
* Negro League Baseball Players Association (NPPBA) website, nlbpa.com.
* Baseball-Reference.com.
* Negro League Baseball Museum "eMuseum" website.
* Negro League Baseball.com.
Luis E. Tiant striking out Babe Ruth and/or keeping him from homering, anecdote from many sources including:
* Steve Jacobson and Newsday, "Tiant wishes famous father had seen him in Yankee suit," Washington Post, Feb. 25, 1979.
"Tiant's only flaw...":
* Peter J. Bjarkman, Diamonds around the Globe—The Encyclopedia of International Baseball, Greenwood Press, 2005, 10.
Luis E. Tiant beating Yankees and Cardinals in exhibition games and getting batter to swing at a phantom pitch:
* Roberto Gonzalez Echevarria, The Pride of Havana: A History of Cuban Baseball, Oxford University Press, NY, 1999, 261.
Cool Papa Bell being "so fast he could flip the light switch..." attributed to Satchel Paige and told often, including in Bell's Hall of Fame bio: https://baseballhall.org/hall-of-famers/bell-cool-papa.
Frank Forbes on Luis E. Tiant being so skinny he "looked like he had consumption," biographical essay from Luis E. Tiant files, National Baseball Hall of Fame.
Ted Page hit-by-pitch story:
* Rory Costello, Luis E. Tiant's Society of American Baseball Research (SABR) biography article; originally by Brent Kelly, Voices from the Negro Leagues, Jefferson City, North Carolina: McFarland & Co., 1998.
Details on Martin Dihigo's career, including 1935 East-West All-Star game, from Dihigo's SABR bio, by Peter C. Bjarkman.
Wilmer Fields quotes and reflections on Luis E. facing Buck Leonard:
* John Holway, "Will the Real Luis Tiant Please Stand Up," Baseball Digest, Feb. 1976, 74–77.
John Holway records from white-black games, ibid.
Ted Page story about beaning by Luis E. Tiant, ibid.
Armando Vazquez quotes from Lost Son of Havana documentary film, director-screenwriter Jonathan Hock, producer Kris Meyer, executive producers Bobby Farrelly and Peter Farrelly; Hock Films, 5-Hole Productions, 2009.
Monte Irvin quote on Luis E.:
* Luis Tiant and Joe Fitzgerald, El Tiante, New York, New York; Doubleday, 1976.
New York Cubans 1947 roster and statistics, Baseball-Reference.com.
Description of Cuban baseball in the 1930s and 40s:
* Steve Fainaru and Ray Sanchez, Duke of Havana: Baseball, Cuba, and the Search for the American Dream, New York, 2001, 17–18. (Some details, including Max Lanier getting money from gamblers, first appeared in The Pride of Havana.)
Cuban/Negro League baseball coverage in New York Times:
* Roscoe McGowen, "Brooklyn Takes Havana Game," March 14, 1941.
* "Negro All-Star Game Listed for Tonight," July 29, 1947.
* Louis Effrat, "Negro Star Game to American Loop," July 30, 1947.

- "Negro Series to Start," Sept. 19, 1947.
- "Buckeyes top Cubans in Negro Game, 10-7," Sept. 22, 1947.

CHAPTER 3: CUBA DREAMS

General insights on Cuban Baseball in 1940s and 50s from:
- Peter C. Bjarkman, "Diamonds around the Globe—The Encyclopedia of International Baseball," Greenwood Press, Westport, Conn., 2005.
- Adrian Burgos Jr., editor in chief, "La Vida Baseball" section of National Baseball Hall of Fame website, lavaidabaseball.com.
- Stephen R. Kenney, "Blurring the Color Line: How Cuban Baseball Players Led to the Racial Integration of Major League Baseball," *National Pastime—2016*, Society of American Baseball Research (SABR).

Fight between Luis E. and Isabel Tiant about Luis C. trying out for Havana, and resulting tryout:
- Luis C. Tiant and Joe Fitzgerald, *El Tiante: The Luis Tiant Story*, Doubleday, NY, 1976, 11–13.

Tiant in 1960 Pan-American games, United Press International (UPI) coverage in *Corpus Christi Caller-Times*:
- Tiant beats Tulsa from article "Mexico Tigers Defeat Oilers," May 12, 1960.
- Dick Hughes beats Tiant for championship from article "Tulsa Gets Title in Pan American," Sept. 24, 1960.

CHAPTER 4: YOU CAN'T GO HOME AGAIN

Details on Bobby Avila's career from his SABR bio, by John Stahl.
Senators Scout Joe Cambria quote from *Sporting News*, March 23, 1960, 14.
Three Cubans make 1959 AL All-Star team, Baseball-Reference.com.
Fidel Castro's ties to baseball, including myths on skills as pitcher:
- Peter C. Bjarkman, "Fidel Castro and Baseball," Society of American Baseball Research.

Insights on Cuban League history:
- Roberto Gonzalez Echevarria, The Pride of Havana: A History of Cuban Baseball, Oxford University Press, NY, 1999.

Castro says government will support Sugar Kings franchise:
- Jimmy Burns, "Maduro Ready to Sell; Castro Offers New Aid," *Sporting News*, July 29, 1959, 32.

Castro pitches in exhibition game:
- International League notes, *Sporting News*, Aug. 5, 1959, 32.

Sources for Gran Stadium incident and aftermath:
- George Beahon, "Nightmare in Havana—Wings in Real Danger," *Rochester Democrat & Chronicle*, July 27, 1959. (Reprinted in edition of March 22, 2016).
- Peter C. Bjarkman, *Diamonds Around the Globe*, Greenwood Press, 2005, 13–15.
- Jimmy Burns, "Int Will Play Out Havana Sked, Despite Shooting, Shag Suggests," *Sporting News*, Aug. 3, 1959, 9.
- "Last U.S. Baseball Team to Play in Havana before Embargo Had Bullets Rain Down on Them," Fox News. com, Dec. 26. 2014.
- Bill Madden, "Orioles' Cuba Trip Opens Old Wounds Havana Shooting Scarred Player," *New York Daily News*, March 28, 1999.
- Tyler Maun, "The Minor Leagues' Last Nights in Havana," MILB.com, March 16, 2017.
- Evan Nagel, *Beyond the Sports Page: Baseball, The Cuban Revolution, and Rochester, New York Newspapers, 1954-1960,*" doctoral thesis by Evan Nagel, the University of Western Ontario, 2014.
- Travis Waldron, "Havana's Forgotten Baseball Team Played Key Role in Cuba-U.S. Relations," *Huffington Post*, March 19, 2016.

Tiant beats Mexican City Reds in both games of doubleheader:
- Roberto Hernandez, Mexican League notes column, *Sporting News*, July 5, 1961, 35.

Details on Julio Moreno from his SABR bio, by Rory Costello.
Overview of Bay of Pigs Invasion, The Learning Network, *New York Times*.
Pan-American All-Star Game, game coverage by John Trowbridge, *Sporting News*, Aug. 9, 1961, 39.
Dodgers and Cubs show interest in Tiant, *Sporting News*, Aug. 9, 1961, 41.
Overview/timeline of U.S.-Cuba relations, Suddath, Claire, Time.com, April 15, 2009.
Mexico City Tigers 1959-1961 statistics, Baseball-Reference.com.

CHAPTER 5: FROM THE BUSHES TO THE BRONX

Tiant in Puerto Rican League 1961-62, all coverage by Miguel Frau in *Sporting News*:
- "Puerto Rican League Roundup," (sets league strikeout record), Jan. 17, 1962, 29.
- "Belters Beltran and Christopher Bomb Twirlers," (duels Juan Pizzaro), Feb. 7, 1962, 35.
- "Santurce Club Gets Jump in Inter-American Series," (gets playoff win), Feb. 14, 1962, 31.
- "Crabbers Cop Latin Title Fourth Time in 14 Years," (faces Bob Gibson in championship), Feb. 21, 1962, 37.

First minor league win:
- "Charleston Hands York 7-1 Setback," *Springfield Union*, April 27, 1962, 45.

Reflections from Luis about when Luis Jr. was born and first Christmas away from Cuba:
- Luis Tiant and Joe Fitzgerald, *El Tiante*, 33.

Eight straight wins in Puerto Rico:
"Tiant's Arm, Beequer's Bat set Hot Pace in Veracruz," *Sporting News*, Dec. 29, 1962.
Reflections of Burlington teammate Barry Levinson from interviews for *Lost Son of Havana* documentary. (not in final film, included with permission of director)

Tiant reflects on racism in minor leagues, 1962-63:
- Pat James, "Unlike Knights protégé, Red Sox legend faced harsh racism. Then he had a revelation," *Charlotte Observer*, April 19, 2017.

Minor league season at Burlington, including no-hitter, covered in *Sporting News*, April-September 1963.

Occidental League season coverage, 1963-64 by Olaf Dixon in *Sporting News*, including:
- "Lara Pegs Flag Bid on Six Tribe Farm Phenoms," Nov. 2, 1963, 24.
- "Hill Lulus for Lara by Tiant and Bailey," Nov. 16, 1963, 24.
- "Tiant and Torres Pushing Redbirds Off to Fast Start," Nov. 23, 1963, 30.
- "Sanders' One-Hit Gem Helps Lara Nab Playoff Lead—Tiant Runs Record to 7-0," Dec. 21, 1963.

Nine straight wins over winter:
- Eduardo Moncada, "Tiant Toys With Batters—Five Runs in 79 Frames," *Sporting News*, Jan. 11, 1964, 19.

Tiant left unprotected in 1963 MLB Draft:
- Hal Lebovitz's Indians notes, *Sporting News*, Jan. 11, 1964, 7.
- Regis McAuley, "Tiant, Overlooked in 1963 Draft, Now Toast of Teepee," *Sporting News*, Aug. 1, 1964, 9.

General insights on Indians in 1950s and 60s:
- David Bohmer, "Cleveland Indians Team Ownership History," SABR Team Ownership Project.

Sam McDowell's opinions on Tiant being a "can't miss" pitcher:
- Gordon Cobbledick, "Plain Dealing," Cleveland *Plain Dealer*, June 20, 1964.

Selected articles on Tiant's 1964 season with Portland in Pacific Coast League:
- L. H. Gregory, "Tiant Thundering Toward Cleveland on Lightening Pitch," *Sporting News*, June 20, 1964, 33.
- Don Fair, "Luis Tiant—A Surprise Even to Beaver Manager," Oregonian, July 17, 1964, 5.
- "Tiant Wins PCL Player of Month Award by Topps," (and sets record for best winning percentage in league history), *Sporting News*, Aug. 1, 1964, 28.

Selected articles on Tiant's MLB debut, by Russell Schneider, Cleveland *Plain Dealer*:
- "Tiant to Join Tribe, Hurl Against Yanks," July 18, 1964.
- "Tiant's First Assignment—Beat the Yankees Today," (includes Yogi Berra-Birdie Tebbetts conversation about Tiant starting), July 19, 1964.
- "Tiant Blanks Yanks on 4 Hits, 3-0," July 20, 1964.

Additional coverage of debut:
- Leonard Koppett, "Bombers Win, 6-2, Before 3-0 Loss," *New York Times*, July 20, 1964.

Cleveland minor league statistics and rosters for Charleston, Burlington, and Portland from Baseball-Reference.com.

Cleveland Indians-New York Yankees box scores, July 1964, Baseball-Reference.com.

CHAPTER 6: COMING OF AGE IN CLEVELAND

General insights on Indians in 1950s and 60s:
- David Bohmer, "Cleveland Indians Team Ownership History," SABR Team Ownership Project.

Cleveland Browns attendance figures vs. Indians, Football-Reference.com box scores and Cleveland *Plain Dealer* game stories.

Indians owners consider moving team:
- Regis McAuley, "Mayor of Cleveland Leads All-Out Fight To Keep Franchise," *Sporting News*, Sept. 26, 1964, 10.

Referred to as "Lightening Luis Tiant, the Indians pitching papoose," Johnny Pesky on Tiant:
- Hal Liebowitz, "Sox Give Tiant 'Little Bull' Tag," Cleveland *Plain Dealer*, July 25, 1964.

Tiant's car troubles:
- Russell Schneider, "Batting Around" Indians notebook, Cleveland *Plain Dealer*, Aug. 19, 1964.
- Hal Lebowitz, "Luis Bought Car, See? Then Repair Bills Boomed, Si!," *Sporting News*, April 9, 1966, 44.

Birdie Tebbetts as player and Indians manager, from various Cleveland *Plain Dealer* articles and Tebbetts's SABR bio, by Tom Simon.

Al Smith as Indians player and coach, from various Cleveland *Plain Dealer* articles and his SABR bio, by Gary Livicari.

Tiant first to twenty wins in organized baseball:
- "Major Flashes," *Sporting News*, Aug. 22, 1964, 27.

Roger Birtwell, "Indians Tiant, McDowell Baffle Red Sox, 5-0, 3-0," *Boston Globe*, Oct. 1, 1964

Tiant at thirty-five wins, including winter ball:
- American League notebook, Sporting News, Oct. 3, 1964. (He won one more, to finish 36-6.)

Tiant, Indians stop Yankees from 100 wins:
- "Indians Topple Yanks, 2-1," Plain Dealer Special, Oct. 5, 1964.

Indians set MLB record for strikeouts by pitching staff:
- *Sporting News*, Oct. 17, 1964, 12.

Tiant, Bob Chance of Indians make all All-Rookie Team:
- Cleveland *Plain Dealer*, Oct. 27, 1964.

Indians pitchers in Puerto Rico League, all by Miguel Frau, *Sporting News*:
- "Lions Corral Tiant To Head Hill Staff; Swift to Pilot Tribe," Oct. 10, 1964, 46.
- "Tiant, Siebert, McBean, Stamp Lipon's Lions as 'Club to Beat,'" Oct. 31, 1964, 27.
- "Latin Leaguers Tip Off Injuns On '65 Outlook," Jan. 23, 1965, 5.

Tommy John out, Rocky Colavito in:
- "Happy Rocky's Return Raises Cleveland Hopes," Sporting News, Feb. 4, 1965, 11.

Indians could be "surprise team of 1965":
- Joseph Sheehan, MLB Preview, New York Times, Feb. 21, 1965.

Hurt in spring training:
* Russell Schneider, "Terry Earning Tip-Top Rating as Injun Hurler," *Sporting News*, April 10, 1965, 19.
Tiant win at Boston gets Cleveland to first:
* "Indians Win 9-2, And Tie For First," United Press International, *New York Times*, June 29, 1965.
Tiant earns spot in starting rotation:
* Russell Schneider, "Doubts Gone—Tiant Earns Major Spurs," *Sporting News*, Sept. 18, 1965, 7.
Tiant success vs. Red Sox compiled from Baseball-Reference.com game logs.
Red Sox racial problems detailed in many sources, most notably in:
* Glenn Stout and Richard Johnson, *Red Sox Century*, Houghton-Mifflin Harcourt, Boston, 2005.
* Howard Bryant, *Shut Out: A Story of Race and Baseball in Boston*, Beacon Press, Boston, 2003.
Tiant loses 2-0 four-hitter at Boston on no-hitter:
* Roger Birtwell, "Morehead Fires No-Hitter—Sox Fire Higgins," Boston Globe, Sept. 17, 1965.
* Larry Claflin, "A Photo Finish to Morehead's No-Hitter," Sporting News, Oct. 2, 1965, 7.
* "Boston's Morehead Pitches No-Hitter," Associated Press, New York Times, Sept. 17, 1965.
Slims down for 1966, starts strong—stories by Russell Schneider for *Sporting News*:
* "Tiant Tantalizes Tribe by Cutting Down Weight," March 12, 1966, 20.
* "I'm Skinny Lucky, Says Winner Luis," May 28, 1966, 3.
"This could be the team to watch in 1966," Baseball Preview, *New York Times*, April 10, 1966.
Cleveland's record start in 1966, fueled by pitching:
* "Indians Tie Mark Beating A's, 4-0," Associated Press, New York Times, April 27, 1966.
* Leonard Koppett, "Indian Hurlers Put Sign on League," New York Times, May 1, 1966.
* Gordon White Jr., "Cleveland Moves Into League Lead," New York Times, May 4, 1966.
Tiant allows mammoth home run to Frank Robinson:
* Russell Schneider, "Birds Sweep 2, Tie Tribe for 1st," Cleveland *Plain Dealer*, May 9, 1966.
* Doug Brown, "F. Robinson Powers First Drive Out of Oriole Park," *Sporting News*, May 21, 1966, 27.
* George Vass, "Frank Robinson—The Game I'll Never Forget," *Baseball Digest*, September 1973.
* Mike Klingaman, "Remembering Frank Robinson's historic, outside-the-park home run, 50 years later," *Baltimore Sun*, May 6, 2016.
Frank Robinson batting "about .150" after his mammoth home run off Tiant, statistics verified in "pitcher vs. hitter" section of Tiant's statistical pages on Baseball-Reference.com, which noted Robinson was 5-for-33 lifetime (.152) off Tiant.
Winter League in Venezuela, 1966-67, by Eduardo Moncada, *The Sporting News*:
* "Looey's Back—Better Beware Of the Sharks!" Nov. 19, 1966, 45.
* "Dietz Grabs Plane For Home in Wake of Missile Barrage," Nov. 26, 1966, 42.
* "Lions Boast Terrific Twosome in T-Men Tartabull and Tiant," Jan. 28, 1967, 39.
* "Tiant, Casanova Cook a Feast for Champion Lions," Feb. 25, 1967, 33.
Appeals to Adcock:
* "Tiant Makes Starting Pitch," Cleveland *Plain Dealer*, March 8, 1967.
Adcock says Luis is throwing "lollipops":
* "Rocky Hits Homer; Indians Wins, 14-5," Cleveland *Plain Dealer*, March 22, 1967.
Gary Bell sent to Red Sox:
* Russell Schneider, "Tribe Obtains Horton, Demeter for Bell," Cleveland *Plain Dealer*, June 5, 1967.
Russell Schneider, "Tribe Drops Chisox 2 Behind," Cleveland *Plain Dealer*, Sept. 23, 1967.
Final week of 1967 season at Fenway Park:
* "We couldn't hit him…" Rico Petrocelli interview, October 2016.
* Rico Petrocelli and Chaz Scoggins, "Tales From the 1967 Red Sox Dugout," Sports Publishing, 2017.
* Russell Schneider, "Indians Drop Red Sox 1 Behind," Cleveland *Plain Dealer*, Sept. 27, 1967.
* Clif Keane, "Have to Eat, Too, Says Tribe's Tiant," *Boston Globe*, Sept. 27, 1967.
* Joseph Durso, "Homers by Hinton and Salmon Help Tiant Turn Back Boston," *New York Times*, Sept. 28, 1967.
* Carl Yastrzemski with Gerald Eskenazi, *Yaz: Fenway, The Wall, and Me*, Doubleday, 1990, 172.
Major League Baseball box scores, statistics, and standings, 1964-67, Baseball-Reference.com.

CHAPTER 7: POOR MAN'S MCLAIN

Change in Managers, by Hal Lebovitz, Cleveland *Plain Dealer*:
* "Adcock Out; See Al Dark In," Oct. 2, 1967.
* "Can Dark Make Tribe See Light?" Oct. 3, 1967. (Gonzalez says Marichal told him Dark is not racist.)
Dark "unlikely" to trade Tiant:
* Russell Schneider, "Dark Seeing Bright Spots in Wigwam," *Sporting News*, Nov. 25, 1967, 43; repeated in Dec. 2, 1967 issue, 36.
Dark "worried about my weight…":
* Russell Schneider, Indians notebook, Sporting News, Dec. 9, 1967, 40.
"I was determined to prove myself, and I did…" Final Venezuela League stats in *Sporting News*, Feb. 10, 1968, 39.
"Man, we're all just floating…"
* Russell Schneider, "Indians Are 'Floating' After First Drill," Cleveland *Plain Dealer*, Feb. 27, 1968.
"Look at the way that guy is working…":
* Russell Schneider, "Batting Around," Cleveland *Plain Dealer*, March 22, 1968.
Leon Wagner "came out flat":
* Russell Schneider, "Daddy Wags Promises 40 HRs 'If They Let Me Play,'" Sporting News, March 16, 1968, 26.

Photographer "gets cute" (batting donuts photo):
- "Luis to Zero In on O's," Cleveland *Plain Dealer*, May 13, 1968. (picture ran in many papers including *Sporting News*, May 25, 1968, 21.)

Tiant on "being a good teammate":
- Chuck Heaton, "Chico Preserved One Shutout—Luis," Cleveland *Plain Dealer*, May 18, 1968. (After shutout string ends at four.)

"We always had a hard time turning double plays..." Indians are ranked last in double plays in American League through May 19, stats from *Sporting News*, June 1, 1968, 27.

Focus on 1968 as "Year of the Pitcher" in MLB:
- Edgar Munzel, "Baseball Keeping Wary Eye on Hitters' Poverty March," *Sporting News*, June 8, 1968, 4.
- Si Burek, "Hat Blames Swat Dip on Little Loop," *Dayton Daily News*, reprinted in *Sporting News*, June 8, 1968, 4. (Harry Walker blames Little League.)
- Henry Aaron on giving batters four strikes, *Sporting News*, June 8, 1968, 31.
- Matt Monagan, "Let's travel back 50 years to the 'Year of the Pitcher,'" April 12, 2018, on *CUT 4*, MLB.com.
- Rex Lardner, "The Pitchers Are Ruining The Game," *New York Times Magazine*, June 16, 1968.

"For me, that edge was never bigger..." Details of nineteen-strikeout game:
- Russell Schneider, "Tiant Fans 19, Captures 13th," Cleveland *Plain Dealer*, July 4, 1968.
- Russell Schneider, "'My Finest Game,' says Tiant After 19-Whiff Effort," Sporting News, July 20, 1968, 11.

Tiant at 1968 All-Star Game:
- Hal Lebovitz, "Tiant Faces Drysdale Today," Cleveland *Plain Dealer*, July 9, 1968.
- "N.L. Stars Win Again," Cleveland *Plain Dealer*, July 10, 1968.

"Wait 'Til Next Time—Tiant" by Hal Lebovitz, Cleveland *Plain Dealer*, July 10, 1968.
- Brendan Bingham, "The 1968 All-Star Game," SABR, *National Pastime*, 2014.
- Stats and details on game from: Wells Twombley, "Show Time! All-Star Game in Astrodome," *Sporting News*, July 13, 1968, 7.

Luis Tiant Jr. reflections on Cleveland Stadium, going on road trip in '68, from interview of Sept. 17, 2018.

"Little Luis gave me a big kiss":
- "Looie Gets Last Word," blurb and photo in Cleveland *Plain Dealer*, June 24, 1968.

McDowell quotes about pitchers competing with another, and Hank Peters on "the best-dressed pitchers in the league":
- Terry Pluto, "The Curse of Rocky Colavito."

Quotes on Tiant's windup and delivery:
- "He's the toughest pitcher in the league to follow," (Mickey Mantle): Ray Robinson, "Luis Tiant—You Got to Be Luckee," from "Baseball Stars of 1969," edited by Ray Robinson, Pyramid Books, NY, 1969.
- Frank Howard on "nightmares" facing Tiant, and John Roseboro "I've never seen," from Tim Wendel, "Summer of '68," 90–91.
- Leigh Montville, "Harper Compares Tiant to Marichal," *Boston Globe*, June 30, 1968. (Montville describes how "Tiant uses the pitcher's rubber like a swivel.")
- Rico Petrocelli on Tiant's delivery, from interview of Oct. 4, 2016.
- Sam McDowell SABR bio, by Joseph Wancho.

Further insights on McDowell:
- Pat Jordan, "Sam of 1,000 Ways," *Sports Illustrated*, Aug. 17, 1970.

CHAPTER 8: DOWN AND (ALMOST) OUT

Al Dark/Gabe Paul say no winter ball for Tiant:
- Indians Notebook, Cleveland *Plain Dealer*, Sept. 27, 1968.

Russell Schneider, "Big Winner Tiant Takes Tribe's Tip, Shuns Winter Ball," *Sporting News*, Dec. 14, 1968, 39.
Russell Schneider, "Tiant Named Indians' Man of Year," Cleveland *Plain Dealer*, Oct. 31, 1968.
Raise for Tiant:
- Russell Schneider, "Tiant Gets $52,000," Cleveland *Plain Dealer*, Feb. 24, 1969.

"Luis Tiant could be better...":
- Chuck Heaton, "Dark Raises Goal to Top," Cleveland *Plain Dealer*, Jan. 28, 1969.

Problems with stiff arm in '69 spring training:
- Hal Lebovitz, "Indians Are Stopped at Nine in Row," Cleveland *Plain Dealer*, March 20, 1969.

Juan Marichal offers gift of snake oil:
- Russell Schneider, Indians notebook, Cleveland *Plain Dealer*, April 3, 1969.

Opening Day 1969 in Detroit:
- Russell Schneider, "McLain Stops Tribe on 3 Hits," Cleveland *Plain Dealer*, April 9, 1969. (Also mentions Tiant's problems with umpire Larry Napp.)

Umpire Larry Napp shows Tiant strike zone diagram:
- Russell Schneider notes, Cleveland *Plain Dealer*, April 11, 1969.

Changes in Strike Zone for 1969 detailed in MLB chronology, "The Strike Zone: A historical timeline" on MLB.com.

"We really don't know what is the matter..." Dark on Tiant's slump:
- "Last Year's Aces Are This Year's Patsies," Associated Press, *Winona Daily News*, Winona, Minn., May 8, 1969.

"No champagne" after first win in eight weeks, four days:
- Russell Schneider, "Tiant Tops Tigers, 5-2," Cleveland *Plain Dealer*, Sept. 12, 1969.

"I think Luis will come back..." Dark quoted after season:
- Chuck Heaton, "Plain Talk," Cleveland *Plain Dealer*, Oct. 3, 1969.

Coverage of Tiant's trade to Twins:
* Overview: "Twins Send Chance to Indians in 6-Player Deal," Associated Press, *New York Times*, Dec. 11, 1969.
* Overview: Russell Schneider, "For Tiant and Williams Tribe Gets…Chance, Uhlaender, Nettles and Bob Miller," Cleveland *Plain Dealer (CPD)*, Dec. 12, 1969.
* Chuck Heaton, "Don't be surprised if Alvin Dark is indicted for theft," *CPD*, Dec. 12, 1969, 5-F.
* Reactions of Al Dark, ibid.
* "Deal Okayed by Most Fans," ibid.
* Stan Williams defending Tiant, from "Chance, 3 Others Traded for Tribe's Williams, Tiant," *Minneapolis Star Tribune (MST)*, Dec. 12, 1969, 29.
* More Stan Williams praise, from Sid Hartman sports column, *MST*, Jan. 19, 1970, 30.
* Dean Chance reaction, from "Chance Happy to be Home," United Press International, *St. Cloud (Minnesota) Times*, Dec. 13, 1969, 13.
* Tiant tells Twins writers he's OK, from "Tiant Says He's Lean, Arm is Fit," *MST*, Dec. 14, 1969, 64.
Signs Twins contract:
* "Tiant signs, claims he still has fastball," *MST*, Jan. 21, 1970, 55.
Meets Calvin Griffith, praised for thinness, pledges pennant:
* Sid Hartman column, *MST*, Feb. 23, 1970, 26.
Works with Bill Rigney and pitching coach Marv Grissom altering delivery, watching video:
* Jon Roe, "Tiant Sharp, But Dodgers Tip Twins 9-5," *Minneapolis Star Tribune*, March 14, 1970.
* Sid Hartman column, *Minneapolis Star Tribune*, March 29, 1970.
Chance throwing better than Tiant (in Cleveland camp):
* Russell Schneider, "Batting Around," Cleveland *Plain Dealer*, March 27, 1970.
Grissom says Tiant is "sound physically":
* Dick Cullum column, *Minneapolis Star Tribune*, April 12, 1970.
"Like with Indians, I kept things loose…"
* Mike Lamey, "Only showers dampen Tiant's humor," *Minneapolis Star*, May 19, 1970.
Tiant after 11-2 win, three hits, over Brewers:
* "Terrorizing teams with his bat as much as with his pitching," Boston Herald Wire Services, *Boston Herald*, May 29, 1970.
Some details of shoulder injury and treatment, including insights of Dr. Phelan:
* Luis Tiant and Joe Fitzgerald, *El Tiante*, 1976.
Dave Boswell SABR bio, by Gregory H. Wolf.

CHAPTER 9: TWIN KILLINGS AND RED SOX

John Dewan, "Tommy John Surgery in Major League Baseball," ACTA Sports, published on SABR.org, Sept. 14, 2018.
"Bert Blyleven took my spot…":
* Tom Briere, "Blyleven Replaces Injured Tiant," *Minneapolis Star Tribune*, June 2, 1970.
* "Twins Recall Blyleven to Replace Injured Luis Tiant," Associated Press, *Daily Journal*, June 2, 1970.
* "Beat the Dutch? Blyleven Tames the Hottest Bats," *Sporting News*, June 13, 1970, 39.
"The fracture is entirely healed…":
* "Twins Face McDowell, McLain on Road," *Minneapolis Star*, July 28, 1970.
"Home plate looked very far away…":
* "Happy Tiant was edgy," *Minneapolis Star*, Aug. 4, 1970.
"I was even more optimistic…":
* "Tiant Registers After His Double," *New York Times*, Aug. 9. 1970.
"Big Frank Howard…could tell the difference":
* "Howard's 'dancing' throws Tiant off-key," *Minneapolis Star*, Aug. 13, 1970.
"I celebrated as hard as anyone…":
* "Twins Win West Division Crown," *Minneapolis Star Tribune*, Sept. 23, 1970.
"There is nothing wrong with me…":
Russell Schneider, "Batting Around," Cleveland *Plain Dealer*, Oct. 4, 1970.
Twins cut Tiant salary maximum from $60,000 to $48,000:
* Sid Hartman column, *Minneapolis Star Tribune*, Dec. 4, 1970, Jan. 6, 1971.
Tiant off-season trade rumors in various sources:
* Russell Schneider, "Schneider Around," Cleveland *Plain Dealer*, Jan. 1, 1971.
"We decided to send Tiant a contract." (Griffith):
* "Griffith optimistic about a comeback by Tiant," Associated Press, *Winona (Minn.) Daily News*, Jan. 20, 1971.
"You can't believe Luis Tiant." (Rigney):
* "Tiant of old cheers Rigney," Minneapolis Star, Feb. 18, 1971.
Tiant denied entry at two Florida golf courses:
* *Minneapolis Tribune* Staff Writer, "Orlando Golf Course Refusal Irks Tiant," MST, Feb. 22, 1971.
* "Tiant Involved in Golf Dispute," United Press International, *St. Cloud (Minn.) Times*, Feb. 23, 1971.
"He [Tiant] has thrown better in spring training than at any time last year." (Rigney):
* *Minneapolis Star Tribune*, March 2, 1971.
"Tiant threw harder today than at any time last year." (Griffith):
* Dan Stineking, *Minneapolis Star*, March 24, 1971.
"I was crushed…":
* Jon Roe, "Cards Rip Tiant, Kaat in 13-2 Twins Loss," *Minneapolis Star Tribune*, March 29, 1971.

How Twins "shit on Luis" with release at end of spring training, and how former teammates "work the phones" to find him a new team, from Stan Williams interview of Nov. 6, 2018.
Tiant released by Indians, picked up by Braves:
- "I've never seen the real Tiant" (Rigney): Griffith, "Tiant, Boswell, Cut by Twins," Plain Dealer Special, Cleveland *Plain Dealer*, April 1, 1971.
- "I tried to make a deal for both men," (Griffith), ibid.
- "If a player is released outright his contract is terminated," from Hal Lebovitz, "Ask Hal the Referee," Cleveland *Plain Dealer*, April 4, 1971.
- Rob Fowler, "Griffith Back on Old Spot, Releasing Tiant, Boswell," *Sporting News*, 15.
Braves give Tiant thirty-day trial, all stories by Jerry Lindquist, *Richmond Times Dispatch*:
- "Braves Ponder Tiant's Status," April 12, 1971. ("Nothing wrong with his arm"—Clyde King.)
- "Tiant Set as Richmond Starter," April 13, 1971. (King puts him in rotation.)
- "R-Braves Get Third Win, Rip Hens, 3-1," April 19, 1971. ("Very impressive"—Paul Richard, Braves GM.)
- "Weatherman Does It Again," April 26, 1971. (Another rainout stops Tiant chance to pitch.)
- "Chiefs Check R-Braves, 6-3," April 29, 1971. (Tiant falls to 1-2.)
- "Chiefs Clip R-Braves, 7-1," May 5, 1971. (Tiant shelled, falls to 1-3.)
- "R-Braves Fritter Away Chances, Lose to Tides in 11ᵗʰ by 8-6," May 11, 1971. (Tiant blows 4-0 lead, lets up grand slam to Jon Milner.)
- "Veteran Tiant Given Release by R-Braves," May 16, 1971.
- "Released by Braves Saturday, Luis Tiant signed with Colonels," May 18, 1971.
Red Sox give Tiant shot with Louisville Colonels:
- "Sox Sign Tiant for Louisville," *Boston Globe*, May 18, 1971.
- "Tiant stands out in Colonels debut," *Courier-Journal* (Louisville, KY), May 19. 1971.
- "Tiant fans 13 batters," *Courier-Journal*, May 23, 1971.
- "Catcher's error gives Colonels split with Chiefs," *Courier-Journal*, May 28, 1971.
- "We've had good reports on him [Tiant]" (Kasko): Ray Fitzgerald, *Boston Globe*, May 31, 1971.
- "Tiant hurls Louisville to 10-0 win." *Boston Globe*, June 2, 1971. (Haywood Sullivan in stands, tells Tiant next morning he's getting called up to Boston.)
Maria encourages Luis not to be discouraged, keep eyes open, chin up, Maria Tiant interviews of 2017-2018.

CHAPTER 10: REBIRTH IN BOSTON

Will McDonough, "Sox add Tiant to roster, option Nagy to Louisville," *Boston Globe*, June 4, 1971.
"My arm is fine…":
- George Sullivan, "Can Tiant pitch? Sox to See Tonight," *Boston Herald*, June 11, 1971.
"The initial investment…":
- Clif Keane, "Tiant fails, Royals sink Red Sox, 6-3," *Boston Globe*, June 12, 1971.
Clif Keane, "Yaz fined; White's homer spoils Tiant 3-hitter, 2-1," *Boston Globe*, July 4, 1971.
Ray Fitzgerald, "Walks take toll on Tiant," *Boston Globe*, July 8, 1971.
"I was still angry at Minnesota…":
- Dave O'Hara, "Petrocelli's Game-Winning Sock Helps Soothe Unnerved Bosox," Associated Press, Paducah (KY) Sun, July 16, 1971.
Larry Claflin, "Pitching Collapse Ends Red Sox Flag Search," *Sporting News*, Aug. 28, 1971.
Tiant's first win for Red Sox:
- Jack McCarthy, "Yaz Single in 9ᵗʰ Tops Orioles, 4-3," *Boston Herald*, Sept. 1, 1971.
"Today, my arm is not really hurt…":
- Eduardo Moncada, "Tovar Swinging Torrid Bat in Venezuela," *Sporting News*, Dec. 4, 1971, 55 (Tiant no-hitter at Caracas.)
"Another Pitcher, Luis Tiant, launches what he hopes will be a strong comeback season today…":
- Bill Kipouras, Spring Training notes, *Boston Herald*, March 1, 1972.
"I did my best to prove myself…":
- Bill Liston, "Hose Pitching Pleases Kasko," *Boston Herald*, March 28, 1972. (Gives up Mike Jorgensen grand slam, but Kasko supportive.)
Sonny Siebert SABR bio, by Joseph Wancho.
Bill Liston, "Yanks' Cater to Red Sox for Lyle," *Boston Herald*, March 23, 1972.
Baseball Strike:
- Denee Freeman, "Strike Halts Baseball Today," Associated Press, April 1, 1972.
- Bill Liston, "Sox Players to Decide Own Fate," *Boston Herald*, April 1, 1972.
- "Bosox camp in turmoil; players given ultimatum," Associated Press, *Lowell Sun*, April 1, 1972.
- Jim Sarni, "Sox get workout at Harvard," *Boston Globe*, April 5, 1972.
- Peter Gammons, "There must be a story," ibid.
- Clif Keane, "Clubs may drop spring training if new player problems develop," *Boston Globe*, April 15, 1972.
Goes back to old wind-up, with a twist:
- "If I do good, maybe I'll start my act again…" Peter Gammons, "Sox eye rerun of Tiant Show," *Boston Globe*, April 24, 1972.
- "I'm going to try something different…" Bob Ryan, "Tiant steals show as Sox win, 5-3," *Boston Globe*, June 29, 1972.
- Fred Ciampa, "Red Sox Cage Tigers, 5-3," *Boston Herald*, June 30, 1972.
- "Back To Old Motion, Says Luis," Associated Press, *Rome (GA) News Tribune*, June 29, 1972.

"The name of the game is to win…":
* Clif Keane, "Tiant, Sox beat Twins, rain, 8-2," July 4, 1972.
Jou Giuliotti, "Luis Tiant Finds The Groove," *Boston Herald*, July 4, 1972.
"Siebert was scheduled to start that night…":
* Clif Keane, "Petrocelli goes 'batty,' drives O's crazy, 6-3," *Boston Globe*, Aug. 6, 1972.
Fred Ciampa, "Lucky Blast, Says Rico," *Boston Herald*, Aug. 6, 1972.
Tim Horgan, "Luis Tiant's No. 1 rooter is Tom Yawkey," *Boston Herald*, Aug. 10, 1972.
"Tiant was all kicks and twists…":
* Clif Keane, "Tiant's 3-hitter gives Sox split," *Boston Globe*, Aug. 13, 1972.
Third-base ump Art Frantz talks to Rico:
* Postgame Notes, *Boston Globe*, Aug. 12, 1972.
Two-hit shutout over White Sox:
* "Zip Job Eludes Tiant," United Press International, Aug. 20, 1972.
"I think he's as good as any right-hander in the American League…" (Chuck Tanner):
* Ken Rappoport, "Boston's Luis Tiant, '72 'Mr. Excitement,'" Associated Press, Aug. 30, 1972.
Yaz lifts elbow higher at bat, gets first homer in nearly a (calendar) year:
* "Yaz's New Style Helps Red Sox," *San Francisco Examiner*, Sept. 30, 1972.
"Both were broken up on September 8…" (shutout and scoreless innings streak):
* "Tiant, Sox Roll On," Boston Herald, Sept. 9, 1972.
"They gave me a standing ovation when I came up to bat…":
* Peter Gammons, "Red Sox romp, 9-1, 4-0; lead by full game," *Boston Globe*, Sept. 21, 1972.
"We finally put the Orioles and the Yankees away…":
* Fred Ciampa, "Yaz, Tiant Tandem Poison for Sox Foes," *Boston Herald*, Sept. 30, 1972.
Playoff tickets would go on sale at Fenway…":
* Joe Trimble, "Chipper Bosox Look Hungrily at Tigers," *New York Daily News*, Oct. 1, 1972.
Steve Buckley on getting playoff tickets, interview of Oct. 18, 2018.
"Aparicio stumbled…":
* Harold Kaese, "Sox hoping for one last, big rebound," *Boston Globe*, Oct. 3, 1972.
Tigers beat Tiant, Red Sox on last weekend:
* Clif Keane, "Tigers eliminate Red Sox, 3-1, win AL East title," *Boston Globe*, Oct. 4, 1972.
* Ray Fitzgerald, "Sox learn Kaline Tiger in the clutch," ibid.
* Larry Claflin, "Detroit Crushes Red Sox Hopes 3-1," *Boston Herald*, Oct. 4, 1972.
* Fred Ciampa, "Yaz Weeps Openly as Sox Fall," ibid.
* Dave O'Hara, "Sox Have no Alibis—Kasko," Associated Press, Oct. 4, 1972.
* "Whatever fate awaits Tiant next year…" Larry Claflin, *Boston Herald*, Oct. 6, 1972.

CHAPTER 11: PUDGE AND ME

Fisk and Tiant "briefly played against one another in spring training…":
* "All-Stars Fall to Hose, 5-1," *Boston Herald*, March 7, 1971. (Red Sox beat team of players from several clubs.)
Kasko says Fisk has "a long way to go," *Boston Herald*, March 14, 1971.
Assorted quotes, insights on Tiant from Carlton Fisk interview of Jan. 21, 2017.
"He has a chance to be one of the best…" (Yawkey on Fisk):
* *Boston Herald*, Sept. 28, 1971.
"Luis has only four basic pitches…":
* Tim Horgan interview with Fisk, *Boston Herald*, Sept. 27, 1972.
Kevin Vahey on Tiant, from interview of Oct. 25, 2018.
Assorted details from Fisk's SABR bio, by Brian Stevens.
Assorted details from Fisk interview:
* Herb Crehan, *Red Sox Heroes of Yesteryear*, Rounder Books, Cambridge, MA, 2005.
Fisk's Hall of Fame induction speech on YouTube (link from National Baseball Hall of Fame website, mentions Tiant at 11:50 mark).

CHAPTER 12: HEART AND SOUL

Bernie Carbo on Tiant, from interview of Oct. 27, 2016.
Memories of Tiant clubhouse pranks, nicknames:
* Carl Yastrzemski with Greg Eskenazi, *Yaz: Baseball, The Wall, and Me*, Doubleday, New York, 1990.
Some also from Yastrzemski interview of March 14, 2017.
Nickname memories from John Kennedy, interview of October 2017.
Origins of "Mullion!" as baseball nickname for "ugly person" found in *Dickson Baseball Dictionary*, by Paul Dickson, Harcourt Brace & Co., New York, 1999.
Cepeda is the talk of 1973 camp:
* Clif Keane, "What about Cepeda?" *Boston Globe*, March 3, 1973.
"After Eddie Kasko named me the Opening Day starter…":
* Peter Gammons, "Moret, all sweetness and light, No. 5 starter," *Boston Globe*, March 27, 1973.
Opening Day 1973—Tiant first to face a designated hitter (Ron Blomberg):
* Murray Chass, "Fisk's 2 Homers Set Boston Pace-Blomber's 'dh' Bat Goes to Hall of Fame," *New York Times*, April 7, 1973.
* Larry Burke and Peter Thomas Fornatale, with Jim Baker, "Change Up: An Oral History of 8 Key Events that Shaped Modern Baseball," Rodale, NY, 2008.
* Steve Wulf, "Distinguished History," *Sports Illustrated*, April 5, 1993.

Cepeda hits his first Green Monster homer:
- Deane McGowan, "Roundup: Cepeda, Tiant Up to Their Old Tricks," *New York Times*, April 9, 1973.

Mike Andrews reflections on batting versus Tiant, from interview of April 4, 2017.
On getting 20th win: "I had brought this cigar with me to Detroit…":
- Clif Keane, "Tiant, Harper, Sox reach goals," *Boston Globe*, Sept. 29, 1973.

New manager shocks the team:
- Bill Liston, "Aparicio, Cepeda Released by Red Sox; Johnson Blasted," *Boston Herald*, March 27, 1974.

Another bad Opening Day start:
- Peter Gammons, "Sox rough around edges, but win on Yaz HR, 9-8," *Boston Globe*, April 6, 1974.

Getting boost from hometown fans:
- Clif Keane, "Tiant three-hitter cools Yanks, 2-0," *Boston Globe*, May 10, 1974.

Fifteen-inning start vs. Angels and Nolan Ryan:
- Clif Keane, "Angels shade Sox in 15th after Ryan strikes out 19," *Boston Globe*, June 15, 1974.
- Bill Liston, "Doyle's Hit Foils Tiant, Sox in 15th, 4-3," *Boston Herald*, June 15, 1974.
- Bill Liston, "Didn't Tire, Says Tiant," *Boston Herald*, June 16, 1974.
- "Ryan Whiffs 19—Angel Hurler Sets One LA Mark, Not Second," Associated Press, *Sacramento Bee*, June 16, 1974.
- Matt Snyder, "Happy 40th Anniversary: Nolan Ryan vs. Luis Tiant," CBSSports.com, June 14, 2014.

"The electricity in the ballpark was amazing…":
- Joe Giuliotti, "35,866 Watch Tiant Whitewash A's for 20th, 3-0," *Boston Herald*, Aug. 24, 1974.

"Naturally, I'm happy…":
- "Tiant Slays A's, 3-0," Associated Press, *Springfield (MA) Times*, Aug. 24, 1974.

Darrell Johnson: "Tiant should be the Most Valuable Player in the American League," ibid.
Peter Gammons, "Some say Jackson or Yaz for MVP; here's vote for Tiant," *Boston Globe*, Sept. 1, 1974.
Robbery story:
- Larry Claflin's column, *Boston Herald*, Sept. 5, 1974.

Some details of Maria Tiant and kids coming to Boston, and family going to Milton home for first time:
- Luis Tiant and Joe Fitzgerald, captured first in El Tiante, 1976.

CHAPTER 13: RACE AND REUNION

Overview on Busing Crisis in Boston:
- Peter Balonon-Rosen, "Boston School Desegregation and Busing: A Timeline of Events," Learning Lab, Sept. 5, 2014.
- Bruce Gellerman, "Busting Left Deep Scars on Boston, Its Students," WBUR News, Sept. 5, 2014.
- "It was Like A War Zone: Busing in Boston," ibid.
- Mike Barnicle, "Joe Timilty's campaign pits 'us' against 'them,'" Boston Campaign Watch, *Boston Globe*, Oct. 12, 1975.
- David Rogers, "Thousands in antibusing march, rally," *Boston Globe*, Oct. 28, 1975.
- Walter V. Robinson, "NAACP to ask Garrity to close S. Boston High," *Boston Globe*, Nov. 16, 1975.
- Arthur Jones and Paul Kneeland, "Two leaders rap Meany's busing stand," ibid.

Luis Tiant Jr. memories of Milton, from interview of Sept. 17, 2018.
On changes to coaching staff:
- Bill Liston, "Pesky, Williams New Sox Coaches," *Boston Herald*, Nov. 11, 1974.

"That summer ride, a right-handed hitter…" (homer past flag pole):
- Clif Keane, "Rice (wham!) Yaz homer; Sox roll, 9-3," *Boston Globe*, July 19, 1975.

"The Yankees outbid several other teams and signed…":
- Murray Chass, "Yankees Sign Up Catfish Hunter In Estimated $3.75-Million Deal," *New York Times*, Jan. 1, 1975.

"The average big-league salary in 1975 would be $44,676":
- Kurt Badenhausen "Average Baseball Salary Up 20,700% Since First CBA in 1968," *Forbes*, April 7, 2016.

Reflecting on how great it would have been to have Hunter:
- "Sox give up on Hunter 'as matter of principle,'" Associated Press, *Boston Globe*, Dec. 31, 1974.

"Luis resented the feelings they had about black folks in some parts of Florida…" restaurant story told by Stan Williams, from interview of Nov. 6, 2018.
Joe Fitzgerald, "How much longer?" *Boston Herald*, Nov. 6, 1983.
Text from Sen. Edward Brooke's letter to Fidel Castro taken from reproduction of letter in *El Tiante*, by Luis Tiant and Ray Fitzgerald, 1976.
"He [Castro] was late for the meeting…" Text of interview with Sen. George McGovern regarding trip to Cuba and appeal to Fidel Castro (through Brooke's letter) to allow Luis Sr. and Isabel Tiant come to Boston, appearing in *Lost Son of Havana* documentary film, used with permission of writer-director and producers.
"My dream appeared to finally be coming true…" (Castro will let his parents visit):
- James Ayres, "McGovern says Castro favors thaw through sports exchanges," *Boston Globe*, May 9, 1975.

Beat Yankees in mid-season to move into first place:
- "Pitch good enough with the stuff you have on any given day…" Greg Erion, "June 26: 1975: Tiant checks Yankees; Fisk homers," from book "'75: The Red Sox Team That Saved Baseball," Society of American Baseball Research (SABR), 2015.
- "Fisk hit his first home run of the year…"(to beat Yankees): Larry Whiteside, "Sox take charge in Round One," *Boston Globe*, June 27, 1975.
- Murray Chass, "Yankees Defeated, 6-1, On 7-Hitter by Tiant," *New York Times*, June 27, 1975.
- "I feel as good as ever…" "Tiant motion dazzles," Associated Press, *Morning Record*, Meridan-Wallingford, CT.

Jeff Anderson on Tiant's importance to people of color, from interview of Oct. 17, 2018.
"When Luis came to Boston, he probably didn't realize…" Boston TV reporter Jorge Quiroga on Tiant's importance to the city's Latino community, from interview used in video shown at ceremony for Tiant's Lifetime Achievement Award from *El Mundo* newspaper, 2017.
Opponents' batting average versus Tiant during mid-season slump courtesy of Baseball-Reference.com.
Luis Sr. and Isabel Tiant (Luis's mother) leave Cuba and come to Boston:
- "Tiant's parents en route to Boston from Cuba for reunion," *Boston Globe*, Aug. 19, 1975.
- Joe Pilati, "Tiant's parents due here today," *Boston Globe*, Aug. 22, 1975.
- Anne Kirchheimer, "Tiants finally reunited; dad, at 69, ready to pitch," *Boston Globe*, Aug. 22, 1975.
- Clif Keane, "The King enjoys good health," (Tiant Sr. to doctor), *Boston Globe*, Aug. 23, 1975.
- Mike Lupica, "At Last Tiant Sr. Has a Chance To See if Jr. Can Pitch Like Dad," *Special to the Washington Star*, Aug. 25, 1975.
- Frank Brown, "Father-and-Son Night on the Mound," Associated Press, *New York Post*, Aug. 27, 1975.
- Peter Gammons, "After one warmup, Tiant Sr. on beam," *Boston Globe*, Aug. 27, 1975.
- Deane McGowan, "Tiant's Best Fans See Him Lose," *New York Times*, Aug. 27, 1975.
- Joe Gergen, "Tiant & Son: Baseball Pitchers," *New York Newsday*, September 1975.
- Additional details captured first by Luis Tiant and Joe Fitzgerald, *El Tiante*, 1976.
On watching film of his delivery with Stan Williams:
- Ray Fitzgerald, *Boston Globe*, Sept. 1, 1975.
"I felt great…":
- Larry Whiteside, "Tiant sings in rain: no pain," *Boston Globe*, Sept. 13, 1975.
"I had a no-hitter until the inning…":
- Clif Keane, "Tiant loses no-hitter in 8th[th], but wins, 3-1," *Boston Globe*, Sept. 12, 1975.
Beats Jim Palmer of Baltimore in big game down stretch:
- "Tiant, Red Sox Top Orioles, 2-0," MLB roundup, *New York Times*, Sept. 17, 1975.
- Ray Fitzgerald, "TV missed the jewel," *Boston Globe*, Sept. 17, 1975.
- Larry Claflin, "Tiant Was His Best in Biggest Game," *Boston Herald*, Sept. 18, 1975.
- Peter Gammons, "Tiant Terrific—And Bosox Fans Let Him Know it," *Sporting News*, Oct. 4, 1975, 19.
"Luis pitched better in big games…" Fred Lynn reflections, from interview of Sept. 19, 2016.
"The thing about pitching is that it's a blank canvas." Jim Palmer reflections, from interview of April 5, 2018.
"At the height of the busing crisis…" Dick Johnson reflections, from interview of Dec. 1, 2017.
"Thank you Mr. Yawkey…":
- Peter Gammons, "A super season…and a low-key ending," *Boston Globe*, Sept. 29, 1975.

CHAPTER 14: THE WORLD IS WATCHING

"Tiant's loved ones…" described at postseason games from World Series broadcasts on NBC (viewed on YouTube), October 1975.
Matraca—Mexican musical instrument / noisemaker played by Maria Tiant and others at World Series games, defined on EcuRed.cu.
Lois Landis, "Maria Tiant's 'Noise' Noisy But To Luis It's Beautiful Music," *Cincinnati Enquirer*, Oct. 16, 1975.
"Luis knows how big the game is to all of us…" (Yaz):
Larry Claflin, *Boston Herald*, Oct. 4, 1975.
"That lever came up from that gate." (Dwight Evans):
- Bruce Shalin, "Oddballs," Penguin, 1989, 170.
"A man can't pitch any better than that…" (Darrell Johnson after ALCS Game One):
- Joe Giuliotti, "Fans Really Stirred Me Up—Tiant," *Boston Herald*, Oct. 5, 1975.
"The way he has been these last few starts…" Fisk after ALCS Game One:
- Peter Gammons, "Act I: Tiant struts on Fenway stage," *Boston Globe*, Oct. 5, 1975.
"This is Louie's palace…" (Yaz after ALCS Game One):
- Will McDonough, "For the Fenway faithful, it's 'Long live King Looie,'" *Boston Globe*, Oct. 5, 1975.
"Louis, you were beautiful out there today…" Al Dark after ALCS Game One, ibid.
"Luis Tiant is the Fred Astaire of baseball" (Reggie Jackson):
- Roger Angell, *Five Seasons: A Baseball Companion*, Simon & Schuster, NY, 1977.
"SEVEN WINS IN OCTOBER" on clubhouse bulletin board:
- Joe Giuliotti, "It's Official—Yaz Will Star in Left, Cooper at 1B," *Boston Herald*, Oct. 3, 1975.
"I can play left field in my sleep," Carl Yastrzemski after ALCS Game Two:
- Chaz Scoggins, "LCS Memories," 2004 League Championship Series Official Program.
"Shake and Bake those National Leaguers…" (Bando to Tiant):
- Peter Gammons, "Wise, Yaz lead the way as Sox humble A's, 5-3," *Boston Globe*, Oct. 8, 1975.
"I played for the Sugar Kings' team…" (Tiant on not getting signed by Reds in Cuba):
- Pat Hanlon, "Luis Tiant: Boston's Favorite Player?" *Cincinnati Post*, Oct. 4, 1975.
"By its simplest definition, a balk occurs when…" balk definition on MLB.com.
Reds stolen base proficiency, from Baseball-Reference.com.
"Thanks to him, all or part of this excerpt…" rule 8.05 of 1975 baseball rules (on balks), *New York Times*, Oct. 11, 1975.
"He couldn't play in the National League in 1975…" (Sparky Anderson on Tiant move to first base):
- Joseph Durso, "Series Opens in Boston Today; Reds UP Against Wall and Tiant," *New York Times*, Oct. 11, 1975.
"Now the drama starts…" NBC broadcast dialogue from 1975 World Series Game One, found on YouTube.
Description and dialogue of 1975 World Series action from NBC broadcasts of games, found on YouTube.
"Tiant has zero…" Pete Rose, *Boston Globe*, Oct. 12, 1975.

"We must have hit fifteen line drives…" Pete Rose after Game One, ibid.
"You forget how to do things…" Luis on baserunning:
- Chaz Scoggins, *Game of My Life: Boston Red Sox*, Sports Publishing Inc., IL, 2006, 102.

"One of the things that I admired about Luis…" Bernie Carbo on Luis Tiant Sr. and Jr. relationship, from interview of Oct. 27, 2016.
"On one pitch, he checked the position…":
- Phil Pepe, "These Guys Didn't Win Cars," *New York Daily News*, Oct. 25, 1975.

"Then there was Roger Angell…":
- Roger Angell, *Five Seasons: A Baseball Companion*, by Roger Angell, Simon & Schuster, NY, 1977, 293–295 (paperback edition).

Luis Sr. said it was "his greatest day too…":
- Russell Schneider, "Tiant's terrific," Cleveland *Plain Dealer*, Oct. 12, 1975.

Bob Parajon on young Cuban pride watching Tiant pitch, from interview of Dec. 7, 2017.
"Of course he interfered with me…" Fisk on Armbrister:
- Kevin Paul Dupont, "Trip Down Memory Lane," *Boston Globe*, Oct. 13, 2013.

"Collision? I thought it was collusion…" Darrell Johnson on Fisk-Armbrister, *New York Times*, Oct. 19, 1975.
"In that game at Cincinnati…" Petrocelli on Game Four of World Series, from interview of Oct. 4, 2016.
"Tiant was his own closer…" (Don Zimmer):
- Don Zimmer with Bill Madden, *Zim: A Baseball Life*, Contemporary Books/McGraw-Hill, NY, 2001.

"Luis absolutely loved his defense…" Fred Lynn on Game Four of World Series, from interview of Sept. 29, 2016.
"I went out to talk to Luis…" Darrell Johnson after Game Four:
- Joseph Durso, "Red Sox Triumph, 5-4, Tying Series," *New York Times*, Oct. 16, 1975.

"The pitch I hit for the last out is the best one Tiant threw me all night…":
- Joe Morgan, "Bosox Square Series," United Press International, Oct. 16, 1975.

"Guts, Guts, Guts…" Yaz on Tiant after Game Four, ibid.
"Yaz was a pretty good battler himself…" Yastrzemski referenced his shoulder injury during 1975, and impact on his first/second half performance:
Carl Castrzemski, *Yastrzemski: Icons of Major League Baseball*, Rugged Land Books, 2007.
"Before we even left the dugout…" On NBC broadcast of Game Four, at very end of tape, you can see Tony Conigliaro talking to Luis with a microphone in dugout before Luis leaves to go to clubhouse.
"I don't care if it's 3,000," Tiant on how many pitches he made in Game Four:
Peter Gammons, "Tiant ready for 7th game? Of course!" *Boston Globe*, Oct. 16, 1975.
"Johnson should have let me pitch Game Six and Luis Game Seven…" Bill Lee on World Series pitching decisions by manager, from interview of Oct. 31, 2016.
"It was a contest between Middle America…" *Boston Globe* editorial on 1975 World Series, Oct. 23, 1975.

CHAPTER 15: DAMN YANKEES

Babe Ruth Award (first time to player on losing team), Baseball-almanac.com.
Description of Milton parade for Tiants:
- Bob Keeley, "El Miltone proves it loves El Tiante," *Boston Herald*, Nov. 3, 1975.
- Joe Pilati, "Milton touches all bases for *Looo-eee*," *Boston Globe*, Nov. 3, 1975.
- Prayer to "bless our favorite right-hander" from parade, ibid.

"You told me there were no guys on three-year deals…":
- Bill Liston, "Tiant claims he's a holdout," *Boston Herald*, March 19, 1976.

"The next day, I stood across from Mr. Yawkey…" (new contract):
- Bill Liston, "Yawkey placates Tiant," *Boston Herald*, March 20, 1976.

"Darrell Johnson said he was worried I'd be out of shape…":
- Peter Gammons, "Johnson ogles his shapely Sox—particularly El Tiante," *Boston Globe*, March 22, 1976.

"Three of our key guys—Fisk, Burleson, and Lynn…" (seeking new contracts):
- Peter Gammons, "Kapstein says no for Red Sox trio," *Boston Globe*, May 18, 1976.

"On Friday, May 20, we went into New York…":
- Peter Gammons, "TAKE ME OUT TO THE BRAWL GAME—Lee may be able to throw in 6 weeks," *Boston Globe*, May 21, 1976.

Lou Piniella reflections on his play at home, fight with Fisk:
- Lou Piniella Maury Allen, *Sweet Lou*, G. P. Putnam's Sons, NY, 1986.

Carlton Fisk on play at home, fight with Piniella on Red Sox 1976 highlight film from WSBK TV-38 (found on YouTube).
Luis Tiant Jr. memories of playing pool with grandfather, from interview of Sept. 17, 1918.
"On Sept. 22, with Dad in the stands…":
- Joe Giuliotti, "Tiant flirts with no-hitter, wins 20th as Sox split," *Boston Herald*, Sept. 22, 1976.

Luis Tiant Sr. and Isabel Tiant (father and mother) pass away:
- "Luis Tiant, pitcher's father," by Ken O. Botwright, *Boston Globe*, Dec. 12, 1976.
- "Luis E. Tiant," Associated Press, *New York Times*, Dec. 12, 1976.
- "Tiant's mother dies three days after husband," *Boston Globe*, Dec. 13, 1976.
- "Both of Tiant's Parents Die Over a 3-Day Period," Associated Press, *New York Times*, Dec. 14, 1976.
- Tiant funeral coverage (no headline), by Shelly Cohen, Associated Press, Dec. 15, 1976.
- "Tiant's Parents Eulogized as Peace Symbols," Associated Press, *New York Times*, Dec. 15, 1976.
- "Luis Tiant's Reunion Ends," by Joseph Durso, *New York Times*, Dec. 16, 1976.

"The team fulfilled Mr. Yawkey's promise…":
- Will McDonough, "Sox butter up Tiant—to tune of $25,000," *Boston Globe*, Sept. 29, 1976.

"My twelve victories, 4.53 ERA, and three complete games (in thirty-two starts)…":
* Ray Fitzgerald, "5 frustrations hindered Sox," *Boston Globe*, Sept. 25, 1977.

CHAPTER 16: OVER MY DEAD BODY

Luis Jr.'s memories of racial challenges faced in teenage years from interview of Sept. 17, 2018.
"What's done is done…":
* Joe Fitzgerald, "Tiant's New Year's resolution simple: Forget '77," *Boston Herald*, Jan. 17, 1978.
"Luis is going to pitch winning ball this year…" (Zimmer):
* Bill Liston, "Tiant, Cleveland don't tame Tigers," *Boston Herald*, March 14, 1978.
"I expect Tiant will be back in the groove this year." (Fisk):
* Jim Morse, "Fisk has suggestion: 'I'll play first base,'" *Boston Herald*, Jan. 9, 1978.
"I think he can still be a big winner." (Yaz):
* Bill Liston, "Yaz—casts his vote for Evans," *Boston Herald*, Nov. 10, 1977.
"I think Luis (Tiant) and Bill Lee are going to come back and have big years." (Evans):
* Bill Liston, "Evans feels he and Sox will be back in running," *Boston Herald*, Feb. 3, 1978.
"One player Zimmer had talked about getting for a while…":
* Leo Monahan, "Remy gives us edge in close games—Zimmer," *Boston Herald*, Jan. 27, 1978.
"Our last move was the biggest." (Eck trade):
* Joe Giuliotti, "Red Sox land man they want—Eckersley," *Boston Herald*, March 31, 1978.
"My finger hurt so bad at first, I thought it was broken":
* Bill Liston, "Tiant dislocates finger, could return for opener," *Boston Herald*, March 18, 1978.
"Tiant loses bid for a no-hitter," *Boston Herald*, April 29, 1978.
"My twelve victories, 4.53 ERA, and three complete games (in thirty-two starts)…":
* Ray Fitzgerald, "5 frustrations hindered Sox," *Boston Globe*, Sept. 25, 1977.
Deane McGowen, "It's close but no cigar for Tiant," (cracks on age, saying he "admits to being 36 years old"), *New York Times*, April 21, 1978.
"Yes We Can, Red Sox Say," by Gerald Eskenazi, *New York Times*, April 10, 1978.
Luck goes bad:
* Joe Fitzgerald, "Tiant takes a fall, but Stanley rises to the occasion," *Boston Herald*, May 9, 1978.
"I had felt something back there last week":
* Larry Whiteside, "Greetings Mr. Hrabosky," *Boston Globe*, May 9. 1978.
Jim Rice on Tiant staying in games, from interview of Jan. 19, 2019.
"It's no longer a question of his coming back." (Zimmer):
* Peter Gammons, "Sox hit-and-run, bunt, steal game," *Boston Globe*, June 11, 1978.
"He's as good as he's ever been." (Fisk):
* Will McDonough, "Now it's 6 straight victories for Sox, Luis," *Boston Globe*, June 15, 1978.
Peter Gammons, "Red Sox-Yankees 'Like World Series Every Day,'" *Boston Globe*, June 18, 1978.
"This is the best team I've ever played with":
* Joe Giuliotti, "It's perfectly (7-0) clear: Tiant, Sox too much," *Boston Herald*, June 25, 1978.
TV stats for Sox-Yanks game:
* Peter Gammons "Red Sox Notebook," *Boston Globe*, June 30, 1978.
"Right now this team is the closest I've ever seen a Red Sox team." (Yaz):
* Paul Zimmerman, "Harsh words—but did Rice say them?" *New York Post*, June 21, 1978.
Fan recommends Tiant pitch once weekly:
* "Fans Speak Out," *Boston Globe*, July 3, 1977.
"A cripple and an old man." (Fisk on Yaz/Tiant):
* Peter Gammons, "Old Reliables (Tiant, Yaz) stop Sox slide, 2-0," *Boston Globe*, Sept. 7, 1978.
This is as big a win as we could ask for," (Yaz), ibid.
"It was a big win for me, a big win for everybody," ibid.
"All right, you guys, let's go." (clubhouse speech vs. Yanks):
* Joe Giuliotti, "Tiant Wakes up Red Sox Wake," *Boston Herald*, Sept. 9, 1978.
"He was in more trouble than a Middle East border guard." (Gammons on Tiant):
* Peter Gammons, "Red Sox 3-1—trail Yankees by 1," *Boston Globe*, Sept. 24, 1978.
"You knew when you went out there and got Luis two or three runs," Jim Rice, from interview of Jan. 19, 2019.
"This team has proven something." (win over Tigers):
* Peter Gammons, "Tiant, Scott take over, keep Red Sox alive, 5-2," *Boston Globe*, Sept. 28, 1978.
"You wanted Tiant to have the ball in those big games," Dan Shaughnessy, from interview of Feb. 7, 2019.
"We had a radio in the bullpen…" Tom Burgmeier, from interview of Oct. 30, 2016.
"They would not lose that day," Dick Johnson, from interview of Dec. 1, 2017.
Micky Rivers on his bat given to Bucky Dent being corked, *14 Back* documentary, 2018.
"When people think back to the 1978 season…" (Goose Gossage):
* Tim Horgan, "KC anticlimax for Yanks," *Boston Herald*, Oct. 4, 1978.

CHAPTER 17: PINSTRIPES AND PLATANEROS

"Yankee Frank" ads recalled in "Accent on Greatness," Roberto Gonzalez and Paul Doyle, *Hartford Courant*, Dec. 13, 2000.
Will McDonough, "Luis Tiant will replace Billy Martin as the new spokesman for Yankee Franks," Jan. 31, 1979.
Will McDonough, "It's official—Tiant enters free agent market," *Boston Globe*, Oct. 24, 1978.
"El Tiante is one of our institutions…":
* Tim Horgan, "Will Sox come through for Tiant?" *Boston Herald*, Nov. 3, 1978.

Sullivan admits Sox will not give Tiant more than a one-year contact:
- Bill Liston, "Sox get their men; will men get money?" *Boston Herald*, Nov. 5, 1978.

"Nobody tells me when to retire…":
- Murray Chass, "Yanks Sign Tiant, 38, to Pitch Two Years for $500,000; Gura Stays With the Royals," *New York Times*, Nov. 14, 1978.

"In my eighteen years with the Red Sox, he was the best…" (Yaz on Tiant):
- Larry Whiteside, "Yaz, Fisk upset; Scott shocked; LeRoux sorry," *Boston Globe*, Nov. 14, 1978.

"It doesn't matter how old you are, it's how good you are," (Fisk on Tiant), ibid.

"How could they let that happen?" (Fisk on Tiant leaving):
- Peter Gammons, "A lot has happened, but not much has changed," *Boston Globe*, Feb. 2, 1979.

"Just like old wine, Luis gets better…" (Al Rosen):
- Bill Liston, *Boston Herald*, Nov. 14, 1978.

"Security for my family…" (contract details):
- Steve Cady, "Tiant, 38, Is Grateful and Ready to Serve Yankees," New York Times, Feb. 12, 1979.

"I'm gonna get my social security…":
- "Tiant Adding Special Zest to Yankees," *New York Times*, Feb. 20, 1979.

Luis Tiant Jr., memories of Yankees, Yankee Stadium, and almost knocking out Tommy John from a ballgame before it started, from interview of Sept. 17, 2018.

"He plays a game with hitters now…":
- Phil Pepe, "Tiant uses brain and little smoke," *New York Newsday*, March 10, 1979.

Hunter, Tiant, and Kaat all two-hundred-game winners on Yanks:
- Peter Gammons, Boston Globe, May 13, 1979.

Tiant talks to Bob Lemon about getting more work:
- Murray Chass, *New York Times*, May 2, 1979.

Yastrzemski/Tiant exchange from first Red Sox Yankee game:
- Peter Gammons, *Boston Globe*, July 1, 1979.

"Fossils can hit fossils…" (Lynn on Tiant):
- Murray Chass, *New York Times*, July 1, 1979.

"I can pitch as long as I can get somebody out." (after shutout vs. A's):
- Murray Chass, "Tiant Pitches One-Hit Victory," *New York Times*, July 9, 1979.

Details from first game after Thurman Munson's death drawn from television broadcast of game, found on YouTube, as well as interview with Scott McGregor, Dec. 10. 2017.

Other details on Munson, Munson/Fisk relationship, and Munson's flying:
- Marty Appel, "Munson: The Life and Death of a Yankee Captain," Doubleday, NY, 2009.

"I think that people understood…" Dan Shaughnessy on Boston fans accepting Tiant back as a Yankee and not booing him like Clemens or Boggs, from interview of Feb. 7, 2019.

"That's the most I can fine him without going into the [grievance] courts." (Howser):
- George Vescey, "Yanks Win, Impose Fine of $500 on Tiant," *New York Times*, May 31, 1980.

"I don't want this to happen." (on fight with Howser):
- "Tiant throws spat after being relieved," United Press International, *Salina (Kan.) Journal*, June 1, 1980.

"Since his last victory on June 20, he [Tiant] has lost six straight games, in which the Yankees scored a total of only eight runs":
- Jane Gross, "Yankees lose, 1-0," *New York Times*, Sept. 1, 1980.

Stan Williams memories of year coaching Tiant on Yankees, from interview of Nov. 6, 2018.

Signed by Pirates, sent to Triple-A Portland, then back up with Pirates:
- Bill Madden, "Tiant Goes To Portland," *New York Daily News*, Feb. 24, 1981.
- "Tiant Takes a Step on the Road Back," (no-hitter vs. Spokane), Associated Press, *New York Times*, April 19, 1981.
- "I've never seen him throw that hard" (Ted Cox, last out of no-hitter), "Tiant no-hits 'minor' foe," Associated Press, April 20, 1981.
- "Tiant Just Misses No-Hitter," (beats Spokane again in next start), Associated Press, *New York Times*, April 26, 1981.
- Jack McCallum, "El Tiante makes his peetch," *Sports Illustrated*, April 27, 1981.
- "Portland's Tiant Easter for Major Move," *New York Times*, July 2, 1981.
- Phil Musick, "Tiant Sets New Goals at the Top," *Pittsburgh Post-Gazette*, Aug. 13, 1981.
- Terrance Moore, "Tiant plans to 'fool them all,'" (back up with Pirates), *San Francisco Examiner*, Aug. 18, 1981.

"His arm is back, as good as it's been." (Cookie Rojas, Angels scout):
- "Tiant Signed By Angels," Associated Press, *New York Times*, Aug. 2, 1982.

"I'm the happiest man on earth today." (signed by Angels from Mexican League):
- "Angels Acquire Veteran Pitcher Tiant," San Diego Union News Service, Aug. 3, 1982.

Beating Red Sox for last MLB win:
- Peter Gammons, "Rejuvenated Tiant sends Red Sox a message," *Boston Globe*, Aug. 18, 1982.

CHAPTER 18: FINALLY BACK AT FENWAY

Scott McGregor on Tiant giving him injury advice, from interview of Dec. 10, 2017.

"He was the best influence on young players we ever had there." (David Hirsch of Portland):
- Peter Gammons, "Yankees hire Tiant as Class A coach," *Boston Globe*, Jan. 11, 1984.

Coaching at Red Sox Fantasy Camp:
- Tim Horgan, "The Sox Exchange: It's a fantasy trip," *Boston Herald*, Jan. 27, 1985.

Reflections of Paul Medici, Fantasy Camp participant, from interview of December 2018.
Playing himself on the TV show *Cheers*:
- Fred Rothenberg, "Toasting A Classy Series: 'Cheers,'" *San Diego Union*, Feb. 10, 1983.

Appearing in "Less filling! Tastes great!" ads for Miller Lite:
- "SPORTS PEOPLE; Hasn't Lost Touch," *New York Times*, Dec. 17, 1985.

Pitching in Equitable Old Timer's Series:
- Wayne Worcester, "Louie serves a last call to grand old gang at Fenway," *Providence Journal-Bulletin*, May 18, 1986.

Mike Dunn memories of playing catch with Tiant, from interview of Oct. 27, 2018.
Getting job with State Treasurer Robert Q. Crane:
- Mark Muro, "The return of Luis Tiant," *Boston Globe*, Nov. 9, 1987.

"You never forget it; there's nothing like the big league." (joins Senior Professional Baseball Association):
- Jeff Schmalz, "Extra Innings for Some Veterans," *New York Times*, Oct. 23, 1989.

Part of a very strange baseball transaction:
- "Teddy Bear—Tiant Trade," Associated Press baseball notes, Oct. 9, 1989.

Minor league instructor for Dodgers: Luis Tiant biography in 2002 Red Sox media guide.
"They won't tolerate discrimination…" (coaching with Dodgers):
- Gordon Edes, "Tiant's A Kid Again, At Least By Association," *Sun-Sentinel*, Nov. 21, 1991.

On helping Tommy Lasorda communicate with Rich Linares:
- "Si habla Espanol," *Arizona Republic*, Feb. 27, 1995.

Pedro Martinez on Tiant and his brother Jesus, from interview of Jan. 19, 2019.
Pitching coach for Team Nicaragua at 1996 Atlanta Olympics:
- Kevin Paul Dupont, "Familiar face on right-hand man," *Boston Globe*, Aug. 3, 1996.

Elected to Red Sox Hall of Fame:
- Marvin Pave, "It's not a ticket to Cooperstown, but…Sox give Tiant Hall space," *Boston Globe*, Aug. 9, 1997.

Luis Jr. on he and father coaching at Savannah College of Art and Design (SCAD), from interview of Sept. 17, 2018.
Danny Tiant on his father's popularity at SCAD, from interview of Sept. 17, 2018.
Tony Blankenship and Bradley Hesser memories of playing for Tiant at SCAD, from interviews of October 2018.
Johnny Papile memories of "adoption" by Tiant family, meeting his wife while with Luis, from interview of November 2018.
Uri Berenguer memories of doing Spanish Radio games with Tiant, from interview of February 2019.
Larry Lucchino on Tiant's return to Red Sox, from interview of February 2019.
Lenny DiNardo on learning from Tiant as a young Red Sox pitcher, from interview of Oct. 15, 2018.
Andrew Benintendi on getting hitting insights from Tiant, from interview of Jan. 19, 2019.
Eduardo Rodriguez on connecting with Latino pitching greats Tiant and Pedro Martinez, from interview of Jan. 19, 2019.
Mike Lowell on impact Tiant had on him as a young ballplayer with Cuban roots, from interview of May 27, 2018.
Danny Tiant cigar stories, from interview of Sept. 17, 2018.
Jim Rice on Tiant's ability to make everyone feel good, from interview of Jan. 19, 2019.
Steve Buckley on Tiant's Cooperstown credentials, from interview of Oct. 18, 2018.
Rico Petrocelli on Tiant's Cooperstown credentials, from interview of Oct. 4, 2016.
Excerpts of "Prime: The Luis Tiant Story," printed with permission of Professor Albert DeCiccio.
Stan Williams on Tiant's Cooperstown credentials, from interview of Nov. 6, 2018.

CHAPTER 19: HOME TO HAVANA

Tiant-Kris Meyer conversation at Fenway:
- John Kelly, "Documentary on Luis Tiant's return to Cuba premieres," WickedLocal.com, April 23, 2009.

Tiant family dialogue from 2007 trip to Cuba, as well as dialogue between Luis Tiant and others visited in Miami and Cuba during trip, excerpted from *Lost Son of Havana* documentary film, with permission of writer-director Jonathan Hock and producers Kris Meyer and Peter and Bobby Farrelly.
Selected articles on *Lost Son of Havana* documentary:
- "Returning Hero," (premiere in Somerville) from "Names," Mark Shanahan & Meredith Goldstein, *Boston Globe*, April 27, 2009.
- Geoff Edgers, "Tracking Tiant's painful homecoming," *Boston Globe*, July 10, 2009.
- Michael Judge, "Stealing Home," ESPN.com (movie review), Aug. 11, 2009.
- Christian Red, "Where are they now? Former Yankee pitcher Luis Tiant goes home again," *New York Daily News*, April 27, 2009.

Selected articles from MLB trip to Cuba (March 2016), Fidel Castro's Death (Nov. 2016):
- Peter Abraham, "Luis Tiant says Cubans thrilled with MLB's return," *Boston Globe*, March 24, 2016.
- Anthony McCarron, "Cuban aces Luis Tiant, Pedro Luis Lazo will throw out first pitch before MLB exhibition game in Havana," *New York Daily News*, March 20, 2016.
- Peter Orsi, "With presidents Obama, Castro watching, Rays beat Cuban team," Associated Press, March 23, 2016.
- Marly Rivera, "Luis Tiant: Castro's Cuba 'took away the freedom, the happiness, the dream,'" ESPN.com, Nov. 26, 2016.
- Jose Pagliery and Ahiza Garcia, "The Cuban baseball smuggling machine behind MLB," CNN.com, Dec. 15, 2016.
- Joe Fitzgerald, "Fidel Castro no hero for Luis Tiant," *Boston Herald*, Nov. 30, 2016.

BOOKS, PERIODICALS, WEBSITES

NEWSPAPERS (1940-2018)

Boston Globe
Boston Herald
Chicago Tribune
Cleveland *Plain Dealer*
Cincinnati Enquirer
Los Angeles Times
Minnesota Star-Tribune
New York Daily News
New York Newsday
New York Times
San Francisco Chronicle
The Sporting News
Washington Post
(Various small dailies and weeklies in which Associated Press stories appeared)

WEBSITES / VIDEO

Baseballhall.org (National Baseball Hall of Fame)
Baseball-Reference.com
GeneologyBank.com (newspaper archive)
MLB.com
Newspapers.com (newspaper archive)
PaperofRecord.com (newspaper archive)
RedSox.com
SABR.org (Society of Baseball Research)
14 Back, directed by Jonathan Hock, Time Inc. studios, 2018
Lost Son of Havana, directed by Jonathan Hock, produced by Kris Meyer and Peter and Bobby Farrelly,
    5-Hole Productions, Hock Films
YouTube (broadcasts of 1975 World Series, other assorted games and highlights)

BOOKS

'75: The Red Sox Team That Saved Boston, edited by Bill Nowlin and Cecilia Tan, Rounder Books,
    Cambridge, MA, 2005.
Baseball's Great Hispanic Pitchers, by Lou Hernandez, McFarland, Nebraska, 2014.
Beyond the Sixth Game, by Peter Gammons, Houghton Mifflin, Boston, 1985.
The Curse of the Bambino, by Dan Shaughnessy, Penguin Books, NY, 1990.
Diamonds Around the Globe: The Encyclopedia of International Baseball, by Peter Bjarkman, Greenwood
    Press, 2005.
El Tiante, by Luis Tiant and Joe Fitzgerald, Doubleday, NY, 1976.
Game of My Life: Boston Red Sox, by Chaz Scoggins, Sports Publishing Inc., Champaign, IL, 2006.
Game Six, by Mark Frost, Hyperion, NY, 2009.
The Greatest Game, by Mark Bradley, Free Press, NY, 2008.
The Long Ball, by Tom Adelman, Little Brown & Co., Boston, 2003.
Munson: The Life and Death of a Yankee Captain, by Marty Appel, Doubleday, NY, 2009.
The Pride of Havana: A History of Cuban Baseball, by Roberto Gonzalez
Echevarria, Oxford University Press, NY, 1999.
Red Sox Century, by Glenn Stout and Richard Johnson, Houghton Mifflin Harcourt, NY, 2000.
Red Sox Heroes of Yesteryear, by Herb Crehan, Rounder Books, Cambridge, MA, 2005.
Saving Bernie Carbo, by Bernie Carbo and Dr. Peter Hantzis, Diamond Club Publishing, 2013.
Shutout: A Story of Race and Baseball in Boston, by Howard Bryant, Routledge, NY, 2002.
Sweet Lou, by Lou Piniella and Maury Allen, Bantam Books, NY, 1986.
Yankees Century, by Glenn Stout and Richard Johnson, Houghton Mifflin Harcourt, NY, 2002.
Yastrzemski, by Carl Yastrzemski, Rugged Land, NY, 2007.

MAGAZINES / GUIDES

Baseball Digest (1990-2018)
Red Sox Magazine / Red Sox Scorebook Magazine (1975-2000)
Red Sox Media Guide (assorted years)

LUIS TIANT has won more games than any other Cuban-born pitcher in the Major Leagues. He played in the MLB from 1964 to 1982, compiling a record of 229 wins and 172 losses to go along with a 3.30 career ERA, 49 shutouts, and 187 complete games. Born in Havana in 1940, the son of a legendary Negro League pitcher, he was 23 years old when he broke into the majors by shutting out the mighty Yankees—three years after leaving Cuba and being forced into exile in the aftermath of Fidel Castro's bloody New Year's Eve takeover in 1959. A star in the 1975 World Series for the Red Sox, Tiant's unique windup, big-game heroics, and exuberant personality made him one of the most popular athletes in New England (and Cuban) sports history. Also a standout performer for the Indians and Yankees, he finally returned home to Havana in 2007, forty-six years after saying goodbye to his parents. Arguably the best 20th-century pitcher not in the National Baseball Hall of Fame, Tiant divides his time between Maine, Florida, and Fenway Park.

SAUL WISNIA has authored, co-authored, or contributed to numerous books on Boston and general baseball history, including *Fenway Park: The Centennial* and *Miracle at Fenway: The Inside Story of the Boston Red Sox 2004 Championship Season.* He is a former sports and news correspondent at the *Washington Post* and feature writer at the *Boston Herald,* whose essays have appeared in *Sports Illustrated, Red Sox Magazine, Boston Magazine,* and the *Boston Globe. For the past twenty years, he* has chronicled the unique relationship between the Red Sox and young cancer patients as senior publications editor at Dana-Farber Cancer Institute. Wisnia lives in his native Newton, Massachusetts five–nine miles away from Fenway Park.